600 GARDEN FAVORITES

600 Garden Favorites

ESSENTIAL PLANTS FOR YOUR GARDEN

TERI DUNN & PAT KITE

MetroBooks

Text for the following chapters by Teri Dunn: 100 Favorite Perennials, 100 Favorite Roses, 100 Favorite Herbs, 100 Favorite Garden Wildflowers, 100 Favorite Plants for Shade

Editor: Susan Lauzau
Art Director: Jeff Batzli
Designer: Christina Grupico
Photography Editor: Jennifer Bove
Production Manager: Ingrid Neimanis-McNamara

Color separations by Ocean Graphic Co. Ltd.
Printed in Singapore by KHL Printing Co. Ltd.

10 9 8 7 6 5 4 3 2 1

For bulk purchases and special sales, please contact:
Friedman/Fairfax Publishers
Attention: Sales Department
15 West 26 Street
New York, NY 10010
(212) 685-6610 FAX (212) 685-1307

Please visit our website:
http://www.metrobooks.com

DISCLAIMER

While many herbal remedies have been used safely for years, even hundreds of years, inexperience can be dangerous. Improper or excessive doses of certain herbs can cause allergic or even toxic reactions. For these reasons, the author has been conservative in describing uses. Neither the author nor the publisher will be held responsible for any adverse reactions.

DEDICATION

For Joe Compito. You will be greatly missed.

—T.D.

For Nancy Neely, my teacher, whose enthusiasm so long ago encouraged

my lifetime interest in science.

— P.K.

CONTENTS

Introduction

If you are becoming more serious about your ornamental garden, or have resolved to finally create one you are proud of, this book is for you. A trip to a busy garden center or a few hours spent poring over colorful catalogs may leave you excited but also overwhelmed. Thumbing through beautiful coffee-table garden books or magazines may leave you inspired yet daunted.

The goal of *Gardeners' Favorites* is to cut through the surfeit of choices and information, and introduce you to some of the best and most common plants worthy of your consideration, garden "all-stars," if you will.

For a plant to be dubbed a "favorite," it must have the important qualities gardeners value, namely attractiveness, dependability, versatility, and easy care. While this information is particularly helpful for novices, the succinct portraits also appeal to more experienced gardeners looking to expand or improve their outdoor spaces. But the favorite plant must also have proven itself over time in the beds and borders of accomplished gardeners in many regions. While there will always be worthy new introductions, and occasionally you may be seduced into acquiring something rare and exotic, the fact remains that the backbone of a lovely and satisfying garden is the "old faithfuls," fine plants that have stood the test of time. Build or add to your garden

with these tried-and-true flowers and foliage, and you will not be disappointed.

In the pages that follow, you will find profiles of the best, most reliable perennials, roses, herbs, garden-worthy wildflowers, shade plants, and flowering shrubs—in sum, the foundations of a good, solid ornamental garden. Each plant is shown in a color photograph, and the accompanying text describes its appearance in more detail, explains its growing requirements, and suggests landscape uses. A quick-reference list lets you assess at a glance the plant's essential characteristics—its ultimate size, bloom time, sun requirements, and so on.

These are not encyclopedia entries, but rather frank and savvy assessments of the plant in question. If a plant has a special requirement or weakness, or looks especially spectacular in a particular setting or with certain other plants, this is noted. Many cultivated plants have been hybridized extensively; instead of exhaustively listing every available cultivar, only the most popular or deserving ones are noted. On the chance that your local garden center doesn't carry a plant, mail-order sources are provided—all of these are attainable plants.

Within each category, a wide range (100 plants) is profiled, giving you plenty of options to choose from even as you move forward with confidence in planning your garden. Each section includes a brief overview that addresses common concerns such as shopping advice, planting tips, information on care, and troubleshooting.

Perennials, of course, are the bedrock of many a beautiful, long-lived, all-season garden, and the ones featured here were chosen with your success in mind. Not all grow well in all regions or soils (facts some catalogs gloss over), so take a

careful look at that information at the outset. Eventual size and habit are also key to your long-range plans, and these tendencies are honestly described.

Roses are included because they remain the world's most popular and beloved flower, and if you wish to grow one or many, you have probably already discovered that there is a bewildering array on the market; those described here are top performers, so you can make wise choices, whether you're seeking a large or small shrub, a climber, or even a groundcover.

Herbs, while always popular for theme gardens (a proper herb garden or even simply a bed or a pot or two), are increasingly making their way into the garden at large, as accents, as foundation plants, and as partners for other plants. They provide unique beauty and, often, enticing fragrance and flowers to cherish. In addition, many of the herbs featured have culinary value or may be dried as decorations or for use in potpourri, and these special uses are detailed.

Certain wildflowers, too, have proven themselves worthy of inclusion in a handsome garden; a number have been selected from the wild and improved by horticulturists. Garden wildflowers also bring a welcome easy-going nature to your garden, as they are frequently a cinch to grow, requiring little or no coddling in return for long periods of interest.

Every garden seems to have an area that receives less light, and the shade plants featured here will open your eyes to the possibility of dressing up such spots in style. You'll discover that you can expect much more than the color green—many of the shade plants featured have appealing flowers. You can also have fun with foliage plants, for many have truly intriguing leaves, stretching the palette of color, form, and texture.

Last but not least are flowering shrubs, which come in an array of sizes and with distinctive personalities—no garden can afford to be without a few. These valuable plants allow you to define (or protect) a boundary, add dimension and heft to your garden's design, and give you the chance to enjoy a diversity of seasonal color. In today's smaller gardens, you want to make a careful choice so your flowering shrub matches your ultimate size and habit requirements, whatever they may be.

Above all, this book is intended to be useful. Many plants are profiled here, but this is not a dry encyclopedia or a comprehensive survey. Rather, you will be given the power to make informed choices about quality plants. For ease of reference, you will find certain extraordinarily useful plants in more than one category—hostas, for example, are stars of both the perennial border and the shade garden. The garden plants offered here are tried-and-true, they are widely available, and they have been richly enjoyed by legions of gardeners before you. This one volume will be a resource you return to again and again, whether you are just starting out or are contemplating new additions. Read before you shop, read before you choose a plant for a spot (or a spot for a plant)—and read when you are in a mood to daydream about the growing beauty of your garden.

—TERI DUNN

1 0 0

Favorite

Perennials

Introducing Perennials

Gardening with perennials can be a great joy. Once planted, they bring wonderful color, texture, and form to your garden for years to come. In the end, they're more gratifying to grow than "flash in the pan" annuals that need to be repurchased and replanted every year. With perennials, you have a lot to look forward to as they mature, spread or billow out, and reach their full character. Perennials are an investment, and when well chosen and well nurtured, they'll repay you handsomely, transforming your garden into a showpiece.

There are many, many perennials in the world. This chapter highlights one hundred of the easiest and most dependable, taking the uncertainty out of your first purchases. None is rare or hard to find. Study the descriptions as well as the photographs, decide which ones are right for you, and rest easy. You're off to a good start.

SHOPPING FOR PERENNIALS

When you buy your perennials locally, you can take them right home and plant them the same day. If you join the mobs down at the local garden center the first warm

Saturday in spring, however, be prepared to accept substitutes for the exact perennials you had in mind. You should return in the less-hectic autumn, which, unknown to some gardeners, is also a great time to plant. The soil is still warm and, when the rains come, the roots will grow quickly and give the plants a head start over their spring-planted counterparts. Another advantage to a follow-up autumn shopping trip is that you'll be armed with a summertime of experience and may shop more wisely.

In any case, the secret to being a savvy garden center shopper is taking your time. Draw up a shopping list beforehand so you don't get overwhelmed by all the choices (though you may still end up making an impulse purchase or two) or the jostling crowds. Examine each plant carefully. Check to see that it's well rooted by turning it over or sideways and thumping the pot lightly. Neither the plant nor the soil mix should fall out, and you may see a few roots peeking out of the drainage holes. Make sure that it's pest-free—look on leaf undersides and in the nodes (where stalks meet stem) for small bugs, sticky residue, or webs. And check that it's disease-free—no spotted, curled, or yellowed leaves, or deformed buds. Don't be seduced by a blooming plant, as the petals may drop on the car ride home or after a few days in your garden. Better to buy a plant that's full of unopened buds, or at least showing signs of fresh, new green growth.

Another option is to buy your perennials from a reputable mail-order catalog; see the list of sources on page 697. You'll find a far wider range of plants and individual cultivars, plus information and inspiring landscaping

ideas—more than you can hope to find at a busy garden center. Mail-order perennials tend to come in two forms: potted and bareroot. Potted ones are generally small (to keep shipping costs down), but don't let size deceive you. They may be one- to two-year-old, well-rooted plants whose foliage has just been chopped back. Once in the ground, they often take off like gangbusters. Bareroot selections offer the further advantage of arriving dormant, so you can plant them a little earlier and let them ease into life in your garden gradually. One last note: always read catalog fine print carefully so you are aware not only of what you are getting but also of substitution and guarantee policies.

As you get more involved in raising perennials, you may wish to save money—or try some rare plants—by growing from seed. There are good books available on seed-starting techniques, but be aware that it can sometimes be an elaborate process. Special harvesting methods, soil mixes, and chilling and warming cycles may be necessary, depending on the plant. It can also be a slow process, taking months or even years. And finally, not all perennials "come true" from seed. An easy, quick way to get carbon copies of perennials you enjoy is by division (see page 17).

PLANTING PERENNIALS

The best thing you can do for your new perennials is prepare the soil ahead of time. Assuming you've picked an appropriate spot in sun or shade, the next step is to improve the bed's quality and texture. Most perennials want a well-drained soil, which means a soil that is neither boggy nor too sandy. To get well-drained soil, dig in some organic matter (compost or rotted cow manure is always a good choice) to a depth of 6 to 12 inches (15 to 30cm). Keep stress to a minimum by planting in the late afternoon, on a gray or rainy day, if possible. And be prepared to protect the young plant from wind, hot sun, and pests like hungry slugs or birds until it gets established.

If your plant is a bareroot, soak it for an hour or two in a bucket of water to rehydrate it. If you're planting a potted perennial, gently pop it out of its container just before planting time. In either case, take a few moments to groom the plant first, snipping off dead or damaged roots or stems. Then place it in an ample hole, firm soil around it, and water it in well.

CARING FOR PERENNIALS

While every plant has its own specific needs, there are general guidelines you can follow for the care and feeding of most perennials. Be sure to water, especially during the first season while the roots are getting established. Don't count on rain and don't wait until you see alarming wilting; water often and generously. Water at the plant's base (this gets to the roots quickly and keeps the foliage dry, which prevents disease). Also, feed your new plants! Mix a standard soluble fertilizer like 5-10-5 in with their water once or twice a month during the growing season. Or sprinkle granular food at their bases and water in well, again once or twice a month. Always follow the label directions so you don't overfeed or undernourish. Your perennials will reward you with lusty new growth and lush blooms — and you will build a foundation for a healthy, solid, and gorgeous performance in years to come.

If you keep up with routine chores in your flower garden, you'll help your perennials prosper and save yourself extra work down the line. Always remove weeds, particularly in the vulnerable first year. Not only are they unsightly, they sap the precious food and water that your plants need to thrive.

Every few days nip out blooms that have passed. This keeps your perennials looking attractive, and it gives them extra energy for more blooming (rather than spending their efforts on going to seed). Harvesting an occasional bouquet can also inspire a plant to bloom some more!

After a few years in the garden, your perennials may become crowded and cease to bloom or grow as well. This is a sure sign that it's time to divide. Most perennials should be divided in the spring or autumn—summer is just too stressful. Simply dig up a plant, taking care to get as much of the root system as possible. Split it into sections, making sure that each section has "growing points" (eyes visible on the rootstock or viable roots with some healthy growth attached). Bare hands alone may not do the trick; you may have to resort to slicing or chopping with a sharp knife, trowel, or shovel. Then, replant the pieces in the same spot or elsewhere in your garden, allowing each one plenty of elbow room. If you have too many, give some away to your neighbors.

If, despite all your kind treatment, your perennials begin to suffer from what appears to be a disease or pest infestation, act quickly. Remove affected foliage and flowers from the plant and from the ground at its feet, and destroy them. Pick off larger bugs and drown them in soapy water, and knock off little ones with a spray of the hose. If the problem remains, you need to move on to diagnosis and treatment. Look up the symptoms in a book, or take a bug or afflicted sample to a more experienced gardener or a good garden center. If you find you must spray your perennials, always use a product that is labeled specifically for the problem, and always follow the directions on the label to the letter.

UNDERSTANDING HARDINESS

First-time perennial gardeners are often bewildered by plant hardiness zones. Don't worry: it's really a simple system, based on the lowest average winter temperatures in different areas. Some perennials are better than others at surviving cold and freezing weather.

First you need to determine which zone you are in (see map on page 696). Then select perennials that are described as hardy in your zone. You can feel confident that these perennials will make it through the winter and live to bloom again next year. Some gardeners take chances; for example, they'll grow a Zone 5 plant in the more northerly Zone 4. If you have a protected warm pocket or spot on your property, and you mulch the plant well in autumn, it may just make it through. Conversely, a Zone 7 plant may survive a steamy Zone 9 or 10 summer if it gets some extra shade and water during the heat of the day.

A little trial and error will teach you about getting your perennials through the winter. Depending on the plants and where you live, some can be chopped back each autumn and left alone until they revive at the return of spring. Others need protection; if an insulating blanket of snow cannot be counted on, and even if it can, mulching is often wise. Wait until late autumn, then lay down several inches of bark mulch, straw, chopped leaves, or evergreen boughs. Don't forget to remove the covering in spring when the soil begins to warm up again and you spot new growth emerging.

Acanthus mollis

Bear's-breeches, acanthus

BLOOM TIME: late spring–summer

HEIGHT/WIDTH: 3'–4' × 2' (90–120cm × 60cm)

LIGHT: full sun–partial shade

ZONES: 7–10

Bear's-breeches

This splendid, clump-forming plant has long been treasured for its big, handsome leaves, which can reach up to 2 feet (60cm) long and half as wide. They're dark green, lustrous, and tough, with deep lobes. You may recognize their bold and elegant form from renderings in art, fabrics, and decorations, and from patterned Corinthian columns.

In fact, acanthus is native to the Mediterranean and grows wild in Greece. It thrives and is more likely to flower in warmer zones in North America. But it may need a little shade in the heat of the day. The bicolor flowers—creamy white with mauve bracts—appear along stiff stalks that rise to about 4 or 5 feet (1.2 or 1.5m) above the foliage.

A plant this imposing needs plenty of elbow room. It makes a great focal point in a flower border, in a tub on a deck, or lining a path or steps. Just be sure to plant it where you want it to stay, because its root system is robust, and you'll never completely remove it if you try to transplant it. Its only enemies are slugs and snails, which can disfigure the gorgeous leaves and spoil their majestic appearance. Make sure it has well-drained soil.

Achillea filipendulina

Yarrow

BLOOM TIME: summer

HEIGHT/WIDTH: 3½'–4' × 1½'–2' (105–120cm × 45–60cm)

LIGHT: full sun

ZONES: 3–8

Yarrow

Achillea has everything going for it: attractive, ferny, olive green foliage, loads of pretty flowers that stay in bloom for weeks, and an agreeable disposition. It adores full sun, and, once established, is drought-tolerant. It is not fussy about soil, growing quickly and lustily in any well-drained spot. (Note that rich or damp soil leads to spindly growth and small flowers.)

The flat-topped blooms, generally 5 inches (13cm) across, are actually tight clusters of tiny flowers. 'Gold Plate' is well named, with slightly larger bright yellow flower heads on a taller plant (to 5 feet [1.5m]) that may need staking. The softer-hued 'Coronation Gold' is smaller (to 3 feet [90cm]) because it's a hybrid between *Achillea filipendulina* and a shorter relative. You'll also find individuals and mixes in pretty shades of white, pink, and salmon-orange; these are also hybrids.

All achilleas are great in sweeps, clumps, or interspersed throughout a flower border where you want dependable color. You'll have plenty for cutting; they're also wonderful for dried flower arrangements.

Aconitum napellus

Common monkshood

BLOOM TIME: summer–late summer

HEIGHT/WIDTH: 3' × 2' (90 × 60cm)

LIGHT: full sun–partial shade

ZONES: 4–8

Common monkshood

Gorgeous spikes of these blue-violet, helmet-shaped flowers appear in late summer, when they are a welcome sight. The divided leaves are attractive, remaining dark green all season and alternating up the stem to just short of the flowers. The plants have an airy, graceful quality. They blend well with other perennials of medium height and will give your yard a nice, cottage garden feel. Their most important requirement is rich, moist (but not soggy) soil.

There are many cultivars and closely related species. In particular, look for the hybrids, including the dense, long-blooming 'Bressingham Spire' and the tall, vivid blue 'Spark's Variety'.

Much has been made of the fact that all the plant parts, especially the roots, are deadly poisonous. The only death-by-aconitum story that comes readily to mind, however, is Romeo in Shakespeare's play. Still, it would be wise to grow this plant out of the reach of curious children.

Agapanthus

Agapanthus

BLOOM TIME: summer–early autumn

HEIGHT/WIDTH: 2½'–4' × 2' (75–120cm × 60cm)

LIGHT: full sun

ZONES: 8–10

'Headbourne' agapanthus

Long a favorite in California gardens, where it grows so well, this terrific "tender perennial" really deserves a chance in other regions. It will grow well in soil of poor-to-average fertility, is drought-tolerant, and blooms for weeks during the first half of the summer. If you have doubts about its ability to survive your winters, grow some in pots and move the plants indoors for the cold months.

The straplike leaves appear first, from the base of the plant. They are later joined by bare stalks bearing show-off flower heads that are between 5 and 8 inches (13 and 20.5cm) across. Composed of small, tubular flowers, these may be loose and carefree, or dense and spherical enough to invite comparison to a flowering allium.

You'll find these plants in a variety of shades of blue and purple, as well as white. The hardiest ones may be the English Headbourne Hybrids, which grow a little shorter and stouter. Newer varieties have been bred to produce loads of flowering stalks—look for the aptly named 'Prolific Blue' and 'Prolific White'.

Ajuga reptans

Bugleweed

BLOOM TIME: late spring–early summer

HEIGHT/WIDTH: 4"–8" × 8" (10–20cm × 20cm)

LIGHT: full sun–full shade

ZONES: 4–8

'Catlin's Giant' bugleweed

An adaptable, fast-spreading (some say invasive) choice for shade, this mat-former will fill in where grass languishes—but will also do perfectly well in sun. It comes in a variety of intriguing forms; if you search the nurseries or catalogs diligently, you can find a handsome, unusual, low-maintenance planting.

The small spike flowers, which appear in profusion in late spring, are usually purple. They look very much like those of mint, which is no surprise, as this plant is a relative. The flowers tend to dry to a dull brown, so keep the display attractive by clipping them off when their looks start to fade.

Among the many choices are 'Burgundy Glow', whose leaves are splashed with pink and cream; 'Pink Surprise', with lance-shaped, bronze-green leaves (and pinkish flowers); and 'Purple Brocade', which sports especially ruffled, duo-tone leaves of purple-bronze and forest green. The most intriguing cultivar is bronze-foliaged 'Catlin's Giant', which has extra-large leaves and taller flowers. (It originated in the garden of a fellow who accidentally sprayed weed-killer on his ajuga patch. Most of the plants died, but one clump survived and came back in this jumbo size.)

Alcea rosea

Hollyhock

BLOOM TIME: summer–autumn

HEIGHT/WIDTH: 5'–10' × 3' (1.5–3m × 90cm)

LIGHT: full sun

ZONES: 5–9

Hollyhock

People love hollyhocks for their gorgeous, stately unbranched bloom stalks. They seem to conjure up the English countryside or Grandma's overgrown, billowy garden. It's true that hollyhocks are usually short-lived; but they do self-seed so you'll always have some if you want them. And it's also true that their leaves are prone to rust (a disfiguring disease), while spider mites, Japanese beetles, and slugs like to nibble on the plants. But love is not rational: hollyhocks are so easy to grow, so charming, and so generous with their blooms, it's easy to forgive them their flaws.

Classic hollyhock clumps can grow quite tall, up to 8 feet (2.4m) or more. Their impressive height makes them perfect for planting at the back of a border or along a fence or wall, where you can admire them swaying in a soft summer breeze. A wide range of colors is available, from white to yellow to pink to lavender. There's even a deep maroon cultivar ('Nigra' or 'The Watchman') that's nearly black. Old-fashioned favorites have single blooms, and more recent "double" cultivars are so fluffy with petals that they look almost like peony blossoms.

Alchemilla mollis

Lady's-mantle

BLOOM TIME: late spring–early summer

HEIGHT/WIDTH: 1'–2' × 1½' (30–60cm × 45cm)

LIGHT: full sun–partial shade

ZONES: 4–7

Lady's-mantle

Every garden should have a spot for this lovely, lush plant, whether it's used as a groundcover, part of the perennial border, or featured in a handsome urn or terra-cotta pot. The scalloped leaves (up to 4 inches [10cm] wide) are lime green and soft to the touch. When it rains or when early morning dew gathers on the leaves, the water beads up like quicksilver and sparkles—a truly enchanting sight.

Unlike some other foliage plants, lady's-mantle has attractive flowers. The frothy flowers are a sharp, clear shade of yellow-green (often described as chartreuse), and appear in profusion each spring. They grow on short stalks that hold them slightly away from the leaves.

Lady's-mantle is easy to grow and adapts well to both sun and partial shade. Just be sure that it gets well-drained but moist soil. If your summers are hot and dry, coddle the plants with fertile soil, some shade, and extra water.

Amsonia tabernaemontana

Bluestar

BLOOM TIME: early summer

HEIGHT/WIDTH: 2'–3' × 2'–3' (60–90cm × 60–90cm)

LIGHT: full sun–partial shade

ZONES: 3–9

Bluestar

If you like blue flowers, try this easygoing native North American plant. A true light blue, the star-shaped flowers are about half an inch (1.5cm) across, and appear in domed clusters at the tops of the stems. The tidy foliage, which is between 3 and 6 inches (7.5 and 15cm) long, is narrow and willowy and encircles the stems. In the autumn, bluestar's foliage is absolutely lovely. Instead of fading away, the leaves turn a vibrant shade of gold that looks wonderful in the company of autumn bloomers such as asters and mums.

Surprisingly strong and tough, these plants stand erect and thrive in moderately fertile soil. (They can be grown in some shade and in richer soil, but will become leggy and need to be trimmed back occasionally to keep their growth dense.) They're also free of disease and pest problems. Bluestar is probably best grown in groups or sweeps, where its fine texture won't be lost and the wonderful shade of blue really stands out. It's also a striking companion for orange- or red-flowered azaleas, which bloom at the same time.

Anemone × hybrida

Japanese anemone

BLOOM TIME: late summer–autumn

HEIGHT/WIDTH: 3'–5' × 2' (90–150cm × 60cm)

LIGHT: full sun–partial shade

ZONES: 5–8

'Queen Charlotte' Japanese anemone

When your autumn garden needs some pizzazz, consider late-blooming, low-maintenance Japanese anemones. They're as fresh as daisies, which they resemble from a distance, and as graceful as old-fashioned single-form roses, which they resemble up close. The plants grow into substantial mounds laden with attractive compound foliage. The 2- to 4-inch (5 to 10 cm) flowers surge above, held high on arching stalks. Occasionally this plant is called windflower: the clouds of flower stalks being tossed gently in an autumn breeze is an irresistible sight. Tuck some into your flower borders, among ornamental grasses, or in a bed with other autumn bloomers. There are several good cultivars available. The white ones are old favorites: 'Honorine Jobert', first introduced in 1858, stands 3 to 4 feet (90 to 120cm) tall; 'Alba' is about a foot shorter, and just as breathtaking. Another short one to look for is 'September Charm', which tops out at between 2 and 3 feet (60 and 90cm), and has unusual rose-pink flowers with a silvery sheen. For best results, Japanese anemones require soil that is moist and rich in organic matter.

Anthemis tinctoria

Golden marguerite

BLOOM TIME: late spring–early autumn

HEIGHT/WIDTH: 1½'–3' × 2½' (45–90cm × 75cm)

LIGHT: full sun

ZONES: 3–7

'E.C. Buxton' golden marguerite

A true yellow-flowered daisy, golden marguerite is an enthusiastic, low-maintenance plant. It produces loads of small flowers—no more than 2 inches (5cm) across—for up to two months running. Give it a spot in full sun and lean soil. And be sure to trim off spent flowers occasionally to encourage continued blooming. Or, better yet, cut bouquets for yourself fairly often. The plant is rather bushy and sprawling, and clothed in ferny, divided daisy foliage. Once established, it will be quite drought-resistant.

Because of its casual appearance, this easygoing plant is a good companion for herbs. But it really looks terrific in the company of blue or red flowers, like 'Johnson's Blue' geranium or any of the red-hued bee balms. No pests ever bother it, and mildew only appears when air circulation is poor, a problem easily remedied by giving it plenty of elbow room.

Aquilegia × hybrida

Columbine

BLOOM TIME: spring–early summer

HEIGHT/WIDTH: 2'–3' × 1½' (60–90cm × 45cm)

LIGHT: full sun–partial shade

ZONES: 3–9

Columbine

The original red-and-yellow wild columbine (*A. canadensis*), simple to grow and long popular with gardeners, has now been joined by a host of fabulous, tall, multicolored hybrids. Their charm is owed to their intriguing flower form—five sepals centered by a boss of perky yellow stamens and backed by five true petals that are usually spurred. Some of the varieties have flowers that nod, and most columbines have sepals and spurs of contrasting colors, which make for a lively display.

Perhaps the best of the lot are the McKana Giants, which grow between 2 and 3 feet (60 and 90cm) tall. They carry lots of extra-large flowers in cream-and-yellow, pink-and-white,

lilac-and-yellow, and other combinations. The durable 'Biedermeier' strain is about half as tall, and has shorter spurs, but comes in an equally diverse color range. If you prefer solid-color columbines, there are plenty of choices, from sherbet yellow 'Maxistar' to pristine white 'Snow Queen'. All are splendid performers in perennial borders.

Columbine's only flaw is that its lacy foliage is prone to leaf miners, which weave their trails inside the leaves until little green is left. The flowers keep on blooming though, seemingly unaffected. Remove all damaged foliage, or wait until flowering is over and cut the entire plant down. A fresh flush of new foliage will appear shortly after.

Arabis caucasica

Rock cress

BLOOM TIME: spring

HEIGHT/WIDTH: 6"–9" × 1' (15–23cm × 30cm)

LIGHT: full sun

ZONES: 4–7

'Spring Charm' rock cress

Some rock garden plants are too fussy for beginning gardeners to bother with, but rock cress will give your garden that elfin look with little trouble. It's an obliging plant, forming a neat, low-growing mat of gray-green 1-inch (2.5cm) leaves that are woolly to the touch. Spring brings stalks (up to 1 foot [30cm] high) of small flowers. The species is a crisp white; the cultivar 'Flore Pleno' has dense, double, longer-lasting white flowers. There is also a pink single-flowered version, named 'Spring Charm'.

Rock cress is happiest in full sun and well-drained soil. It sulks in humid summers. To encourage denser growth, trim back the entire plant after flowering.

Try this plant along a walkway or rock wall. Or you may wish to include it in your bed of spring-flowering bulbs; its delicate flowers will be good company, and the foliage will remain to help distract from the dying-back bulb leaves as summer approaches.

Armeria maritima

Thrift, sea pink

BLOOM TIME: late spring–early summer

HEIGHT/WIDTH: 6"–1' × 1½' (15–30cm × 45cm)

LIGHT: full sun

ZONES: 4–8

'Dusseldorf Pride' thrift

As the name *maritima* suggests, this is a good plant for a seaside garden or, indeed, for any garden with sandy soil. The foliage is fine and dense, almost like grass. It forms little tufted mounds that don't sprawl out much, so it looks good in rock garden settings or in front of other plants as an edging.

The gorgeous flowers appear in profusion just above the foliage in spring, with occasional repeats throughout the summer. These perky 1-inch (2.5cm) balls, borne on bare stalks, look like little flowering alliums. The most popular form is white 'Alba', which mixes well with spring bulbs and other early-flowering perennials. There are also pink cultivars, including the vibrant (and dauntingly named) 'Vindictive' and a stunning new red cultivar called 'Dusseldorf Pride'.

Artemisia

Wormwood, mugwort

BLOOM TIME: spring–summer
(not grown for its flowers)

HEIGHT/WIDTH: varies

LIGHT: full sun

ZONES: 4–8

'Silver King' wormwood

There are more than two hundred species of artemisia, but many are too rangy for use in gardens. Luckily, horticulturists have recognized the value of the silvery foliage, the ease of culture and dependability, and, in many cases, the wonderful, sagelike scent. Today, we can choose from a number of improved selections. The most widely grown is probably *A. schmidtiana* 'Silver Mound', whose thin, silky leaves grow closely to form a compact clump up to 1 foot (30cm) high and at least that wide. Ideal for edging, it also mixes well in the flower border. It looks especially good in the company of purple, blue, and lavender blooms. For taller, lacy plants that blend in beautifully with perennials of similar height, try the

A. ludoviciana cultivars: 'Silver King' is 3 feet (90cm) tall; 'Silver Queen' is 2 feet (60cm) tall; and 'Valerie Finnis', between 2 and 3 feet (60 and 90cm) tall with broader leaves. *A. stellerana* 'Silver Brocade' looks a lot like dusty miller, but is perennial. Note that artemisia is grown for its foliage; the small white or yellowish flowers are nothing to write home about, and are best clipped off.

All of these artemisias do well in poor-to-medium soil, and can spread if you don't keep after them. They keep their cool in the heat of summer, look lovely among pastel flowers, make bright flowers seem more vibrant, and flatter dark green foliage. No garden should be without them.

Aruncus dioicus

Goatsbeard

BLOOM TIME: early summer

HEIGHT/WIDTH: 4'–7' × 3'–4' (1.2–2.1m × 90–120cm)

LIGHT: full sun–partial shade

ZONES: 2–6

Goatsbeard

This shrublike plant has a short moment of glory, but what a show! Great, stately, feathery wands of creamy white flowers bloom for a week or two in early summer. Rising above the light green foliage, they look for all the world like big astilbe blossoms. The male and female flowers are borne on separate plants and the male flowers are fuller. Unfortunately, nurseries don't differentiate and you won't know what you have until it blooms. Staking isn't necessary.

When grown in the partial shade it prefers, goatsbeard lights up the scene like few other shade bloomers can,

thanks to its size. It's dazzling in a woodland garden, and can also be grown out in the open, provided the soil is constantly moist.

After the flowers pass, you'll still appreciate the plant for its foliage. The delicate, textured leaves are compound, dissected, toothed, and clothe the plant from head to toe. They are untroubled by pests and look fresh all season. If the species is too big for your purposes, seek out the shorter cultivars 'Child of Two Worlds' (3 to 4 feet [90 to 120cm]) or 'Kneiffii' (3 feet [90cm]).

Asarum europaeum

European wild ginger

BLOOM TIME: spring (not grown for its flowers)

HEIGHT/WIDTH: 5"–6" × 8"–1' (13–15cm × 20.5–30cm)

LIGHT: partial–full shade

ZONES: 4–7

European wild ginger

If your yard has a shady spot with moist soil, you already know that not much will grow there. Time to turn it over to this fast-growing, glossy-leaved, tidy groundcover—you'll be delighted with the transformation. There are other wild gingers, but European wild ginger is the choicest and easiest to grow. The kidney-shaped leaves are uniform, about 2 to 3 inches (5 to 7.5cm) across, and evergreen in most parts of North America. Carried on short stems, they're thick, leathery, and shiny, retaining their crisp look even in the heat of summer. Tiny brownish or purplish flowers appear in the spring, but they get lost under the foliage and aren't especially noteworthy anyway.

European wild ginger forms a full carpet. You may wish to inject a few shade-loving companions in its midst, such as a groundcovering phlox or some dwarf hostas. Or try pairing it with smaller spring-flowering bulbs, such as scilla or crocus. The ginger leaves will cover over the fading foliage after the bulbs have bloomed.

Aster novae-angliae

Michaelmas daisy, New England aster

BLOOM TIME: late summer–autumn

HEIGHT/WIDTH: 3'–6½' × 2'–3' (90cm–1.9m × 60–90cm)

LIGHT: full sun

ZONES: 4–8

'Purple Dome' Michaelmas daisy

Late summer and early autumn wouldn't be complete without exuberant blooming asters. There are plenty to choose from, but the very best are the Michaelmas daisies, selections of *Aster novae-angliae*. Ironically, a number of these were bred in Europe from native North American species—a case of European gardeners spotting potential where we only saw weeds. 'Alma Potschke' is a splendid plant, sporting gorgeous 2- to 3-inch (5 to 7.5cm) rosy pink blooms with bright yellow centers. Growing up to 4 feet (1.2m) tall, it may need staking. At 20 inches (51cm) tall, 'Purple Dome' is a more compact prize. As its name suggests, this cultivar becomes covered with flowers, to the point of nearly obscuring the foliage. The flowers are approximately 2 inches (5cm) across, and a rich dark purple with a contrasting yellow center. And there are many others, all of which stay in bloom for several weeks running.

Michaelmas daisy selections are robust plants, forming clumps and developing woody stems. The leaves are lance-shaped, and the lower ones tend to drop, leaving the plant bare-kneed. If this bothers you, plant something shorter in front of them.

Astilbe × arendsii

Astilbe

BLOOM TIME: varies; early–late summer

HEIGHT/WIDTH: 1½'–4'× 1½'–2½' (45–120cm × 45–75cm)

LIGHT: partial shade–full sun

ZONES: 4–9

'Deutchland' astilbe

Astilbes are among the finest of the shade-loving perennials. But they require rich, moist, well-drained soil, and must be grown in areas not given to extremes of heat or humidity. Many of the best varieties were bred in Germany at the turn of the century by accomplished plantsman George Arends. The magnificent feathery plumes, actually a mass of tiny flowers, come in a range of colors, from white to lavender to pink to red.

Planted in a sweep in a woodland setting or even as a formal circle around the base of a tree, astilbes are delightful. You can try them in full sun, too, so long as they still get plenty of moisture. They're a popular choice for along the banks of a pond, stream, or pool.

After the flowers go by, the plant remains attractive. A clump-former, it is clothed in toothed leaflets that look somewhat ferny. Problems with diseases and pests are rare.

Aurinia saxatilis

Basket-of-gold

BLOOM TIME: spring

HEIGHT/WIDTH: 1'–2' × 1' (30–60cm × 30cm)

LIGHT: full sun

ZONES: 3–7

Basket-of-gold

Basket-of-gold looks like it should be easy to grow, and it is. It loves to spill over walls, to froth over the edge of containers, window boxes, or raised beds, and to weave its cheerful color into the early-season garden. A trailing, sprawling plant, it bears cluster after cluster of densely packed, tiny yellow flowers. (They may remind you of their relatives—the mustard flowers that coat hillsides in California in the spring and summer.) For variation, you could grow 'Citrinum', which has lemon yellow flowers, or the more recent introduction, 'Sunny Border Apricot', whose blooms have a peachy hue.

The profuse flowers nearly blanket the fuzzy, gray-green leaves. After blooming is over, the hummock form can get a bit rangy and ratty looking, especially if your summers are humid. Step in with your clippers and chop the plants back by about a third, and they'll return in full glory next spring.

Baptisia australis

False indigo, false blue indigo

BLOOM TIME: early summer

HEIGHT/WIDTH: 3'–6' × 3' (90cm–1.8m × 90cm)

LIGHT: full sun–partial shade

ZONES: 3–9

False indigo

This shrubby perennial has blue-green foliage and 10-inch (25.5cm) spikes of lavender-blue flowers that stay in bloom for up to a month. A member of the pea family, there is a resemblance both in the leaflets and in the classic flower form to other members of this family—including sweet peas and lupines.

Super-easy to grow, false indigo requires only well-drained soil; it does well in poor-to-average soil. Just be sure to place it where you want it to stay, because it forms a deep taproot that makes later transplanting an ordeal. False indigo holds its own in a formal flower border, but is equally at home in a more casual, cottage garden setting. It is disease- and pest-free.

When the flowers fade, they are replaced by brown, pendulous pods. Some people harvest the pods for dried flower arrangements or as rattling toys for a cat. But you can also coax the plant into blooming longer if you cut off the blooms before they go to seed.

Bergenia cordifolia

Heart-leaved bergenia

BLOOM TIME: spring

HEIGHT/WIDTH: 1'–1½' × 1' (30–45cm × 30cm)

LIGHT: partial shade

ZONES: 3–8

Heart-leaved bergenia

Bergenia forms big, bold cabbagelike clumps with sturdy, glossy leaves. The oval or heart-shaped leaves can be up to 1 foot (30cm) across; while they look almost tropical, the plants are very hardy. Leathery and shiny, the leaves can develop brown edges if you expose them to too much sun in the summer or if you neglect to mulch for a harsh winter. Otherwise, the plant is handsome in all seasons, remaining evergreen in most areas. The onset of cool autumn weather inspires the leaves to turn an attractive shade of bronze, russet, or purple. Heart-leaved bergenia is a dramatic choice for mass plantings; try it under a tree or at the base of a shrub border.

In the spring, lush trusses of pink blossoms appear on strong stalks just above the leaves. There are a number of worthy hybrids. 'Abendglut' ('Evening Glow') has nearly crimson flowers and foliage that turns maroon in winter. 'Perfecta' has rosy red flowers and purplish leaves. And 'Silberlicht' ('Silver Light') has pink-blushed white flowers with red centers.

Boltonia
asteroides

Boltonia

BLOOM TIME: late summer–autumn

HEIGHT/WIDTH: 4'–6' × 2'–4' (1.2–1.8m × 60–120cm)

LIGHT: full sun

ZONES: 4–9

'Snowbank' boltonia

In recent years, boltonia has become the darling of gardeners who want weeks of showy color in late summer and autumn. This large, billowing plant foams with hundreds of small 1-inch (2.5cm) daisies. White flowers with yellow centers look perky all day and light up the garden in the evening hours. They're carried on strong stems on a casual mound of thin, willowy gray-green foliage. The plant can get quite large, up to 6 feet (1.8m) tall, so you may want to seek out the more modest-size cultivars. 'Snowbank' grows to between 3 and 4 feet (90 and 120cm). 'Pink Beauty' has pink flowers and grows to about the same size.

An easy plant to grow, boltonia requires only plenty of sun. If the soil is naturally moist and fertile, the plant will prosper for years with little attention. It does well even in drier soils, though it may not grow as tall or lush. Only the species will need staking. Grow it with yellow flowers for a pretty picture: try garden-variety goldenrods, sneezeweed, or one of the smaller-flowered sunflowers.

Brunnera macrophylla

Siberian bugloss, perennial forget-me-not

BLOOM TIME: late spring–early summer

HEIGHT/WIDTH: 1'–1½' × 2' (30–45cm × 60cm)

LIGHT: full sun–partial shade

ZONES: 3–8

Siberian bugloss

If you love forget-me-nots, try this perennial charmer. It features loose sprays of tiny (¼ inch [6mm]), star-shaped, periwinkle flowers. They appear early, along with the spring bulbs and forsythia, and bloom with abandon for several weeks. The plant makes a wonderful "weaver" in areas where you've planted a variety of flowers, because the color goes with almost everything. An easy plant to grow, it does well in full sun and in shade—even dry shade. It will spread, but unwanted volunteers are easy to pull out.

Even if it didn't flower, Siberian bugloss would be a valuable addition to a lightly shaded garden as a ground-cover because its heart-shaped leaves are attractive in their own right. They start out small, form a pretty carpet that disguises fading bulb foliage, and expand in size (sometimes to nearly 8 inches [20.5cm] across) as the summer goes by. Watch out for nibbling slugs, though, and set out bait if they start to disfigure the planting.

Campanula

Bellflower

BLOOM TIME: late spring–summer

HEIGHT/WIDTH: varies

LIGHT: full sun–partial shade

ZONES: 3–9 (most)

Bellflower

Campanula is a large genus, with all sorts of varieties, ranging in habit from stately border plants to rock garden specimens. Most are a cinch to grow, preferring full sun (light shade if your summers are especially hot) and decent soil that is neither too wet nor too dry. Slugs and snails adore them, however, so be prepared to do battle if these creatures are already present in your yard.

If you want a low-grower, try *C. carpatica*, which forms a mound 6 to 12 inches (15 to 30cm) tall. It covers itself in stalks of 1- to 2-inch (2.5 to 5cm) blue or white blooms for weeks in early summer to midsummer. And it can be per-suaded to keep blooming if you deadhead regularly. It's a charmer in a pot, and fits in well in rock garden settings or the front of a flower border.

A taller choice, ideal for a starring role in your summer perennial border, is the peach-leaved bellflower, *C. persicifolia*. It grows up to 3½ feet (1m) tall, and displays its pretty, open-bell flowers (1½ to 2 inches [4 to 5cm] across) along the top half of its graceful stems. For a different effect, consider others whose flowers, still bell-shaped, appear in dense clusters, like the 2- to 5-foot (60 to 150cm) *C. lactiflora* or 1- to 3-foot (30 to 90cm) *C. glomerata*.

Catananche caerulea

Cupid's dart

BLOOM TIME: summer–early autumn

HEIGHT/WIDTH: 2' × 1' (60cm × 30cm)

LIGHT: full sun

ZONES: 4–9

Cupid's dart

A tough, charming plant, Cupid's dart forms neat, small clumps of grassy, gray-green foliage. It tosses up adorable little button buds (on long, wiry stems) that open to 2-inch (5cm) flowers of lilac-blue with a darker center. The flowers look a bit like those of their wild cousin chicory, and are a nice addition to summer bouquets. They dry as well as strawflowers, making them a favorite of flower arrangers and wreath-makers. For best drying results, harvest the flowers shortly after they open. The plant looks best massed, with all those small flowers and buds waving in unison in a summer breeze. Several color variations are available, among them var. *alba*, which has silvery white flowers, and 'Bicolor', which features white petals and a contrasting dark blue center.

Cupid's dart prefers soil on the dry side and tolerates drought. The plant's only real drawback is that it is seldom long-lived, though annual spring division helps. It also self-sows readily.

Centaurea montana

Mountain bluet, perennial cornflower

BLOOM TIME: early summer–early autumn

HEIGHT/WIDTH: 1'–2' × 2' (30–60cm × 60cm)

LIGHT: full sun–partial shade

ZONES: 3–8

Mountain bluet

There are other perennial cornflowers, but none with flowers quite as striking as these—they're an electric shade of dark blue, with a dark red eye in the center. About 2 to 3 inches (5 to 7.5cm) across, they have a loose, frilly look thanks to a relatively low petal count. Best of all, the plant blooms continually all summer, especially if you keep it well watered and deadheaded.

This plant grows about 2 feet (60cm) tall. It is well covered in dark green, lance-shaped foliage that provides a good contrasting stage for the remarkable flowers. It's not fussy about soil, and will spread rapidly to form robust colonies.

Like its wild relatives, mountain bluet has a generous, informal look that makes it a welcome addition to casual herb gardens or flower borders. Plant it with red-hued bee balms for a bold color duet, or aim for a softer look by pairing it with one of the lacy, silver-gray artemisias.

Centranthus ruber

Red valerian

BLOOM TIME: late spring–early autumn

HEIGHT/WIDTH: 1½'–3' × 1'–1½' (45–90cm × 30–45cm)

LIGHT: full sun–partial shade

ZONES: 4–8

Red valerian

Long popular in British and European gardens, this tough, agreeable valerian does splendidly in North America as well, sulking only in the South's hot, humid summers. The tiered flower stalks, up to 3 feet (90cm) tall, bear plenty of neat, lightly fragrant ½-inch (1.5cm) flowers in clusters. Usually they are raspberry or bright red, but white ones are also available and are easier to match with other perennials. All the varieties self-sow readily, and sometimes find homes in the most unlikely spots—between paving stones, or wedged into a rock wall.

The branching stems are sturdy and clothed in smooth, bluish green leaves. When the plant is given a prime spot in average-to-sandy soil, it looks terrific and may bloom for months, even all summer long. If it starts to become floppy, or if you'd like to induce a repeat bloom, it's safe to chop back the plant in the middle of the season—it will rebound.

Chrysanthemum

Garden mum

BLOOM TIME: autumn

HEIGHT/WIDTH: 1'–6' × 1½' (30cm–1.8m × 45cm)

LIGHT: full sun

ZONES: 4–9

'Cymbals' garden mum

Apparently the botanists have been hard at work on this group, shifting plants into new categories and assigning new botanical names. But gardeners and nurseries are paying little heed, and you'll still find your favorites (traditionally *C. × morifolium* or *C. × hortorum*) labeled as "mums."

If you've always just plunked a few red, yellow, or orange mums in your borders or flower boxes in the autumn perhaps it's time to take a fresh look at this group. The hybridizers have also been busy, and there are scads of exciting alternatives. Mums now come in a wide range of sizes, from little button blooms to robust 6-inch (15cm) flowers. As for color, you'll discover everything from rich, unfettered crimson to bicolors and tricolors that seem lit from within. You'll find these mainly in the mail-order catalogs (a couple specialize in a stunning array of mums; see Sources on page 697). You will probably be urged to order in the spring, so your plants can get a good start and give their best by the time autumn rolls around. Early planting also gives you the opportunity to pinch back the stems in midsummer to encourage the bushiest possible form.

Chrysogonum virginianum

Goldenstar, green-and-gold

BLOOM TIME: spring–autumn

HEIGHT/WIDTH: 4"–1' × 1' (10–30cm × 30cm)

LIGHT: full sun–partial shade

ZONES: 5–9

Goldenstar

For a shady spot that needs brightening, a little goldenstar is unbeatable. A low, spreading (but not invasive) ground-cover, it has rich green leaves and bears marvelous glowing yellow, 1½-inch (4cm) daisylike blooms on short stalks. If you grow it in soil that is neither boggy nor dry, it will bloom generously, perhaps even for the whole summer.

This plant is native to the Appalachians on south to Florida, and will surely thrive in gardens in that region. But it also does just fine further north, provided you give it a good winter mulch.

Mass plantings always look great and call attention to goldenstar's vivacious little flowers. Try massing it along a woodland walkway or bordering a line of shrubs. You can also successfully combine goldenstar with other perennials—plant it with native columbines, grape hyacinths, or even something taller, like Virginia bluebells.

Cimicifuga racemosa

Bugbane, black snakeroot

BLOOM TIME: midsummer

HEIGHT/WIDTH: 3'–6' × 3' (90cm–1.8m × 90cm)

LIGHT: full sun–partial shade

ZONES: 3–8

Bugbane

This is a tall, full plant, not for every garden, but spectacular in the right setting. It is best used in the back of a large border, where its imposing presence enhances rather than overwhelms. You might also place it in the middle of an island bed, where it can be admired from all sides.

Dark green, much-divided foliage creates a bushlike form up to about 3 feet (90cm) tall and wide. And the creamy white flower plumes, which rise an additional 2 to 3 feet (60 to 90cm) above the foliage, are quite a sight. The flowers are branched rather than in individual spires, so the effect is like a candelabra. They put on their regal show for several weeks in midsummer and never need propping up. Some nurseries don't mention the scent, while others tell you it's "rank," but the truth is that it's not very obtrusive.

Bugbane is long-lived and trouble-free, unfussy about soil, and asks only for sufficient moisture. In hot climates, or if you want extra drama from those remarkable flower plumes, grow it in partial shade.

Clematis hybrids

Clematis

BLOOM TIME: spring–early summer (some later)

HEIGHT/WIDTH: varies

LIGHT: full sun

ZONES: 3–9

'Nelly Moser' clematis

Clematis varieties may well be the most beautiful flowering vines in the world. This group includes many excellent old favorites, and worthy new varieties make their debut each season. You can plant them in the spring, but you may want to give them a head start by planting in the autumn. Your clematis won't appear to be doing much the first season but it is actually building its root system. In years to come, you will be delighted by its profuse flowering.

Hybrid clematis flowers come in nearly every color of the rainbow. They are big and broad, usually in the 4- to 9-inch (10 to 23cm) range, and often centered with a boss of yellow stamens (some are tipped with purple for even more impact). The ever-dependable *C. × jackmanii* is a heavy bloomer in royal purple from midsummer to autumn. 'Nelly Moser' is a late-spring bloomer that repeats in autumn. Its bicolor blooms of soft pink with a dark pink stripe in the center of each petal are as tempting as a peppermint stick. The double-flowered 'Duchess of Edinburgh' features fluffy white blooms in the summer.

Although hybrid clematis vines perform best in full sun, their roots need the cooling influence of a little shade and a few inches (centimeters) of mulch. So plant them at the bottom of a porch, tree, or shrub, or skirt their bases with shallow-rooted perennials or annuals.

Conradina verticillata

Cumberland rosemary

BLOOM TIME: late spring

HEIGHT/WIDTH: 15″ × 1′–2′ (38cm × 30–60cm)

LIGHT: full sun–partial shade

ZONES: 5–8

Cumberland rosemary

Unfortunately, we don't often see this plant in gardens. Its needled foliage looks very much like rosemary—but it is far hardier than rosemary. Tiny, pinkish mauve flowers cover the plant each spring. And it has a powerful fragrance, somewhere between mint and camphor. It would make a nice groundcover in a spot where you don't want to do any elaborate landscaping, or you could add it to a rock garden or plant it for ornamental effect in an herb garden.

Gardeners sometimes call it "rabbit bane" because rabbits seem never to nibble on it.

Native to a limited area in the Cumberland Mountains of eastern Kentucky and Tennessee, it has been listed as a federally protected plant. But nurseries have begun to propagate it and it is bound to grow in popularity as more gardeners discover its easygoing charms. Cumberland rosemary does best in lean, sandy soil—just like in the wild.

Coreopsis hybrids

Coreopsis

BLOOM TIME: summer

HEIGHT/WIDTH: 1′–3′ × 2′–3′ (30–90cm × 60–90cm)

LIGHT: full sun

ZONES: 5–9

'Moonbeam' threadleaf coreopsis

This genus contains some of the finest, toughest perennial border plants going, and no sunny garden should be without a few. All bloom generously over a long period, do well in a wide range of soils, adapt easily to drought once established, and combine nicely with other flowers. The daisylike blossoms are usually yellow.

Among the best cultivars are those derived from *C. grandiflora*. The widely available and deservedly popular 'Sunray' has very full-petaled, bright yellow double flowers on 18- to 24-inch (45 to 60cm) plants. 'Early Sunrise' also bears double yellow flowers in incredible profusion, and is about the same height, but has a more compact habit.

The threadleaf coreopsis, *C. verticillata*, includes several worthwhile cultivars. Perhaps the best of these is the 2-foot (60cm) 'Moonbeam', which billows with lovely pale yellow flowers. The thin, needlelike leaves and graceful stalks give the plant an airy quality. It makes an excellent addition to perennial borders, where it flatters rather than overpowers its companions. Try it with blue campanulas, verbenas, or lavenders.

Crambe cordifolia

Colewort

BLOOM TIME: late spring–early summer

HEIGHT/WIDTH: $4'–7' \times 3'$ (1.2–2.1m ×90cm)

LIGHT: full sun

ZONES: 6–9

Colewort

A tall, striking plant, colewort is easy to grow and always excites comments from garden visitors. It does need full sun to do its best, and the soil should be more alkaline than acid, making it a better choice for gardens of the Northwest and the prairie states and provinces. It forms a substantial mound of broad, cabbagelike leaves (up to 2 feet [60cm] across!) that remain dark green all season. In early summer, it sends up stout, multibranched stalks, to an imposing height of 5 feet (1.5m). These are laden with clouds of tiny white blooms that look very much like baby's breath. You may have to provide stake support.

Colewort asks little of the gardener in exchange for this magnificent show, except adequate water to support the massive leaves. You'll also want to give it an open spot where it can live up to its full, dramatic potential.

Crocosmia

Montebretia

BLOOM TIME: mid–late summer

HEIGHT/WIDTH: 1½'–3' × 1' (45–90cm × 30cm)

LIGHT: full sun

ZONES: 5–9

'Lucifer' montebretia

This is not a plant for the fainthearted. The sprays of tubular flowers, borne along arching stalks, are a fiery shade of reddish orange and bloom for weeks at a time. The most widely available cultivar, 'Lucifer', has brilliant scarlet flowers. All make for splendid bouquets. In the garden and in the vase, the best companions for montebretia are other hot-colored bloomers—try it with any yellow or orange daisylike flower.

A clump-former, it grows from small corms similar to those of gladiolus. But montebretia is hardier and you need not dig up the corms for the winter unless you live north of Zone 5. The foliage is dark green and swordlike, and blends well in the garden when the plant is not in bloom. In order to thrive, this plant needs moist soil. If you are concerned that the soil will dry out between waterings, lay down a mulch. In the South, give it some shade.

Delphinium hybrids

Delphinium, larkspur

BLOOM TIME: spring–summer

HEIGHT/WIDTH: 3′–8′ × 2′–3′ (90cm–2.4m × 60–90cm)

LIGHT: full sun

ZONES: 3–9

Delphinium

A foolproof delphinium? Can such a thing exist? If you're intimidated by these beauties, or have been disappointed in the past, vow first and foremost to give them the best conditions you can. You will be richly rewarded.

It's true that the magnificent flower stalks are prone to toppling or breaking in strong breezes or summer rain showers. Staking the stalks early is always wise, but you should also be sure to plant your delphiniums in a protected spot. A fence, wall, porch, or hedge can all act as buffers.

The soil should be rich in organic matter, and you ought to fertilize them monthly—delphiniums are greedy feeders.

Arguably the best of the delphiniums are the widely available *D. × elatum* hybrids, which have dense, full spikes of flowers. These come in an extensive range of colors—white, near pink, lavender, purple, and many variations on blue, often with contrasting "bees" in the centers. The Blackmore & Langdon series is of superior quality, as are the Pacific hybrids.

Dianthus

Pinks

BLOOM TIME: varies depending on species

HEIGHT/WIDTH: 6″–1½′ × 8″–12″ (15–45cm × 20.5–30cm)

LIGHT: full sun

ZONES: 4 or 5–10

Maiden pinks

Dianthus is a big genus that features numerous lovely, clove-scented beauties. Many are perfectly simple and satisfying to grow. Most are mound- or mat-forming plants well suited to flower borders, edgings, and containers. The blooms, which are produced in profusion, are usually on the small side, with "pinked" or fringed petal ends. The leaves are generally thin, needlelike, and gray-green. Pinks require quick-draining soil (sandy loam is perfect) that's on the alkaline side. You can cheat by sprinkling lime chips at the bases. The plants are rarely bothered by pests or diseases.

The maiden pink (*D. deltoides*) is a drought-tolerant mat-former that grows to between 6 and 12 inches (15 and 30cm) high. The small, ⅞-inch (2cm) flowers come in pink, rose, red, and white. Cheddar pink (*D. gratianopolitanus*), at 9 to 12 inches (23 to 30cm) high, forms neat, dense mounds from which emerge wiry stems that bear small, solitary flowers about ½ inch (1.5) across, usually in pink, sometimes in red. 'Bath's Pink' wins raves for its old-fashioned beauty and spicy fragrance. It is especially beloved by Southerners, who prize its ability to weather their hot, humid summers. The cottage pink (*D. plumarius*) is a larger, hummock-forming plant (up to 2 feet [60cm] tall) whose long-blooming 1-inch (2.5cm) flowers are often found in fluffy, double hybrids of white, pink, and red.

Dicentra spectabilis

Bleeding-heart

BLOOM TIME: spring

HEIGHT/WIDTH: 2′–3′ × 2′ (60–90cm × 60cm)

LIGHT: partial–full shade

ZONES: 3–9

Bleeding-heart

Bleeding-heart is a terrific plant that has stood the test of time. It is a favorite choice for the woodland garden, and often mixed to good effect with spring-flowering bulbs. If you've had trouble growing this so-called "easy" plant in the past, remember that it requires moist soil and at least partial shade. With the proper conditions, it is sure to prosper.

Bleeding-heart's ferny, much-divided foliage forms a beautiful, loose mound about as wide as it is tall. The endearing 1-inch (2.5cm) locket-shaped flowers line lovely arching stems. The plain species is pink-and-white flowered. A cultivar, 'Alba', is all white, and not quite as vigorous a grower. Both will stay in bloom for up to six weeks, provided that your spring weather is not too capricious. After the flowers are finished blooming, the attractive foliage remains and holds its own fairly well for the rest of the season. In warmer areas or drier soils, however, the plant may simply throw in the towel and go dormant by midsummer.

Digitalis

Foxglove

BLOOM TIME: early–midsummer

HEIGHT/WIDTH: $3'$–$5' \times 2'$ (90cm–1.5m $\times$ 60cm)

LIGHT: full sun–partial shade

ZONES: 4–7 (most)

Foxglove

Foxgloves have been cherished by generations of gardeners because they are so handsome and so low-maintenance. Most are short-lived, and are better considered biennials—which simply means that they generally delay bloom until their second season. But if you grow them in moist, fertile soil, you'll always have them, for they self-sow with abandon. There are many enchanting cultivars and mixes from which to choose. But you'll notice that the self-sown seedlings of later years have their own ideas about what color to be, due to rather complex foxglove genetics. So foxgloves are not for color purists, but rather for gardeners who enjoy exuberant variability.

The old-fashioned *D. purpurea* is 2 to 5 feet (60cm to 1.5m) tall and comes in purple as well as pastel shades of pink, mauve, yellow, and white. 'Alba', an all-white variety, is a real stunner, especially when grown in partial shade with dark green foliage as a backdrop. Shade gardeners who want a break from white flowers will appreciate the chiffon yellow bells of *D. ambigua* (also known as *D. grandiflora*), borne on stalks that are 2 to 3 feet (60 to 90cm) tall.

Doronicum orientale

Leopard's-bane

BLOOM TIME: spring–early summer

HEIGHT/WIDTH: 1½′–2′ × 1′–1½′ (45–60cm × 30–45cm)

LIGHT: full sun–partial shade

ZONES: 3–8

Leopard's-bane

Unlike most yellow daisies, leopard's-bane blooms in spring, which suggests a whole different range of plant combinations. Its cheerful, butter yellow blooms (1 to 2 inches [2.5 to 5cm] across), produced in profusion and held up proudly, look terrific in the company of bold red tulips, for instance, or the blue flowers of brunnera. The plant is neither tall nor sprawling, which is a plus when you have specific plans for it. Its leaves are dark green, heart-shaped, and toothed.

They grow thickly at the base and line the stems but stay short of the flowers. This plant tends to go dormant in the summer, particularly where summers are hot.

Grow leopard's-bane in sun or shade, but make sure the soil is on the moist side. Mulching helps; otherwise, this energetic plant will ask little and give much.

Echinacea purpurea

Purple coneflower

BLOOM TIME: summer

HEIGHT/WIDTH: 2′–4′ × 1½′–2′ (60–120cm × 45–60cm)

LIGHT: full sun

ZONES: 3–8

Purple coneflower

Perhaps the most dramatic of the daisylike perennials, purple coneflower has big, splendid blooms. The petals are long, up to 2 ½ inches (6.5cm), and are generally light purple. The orange-to-bronze cone in the center is symmetrical and very prominent. Often the petals droop downward from the cone, giving the plants a whimsical, shuttlecock appearance and providing a welcoming stage for visiting butterflies. Carried in great numbers on a coarse, well-branched plant, these blooms make for wonderful bouquets. Flower arrangers love to collect and dry them for the central cones alone—though if you leave them be, the plant will often self-sow and add to your display with each passing year.

A native of the prairies, this stalwart plant loves full sun and is content with average, not overly rich, soil. It has a hefty root system, and develops a deep taproot, so moving and dividing is not recommended. However, this means it will weather periods of drought well and contribute many years of beauty to your garden.

Echinops ritro

Globe thistle

BLOOM TIME: summer

HEIGHT/WIDTH: 2′–4′ × 1½′ (60–120cm × 45cm)

LIGHT: full sun

ZONES: 3–8

Globe thistle

Ordinarily, thistles are considered weeds, but not this lavender-blue beauty. The 1- to 2-inch (2.5 to 5cm) globe-shaped flower heads are actually composed of many tiny florets, and are attractive viewed from any angle. There are a couple of nice cultivars in different shades. Look for 'Taplow Blue', which is more silvery blue or steel blue, and 'Veitch's Blue', a darker blue. Globe thistle makes a wonderful color contribution to perennial borders—and is especially terrific in the company of yellow daisies or daylilies. If you wish to cut some to dry, do so before the blooms have opened or they'll shatter.

The plants themselves are admittedly a bit rough. The leaves are dark green and bristly, with spiny tips. But the prickles are not as dangerous as those on some wild thistles. Over the course of a summer, the lower leaves may dry up and fall off, so plant globe thistle well back in the border where this tendency won't be exposed.

Epimedium × rubrum

Epimedium

BLOOM TIME: spring

HEIGHT/WIDTH: 6″–1′ × 1′–1½′ (15–30cm × 30–45cm)

LIGHT: partial–full shade

ZONES: 4–8

Epimedium

If you find the ubiquitous pachysandra boring or too bold as a groundcover, you might try the delicate-looking but naturally tough epimedium instead. Its preference is for damp shade, but it will also do well in traditionally difficult settings, such as under a tree or in a dry shade area. Epimedium is not a fast increaser, so you should plant individuals fairly close together—approximately 1 foot (30cm) apart.

Like all epimediums, this species has pretty, oblong heart–shaped leaflets on wiry stems. The leaves are red when they emerge in early spring, and change to red-tinged green over the course of the summer. They are not evergreen over the winter. The spurred flowers appear for a brief but generous display in spring. They are about 1 inch (2.5cm) across and bright pink to almost crimson, sometimes flushed with yellow.

Eupatorium purpureum

Joe-Pye weed

BLOOM TIME: summer–early autumn

HEIGHT/WIDTH: 4′–6′ × 2′–4′ (1.2–1.8m × 60–120cm)

LIGHT: full sun–partial shade

ZONES: 4–8

'Gateway' Joe-Pye weed

Big and imposing, Joe-Pye weed is best planted in groups at the back of the border. It is sure to dazzle visitors to your garden and draw butterflies like a magnet. The strong, erect but hollow stems are wine red and tall, and are clothed in handsome, toothed leaves that may grow as long as 1 foot (30cm). Flowers don't appear until later in the summer, but they're worth the wait. They foam forth in clusters of rose pink to light purple, and have a sweet, enticing fragrance.

A native North American plant, Joe-Pye weed is tough and hardy. Its only preference seems to be for damp soil. Otherwise, it needs little attention to maintain its spectacular form and annual performance.

Other types of Joe-Pye weed come in different sizes and colors. The most widely available cultivar is probably 'Gateway'. This handsome hybrid between *E. purpureum* and *E. maculatum* features darker, reddish purple blooms.

Euphorbia

Spurge

BLOOM TIME: spring–early summer

HEIGHT/WIDTH: varies

LIGHT: full sun–partial shade

ZONES: varies

'Wulfenii' spurge

Euphorbia is an intriguing and enduringly popular genus of diverse plants. The plants have long, thin leaves, dense along their stems, and unusual "flowers" that are really colored bracts. You will find that they are trouble-free where the summers are not too hot or humid. Insects and diseases are not a problem, and the plants grow well in many soils (if you avoid clay and waterlogged areas). Do place them where you want them to stay, because they develop substantial taproots.

The popular *E. characias* is dramatic and tall, growing to 4 feet (1.2m). It has big, chartreuse, nearly globe-shaped flower heads. These contrast dramatically with the blue green leaves. *E. griffithii* 'Fireglow' is also widely grown, and is valued for its orange-red bracts and red-veined leaves. It reaches 2 to 3 feet (60 to 90cm) tall. Both are noble contributions to a perennial border, or can be used for impressive mass or bank plantings. *E. polychroma* (also known as *E. epithymoides*) is a stout smaller plant, growing in mounds of 1 to 2 feet (30 to 60cm). It owes its name to the fact that it displays different colors in different seasons: citrus yellow flowers in spring, lime green foliage by summer, and russet or red leaves in autumn. Beware of the sap of all these plants; some people have found it causes skin irritation.

Filipendula rubra

Queen-of-the-prairie

BLOOM TIME: summer

HEIGHT/WIDTH: 6'–8' × 3'–4' (1.8–2.4m × 90–120cm)

LIGHT: full sun–partial shade

ZONES: 3–9

Queen-of-the-prairie

Queen-of-the-prairie is a towering, bushy beauty. Its elegant flower plumes resemble those of the shrub spirea, but these are longer—up to 9 inches (23cm) in length. The plumes are composed of myriad tiny pink flowers. For a deeper pink-rose show, try the cultivar 'Venusta'. You'll find that deadheading prolongs the already generous bloom period. The flowers are joined by jagged forest green leaves that cover the especially strong stems. This plant stands up well to wind and weather.

Queen-of-the-prairie is not a dryland plant, despite what the name suggests. It requires damp or even wet soil, so it might be just right for a boggy spot along a back stone wall or fence. Some water gardeners border the far side of their pools with it—with spectacular results.

When well-situated, queen-of-the-prairie will grow exuberantly and spread by means of runners. So unless you've planted it in a slightly wild spot, you may have to intervene to control it.

Gaillardia × *grandiflora*

Blanket flower

BLOOM TIME: summer

HEIGHT/WIDTH: 2′–3′ × 1′–2′ (60–90cm × 30–60cm)

LIGHT: full sun

ZONES: 3–9

'Goblin' blanket flower

Big, cheerful, daisylike flowers cover this sturdy plant for most of the summer. Up to 4 inches (10cm) across, their rosy red or orange-red petals are tipped with bright yellow; the centers are broad and usually in a complementary shade of bronze or orange. The best cultivar is 'Goblin', a dwarf plant that grows only 1 foot (30cm) tall and is constantly covered with vibrant red-and-yellow blooms. The well-named 'Burgundy' is worth seeking out if you want a solid-colored flower.

The plant forms tidy clumps of handsome, somewhat fuzzy foliage. Blanket flower is undemanding, thriving easily in poor soil, drought conditions, and long, hot summers. A natural for low-maintenance flower borders, this sunny beauty looks terrific in the company of other primary-color flowers such as yellow coreopsis, red salvia, and blue veronica.

Galium odoratum

Sweet woodruff

BLOOM TIME: spring

HEIGHT/WIDTH: 6"–1' × 1' (15–30cm × 30cm)

LIGHT: partial–full shade

ZONES: 3–9

Sweet woodruff

It's hard to imagine a prettier groundcover for shade. The long, thin, apple green leaves occur in whorls, and spread slowly but surely over the years to densely cover large areas. When they are joined by the tiny, dainty, white- to cream-colored flowers (only ¼ inch [6mm] across), the effect is downright enchanting. The name refers to the fact that both leaves and flowers exude a sweet, spicy scent when dried. Some craftspeople like to add sweet woodruff to the stuffing in pillows and mattresses, and it has also been used to enhance homemade wine.

Plant this charmer on banks, along walkways, under trees, or even in the gaps between walkway stones. It will grow in damp or dry soil alike, and is very durable. "Volunteers" that appear beyond their bounds are easily pulled out.

 Gaura lindheimeri

White gaura

BLOOM TIME: summer

HEIGHT/WIDTH: 3'–4' × 1'–2' (90–120cm × 30–60cm)

LIGHT: full sun

ZONES: 5–9

White gaura

It's surprising that this extremely tough and exuberant plant isn't grown more widely. All summer long, it's a fountain of lovely, delicate-looking white flowers that age to a pretty shade of light rosy pink. These are carried on the upper part of long, willowy stems. The leaves, which are dark to medium green and spear-shaped, tend to remain low on the plant and don't steal the show.

To give its best, gaura deserves a place out in the open or a spot in the perennial border with ample elbow room.

Established plants have a sturdy, fleshy root (like a carrot) and are quite drought-tolerant, but well-drained soil is still an important requirement. Gardeners in the hot, humid South are especially enthusiastic about this lovely plant, as it thrives in scorching sun, enervating heat, and poor soil. It also does well up North, but may not grow as large and may not bloom until later in the summer in cooler areas. It falters in the shade, so make sure to give it a site in full sun.

Geranium

Cranesbill, hardy geranium

BLOOM TIME: varies

HEIGHT/WIDTH: 1'–2' × 1'–2' (30–60cm × 30–60cm)

LIGHT: full sun–partial shade

ZONES: 5–9

'Wargrave Pink' and 'Johnson's Blue' cranesbills

Hardy geraniums are sprawlers or mound-formers that cover themselves with pretty saucer-shaped flowers. These come in a range of colors from white to pink to blue, and the dainty petals often have darker-colored veining. The attractive leaves are usually palm-shaped and deeply lobed or cut. They may turn red in autumn, adding a nice late splash of color. The cranesbills are a versatile, easygoing addition to any flower border. They thrive in good, but not overly rich soil and benefit from some shade in the heat of the day.

Probably the finest and, not surprisingly, the most widely planted cranesbill is a hybrid named 'Johnson's Blue'. It produces loads of wonderful, true-blue 2-inch (5cm) flowers. The plant sprawls, so let it act as a "weaver" among other plants. Another choice selection is the lovely and vigorous *G. endressi* 'Wargrave Pink'; the 1-inch (2.5cm) blooms are bright pink. *G. sanguineum* 'Album' has pure white 1½ -inch (4cm) flowers against a backdrop of dark green leaves.

Gypsophila paniculata

Baby's-breath

BLOOM TIME: summer

HEIGHT/WIDTH: 1½'–4' × 3'–4' (45–120cm × 90–120cm)

LIGHT: full sun

ZONES: 3–9

Baby's-breath

It's easy to grow your own baby's-breath. And this plant blooms so generously that you'll have a sweet, airy addition to your garden plus plenty of opportunities to harvest sprays for bouquets. There are many cultivars to choose from beyond the familiar white species. The double-flowered ones are especially desirable—the flowers are a little bigger and a bit fluffier. Look for 'Bristol Fairy' (white) and 'Pink Fairy'. They make nice fillers for sunny parts of the yard.

They billow right over fading bulb foliage and other spring bloomers, and make spiky-flowered plants look less stiff. It's fine to cut flowers for drying even when the plant is in full bloom.

Baby's-breath will do best in soil that is neutral to slightly alkaline, fertile, and moist. The bushes can get a tangled, unkempt look unless you offer support in the form of stakes and string early in the season.

Helenium autumnale

Sneezeweed

BLOOM TIME: late summer

HEIGHT/WIDTH: 4' × 1'–2' (120cm × 30–60cm)

LIGHT: full sun

ZONES: 3–9

Sneezeweed

A perky late-season bloomer, this clump-forming plant began as a pretty wildflower and is now available in a wide range of cultivated varieties. (The common name is a misnomer, perhaps acquired because it blooms at the same time as the real culprit, ragweed.) All of the cultivars are as hardy and eager to bloom as their parent. The branched stems bear loads of 2-inch (5cm) daisylike flowers. The centers are often darker than the notched petals, which droop slightly. 'Moerheim Beauty' has bronze-red flowers that age to burnt orange. The aptly named 'Brilliant' has rich orange flowers with a darker center. A hybrid called 'Kugelsonne' has sunny yellow blooms and a chartreuse center. Try combining some of these with the various autumn-blooming asters for a spirited display.

Give sneezeweed moist soil for best results. In any case, it tends to get rangy, so some gardeners cut it back to about a foot (30cm) high in midsummer. It will bloom about six to eight weeks later.

Helianthus × multiflorus

Perennial sunflower

BLOOM TIME: summer

HEIGHT/WIDTH: 4′–6′ × 2′ (1.2–1.8m × 60cm)

LIGHT: full sun

ZONES: 3–9

'Flore Pleno' perennial sunflower

These hybrid sunflowers are derived from the familiar annuals, and share with their relatives an enthusiasm for growing tall and wide. But these are perennial, of course, and the flowers are substantially smaller—generally between 3 and 5 inches (7.5 and 13cm) across. They are usually a sunny yellow color. A number of the cultivated varieties are double, and some (notably 'Flore Pleno' and 'Loddon Gold') contain so many petals that the blossoms look almost like those of chrysanthemums.

You can expect loads of these bright flowers starting in midsummer and continuing well into autumn. The plant may need staking. It is probably best situated toward the back of your display where its size and exuberance won't overwhelm its neighbors. Such a setting will also downplay the coarse foliage. Despite these seeming drawbacks, sunflowers are hard to beat for dependable, late-season splendor.

Helleborus orientalis

Lenten rose

BLOOM TIME: early spring

HEIGHT/WIDTH: $2' \times 2'$ (60cm $\times$ 60cm)

LIGHT: partial–full shade

ZONES: 4–8

'Atropurpureus' Lenten rose

Easier to grow than its cousin the Christmas rose (*H. niger*), just as gorgeous, and somewhat larger-flowered, this hellebore is often among the first signs of spring. The nodding flowers are slightly cup-shaped, 3 to 4 inches (7.5 to 10cm) across, and come in shades of cream, pink, rose, lavender, or purple, often blushed or speckled with a darker hue. At first glance, they are reminiscent of old-fashioned, single-form roses. The leaves are carried in compound leaflets, and may be evergreen if your winters are not too harsh.

Named cultivars are hard to come by, but you might try some seed-grown hellebores in a shady spot and wait to see what comes up. To ensure a great performance, pamper them with cool, moist, and slightly alkaline soil. Beware: both leaves and roots are poisonous.

Hemerocallis

Daylily

BLOOM TIME: summer

HEIGHT/WIDTH: varies

LIGHT: full sun–partial shade

ZONES: 3–9

Daylily

Where would the perennial garden be without daylilies? They are so dependable, so long blooming, and so handsome, that few plants are their equals. There are literally hundreds of named varieties available, so don't settle for plain old yellow or orange if you want something more exciting. Order a catalog from a specialist (see page 697), and feast your eyes on the amazing range of choices. Some newer, sunfast reds are actually a glorious crimson, and there are countless worthy bicolors (how about a peach-colored daylily with a lavender throat?). For a stouter plant and a fuller flower, consider one of the "tetraploid" hybrids.

Daylilies will grow in many settings and soils, and will be utterly spectacular if you don't take them for granted. Grow them in fertile soil that is adequately drained. Water deeply when the weather is dry and remove spent blossoms regularly—they owe their name to the fact that individual blossoms really do only last one day.

Heuchera × brizoides

Coralbells

BLOOM TIME: spring–summer

HEIGHT/WIDTH: 1'–2½' ×1' (30–75cm × 30cm)

LIGHT: full sun–partial shade

ZONES: 3–9

'Bressingham Hybrids' coralbells

Coralbells are often treasured for their foliage. The leaves, generally green, are produced in mannerly clumps, and look a bit like those of ivy, though more rounded. They remain attractive all season long, making the plant an ideal choice for a semishady perennial border or even a groundcover. *H. × brizoides* hybrids, however, are also treasured for their petite but splendid flowers. Arrayed along tall, graceful stalks above the leaves, these remain in bloom for several weeks in spring or early summer. 'Mt. St. Helens' has red flowers, 'Coral Cloud' has pinkish coral flowers, and 'June Bride' and 'White Cloud' have white flowers. When planted in groups, coralbells in bloom bring an enchanting, fairyland quality to the garden. Relatives and parents of *H. × brizoides* offer an expanded range of leaf colors. The renowned 'Palace Purple' sports rich leaves ranging from maroon to royal purple. Other selections are bronze, russet, or silvery, or feature these colors on their veins for a rich, tapestrylike appearance.

Hibiscus moscheutos

Rose mallow

BLOOM TIME: summer

HEIGHT/WIDTH: 4′–6′ × 3′ (1.2–1.8m × 90cm)

LIGHT: full sun

ZONES: 5–9

Rose mallow

This perennial produces flowers of amazing size—up to 10 inches (25.5cm) across! They're in the classic hibiscus form, complete with five broad, silky petals and that distinctive bottlebrushlike center part. These appear in profusion for weeks on end in the latter part of the summer. You'll find rose mallow offered in red, pink, and white. Unless you have the space and are willing to let several plants steal the scene, your best bet is to tuck just a plant or two into a border with other bold performers.

The plant itself grows quickly, especially in organically rich soil, which it relishes. It is large enough to be mistaken for a shrub, and has strong stems that stand up well to wind, rarely requiring staking. The soft lime green foliage is attractive but vulnerable to Japanese beetles. As with other hibiscus, the rose mallow is also susceptible to white fly. Try to keep the plant healthy, and spray with insecticidal soap if need be.

Hosta

Hosta, plantain lily

BLOOM TIME: varies

HEIGHT/WIDTH: varies

LIGHT: partial–full shade

ZONES: 3–9

'Golden Tiara' hosta

Hostas are popular because they are so simple to grow and bring a cool beauty to shady spots. The trick is to choose wisely from among the many selections. Consider size first: there are small mounding types that stay under 12 inches (30.5cm) across, as well as great broad-shouldered ones that spread out at maturity to 2 ½ feet (75cm) across. There is also great diversity in leaf color, perhaps more so than with any other foliage plant. Hostas range from soft blue-green to shiny, minty bright green. Many varieties are white- or gold-rimmed or feature light green or creamy variegation. And last but not least, there is texture—some hosta leaves

are almost smooth, some are ribbed, and some are quite puckered. All this variety means irresistible opportunities for dressing up your shade garden, whether you plant masses under the high trees or use only a few as accent plants. Although its greatest value is as a foliage plant, don't overlook hosta flowers, which come in either white or various shades of lavender. The blooms line arching stalks and appear anywhere from late spring to late summer, depending on the variety. They can be quite a show in their own right, especially if you've planted a grouping.

Iberis sempervirens

Candytuft

BLOOM TIME: late spring

HEIGHT/WIDTH: 6″–1′ × 2′ (15–30cm × 60cm)

LIGHT: full sun–partial shade

ZONES: 3–9

Candytuft

Why plant the same old annual white alyssum as an edging or in a rock garden when you can get bigger, brighter flowers on a perennial plant? Candytuft has much to recommend it: the plant forms tidy mounds or mats of thin, glossy leaves that look good before, during, and after blooming. And the 1- to 2-inch (1.2 to 2.5cm) flowers are fabulous. Carried in dense, lacy clusters, they literally cover the plant every spring. A popular variety, 'Snowflake', has slightly larger flower heads and stays around 10 inches (25.5cm) tall. 'Little Gem' is a perky dwarf edition.

This plant adores full sun, and needs well-drained soil. It's a good idea after flowering to chop back the plants a few inches (centimeters) to maintain their compact form. For a spectacular, low-maintenance display, try underplanting a maroon-leaved weeping Japanese maple with a skirt of candytuft—it'll stop traffic.

Iris spp.

Tall bearded irises

BLOOM TIME: late spring

HEIGHT/WIDTH: generally 3'–4' × 2'–3' (90–120cm × 60–90cm)

LIGHT: full sun

ZONES: 4–9

Tall bearded iris

There are few sights as splendid as a stand of blooming tall bearded irises, backlit by the sun. They come in practically every color of the rainbow, including bicolors. Some are sweetly fragrant. Check out the newer introductions, and watch the nurseries for special deals on large quantities, because mass plantings are truly an unrivaled spectacle. Unfortunately, these flowers do not bloom for very long, but gardeners continue to lose their hearts to them, anyway.

The secrets to growing terrific bearded irises are simple. They need well-drained soil so their rhizomes don't rot or succumb to disease. Never bury the rhizomes completely; they should be planted only halfway into the ground.

Always keep your irises groomed, both of spent leaves and passed flowers. Also, clean up the ground around your planting so diseases and pests are not harbored in dead leaves or other garden debris. Don't mulch. Tall bearded irises are vulnerable to the dreaded iris borer. If you catch borers before the rhizomes become hollow shells, remove and discard all affected plants and check the surrounding soil. Don't spare the life of a single fat pink grub.

Iris sibirica

Siberian iris

BLOOM TIME: early summer

HEIGHT/WIDTH: $2'-4' \times 2'-3'$ (60–120cm $\times$ 60–90cm)

LIGHT: full sun–partial shade

ZONES: 4–9

Siberian iris

There are many excellent reasons why Siberian irises are so prized by perennial gardeners. Flocks of pretty 2- to 3-inch (5 to 7.5cm) flowers appear dependably year after year. And after the irises are finished blooming, the neat clumps of straplike green foliage remain an attractive contribution to the flower border. Siberian irises grow well in most areas and most soils, and they are hardly ever prey to any pests or diseases.

Traditionally blue, purple, or white, these tough irises have received attention from hybridizers, and the result is many lovely variations on those colors. 'Ewen' has wine red flowers; 'Summer Sky' has soft, sky blue blooms; and 'Orville Fay' has delphinium blue flowers with darker veining. The whimsically named 'Butter and Eggs' is a white-and-yellow bicolor. If you shop around, you'll find dozens of other tempting choices.

Kniphofia uvaria

Red-hot-poker, torch lily

BLOOM TIME: late summer–early autumn

HEIGHT/WIDTH: 2½'–3½' (75–105cm) × 1½'–2'
(45–60cm)

LIGHT: full sun

ZONES: 6–9

Red-hot-poker

These brilliantly colored bloomers are a wonderful contribution to the late-season garden. For most of the summer, the tufts of ordinary-looking grassy leaves (usually blue-green in color), call little attention to themselves. Then the flower spikes emerge and rise a foot (30cm) or more into the air. They bear tapering spires of 1- to 2-inch (2.5 to 5cm) drooping, tubular flowers; these take on a bicolor look because the lower flowers (which open first) are one color, and the upper ones another color. The species is yellow below and fiery orange above. Plant them in a row, along a wall or fence, for example, if you want a real showstopper.

Most red-hot-pokers these days are actually hybrids. Many are in the yellow-orange-red range, but some are solid colors that are a little easier to combine with other flowers. Among these, you'll find the aptly named 'Vanilla', and the similar 'Little Maid' (whose creamy white spikes are especially long). Gold and yellow ones are also pleasant choices; look for 'Ada' and 'Primrose Beauty'.

Lamium maculatum

Lamium

BLOOM TIME: summer

HEIGHT/WIDTH: $1'-1\frac{1}{2}' \times 1'$ (30–45cm $\times$ 30cm)

LIGHT: partial–full shade

ZONES: 4–8

'White Nancy' lamium

An easygoing, creeping groundcover for shade, lamium offers unique, variegated foliage. The oval leaves are a fresh green, spotted, ribbed, or marked with white, light green, or silver. 'White Nancy' and 'Beacon Silver', the most commonly seen cultivars, have green-rimmed foliage that is otherwise entirely silver.

A nice plus about these plants is their flowers, which nearly steal the show when they appear for several weeks each summer. They're only ½ to 1 inch (1.2 to 2.5cm) long, and have a hooded shape. But they're borne in tight little clusters that stand slightly above the foliage. 'White Nancy' has white flowers, which combine with the leaves to make the plants "pop" out of the shade. 'Beacon Silver' has pretty pink flowers.

Essentially a trouble-free plant, lamium will obligingly carpet great areas, even in deep shade. Moist, well-drained soil is best, but the plant will manage even without perfect conditions.

Leucanthemum × superbum

Shasta daisy

BLOOM TIME: summer

HEIGHT/WIDTH: 1'–3' × 2' (30–90cm × 60cm)

LIGHT: full sun–partial shade

ZONES: 5–9

'Little Princess' Shasta daisy

This classic daisy is an old favorite. The large flowers (up to 5 inches [13cm] across) are a crisp white centered with sunny yellow. They cover a somewhat rounded bush of strong stems, loosely lined with skinny, toothed leaves. Don't hesitate to pick plenty of bouquets—it will inspire the plant to continue pumping out blooms all summer long.

You'll discover a number of worthwhile cultivated varieties, including many with double or semidouble flowers. For smaller gardens or tighter spots, consider growing a more compact selection, such as 'Little Princess' or 'Little Miss Muffet'. A newer variety named 'Becky' is bushier and leafier than its parent, blooms a little later, and has been winning raves from Southern gardeners for its ability to endure heat and humidity.

Generally speaking, Shasta daisy is no trouble to grow. But it does need well-drained, fertile soil. If the plant sits in a puddle all winter, it may falter or even die. Also, it performs best in cooler summers, so if yours are hot and steamy, offer Shasta daisy some afternoon shade and keep it well watered.

Liatris spicata

Spike gayfeather

BLOOM TIME: summer

HEIGHT/WIDTH: $2'–5' \times 1\frac{1}{2}'$ (60cm–1.5m $\times$ 45cm)

LIGHT: full sun

ZONES: 3–9

Spike gayfeather

Treasured by bouquet lovers, spike gayfeather is a champ. It blooms eagerly and handsomely, bearing wonderful, dense spires of small purple flowers. These are carried one to a stem, making harvesting easy. They last a long time in a vase and dry beautifully, too. If you can hold back from picking them, however, your garden will soon be hosting lots of butterflies.

A native of the American prairies, spike gayfeather is a tough plant. It does best in somewhat sandy, fertile soil, and develops a strong tuberous rootstock that stores water for survival during dry spells.

A number of terrific cultivars have been developed from the species. The popular 'Kobold' is shorter, around 2 feet (60cm) tall, and has dark reddish purple blooms. (Try it alongside a yellow flower, such as coreopsis, for a striking combination.) 'Floristan White' has gorgeous, pure white spikes.

Linum perenne

Blue flax

BLOOM TIME: late spring–summer

HEIGHT/WIDTH: 1′–2′ × 1′–2′ (30–60cm × 30–60cm)

LIGHT: full sun

ZONES: 5–9

Blue flax

A must for casual cottage garden planting schemes, this lovely blue flower has many endearing qualities. The slim, arching stems bear clouds of sweet, almost delicate 1- to 2-inch (2.5 to 5cm) blooms over a long period. They need sun to open. On hot days, they drop their petals by midafternoon—but the flowers are replaced the next day.

The plant has an appealing, vaselike profile. It sports very thin—almost wispy—foliage in a complementary shade of bluish green. You'll find it easy to slip blue flax into perennial borders. It looks lovely in the neighborhood of many different plants, from pale yellow 'Moonbeam' coreopsis to pink roses.

Blue flax is not long-lived, even when grown in the well-drained, sandy soil it prefers. But it always self-sows, so you'll never be without it.

Liriope muscari

Lilyturf

BLOOM TIME: late summer–autumn

HEIGHT/WIDTH: 1'–2' × 1½' (30–60cm × 45cm)

LIGHT: partial–full shade

ZONES: 6–10

'Variegatum' lilyturf

Lilyturf is a staple in areas with long, hot, and steamy summers. It is one of the few edging or groundcover plants that maintains a cool freshness in those conditions. The spiky leaves are grasslike and narrow, but still substantial. A naturally compact grower, the plant usually stays under 2 feet (60cm), and some of the cultivars are even smaller. (One, 'Christmas Tree', is a mere 8 inches [20.5cm] tall.) The plant readily lends itself to formal edging schemes and is also a superb choice for carpeting the area under tall trees.

Its only drawback is its vulnerability to snails and slugs. So if these pests are in residence in your garden, be prepared to protect your lilyturf.

As the name suggests, the blooms look like taller versions of the spring-flowering bulb *Muscari*, also known as grape hyacinth. They appear on narrow 10- to 20-inch (25.5 to 51cm) spikes late in the season, and are generally purple, though white varieties also exist.

Lobelia cardinalis

Cardinal flower

BLOOM TIME: mid–late summer

HEIGHT/WIDTH: 3′–5′ × 1′ (90cm–1.5m × 30cm)

LIGHT: full sun–full shade

ZONES: 2–9

Cardinal flower

If your garden has a damp spot in need of manageable, low-maintenance color, look no further. The cardinal flower is robust, but not rangy or invasive. Its striking flower spires are carried on tall stalks that emerge from a low rosette. The oblong, slightly serrated leaves are medium to dark green. They ascend the stalk to just short of the blooms. Usually no more than 1½ inches (4cm) long, the flowers have the distinctive fanlike shape found on blue garden lobelias. The species is scarlet, but variations can be found if you hunt for them (some may be crosses with other, similar lobelias). 'Ruby Slippers' is an especially gorgeous choice, as is the richly hued, more subtle 'Garnet'. There's also a white ('Alba') and a soft pink ('Heather Pink'), and many others.

Although this handsome native North American plant is found growing along streams and ponds in the wild, such naturally wet conditions are not mandatory. It will adapt well to the garden proper, just so long as the soil is moist or you water often and mulch.

Lupinus

Lupine

BLOOM TIME: late spring–early summer

HEIGHT/WIDTH: 3′–4′ × 1½′–2′ (90–120cm × 45–60cm)

LIGHT: full sun–partial shade

ZONES: 4–8

Lupine

Stately and gracious, lupines are a mainstay of the classic perennial border. Commonly offered in mixes, the widely available 'Russell Hybrids' is clearly the best choice for its beauty as well as its vigor and durability. This mix offers a full range of showy colors and bicolors, including white, cream, yellow, orange, pink, red, lavender, royal blue, and purple. In full bloom, the tall, dense stalks may need staking.

Even the foliage of lupines is beautiful. It's lance-shaped, between 6 and 12 inches (15 and 30cm) long, and gathered in palmate leaflets. The leaves have a light coating of tiny silky hairs that capture water droplets—a truly fetching sight.

The secret to growing spectacular lupines is in the soil; it should be deep, moist yet well drained, acidic, and moderately rich. These plants are very sensitive to hot, dry weather—a mulch and some shade may help, but they won't be able to take too much of that sort of stress.

Lychnis coronaria

Rose campion

BLOOM TIME: early summer

HEIGHT/WIDTH: 2′–3′ × 1½′ (60–90cm × 45cm)

LIGHT: full sun

ZONES: 4–8

Rose campion

There's nothing else quite like these flowers: they're a bold, vivid shade of pink, almost fluorescent. The easygoing plant produces them in great numbers, so although each flower is only 1 inch (2.5cm) across, the effect is bright and vivacious. Fuzzy, grayish white foliage makes a cool, calming contrast to the loud flowers and lends interest to a border when the plant is not blooming. The plant has rather a loose profile and is multibranched. It may sprawl. Rose campion is rarely long-lived, but it self-sows, so you'll never lose it.

Needless to say, such an unusual-looking plant is not easy to combine with others. You might tuck it into a spot where later-blooming plants won't overlap with it. Or try it in an herb garden setting, or among other gray-leaved plants.

Lysimachia clethroides

Gooseneck loosestrife

BLOOM TIME: summer

HEIGHT/WIDTH: 2'–3' × 3' (60–90cm × 90cm)

LIGHT: full sun–partial shade

ZONES: 3–9

Gooseneck loosestrife

To say that gooseneck loosestrife is easy to grow would be an understatement. Some gardeners find it downright invasive, especially in moist soils. But it is a great beauty. So if you have a spot where this tendency will not be a problem (say, an area under the high shade of trees in need of brightening), go ahead and plant it.

The common name refers to the slender white spikes, which arch over at their tips. This quality becomes absolutely charming when the plant is grown in groups. One writer has likened the sight to "a flock of eager geese on the run." The spikes vary from a mere 3 inches (7.5cm) long to a generous 12 inches (30.5cm). Close inspection reveals that they are composed of dozens of tiny, densely packed flowers. As for the leaves, they're a basic, tapered oval shape, slightly furry, and line the stems right up the base of the flower spikes. The plant's profile is lush and casual.

Malva alcea

Hollyhock mallow

BLOOM TIME: midsummer–autumn

HEIGHT/WIDTH: 3′–4′ × 1′–2′ (90–120cm × 30–60cm)

LIGHT: full sun

ZONES: 4–9

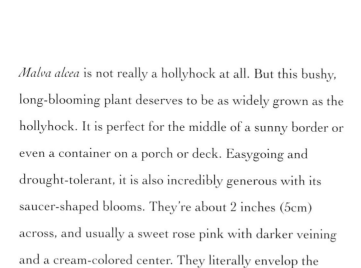

'Fastigiata' hollyhock mallow

Malva alcea is not really a hollyhock at all. But this bushy, long-blooming plant deserves to be as widely grown as the hollyhock. It is perfect for the middle of a sunny border or even a container on a porch or deck. Easygoing and drought-tolerant, it is also incredibly generous with its saucer-shaped blooms. They're about 2 inches (5cm) across, and usually a sweet rose pink with darker veining and a cream-colored center. They literally envelop the entire plant for weeks on end. The sometimes lax stems are lined with rather dainty, lobed palmate leaves. The plant owes its tough constitution to a thick, fibrous root system. And if that doesn't assure its survival in your garden, its propensity to self-sow will.

The most widely available form is a cultivar named 'Fastigiata', which is a neater, more upright plant. But, like the species, it may need to be staked later in the season.

Mertensia virginica

Virginia bluebells

BLOOM TIME: spring

HEIGHT/WIDTH: $1'$–$2' \times 1\frac{1}{2}'$ (30–60cm $\times$ 45cm)

LIGHT: partial–full shade

ZONES: 3–9

Virginia bluebells

Looking for a sweet companion for your spring-flowering bulbs? Something versatile and dependable? Virginia bluebells may be your perennial. A native of southeastern woodlands, it likes similar conditions in the garden: organically rich soil in cool shade. The thin, lance-shaped leaves are mainly basal, but also ascend the stems on short, succulent stalks. At the top of these stalks are clusters of nodding little bells. They begin as pink buds, then open to lilac-blue flowers. The blue will be darker in deeper shade. In any case, the color seems to go with everything, but is particularly fetching combined with small-flowered yellow or white narcissus.

Like the bulbs, though, Virginia bluebells' show ends as summer arrives. The stems die down after bloom, and the plant gradually goes dormant and disappears from view, until next year. So mark its spot if you wish to move or divide it in the autumn, and to avoid trampling it or planting something else right above it.

Monarda didyma

Bee balm

BLOOM TIME: mid–late summer

HEIGHT/WIDTH: 2½′–3′ × 1½′ (75–90cm × 45cm)

LIGHT: full sun–partial shade

ZONES: 4–9

'Cambridge Scarlet' bee balm

This showy relative of mint is just as easy to grow, so long as your garden has the rich, moist soil it needs to thrive. Like mint, it has aromatic dark green leaves and square stems, and can be invasive (keep it in bounds by chopping back at the roots' outer perimeter). The big flower heads, up to 4 inches (10cm) across, are a knockout in full bloom. And hummingbirds find them irresistible.

It is most often seen in scarlet ('Cambridge Scarlet', 'Gardenview Scarlet'), but recent years have seen a flurry of new introductions in other colors. 'Marshall's Delight' is peppermint pink, 'Raspberry Wine' is a clear, unmuddied wine red, 'Claire Grace' is lavender, and 'Snow Queen' is pure white. All offer wonderful possibilities for perennial border combinations, and also look terrific in each other's company.

Traditionally, this stalwart plant has been susceptible to mildew, which disfigures it later in the season. Breeders are well aware of this problem, however, and many of the new varieties mentioned above, while not immune, are touted as "resistant." You can do your part by offering each plant enough elbow room to allow for air circulation, and spraying with a sulfur fungicide if need be.

Nepeta × faassenii

Catmint

BLOOM TIME: early–midsummer

HEIGHT/WIDTH: $1'-1\frac{1}{2}' \times 1\frac{1}{2}'$ (30–45cm $\times$ 45cm)

LIGHT: full sun

ZONES: 4–9

Catmint

Some herblike plants for the garden are a little rangy or sparse flowering. But this is not true of the robust, free-blooming catmint. It produces many generous spires of small, light purple, long-lasting flowers that always look perky and fresh. The fragrant foliage below is a neat gray-green.

The best thing about this plant, though, is its habit. Despite its profuse blooms, it has a natural grace and remains compact and tidy looking. You could certainly use it as an edging in the front of a border, along a path, or in front of rosebushes or other shrubs. Or try massing it as an unusual groundcover in a sunny spot. After the catmint is finished flowering, some gardeners chop it back about halfway. This keeps it neat and may inspire a second round of blooms later in the summer.

Oenothera tetragona

Yellow evening primrose, sundrops

BLOOM TIME: early summer

HEIGHT/WIDTH: 2′ × 1′ (60cm × 30cm)

LIGHT: full sun

ZONES: 4–8

Yellow evening primrose

Few other plants offer the exuberant bright yellow that you get from this clump-forming, but sprawling, plant. Evening primrose sends up fuzzy branched stems that bear spikes of butter yellow, cup-shaped 1- to 2-inch (2.5 to 5cm) blooms in early summer. 'Fireworks' is an improved variety with slightly bigger flowers; it also flowers longer and often has an autumn encore. Other closely related species that are worth growing include *O. fruticosa* and *O. missouriensis* and cultivars of them. Some of these have reddish stems or buds, which add to the plant's overall appeal. You may well be tempted to combine evening primroses with blue or purple flowers, but try it also with yellow-centered white daisies for a fresh-looking display.

Evening primrose is not particular about soil, and will do well in moist or dry settings. However, don't let it sit in saturated, poorly drained soil or it will succumb to rot. It is drought-tolerant and untroubled by pests and diseases.

Paeonia

Herbaceous peony

BLOOM TIME: spring

HEIGHT/WIDTH: 1½'–3½' × 2'–3' (45–105cm ×
60–90cm)

LIGHT: full sun

ZONES: 3–7

'Largo' herbaceous peony

If you live where the winters are long and cold (Zones 3 and 4), you already know your choices of hardy perennials are somewhat limited, and you would be crazy not to grow peonies. Even if you live further south, you would be crazy not to grow them. Peonies have a well-deserved reputation for being as tough as they are gorgeous. The double-flowered varieties are more popular, but the single-flowered ones offer a contrasting center boss of golden stamens. Some new hybrids sport a tuft of extra petals at the center of the bloom. All peonies have handsome divided foliage that is an asset to the garden long after the blooms are gone.

Generally derived from *P. lactiflora* and *P. officinalis*, the hybrids are legion. One of the oldest and still one of the best is the sweetly fragrant 'Festiva Maxima', which has plush white blooms flecked with crimson. Another favorite is the deliciously scented, soft pink 'Sarah Bernhardt'. Do yourself a favor and order a fall catalog (because peonies should be planted in autumn) from a peony specialist or a perennial nursery that devotes many pages to this group.

There's no real mystery to growing fabulous peonies. Just plant the stout rootstocks 1 or 2 inches (2.5 to 5cm) deep in organically rich, well-drained soil.

Papaver orientale

Oriental poppy

BLOOM TIME: early summer

HEIGHT/WIDTH: $2'-4' \times 2'-3'$ (60–120cm $\times$ 60–90cm)

LIGHT: full sun

ZONES: 3–7

Oriental poppy

They may look exotic, but Oriental poppies are no trouble to grow. Just plant them in light or heavy well-drained soil. The large, 4- to 6-inch (10 to 15cm) crepe-paper blossoms open to a graceful goblet shape. When the blossoms are open, you will see black accent markings at the petal bases and a fat, distinctive center mound of stamens. The effect is sensational, especially in the fiery red- and orange-flowered varieties. But the drama is not lost on the pink-flowered varieties either. If you cut some for bouquets, you'll notice a milky sap. Stop the flow and assure longer vase life by searing the cut base with a lit match.

The light green, furry foliage is rather rough looking, but the flowers steal the show anyway. By midsummer, the plant dies back and fades away. The best way to capitalize on Oriental poppy's brief but exciting show is to use it to bridge the gap between spring-flowering bulbs and summer bloomers. A popular and successful perennial companion is baby's-breath (*Gypsophila*), which begins to bloom just as the Oriental poppies fade and quickly billows over the gaps they leave behind.

Penstemon digitalis

Foxglove penstemon

BLOOM TIME: early summer

HEIGHT/WIDTH: 2′–5′ × 2′–3′ (60cm–1.5m × 60–90cm)

LIGHT: full sun

ZONES: 4–8

'Husker Red' foxglove penstemon

There are many species of penstemon, and they all share a more or less erect profile and arching, unbranched spires of small, pretty tubular flowers. But some are tricky to grow well outside of their native habitat (usually the mountains of the West). Foxglove penstemon is one of the more adaptable species. Taller than some of its relatives, it starts from a tufted rosette on the ground, then sends up stout stalks lined with long, lance-shaped leaves. These are topped with jaunty clusters of 1-inch (2.5cm) flowers.

The cultivar 'Husker Red' recently won the Perennial Plant Association's "Plant of the Year" award, an honor bestowed on a perennial that is considered superior and particularly easy to grow. The name 'Husker Red' comes from the reddish foliage and stems. The flowers are white, but sometimes they develop a pink cast. Like all penstemons, *P. digitalis* cannot tolerate sodden soil, so plant it in a well-drained spot. The fibrous root system will help it through periods of drought.

Perovskia atriplicifolia

Russian sage

BLOOM TIME: midsummer–autumn

HEIGHT/WIDTH: 3′ × 2′ (90 × 60cm)

LIGHT: full sun

ZONES: 5–7

Russian sage

Always fresh-looking, always pretty, Russian sage is a great addition to any perennial garden. Great spires of fuzzy, soft lilac-blue flowers bloom for weeks on end in late summer. And silvery gray, cut-leaf foliage emits a pleasant, sagelike scent when handled. This enchanting combination seems to enhance many other colors, from darker purple blooms to softest pink to pastel yellow. The branches also make a splendid contribution to homegrown bouquets.

Because it is broad and bushy, and develops woody stems over time, Russian sage might be taken for a shrub. But in order to encourage the best performance, you should cut it back to the ground in late autumn or early spring so new growth can take the stage. Truly a trouble-free plant, it is immune to pests and withstands heat and drought with style.

Phlox paniculata

Summer phlox

BLOOM TIME: midsummer

HEIGHT/WIDTH: $2'-5' \times 2'$ (60cm–1.5m $\times$ 60cm)

LIGHT: full sun

ZONES: 3–9

Summer phlox

For a carnival of bright, lively color and a bonus of sweet scent, summer phlox is hard to beat. The hybrids come in a broad range of hues, from snowy white to pink, red, lavender, and purple. Many have a contrasting center eye that adds extra sparkle. If you have the space, by all means plant a mixture. Otherwise, you are sure to find at least one or two individual varieties that capture your imagination and fit well into your garden's color scheme. One of the best is 'Bright Eyes', pastel pink with a crimson center—plant it near purple liatris or blue echinops. If you prefer a solid-color phlox, try beet red 'Starfire' or all-white 'David'.

Phlox bloom heavily for weeks on end, provided they're planted in rich soil and get plenty of water. Their only flaw is susceptibility to powdery mildew, which attacks the plants toward the end of the season. A little extra room for air circulation may help. Plant individuals fairly well apart at the outset or do some thinning after the plants are up and growing in the spring. Spraying with an "anti-transpirant" (a product used to prevent foliage from dehydrating—ask at your local garden center) also seems to help. An easier recourse, though, is to plant resistant varieties. Ask for them, or read catalog descriptions carefully.

Platycodon grandiflorus

Balloon flower

BLOOM TIME: summer

HEIGHT/WIDTH: 1½'–2½' × 1' (45–75cm × 30cm)

LIGHT: full sun–partial shade

ZONES: 3–9

Balloon flower

This easygoing, attractive plant gets its name from its buds, which puff out like balloons prior to popping open. The flowers are cup-shaped, and are about 2 inches (5cm) across. They look a lot like campanulas, which is no surprise, since they're in the same family. At any given point over the course of the summer, you'll have both buds and open blooms on the same plant, making for a fun and pretty display. If you deadhead regularly, the blooms will keep on coming. Another plus: the plants will self-sow. Balloon flower provides lots of reliable color in perennial borders.

And you'll find that the blue mixes well with many other colors. You might wish to try other cultivars—balloon flower also comes in pink and white.

Balloon flower demands little of the gardener. It will grow in a variety of soils, but is at its best in sandy, well-drained soil. Note that it is slow to come up in the spring—don't give up on it (it is very hardy). The thick roots help the plant endure periods of drought but also make transplanting tricky.

Polygonatum commutatum

Great Solomon's-seal

BLOOM TIME: spring

HEIGHT/WIDTH: 3′–5′ × 2′–3′ (90cm–1.5m ×
  60–90cm)

LIGHT: partial–full shade

ZONES: 4–8

Great Solomon's-seal

One of the finest and easiest of all shade plants, Solomon's-seal has a wonderful presence in the garden. Strong, gracefully arching stems spread outward, bearing along their length oval-shaped, parallel-veined leaves. In the spring, a jaunty row of lightly perfumed, pale green to white, bell-shaped flowers dangle along the undersides of the stems. These become blue-black berries by late summer.

This is the largest of the Solomon's-seals. If your garden is smaller, you'll find very similar ones that are up to half the size. Or try the closely related, medium-size *P. odoratum* cultivar 'Variegatum', whose leaf edges and tips are splashed with white markings.

In any case, this plant is eager to please. Just give it the woodland soil and shade it prefers, and enjoy the show. If you are building a many-textured shade display, note that great Solomon's-seal combines well with hostas and ferns.

Potentilla atrosanguinea

Himalayan cinquefoil

BLOOM TIME: early summer

HEIGHT/WIDTH: 1½'–2' × 1'–2' (45–60cm × 30–60cm)

LIGHT: full sun

ZONES: 5–8

Himalayan cinquefoil

This groundcovering potentilla is a relative of the bigger, mounding shrubs. It offers a season of attractive foliage and, in late spring, especially vivid color. It grows densely, outcompeting weeds, and spreads gradually, so it's easy to keep in bounds. The medium green foliage, underlaid with silver, consists of compact rosettes of five-fingered leaflets. The 1-inch (2.5cm) red flowers come in clusters. Among the cultivars are some real knockouts, many of which are longer-blooming than the species. Try 'Gibson's Scarlet' (bright red), 'William Rollison' (semidouble, fiery orange and yellow), or 'Fire Dance' (salmon red, edged in yellow).

Use Himalayan cinquefoil in rock garden settings, or plant a row along the front of a warm-colored perennial border. It grows best in fertile soil, is untroubled by pests and diseases, and is happy in sun or part shade. There's only one catch: it struggles in areas with very hot summers or very cold winters.

Primula japonica

Japanese primrose, candelabra primrose

BLOOM TIME: spring

HEIGHT/WIDTH: 1′–2′ × 1′ (30–60cm × 30cm)

LIGHT: partial shade

ZONES: 5–8

Japanese primrose

Of all the beautiful members of the large primrose family, the Japanese primrose is perhaps the easiest to grow. It does require a cool climate, shade, and damp soil, but once these basic needs are met, it will flourish. In fact, it is likely to self-sow, so you might as well plan to devote a broad area to this enthusiastic plant.

The flowers are unique. They line the stalks on all sides, in whorls, and appear in tiers, not just at the top. Individual blossoms are a mere ½ inch (1.5cm) across, but they are clustered so there's no missing them. The flowers range from white to pink to lavender, and are accented with contrasting eyes (darker pink or red, sometimes yellow). As with other primroses, the leaves remain basal (that is, at ground level) and are broadly paddle-shaped.

Combine Japanese primroses with other shade-lovers, but try to stay with foliage plants such as ferns or hostas. You won't want anything to distract from these sensational flowers.

Pulmonaria saccharata

Bethlehem sage

BLOOM TIME: spring

HEIGHT/WIDTH: 9"–1½' × 2' (23–45cm × 60cm)

LIGHT: partial–full shade

ZONES: 3–8

'Mrs. Moon' Bethlehem sage

Large, sturdy leaves dappled with silvery spots and blotches make this groundcovering plant stand out in the shade. The leaves are mostly basal and lance-shaped, and can grow up to 1 foot (30cm) long and 6 inches (15cm) wide. In mild climates, the leaves may weather the winter. When planted en masse, Bethlehem sage forms an elegant, luminous carpet. Do give it shade—the more, the better—and moisture is essential as well. One of its favorite spots is under the shade of tall deciduous trees.

The blossoms, while fleeting, are lovely. Loose clusters of rosy pink buds open to sweet, violet-blue bells. The most widely available variety, 'Mrs. Moon', has pink flowers that age to blue and more prominently spotted leaves. 'Sissinghurst White' has white flowers.

Bethlehem sage is easy to incorporate into a spring bulb display, and the leaves will remain to help disguise the fading bulb foliage. It's also nice with other spring-blooming perennials, particularly white-flowered bleeding-heart.

Rudbeckia fulgida

Black-eyed Susan

BLOOM TIME: midsummer–autumn

HEIGHT/WIDTH: 2′ × 2′ (60cm × 60cm)

LIGHT: full sun

ZONES: 3–10

'Goldsturm' black-eyed Susan

Perennials don't get any easier than this tough, bright, long-blooming daisy. The plant smothers itself in 2- to 3-inch (5 to 7.5cm) blooms for weeks on end. Vibrant, yellow-orange petals surround a chocolate brown center. These not only keep well on the plant but make for exceptional summertime bouquets. The rough-textured leaves are an attractive oval to lance shape. They are a neat, contrasting shade of dark green. The plants don't get leggy, don't flop, and don't give up in heat and drought conditions. A superior selection with even larger flowers (to 4 inches [10cm] across) and a more compact habit is *R. fulgida* var. *sullivantii* 'Goldsturm'.

There are many ways to use this terrific plant. The popular "new American garden" look (not so new now, but still in vogue) pairs it with plain and variegated ornamental grasses for a display that is both exciting and casual. But it is just as easily combined with flowering partners, preferably also in bold colors, such as red bee balm.

Ruta graveolens

Rue

BLOOM TIME: summer

HEIGHT/WIDTH: 1′–3′ × 1′–2′ (30–90cm × 30–60cm)

LIGHT: full sun

ZONES: 4–9

Rue

A mound-forming foliage plant, rue has beautiful, smooth blue-green leaves. Individual leaves are rather small and almost spoon-shaped. They are borne in symmetrical leaflets that are much divided, giving the plant an almost fernlike delicacy. You can promote a bushier, more compact habit by pruning back the plant each spring.

The soft-hued leaves provide a wonderful cooling effect in sunny borders where silver-leaved foliage plants aren't appropriate. Try interplanting with blue-flowered campanu-las or verbenas for a stunning show. (The small, not especially striking mustard yellow flowers appear in early summer to midsummer. If they don't appeal to you, they can be easily removed.)

Rue is gratifyingly easy to grow. It likes sandy or loamy soil best, and is drought-tolerant. Pests and diseases never bother it. The only thing to watch out for is contracting dermatitis when handling the plants—some people develop a rash.

Salvia

Sage

BLOOM TIME: summer

HEIGHT/WIDTH: varies

LIGHT: full sun

ZONES: 4–9

'May Night' sage

The Cinderella of herbs, perennial sage has moved out of the herb garden and into the flower borders and hearts of gardeners in all regions. There are dozens of intriguing and beautiful species and cultivars. All are long blooming and thrive in the heat of summer, making them especially valuable players. A good list from a specialty nursery will set you to dreaming.

Among the many worthy choices are some especially dramatic flowering selections. *Salvia coccinea* adorns its 1- to 2-foot (30 to 60cm) stalks with remarkable scarlet blooms accented with purple. The slightly taller *S.* × *superba* (1½ to 3 feet [45 to 90cm]) features stunning hybrids with dense flower spikes—look for royal purple 'East Friesland' or maroon-tinged purple 'May Night'. Autumn-blooming *Salvia leucantha* 'Emerald' grows to 4 feet (1.2m) tall and has red-violet buds that open to reveal white petals.

Generally speaking, these salvias are clump-forming plants with woody bases. They have gray-green to green foliage (which may be scented), and their flower spires appear in profusion above the leaves. Some spires are sturdy and erect, suggesting use in a formal setting, while others are arching wands perfect for casual plantings.

Scabiosa columbaria

Pincushion flower

BLOOM TIME: summer

HEIGHT/WIDTH: 1½'–2' × 1½'–2' (45–60cm × 45–60cm)

LIGHT: full sun

ZONES: 5–10

'Butterfly Blue' pincushion flower

This little charmer is a hard worker. It produces clouds of lacy 1½-inch (4cm) blooms for most of the summer, especially if you deadhead or pick for bouquets. The plants maintain themselves as tidy clumps and have slightly fuzzy stems and small, cut leaflets of sage green. 'Butterfly Blue' is widely sold and is actually more lavender than blue; 'Pink Mist' is also available. Use both together to bring an instant, cottage garden feel to your yard. Pincushion flowers are also perfect for tucking into a perennial border where all-season color is desired.

Encourage pincushion flower's exuberant performance by planting it in full sun in a light, loamy soil that is toward the alkaline side. It doesn't like excessive heat and humidity, but southern gardeners may have success if there's some cooling afternoon shade.

Sedum spectabile

Stonecrop

BLOOM TIME: late summer

HEIGHT/WIDTH: 1½′–2′ × 1½′ (45–60cm × 45cm)

LIGHT: full sun–partial shade

ZONES: 4–9

'Autumn Joy' stonecrop

Some plants are touted as three- or four-season plants, but the claim often turns out to be unfounded. But this hardy, versatile sedum truly is a chameleon. Technically it is a succulent—it has durable, fleshy, pest- and disease-free foliage. The best hybrid (experts don't agree about the exact parentage), and the one you see everywhere, is named 'Autumn Joy'. Its rounded leaves begin lime green and darken somewhat over the ensuing months. Meanwhile, the 3- to 4-inch (7.5 to 10cm) domed flower heads start out as tight, little gray-green buds, and gradually open to a pleasant shade of pink. As autumn approaches, the flowers start to turn rosy red, then russet, and finally, rust brown. If your winters are not overly harsh, the rust brown heads will remain all through the cold weather. Other cultivars with flower heads in variations of pink and red are also available.

Plant this sedum in decent, well-drained soil. Don't overwater. In fact, don't fuss much over this low-maintenance classic. With very little effort or intervention on your part, it will delight for years to come.

Solidago

Ornamental goldenrod

BLOOM TIME: midsummer–autumn

HEIGHT/WIDTH: varies

LIGHT: full sun

ZONES: 3–9

Ornamental goldenrod

If you think this is a weed plant, look again. Nowadays, thanks more to European horticulturists than to North American ones, there are some terrific hybrids. The best are well behaved enough to stay in bounds in your perennial borders, and feature glorious plumes composed of tiny golden flowers. The only thing they share with their wild cousins is an eagerness to bloom and easy maintenance. There's nothing quite like them in late summer. In both color and form, they make a great contribution to the garden. You'll love them with the yellow-centered Michaelmas daisies (New England asters).

Nurseries that specialize in native plants carry many of these desirable goldenrods. The aptly named *S. rugosa* 'Fireworks' is a compact, dome-shaped, clump-forming plant (3 to 4 feet [90 to 120cm] tall) that cascades with bright yellow color. *S. sphacelata* 'Golden Fleece' is a dwarf selection (1½ to 2 feet [45 to 60cm] tall) that carries its cheery sprays in a tidy, pyramidal fashion. *S. virgaurea* 'Crown of Rays' (2 feet [60cm] tall) has such full, lush plumes that it looks like a golden waterfall. All of these do well in poor-to-average soil—in fact, soil that is too rich will cause them to grow more rampantly than you might wish.

Stachys byzantina

Lamb's-ears

BLOOM TIME: late spring

HEIGHT/WIDTH: $1'–1\frac{1}{2}' \times 1'$ (45cm $\times$ 30cm)

LIGHT: full sun–partial shade

ZONES: 4–9

Lamb's-ears

This silver-leaved plant is a perennial garden classic, and with good reason. So long as it is growing in poor-to-average soil, it will produce wonderful oblong leaves in a consistently lovely shade of silvery gray. The sweet name comes from the texture, which is as soft as felt ... or a lamb's ear.

Because the plant likes to sprawl, it is perfect for soft edging along a path or planter. Or include it in a casual flower border, with pink, lavender, purple, or red perennials or roses. It is also lovely interwoven with irises—it seems to go with all types and colors.

Although some gardeners don't like lamb-ear's blooms and cut them off as soon as they appear, the flowers are hardly offensive. Stout, woolly spikes bear lavender flowers that pass by the time summer is in full swing. If you're in the antiflower camp, you can always grow a nonflowering cultivar. 'Silver Carpet' is considered the best one.

Stokesia laevis

Stokes' aster

BLOOM TIME: summer

HEIGHT/WIDTH: 1'–2' × 1'–2' (30–60cm × 30–60cm)

LIGHT: full sun

ZONES: 5–9

Stokes' aster

Although the blooms of Stokes' aster are wonderfully intricate and delicate looking, they are durable and long lasting, and borne on a tough, vigorous plant. The flower heads are about 4 inches (10cm) across, and feature two rows of numerous petals. The outer petals spray outward in a loose, open fashion, while the shorter, inner ones hug close to the center. The effect is reminiscent of a Chinese aster or a bachelor's button. In any event, they're produced one to a stalk, which is convenient for bouquet-lovers. They also tend to have a long vase life. The species is usually lavender-blue, but there are many fine cultivars. 'Alba', of course, has white flowers. 'Klaus Jelitto' has powder blue blooms. Those of 'Wyoming' are dark blue.

The plant itself is a mound-former, and covered in smooth, spear-shaped leaves that make a nice contrast to the interesting flowers. It is no trouble to grow, and is happiest in soil that is neither too fertile nor too poor. Just avoid letting its area get waterlogged during the winter and don't overwater it.

Thalictrum aquilegifolium

Meadow rue

BLOOM TIME: late spring

HEIGHT/WIDTH: 2′–3′ × 1′ (60–90cm × 30cm)

LIGHT: full sun–partial shade

ZONES: 5–9

Meadow rue

Meadow rue greets spring with powder-puff lavender blooms atop slender, swaying stalks. If lavender doesn't fit in your color plans, look for the white version, 'Alba'. *T. aquilegifolium* is shorter than the other species and doesn't require staking. But it is still tall enough to bring a little height to the middle or back of a flower bed. The "aquilegifolium" part of the name refers to the fact that the dainty, lacy leaves are similar to those of *Aquilegia* (columbine).

These are bluish green and clothe the stems at loose intervals, stopping short of the flower heads. Thanks to the leaves, the plant remains a welcome, graceful presence in the garden even after the flowers have come and gone.

The key to a sterling performance from meadow rue is moist soil, which is what it has in its native habitat. A light mulch and some afternoon shade is a good idea, especially in areas with hot summers.

Tradescantia × andersoniana

Spiderwort

BLOOM TIME: summer

HEIGHT/WIDTH: 1½'–3' × 2' (45–90cm × 60cm)

LIGHT: full sun

ZONES: 5–9

Spiderwort

Spiderwort's clumps of grassy, spear-shaped foliage will enthusiastically cover a sunny bank or serve as a foundation planting. And it has the added bonus of a constant supply of flowers. The leaves can be as long as 1 foot (30cm). They interweave and overlap, generally to the exclusion of weeds. The distinctive, three-petaled flowers look a bit like little tricorner colonial hats. Centered with a small boss of yellow-tipped stamens, they are carried in umbels. About 1½ inches (4cm) across, the flowers are usually a vivid shade of purple, but almost-blue hybrids exist, as do crisp white and rich magenta ones. All appear over a very long period, for weeks or even months. Deadheading is not necessary—the petals fade and drop unobtrusively. If the show begins to dissipate, simply cut back the entire plant hard; by autumn, you should get a repeat performance.

A truly low-maintenance plant, spiderwort is perfectly content with soil that is so poor nothing else seems to thrive in it. Feeding and regular watering are not a good idea, unless you want to encourage excessive foliage growth.

Trollius ✕ _cultorum_

Globeflower

BLOOM TIME: late spring

HEIGHT/WIDTH: $2'-3' \times 1'$ (60–90cm $\times$ 30cm)

LIGHT: full sun–partial shade

ZONES: 3–9

Globeflower

Extra-hardy and extra-vibrant, globeflowers are a wonderful choice for locations with moist soil. Once that basic soil need is met, they are sure to bloom for weeks. Regular deadheading will extend the performance even further. The traditionally yellow blossoms begin as fat, round buds. They spring open to become many-petaled, 1- to 2-inch (2.5 to 5cm), globe-shaped blooms that look a bit like tiny lotus blossoms (though trollius is actually cousin to the buttercup). Because the flowers are usually borne on single, strong stalks, they are a natural for sweet, cheerful bouquets.

The plant forms rather loose, open clumps. The attractive foliage is dark green, palmate, deeply divided, and lines the stems at intervals. A slow grower, globeflower will stay easily within the bounds you allot it.

Some exciting cultivars have appeared in recent years and are as easy to grow as the species. The bicolor 'Be Mine' has butter yellow outer petals and a rich orange center. 'Alabaster' has creamy white blooms. And 'Fireglobe' has fiery orange-yellow flowers.

Verbascum chaixii

Nettle-leaved mullein

BLOOM TIME: summer

HEIGHT/WIDTH: 2′–3′ × 1½′ (60–90cm × 45cm)

LIGHT: full sun

ZONES: 6–9

'Album' nettle-leaved mullein

This is a terrific plant for the middle of a border, especially in the company of purple or blue flowers. Unlike some of its weedy roadside relatives, *V. chaixii* has nice foliage and numerous densely blooming flower stalks. It does retain a preference for well-drained or even dry soil and is easy to grow. This species is perennial, while many other mulleins are short-lived biennials.

The yellow flowers centered with woolly purple-to-maroon stamens are up to 1 inch (2.5cm) across. A wonderful cultivar named 'Album' has white petals and the same attractive centers. It is ideal for a cottage garden setting with other soft-colored flowers.

The sage green leaves, which are 3 to 6 inches (7.5 to 15cm) long, and the strong stems are both coated with a soft fuzz. The best thing about this plant is its stately profile. It always holds itself erect, and never needs staking. However, if you plant it in anything less than full sun, the stalks will bend and contort themselves in their efforts to reach for the sun.

Veronica spicata

Spike speedwell

BLOOM TIME: summer

HEIGHT/WIDTH: 1′–2′ × 1′–2′ (30–60cm × 30–60cm)

LIGHT: full sun–partial shade

ZONES: 4–9

'Red Fox' spike speedwell

Veronica is an upright-growing plant that doesn't get very tall. It is ideal for edging a walk, and well suited to life in a sunny perennial border. Sporting handsome spires of blue-purple blooms, it looks terrific for up to two months running in early summer to midsummer. And diligent dead-heading will prolong the show. The plant spreads out a bit, but has a neat appearance. The lance-shaped, tapered leaves are only about 2 inches (5cm) long and are usually a nice, contrasting matte green.

Veronica is simple to grow. It prefers moderation in all things—moderate soil, not too damp or too dry, and does just as well in full sun as in partial shade. No pests or diseases ever trouble it.

This agreeable plant also comes in colors other than blue-purple. The especially long-blooming 'Icicle' is pure white, and 'Red Fox' is a splendid shade of rosy red. If you have an exact color scheme in mind, you will be happy to learn that there are gradations of shade between blue and purple. The best of these is dark blue 'Sunny Border Blue', which was the Perennial Plant Association's "Plant of the Year" in 1993.

Viola odorata

Sweet violet

BLOOM TIME: spring

HEIGHT/WIDTH: 2″–8″ × 8″ (5.0–20.5cm × 20.5cm)

LIGHT: partial shade

ZONES: 6–9

Sweet violet

This dainty, fragrant violet immediately conjures up visions of Victorian-style Valentine's Day cards. The little leaves, 2 to 3 inches (5 to 7.5cm) long, are appropriately heart-shaped. Unlike some other violets, the flowers rise directly from the center of the plant on short stems. They're only about ¾ inches (2cm) across, but appear in great numbers and waft such an enticing perfume into the air that you almost forget how small they are. Traditionally violet, you can also find *Viola odorata* in other enchanting colors: 'White Czar' is pure white, 'Rosina' is rose pink, and 'Royal Robe' is a deep dark blue.

The most appropriate use of sweet violets is in a woodland setting, where they can enjoy the cool, moist soil and semishade they need to thrive. When happy, they will spread eagerly, making for a sweet groundcover. You can also employ them as edging for a shady border. But your greatest joy in growing these will be slipping out to pick a handful for a bouquet for the house or as a gift.

1 0 0

*F*AVORITE

*R*OSES

Introducing Roses

Everybody knows roses are among the most splendid, most beloved flowers in the world. But not everybody grows them, perhaps because there are some unfortunate misconceptions about them. Traditional rows of hybrid tea roses emerging from a bed of bare earth or bark chips may strike present-day gardeners as boring or stilted. But roses, from hybrid teas to climbers to the newer groundcovering varieties, don't have to be confined to bedding schemes. They can contribute wonderful exuberance to today's popular "mixed" or "naturalistic" gardens of perennials and shrubs. And they often have the bonus of providing more constant color than their companions throughout the course of a summer.

It's also a myth that roses are high-maintenance, requiring all sorts of special pruning and continual spraying just to remain presentable. Rose breeders have been hard at work dispelling these problems. And dedicated rosarians keep tabs on roses past, present, and future, winnowing out the very best. These factors should certainly ease a beginner's worries. A well-chosen rose requires no more special maintenance than many other garden plants. The truth is, there's a great deal of variety in the rose world, and any gardener, no matter where he or she lives, can grow at least one showpiece rose easily and well.

The roses in this chapter were selected based on two sets of criteria. First, they exhibit some of the finest qualities a gardener could wish for: dependable growth, longevity, winter-hardiness, beautiful blooms, and, in many cases, heady fragrance. Second, they are readily available (check your local garden center or order from the mail-order catalogs listed on page 697). Some are old favorites that have stood the test of time, others are terrific new hybrids—the goal was to include a cross section.

Not all of these will grow well everywhere, so read the individual descriptions to see if the rose of your dreams will be happy in your garden. You may also wish to double-check with your local consulting rosarian. The American Rose Society has an entire network of these experts; call or write the society for the one nearest you (see the appendix for the address and phone number).

How to Select a Rose Plant

There are many different kinds of roses, from low-growing groundcovers to classic bushes and hedge types to lusty, towering climbers. Some produce flowers in clusters (these are called floribundas) and others are primarily one-to-a-stem (hybrid teas). Some bloom with abandon just once in the spring or early summer, and others repeat on and off throughout the summer.

No matter where you buy a rose plant, you will find yourself confronted with two choices: potted or bareroot. It's easy to be seduced by the container-grown roses that look already established in potting mix, leafed out and maybe even showing colored buds. But these plants are not the best choice. Rose roots require plenty of room, and too often pot-grown roses are crammed in or potbound, which damages them and inhibits future good growth. Also, the potting mix is quite different (lighter, less dense, and often less fertile) than your garden's soil. The container-grown rose plant is likely to have trouble "leaving home," that is, spreading out beyond its original boundaries as it must to grow and thrive.

If you shop for your rose at a garden center in the spring, choose what looks like the best plant. Look for strong, healthy canes and roots—avoid those that show signs of damage or dehydration. If you're buying a pot-grown plant, at least insist on one in a relatively large container in the hope that the roots are still in good shape. It'll experience less transplant trauma and you'll have more to look forward to if it's just beginning to show signs of life rather than fully leafed out or blooming.

Bareroot plants are sometimes available at garden centers and are the form of choice for mail-order houses. They may look like dry sticks, but don't be deceived by appearances—these are always your best buy. Bareroot plants are dormant, which means that they can be planted earlier than potted roses. They will adapt to the soil in your garden gradually and without transplant trauma, easing into growth at a natural pace.

At garden centers, you'll sometimes find bareroot plants tucked into cardboard or plastic sleeves, protected by a moisture-retaining medium like wood shavings. If possible, slide out your choice and examine it carefully. Don't buy one with dried-out or blackened, wiry roots. The canes should also be in good shape and not yet leafing out.

Mail-order specialists offer a tantalizing array of roses, including many wonderful varieties you'll never find locally. You'll also get the expert information and landscaping ideas, customer service, and a guarantee that a garden center rarely offers.

How to Plant a Rose

If you plant a rose correctly—not a mysterious or difficult process—the plant is sure to do well for you. First of all, though, pick a good site, one in full sun with decent, well-drained soil and a little shelter from drying winds.

Prepare a good hole. Make it about 2 feet (60cm) wide, and, for the bareroot plant, about 18 inches (45cm) deep. A potted rose's hole should be just a little deeper than the depth of the container you bought it in. Then, loosen the bottom and sides of the hole to make it easier for the roots to penetrate the surrounding soil.

BAREROOT ROSES

Soak the plant in a bucket of water for a few hours or overnight before planting to rehydrate it. If you wish, add a small amount of liquid fertilizer to stimulate root growth, plus a tablespoon or two of household bleach to prevent the growth of unwanted bacteria.

When you're ready to plant, take some of the soil you removed while digging the hole and make a mound or cone all the way up. Pack it in place firmly with your hands. You'll find that the bareroot plant's root system's naturally splayed-out form rests easily on the mound. While holding the stem in place with one hand, check that the roots are not tangled and are facing downward. The "bud union" area—the knob where the rose stem meets the root system—should be at ground level (a little lower if you have cold winters, that is, Zones 6 and north). If it's not at ground level, simply add or take away soil on the mound until it's right.

You will refill the hole in two steps. Mix some organic matter, such as compost or aged cow manure, into the soil you've removed and scoop this mix into the hole until it's about halfway full. Sprinkle in some slow-release rose fertil-

izer, bonemeal, and/or superphosphate to nourish the roots. Then add water until the hole is filled to the top. After it drains, finish backfilling. Finally, lay an inch or two (2.5 or 5cm) of mulch such as compost or bark chips to suppress weeds and retain soil moisture.

POTTED ROSES

Gently ease the plant out of the pot and score the sides of the root ball with the side of your trowel or a knife—this loosens it up and allows new roots to form. Place the plant in the hole, and fill in around it with soil amended as described above for the bareroot rose. Firm it into place with your hands, and water well to make sure there are no air pockets. Then mulch around the base of the plant.

BASIC ROSE CARE

WATER

Roses should be watered at least once or twice a week during the summer, and more often only if the plants are obviously wilting. They prefer deep soakings. Always water at ground level, as damp foliage is more susceptible to disease.

FERTILIZER

Roses love food, rewarding the gardener with vigorous growth and fabulous blooms. What to feed roses is a matter of debate. There are products labeled "just for roses" as well as general-use, balanced fertilizers that serve perfectly well. Epsom salts (magnesium sulfate) are often recommended as

a supplement because they stimulate "basal growth," that is, new, major canes. Whatever you use, distribute it generously around the rose's "drip line" (the imaginary line along the bush's outer perimeter) and water it in well.

PRUNING

Wait until early spring, after danger of hard frost is past so new growth doesn't get nipped. Begin by cutting out all "nonnegotiable" growth, such as canes that are winter-damaged, diseased, unshapely, or rubbing against others. Then remove all thin growth, anything smaller in diameter than a pencil. Finally, remove all but five to ten strong canes. Prune the canes that are left, cutting back up to, but no more than, half of a cane's length. That's all there is to it. Your rose will be reinvigorated and soon burst into robust growth. Note: there are some roses that do not require such drastic pruning every single spring. Over the years, keep an eye on yours and the way it's growing and decide if you wish to be more conservative.

ROSE TROUBLESHOOTING

While it's true that roses can fall prey to pests and diseases, it's not true that a rose gardener has to spend the summer doing constant battle. Begin by choosing a rose that is known to grow well in your area. And remember that a rose that starts out healthy is much more likely to remain that way; so plant it well and care for it as described above. Other tips: be sure each rose has plenty of air circulation.

And keep the area around the plant tidy: rake up fallen leaves and clip out growth that looks unhealthy. Prevention is always easier than crisis intervention!

Should your rose show signs of trouble, diagnose and treat it early rather than letting the problem continue. When you must spray, use a product specifically labeled for the problem, follow label directions to the letter, and treat the plant on a dry, windless day.

'Abraham Darby'

TYPE/CLASS: English shrub

HEIGHT: 5 feet (1.5m); 10 feet (3m) as a climber

BLOOM SIZE: 4½ to 5 inches (10cm)

BLOOM TIME: repeats all summer

FRAGRANCE: strong

'Abraham Darby'

This lush-flowered rose is romance itself. The color is downright glorious, a warm apricot with yellow undertones that make the blossom seem lit from within. And the fragrance is delicious—rich and generous, especially in hot sun. The plant makes a big, splendid bush, and because it has lanky, arching stems, you can also train it as a climber. Just watch out for the thorns, which are stout and sharp, up to an inch (2.5cm) long! Fortunately, it doesn't require much pruning and maintains a naturally tidy shape.

'Abraham Darby' is the work of famous English rose breeder David Austin, and like all of his roses, it combines the best qualities of the old-fashioned varieties (sumptuous yet soft color, powerful fragrance, loads of petals for a very full blossom) with the best of the newer hybrids (constant bloom, disease-resistance). Indeed, 'Abraham Darby' may be one of the most disease-resistant English roses around.

'Agnes'

TYPE/CLASS: rugosa hybrid

HEIGHT: 4–7 feet (1.2–2.4m)

BLOOM SIZE: 3½ inches (8cm)

BLOOM TIME: early summer

FRAGRANCE: strong

'Agnes'

Here's your opportunity to grow a very tough rose with delicately beautiful blooms. 'Agnes' is an older cultivar that has stood the test of time, particularly in cold northern gardens. She was also the first yellow-flowered rugosa, and is still considered by many to be the best.

The blooms are a wonderful shade of pastel yellow (the intensity of the color varies, depending on the weather), fluffy with petals, and have a heady, fruity fragrance. Like all rugosas, this plant has dark green, crinkly leaves, plenty of thorns, and is extremely disease-resistant. If the rest of your garden follows a soft-colored theme, try 'Agnes' as an ideal "garden room" boundary or property-line hedge.

'Altissimo'

TYPE/CLASS: climber

HEIGHT: 8–12 feet (2.4–3.7m)

BLOOM SIZE: 5–6 inches (13–15cm)

BLOOM TIME: repeats all summer

FRAGRANCE: medium

'Altissimo'

Somewhat unusual among climbers, this lusty bloomer has single flowers, which simply means they have few petals (five to seven per flower). They're a brilliant shade of crimson, centered by golden stamens, and when they open fully, the flower is breathtaking. They also have a sweet — but not overpowering — rose-perfume fragrance. The dark green foliage is large, robust, and especially disease-resistant.

Another nice thing about 'Altissimo' is that it blooms along its full length, not just toward its top. Be sure to showcase this one; don't relegate it to the back fence. 'Altissimo' would be terrific clambering up a pergola or wide archway, or even just trained up a pillar. It can also be espaliered against a wall.

'America'

TYPE/CLASS: climber

HEIGHT: 9–12 feet (2.7–3.7m)

BLOOM SIZE: 3½–4½ inches (8–11cm)

BLOOM TIME: repeats all summer

FRAGRANCE: medium

'America'

The American Rose Society has given out plenty of awards over the years, but rarely to climbers, so it's significant that 'America' was so honored in 1976. It's a classy rose, with handsomely formed blossoms of coral-pink. Loaded with petals, these blossoms retain the classic hybrid-tea shape and are quite symmetrical. They're also fragrant, with a rich, orange blossom scent. Plus, they appear in clusters, creating a feeling of graceful abundance. The plant itself is a vigorous grower, bushy with medium green leaves, and disease-resistant. (If mildew is a concern in your area, make sure the plant gets good air circulation.)

'America' can be used any number of ways; plant it as a tall upright shrub or train it as an archway showpiece. The form and color are both versatile enough to lend charm to a cottage garden or dignity to a more formal setting.

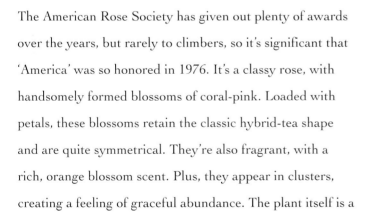

'American Pillar'

TYPE/CLASS: climber/rambler

HEIGHT: 12–20 feet (3.7–6m) or more

BLOOM SIZE: 2–3 inches (5–7.5cm)

BLOOM TIME: late spring–early summer

FRAGRANCE: none

'American Pillar'

This classic rose from the turn of the century has a casual, summer-vacation feel to it, perhaps because we've seen it adorning old summer cottages or cascading over a venerable tree in someone's "back forty." It flowers in extravagant sprays, with literally dozens of blooms per cluster. Each one sports only five hot pink petals, with a crisp white center and a sunburst of yellow stamens. The plant pumps out blooms for weeks, often up to a full month running. A performance this exuberant makes you forgive the lack of fragrance!

The plant itself is easygoing, with glossy green leaves and long, somewhat thorny, pliable canes that lend themselves well to training if you keep after it. Indeed, it will submit willingly to life on an arbor or arch. But left to its own devices, 'American Pillar' is a rambler at heart.

'Angel Face'

TYPE/CLASS: floribunda

HEIGHT: 2–3 feet (60–90cm)

BLOOM SIZE: 3½–4 inches (8–10cm)

BLOOM TIME: repeats all summer

FRAGRANCE: strong

'Angel Face'

You get a lot of fabulous, rich fragrance from this low-growing, mounding rose. Like all floribundas, it blooms mainly in clusters rather than one-to-a-stem, displaying the flowers in all stages of development, from full, pointed buds to completely open. The open flowers are truly gorgeous: a rich, deep mauve, touched with red. They're thick with ruffle-edged petals, so the effect is as lush and feminine as a Victorian greeting card.

The bush is healthy, with lots of dark foliage that has a slight coppery tint to it, a nice complement to the flowers. It is also of a manageable size, making it well-suited to smaller gardens or bedding schemes. You could even tuck one into a perennial border for color and fragrance throughout the summer. For all its superb qualities, 'Angel Face' won an All-America Rose Selections award in 1969.

'Ballerina'

TYPE/CLASS: hybrid musk/polyantha

HEIGHT: 3–6 feet (1–1.8m)

BLOOM SIZE: 1–2 inches (2.5–5cm)

BLOOM TIME: repeats all summer

FRAGRANCE: slight

'Ballerina'

No doubt this lovely rose got its name from its graceful arching stems. Yet the plant has discipline—it is dense with smallish, dark leaves and stays compact, growing about as wide as it does tall. This makes it ideal for a specimen plant, placed out in the open where nobody can fail to admire its charms. But it will also work well as a natural-looking hedge or draped over a low fence.

The dainty, single-form flowers are on the small side, but produced in generous numbers on luxurious tresses of up to a hundred individual blooms. The petals are a fancy pink that darkens toward the outer edges and are centered with a creamy white eye and dark yellow stamens. Like others of its kind, 'Ballerina' has a musky, but subtle, perfume.

'Barbara Bush'

TYPE/CLASS: hybrid tea

HEIGHT: 5 feet (1.5m)

BLOOM SIZE: 5 inches (13cm)

BLOOM TIME: repeats all summer

FRAGRANCE: slight

'Barbara Bush'

There are many pink roses in the world, but this one, named for the former U.S. First Lady, has a robust character and splendid, high-quality blooms. While other pinks flag in the heat of summer, 'Barbara Bush' continues to produce a steady parade of beautiful blossoms. Not a pure pink, they are softer, almost porcelainlike, toward the center, and have a darker, watercolor-brushed pink to the outer petal edges.

As with most hybrid teas, the flowers are produced on single stems, and you'll certainly be tempted to harvest them for bouquets.

The plant itself is strong-growing and disease-resistant, with glossy, dark green leaves that set a handsome stage for the blooms. Its shape is upright and vaselike, making it a regal addition to any garden.

'Beauty Secret'

TYPE/CLASS: miniature

HEIGHT: 10–18 inches (25–45cm)

BLOOM SIZE: 1½ inches (4cm)

BLOOM TIME: repeats all summer

FRAGRANCE: strong

'Beauty Secret'

The American Rose Society bestowed an Award of Excellence upon this precious little plant in 1975. All season long it is laden with terrific, double, dark red blooms that have the formal perfection of larger hybrid tea blooms. Even the buds are fancy, looking just like tiny replicas of those on the long-stemmed red roses of Valentine's Day. All this, plus they're sweetly fragrant.

Like the best minis, the plant is clothed in glossy, dark leaves, and grows vigorously to its full height. 'Beauty Secret' makes a wonderful container-grown rose, particularly if you have an especially pretty pot in mind, something fancier than mere terra-cotta. It can also be grown directly in the ground, but will require winter protection.

'Betty Prior'

TYPE/CLASS: floribunda

HEIGHT: 5–7 feet (1.5–2m)

BLOOM SIZE: 3–3½ inches (7.5–8cm)

BLOOM TIME: repeats all summer

FRAGRANCE: medium

'Betty Prior'

For gardeners who live in the cold North (Zones 5 on up), this rose is a godsend. Not only is it especially hardy, it is a generous bloomer. The flowers are often likened to those of a pink-flowering dogwood tree. Sporting only five slightly ruffled petals and centered with a small boss of yellow stamens, they open to a saucer shape and hold that form well for days. Borne in bountiful clusters, they literally cover the plant with color. Their delicious (though not overpowering) scent can be detected from several feet away.

Many rosarians have remarked that 'Betty Prior' has a nice "wild rose" look—but it is better-behaved. Given that quality, and the fact that it is tall for a floribunda, and rather full, the best use for this agreeable rose may be as a hedge or in a row along a fence.

'Blanc Double de Coubert'

TYPE/CLASS: rugosa hybrid

HEIGHT: 5–7 feet (1.5–2m)

BLOOM SIZE: 2½–3 inches (6.5–7.5cm)

BLOOM TIME: repeats all summer

FRAGRANCE: strong

'Blanc Double de Coubert'

The crisp combination of pure white blooms and dark green leaves makes this shrubby rose a knockout. The flowers are flush with a double load of petals, giving them an almost camellialike appearance, and they have an intense clove fragrance. The peak show is in early summer, but you'll have encores throughout the summer. Nor is that the end: autumn brings another remarkable color duet, this time showcasing big, orange-red hips against a backdrop of bright yellow foliage.

'Blanc Double de Coubert' is a rugosa type, which means that it is exceptionally tough, tolerating poor soil, cold winters (to Zone 3), wind, and salt, and shrugging off pests and diseases. The trade-off comes in the somewhat coarsely textured foliage, the thorny canes, and the vigorous growth habit. But if you need a hardy rose for a difficult spot, 'Blanc Double de Coubert' is a spectacular choice.

'Blaze'

('Improved Blaze')

TYPE/CLASS: climber

HEIGHT: 7–9 feet (2–2.7m)

or more

BLOOM SIZE: 2½–3 inches (6.5–7.5cm)

BLOOM TIME: repeats all summer

FRAGRANCE: slight

'Blaze'

Ablaze with bloom for practically the whole summer, this fabulous climber has generous clusters of big flowers. They're more cherry red than crimson, full of petals, and tend to open all at once—so each spray looks like its own festive bouquet. Unlike some other climbers, 'Blaze' produces blooms along its entire length, which makes it especially suitable for high-traffic areas where it can be admired close at hand.

The plant itself is a vigorous grower, eagerly mounting whatever support you provide it. Its leaves are medium green and disease-resistant. A real prize, this exuberant and trouble-free rose is easy and satisfying to grow. Plants labeled 'Improved Blaze' are touted as extra-disease-resistant.

'Bonica'

('Bonica '82')

TYPE/CLASS: shrub

HEIGHT: 2–4 feet (60–120cm) or more

BLOOM SIZE: 1–2½ inches (2.5–6.5cm)

BLOOM TIME: repeats all summer

FRAGRANCE: none

'Bonica'

Before 1987, no shrub rose had ever won an All-America Rose Selection award, but this one swept the competition that year. It has long, arching branches that are often completely covered by wide sprays of small, full, delicate pink blooms. The leaves are also diminutive and generally disease-free.

But the bush is hardly dainty. It is tough as nails, enduring hot summers and cold winters with equal aplomb.

'Bonica' naturally maintains a compact habit, and asks little from the gardener. It might be the perfect rose if you need a tallish cover for an embankment, but it's also pretty enough to merit a spot in the garden proper. (Note: To avoid confusion with an earlier, obscure rose of the same name, some suppliers use the name 'Bonica '82'.)

'Brandy'

TYPE/CLASS: hybrid tea

HEIGHT: 4–5 feet (1.2–1.5m)

BLOOM SIZE: 4–5 inches (10–13cm)

BLOOM TIME: repeats all summer

FRAGRANCE: strong

'Brandy'

An elegant and perfectly formed rose, the aptly named 'Brandy' has blossoms in a unique shade of coppery apricot, which is a little darker on the interior of the petals than on the outside. Their fragrance is sweet yet slightly spicy, like that of orange blossoms. The leaves have a touch of mahogany to them, especially when new, which makes a gorgeous counterpart to the flowers.

The plant is a strong grower, with a vaselike profile, and bears these wondrous blooms on long cutting stems. Its only flaw seems to be that it is not very winter hardy, but gardeners north of Zone 6 can nurse it through with diligent mulching and wrapping. For a stunning effect, try growing 'Brandy' in the company of white-flowered perennials, such as certain foxgloves or campanulas.

'Brass Band'

TYPE/CLASS: floribunda

HEIGHT: 3–3½ feet (90–105cm)

BLOOM SIZE: 3½–4 inches (8–10cm)

BLOOM TIME: repeats all summer

FRAGRANCE: medium

'Brass Band'

This sprightly rose took top honors in All-America Rose Selections in 1995, and it's easy to see why. A 'Brass Band' bush in full bloom is downright vivacious with bright color. And close inspection reveals that the individual flowers are also splendid. Like all floribundas, this one blooms in clusters, displaying everything from sunny yellow buds to partially open apricot-coral flowers, to fully open showpieces of orange-pink enriched with undertones of coral-pink. The petals are slightly scalloped and substantial, so they keep very well on the bush and are long-lasting in bouquets.

The plant is of top quality, too, with loads of glossy green leaves borne on a compact, somewhat mounding bush. Add 'Brass Band' to a border that features other bright flowers, or plant this shrub in groups for clouds of glorious color.

'Carefree Wonder'

TYPE/CLASS: shrub

HEIGHT: 3–5 feet (1–1.5m)

BLOOM SIZE: 4 inches (10cm)

BLOOM TIME: repeats all summer

FRAGRANCE: slight

'Carefree Wonder'

Admittedly, 'Carefree Wonder' is not the sexiest name, but it certainly is accurate. This plant is a classic example of the best a landscape rose can be: It grows vigorously in an upright yet casual shape, its fresh green foliage is impervious to disease, and it blooms abundantly throughout the summer. The small, perky flowers are a bright candied pink, with a creamy reverse, and are carried in sprays.

Perhaps the best use for this rugged rose would be in a long hedge. You probably won't have to spray it, but be sure to give it plenty of water and fertilizer so it will thrive.

'Chicago Peace'

TYPE/CLASS: hybrid tea

HEIGHT: 4½–5½ feet (1.3–1.5m)

BLOOM SIZE: 5–5½ inches (13–14cm)

BLOOM TIME: repeats all summer

FRAGRANCE: slight

'Chicago Peace'

A justly popular "sport," or chance mutation, of the famous 'Peace' rose, this one has all the best qualities of its parent, including lush, full-petaled blooms, a long bloom period, and a well-branched, husky habit. The main difference is in the flowers; these are decidedly livelier, more pink, and more ruffled. They're still a blend of colors, though, and you'll cherish the enriching tints of copper and the blossom's overall warm glow (thanks to yellow petal bases).

'Chicago Peace' is hardy (to Zone 6). Although its foliage is leathery and dark forest green, it does fall victim to blackspot, so if that disease is a problem in your area, you'll have to spray. Otherwise, it is a terrific rose, eager to please and adaptable to formal and informal garden schemes alike.

'Child's Play'

TYPE/CLASS: miniature

HEIGHT: 15–20 inches (38–51cm)

BLOOM SIZE: 1¾ inches (4.4cm)

BLOOM TIME: repeats all summer

FRAGRANCE: none

'Child's Play'

The first mini ever to sweep both the All-America Rose Selections and win an American Rose Society Award of Excellence (in 1993), this little charmer is as durable as it is pretty. The flowers are of exhibition quality, which means that they have the superb form of their larger cousins the hybrid teas, and that they keep well on the bush or in a vase. They're an unusual, enchanting color combination of crisp white with brushed-pink edges—small as they are, nobody will ever overlook them!

The plants display outstanding resistance to disease, and grow to their dwarf size full of crisp little leaves. Plant a row of 'Child's Play' in a deck planter for a real conversation piece, or tuck them into flower beds where their color will harmonize with the neighboring flowers.

'Chrysler Imperial'

TYPE/CLASS: hybrid tea

HEIGHT: 4–5 feet (1.2–1.5m)

BLOOM SIZE: 4½–5 inches (11–13cm)

BLOOM TIME: repeats all summer

FRAGRANCE: strong

'Chrysler Imperial'

Nowadays, probably no one would name a rose after a car. But when this one appeared in the early 1950s, Americans were in love with automobiles, and 'Chrysler Imperial' immediately conferred a certain panache and romance. The blooms are fabulous, in a rich, velvety shade of crimson, and they perfume the air with an irresistible, almost tangy orange scent. Prior to opening (at the stage when you'll probably want to cut some), the long, strong stems bear shapely, pointed buds. The plant blooms profusely, so you shouldn't hesitate to use your clippers!

The bush is upright yet compact, and laden with matte-green leaves. 'Chrysler Imperial' isn't without its flaws, but for years it remained a sentimental favorite, winning an All-America Selections Award and an award for its fragrance. Its main weakness is its susceptibility to mildew, so gardeners who live in damp climates may have to forego growing it (though it can tolerate humidity). Hot summers are best because the blossoms will open completely.

'Climbing Cécile Brünner'

TYPE/CLASS: climber

HEIGHT: 15–20 feet (4.6–6m)

BLOOM SIZE: 1½ inches (4cm)

BLOOM TIME: repeats all summer

FRAGRANCE: slight

'Climbing Cécile Brünner'

A climbing version of the immensely popular "sweetheart rose" (used so often in corsages and boutonnieres), this special plant has a lot to recommend it. The adorable pastel pink flowers are perfect, tiny versions of hybrid teas, lightly but sweetly scented, and carried in generous sprays. The plant blooms well in early summer, and continues on and off for months until cold weather stops it. Unlike some climbers, the canes aren't very thorny, which makes them easy to work with if you're training the rose on a large trellis, archway, or wall.

'Climbing Cécile Brünner' has demonstrated an ability to perform well in average to poor soil and to tolerate partial shade. So if you're seeking a large, yet delicate-looking climber, and don't have the best conditions to offer, this sweetheart may be your rose.

'Complicata'

TYPE/CLASS: shrub (gallica)

HEIGHT: 5–10 feet (1.5–3m)
   or more

BLOOM SIZE: 4–4½ inches (10–11cm)

BLOOM TIME: once, early summer

FRAGRANCE: medium

'Complicata'

A hybrid that hails from an ancient tribe of European roses, most of which are pink and all of which are fragrant, 'Complicata' is perhaps the best of the old-fashioned gallicas. Its blossoms are large yet single (only five petals) and a brilliant shade of pink, creamy white toward the center, and accented with a dainty boss of small yellow stamens. The scent is reminiscent of ripe berries, and the petals are treasured for potpourris and sachets because the fragrance keeps so well even when they're dried.

The foliage is a paler shade of green than the leaves of most roses, but it complements the flowers well. 'Complicata' is, however, vulnerable to mildew, so gardeners in damp climates beware. The plant is an enthusiastic grower, and will cause you less frustration if you grant it room to roam—it might make a good hedge along a back fence, for instance.

'Constance Spry'

TYPE/CLASS: English shrub

HEIGHT: 5–10 feet (1.5–3m)

BLOOM SIZE: 4½–5 inches (11–13cm)

BLOOM TIME: once in early summer

FRAGRANCE: strong

'Constance Spry'

This pure pink rose is famous thanks to one gorgeous, much-photographed specimen that drapes over a wall and around an elegant white wooden bench in the renowned rose garden at Mottisfont Abbey in Hampshire, England. As that display hints, 'Constance Spry' is a large rose, so while you don't necessarily need the white bench in order to grow it, you will certainly need plenty of space.

It is also famous among rosarians because it is a parent of David Austin's English roses. It has the same wonderful, huge, petal-laden blossoms that look almost like double peonies. Alas, however, the blooms of 'Constance Spry' appear only once a summer (while its successors repeat their bloom). The bloom period is long, though, and the fragrance is utterly luscious.

'Country Dancer'

TYPE/CLASS: shrub

HEIGHT: 4½ feet (1.3m)

BLOOM SIZE: 4 inches (10cm)

BLOOM TIME: repeats all summer

FRAGRANCE: medium

'Country Dancer'

'Country Dancer' was bred at Iowa State University by Griffith Buck, who dedicated years to developing what he and many others consider ideal roses: long-blooming, disease-resistant, and cold-hardy. Its toughness is indisputable, and sure to make this rose very popular with gardeners in the Midwest and North. But its beauty is a wonderful plus: the blooms are a vibrant watermelon pink, and full (but not overfull) of petals, somewhat resembling a double camellia flower. The fragrance is pleasantly fruity.

This is a vigorous shrub, growing taller than wide, so you'll find it easy to tuck in toward the back of a flower border. Just remember that it is constantly in bloom, so place it among companions that are flattered by the bright pink flowers.

'Cupcake'

TYPE/CLASS: miniatures

HEIGHT: 12–16 inches (30–40cm)

BLOOM SIZE: 1½ inches (4cm)

BLOOM TIME: repeats all summer

FRAGRANCE: none

'Cupcake'

Actually, this lovely little rose looks for all the world like the frosting roses found on wedding cakes. Borne in small clusters, each bloom is symmetrical, neat, and dainty, in a clear shade of pink that strays neither to white nor to rose. The petals are heavily textured, so they last well on the bush or when cut.

The bush is compact and covered with glossy green leaves. The stems are fairly thornless, which is another agreeable feature of this endearing plant. 'Cupcake' won a well-deserved Award of Excellence from the American Rose Society in 1983.

'Don Juan'

TYPE/CLASS: climber

HEIGHT: 8–10 feet (2.4–3m)

BLOOM SIZE: 4½–5 inches (11–13cm)

BLOOM TIME: repeats all summer

FRAGRANCE: strong

'Don Juan'

If you live in an area with relatively mild winters (Zones 8 and south), you will find no finer red climber than 'Don Juan'. Gardeners farther north who simply *must* have this rose may be able to get it through the cold weather by gingerly detaching the canes from their support, laying them along the ground, and mounding a mulch of soil and hay over the entire plant until spring returns.

As compared to the cherry red blossoms of the climber 'Blaze', these are a passionate, velvety crimson. With a classic hybrid tea shape, most blooms appear in clusters, but some are on single stems. The fragrance is heady, tawny, almost musky—enough to make you swoon! The dark, leathery leaves are disease-resistant. 'Don Juan' makes a spectacular pillar-trained specimen.

'Dortmund'

TYPE/CLASS: climber

HEIGHT: 10–30 feet (3–9m)

BLOOM SIZE: 3–3½ inches (7.5–8cm)

BLOOM TIME: repeats all summer

FRAGRANCE: medium

'Dortmund'

A super-hardy climber (to Zone 4), 'Dortmund' has been around for years, and has certainly stood the test of time. The flowers are single (they have just five petals), bright red, and glow in the center with a white eye. The petal edges are slightly scalloped, which lends a touch of welcome fancy. Handsome orange-red hips follow the blooms, but you ought to deadhead before they appear or clip them off early to encourage the plant to continue its profuse blooming a little longer. The foliage is quite dark and glossy, providing a nice contrast to both blooms and fruits.

This vigorous climber would be an appropriate accent in a garden of old-fashioned flowers because it has a nice, unpretentious charm. After one initially heavy bloom period, it repeats reliably for the rest of the summer. Only one caveat: without pruning, it may become rather big and sprawling.

'Double Delight'

TYPE/CLASS: hybrid tea

HEIGHT: 3½–4 feet (1–1.2m)

BLOOM SIZE: 5½ inches (14cm)

BLOOM TIME: repeats all summer

FRAGRANCE: strong

'Double Delight'

There is no other hybrid tea quite like 'Double Delight'. Winning raves from gardeners for years, it took top All-America Selections honors in 1977. The big blooms display unusual and spectacular coloration: The scarlet bud whirls open to a creamy white-washed pink blossom, ending in buttery yellow and strawberry red. (The amount of red seems to vary according to the weather.) The powerful scent is ravishing: rich, spicy, and fruity. Needless to say, these flowers make for superb bouquets. Pick them early in the opening process so you can savor the show indoors. As for fitting this unique rose into the garden, well, frankly, it's not easily paired with other roses or many other flowers. But after you've been smitten, you'll find a way.

Be forewarned that 'Double Delight' is a slow starter. It comes into full glory in its second and third seasons. Also, the medium green foliage is prone to mildew in damp climates, so spraying will be necessary for gardeners in those areas.

'Dreamglo'

TYPE/CLASS: miniature

HEIGHT: 18–24 inches (45–60cm)

BLOOM SIZE: 1 inch (2.5cm)

BLOOM TIME: repeats all summer

FRAGRANCE: slight

'Dreamglo'

The blooms of 'Dreamglo' are bicolor, with creamy white petals edged in rosy red, and are prized because they do not fade or wash out in the heat of summer. They have a formal, hybrid tea form, which means that they unfurl evenly from a high center. The overall impression is of a carefully crafted miniature ceramic replica of a rose. Not surprisingly, it is a favorite of rose aficionados who exhibit. The accompanying leaves are medium green, somewhat glossy, and moderately disease-resistant.

On the tall side for a miniature, this vigorous plant easily reaches a height of 2 feet (60cm) so it would be a nice choice for a border along the front of the house, or following a walkway. Winter protection is recommended north of Zone 7.

'Dublin Bay'

TYPE/CLASS: climber

HEIGHT: 8–14 feet (2.4–4.2m)

BLOOM SIZE: 4½ inches (11cm)

BLOOM TIME: repeats all summer

FRAGRANCE: medium

'Dublin Bay'

An excellent climber, this rose has everything going for it. Its deep red flowers are big but not blowsy and double-petaled but not overfull. They appear in loose clusters, so a plant in full bloom is literally clothed in flowers. The large, handsome, leathery leaves are disease-resistant. Growing vigorously but not rampantly, the stems are only moderately thorny, and are easily trained on anything from a pillar to a trellis.

The plant tends to have a lush blooming in early to mid-summer. But since it continues to pump out a steady parade of quality blooms, it won't disappoint through the rest of the season. 'Dublin Bay' is a particular favorite of gardeners in the damp Pacific Northwest because its buds and flowers still look great even if it's been raining on and off all week.

'Europeana'

TYPE/CLASS: floribunda

HEIGHT: 2½–3 feet (75–90cm)

BLOOM SIZE: 3 inches (7.5cm)

BLOOM TIME: repeats all summer

FRAGRANCE: slight

'Europeana'

As an alternative red rose to the generally one-to-a-stem hybrid teas, the cluster-blooming 'Europeana' can't be beat. In any given spray, you'll find the handsome flowers in all stages of development. The stout buds are a classic crimson; they open to reveal medium-size, cupped flowers in a fancy ruby red hue that holds its color well.

This low, spreading shrub also owes its enduring appeal to its foliage, which starts out mahogany (a beautiful backdrop for the blooms) and eventually goes to a rich dark green. It won an All-America Selections award in 1968.

Tall, commanding red hybrid teas are not always easy to place in the garden. Because of its generous sprays of flowers, 'Europeana' is more obliging, particularly if your flower borders include a range of perennials and annuals. It doesn't take up much space, it blooms dependably, and it flatters other bright colors. The only complaint made about 'Europeana' is its occasional bouts with mildew; good air circulation and spraying will prevent that.

'Fair Bianca'

TYPE/CLASS: English shrub

HEIGHT: 3 feet (1m)

BLOOM SIZE: 3–3½ inches (7.5-8cm)

BLOOM TIME: repeats all summer

FRAGRANCE: strong

'Fair Bianca'

It's hard to imagine a prettier, more romantic rose. The stout, round buds are rosy pink, but open to a very lush, symmetrically arranged creamy white blossom. Both stages of bloom are on the bush at any given time, and the effect is adorable. As for the fragrance, it is intense and reminiscent of anise— not too sweet. You won't be able to resist picking bouquets for the house, and you'll be pleased to see that these roses have a long vase life.

Most of the David Austin English roses are medium to large plants; this one is small and compact, ideal for a smaller garden or incorporating into a flower bed. Still, the bush maintains a graceful upright habit. The foliage is matte green and not very dense, lending this rose an overall lacy effect.

'The Fairy'

TYPE/CLASS: shrub (polyantha)

HEIGHT: 1 ½–3 feet (45–90cm)

BLOOM SIZE: 1–1 ½ inches (2.5–4cm)

BLOOM TIME: repeats all summer

FRAGRANCE: none

'The Fairy'

Visitors to your garden might not realize, at first glance, that this is a rose. 'The Fairy' is unique. The adorable pink flowers are tiny, round, and so fluffy with petals that you could almost take them for itsy-bitsy peony blooms. They're borne on abundant sprays that emerge from the equally diminutive shiny green leaves. Blooming occurs a little later than other roses, but the show is certainly in full swing by midsummer, and it doesn't quit until the cold weather comes.

Speaking of cold weather, 'The Fairy' is also exceptionally hardy. It can be grown, and grown well, as far north as Zone 4. And thanks to its unusual appearance, it neither requires nor especially benefits from being grown in a traditional rose garden. This rose really fits in beautifully in a perennial border. It will billow around its companions as they go in and out of bloom, and offer a pretty counterpart to everything from mound-forming blue campanulas to spiky white or purple veronicas.

There seems to be a natural variability in this rose, or perhaps alternate versions are on the market. It can be found as a low, sprawling near-groundcover and as a more upright, though not tall, bush.

'First Prize'

TYPE/CLASS: hybrid tea

HEIGHT: 4–5 feet (1.2–1.5m)

BLOOM SIZE: 5–5½ inches (13–14cm)

BLOOM TIME: repeats all summer

FRAGRANCE: slight

'First Prize'

As the name suggests, this rose has won many awards, including All-America Selections in 1970. The lovely, unique blooms are big, pleasantly scented, and meet the rose aficionado's standard of perfect form. They begin as long, ivory buds but spiral open to reveal a painterly shade of medium pink (almost as if they'd been touched with an artist's brush). This gradually flushes on the outer edges to a richer rose color. The original ivory remains to lighten the very center of the bloom. A fully open flower is a breathtak-ing sight. Like most hybrid teas, 'First Prize' has nice long stems, ideal for cutting—you'll want to pick some just as the buds are beginning to unfurl so you can savor the full effect.

The leaves are dark and leathery, but, alas, not immune to disease. Mildew and blackspot are often a problem. Yet the bush grows vigorously and continues to bloom on and off all summer. It is not especially hardy, so is best enjoyed by gardeners in Zones 7 and south.

'Flower Carpet'

TYPE/CLASS: groundcover

HEIGHT: 1 foot (30cm)

BLOOM SIZE: 2–3 inches (5–7.5cm)

BLOOM TIME: repeats all summer

FRAGRANCE: none

'Flower Carpet'

This rose, officially introduced to North America in 1990, is still quite new. Although the jury's still out, it certainly looks terrific—you'll find it showcased at many garden centers these days. It is marketed as hardy and extra tough, and is touted as tolerating all soil types, even clay. It is also billed as "the environmental rose," meaning that the dark green, glossy foliage should remain healthy and does not require spraying.

But the most remarkable quality of 'Flower Carpet' is its profuse blooms: it foams with clusters of pretty, dark pink blooms for months on end. So if you use it as a groundcover, you can count on a big sweep of color. It would also be an exuberant container plant. In any event, watch for this unique newcomer to grow in popularity—and, no doubt, for more color options to appear in the near future.

'Fragrant Cloud'

TYPE/CLASS: hybrid tea

HEIGHT: 3–5 feet (1–1.5m)

BLOOM SIZE: 4–5 inches (10–13cm)

BLOOM TIME: repeats all summer

FRAGRANCE: strong

'Fragrant Cloud'

The old phrase about 'Fragrant Cloud' is true: "One bloom can scent an entire room!" Indeed, this rose has won many awards for its fragrance, including the prestigious Gamble medal. Rich and intoxicating, it smells of tangerine and mandarin orange.

The blossom's color is the perfect complement to its fabulous fragrance. A pure coral-red from petal tip to petal base, it is simply gorgeous. The large bloom size also adds to the impact (unlike some hybrid teas, it blooms in clus-ters). And you can expect a steady parade of blooms throughout the summer.

All this splendor is borne on an upright bush of luxuri-ous, dark green foliage that resists disease. The plant is also winter-hardy to Zone 7 at least. Give it a prominent spot in your garden and bring your clippers when you're showing it off, so you can send visitors home with a memo-rable bouquet.

'French Lace'

TYPE/CLASS: floribunda

HEIGHT: 3–3½ feet (90–105cm)

BLOOM SIZE: 3½–4 inches (8–10cm)

BLOOM TIME: repeats all summer

FRAGRANCE: medium

'French Lace'

Neither white nor pink, but falling in some sweet, romantic spot between the two, 'French Lace' is an utterly captivating rose. It bears clusters of three to twelve buds, which are ivory to light apricot. The flowers open to porcelain-perfect ivory blooms blushed with a soft pink glow. The blooms are full of petals, giving them an endearing old-fashioned look. Hot sun releases their delicate, carnationlike fragrance.

The dark, smallish leaves (which are rarely troubled by disease) and the thin but strong stems give the bush a lacy look. 'French Lace' grows taller than most floribundas, and combines well with pastel-colored cottage-garden flowers. Not super-hardy, it should be protected for the winter months if you garden in Zones 7 and north. This rose was bestowed with top All-America Selections honors in 1982.

'Fru Dagmar Hastrup'

('Frau Dagmar Hartopp')

TYPE/CLASS: rugosa hybrid

HEIGHT: 3–4 feet (90–120cm)

BLOOM SIZE: 3–3½ inches (7.5–8cm)

BLOOM TIME: repeats all summer

FRAGRANCE: strong

'Fru Dagmar Hastrup'

Considered by some rosarians to be a classic among rugosas, this older variety (bred in Denmark in 1914) has many virtues. In addition to the winter hardiness and immunity to disease we've come to expect from rugosas, this one has especially enchanting blooms. They're large and single, with nearly white stamens, but open cupped rather than flat, which gives them a more refined look. Petal color is beautiful: a soft, elegant, pewter-tinted pink with darker pink veins, almost reminiscent of a geranium petal.

Plus, they're fragrant, smelling strongly of spice. The blooms literally envelop the plant for most of the summer— an unbeatable performance. And in the autumn, look forward to a showing of large, bright red hips.

Possessed of a tidier, better-mannered growth habit than some of its peers, this rose might be the perfect candidate for a low hedge or a property-line planting. Just be warned, 'Fru Dagmar Hastrup' is very thorny.

'Gold Medal'

TYPE/CLASS: grandiflora

HEIGHT: 4½–5½ feet (1.3–1.6m)

BLOOM SIZE: 4 inches (10cm)

BLOOM TIME: repeats all summer

FRAGRANCE: slight

'Gold Medal'

A real powerhouse of big blooms all summer long, 'Gold Medal' flowers in clusters like a floribunda. The difference is that grandifloras tend to open all their flowers at once, so you get quite a blast of color. And what color! A rich, enduring butter yellow, their edges are touched with orange or, in some cases, red, which helps to define their size and beauty from a distance. The blooms of 'Gold Medal' sport a slight, pleasing, citrusy fragrance. They are at their best in warm climates.

A tall, vigorous plant, you can expect a dependable performance from it year after year. It is generally the picture of health, although occasionally it suffers from blackspot.

'Gourmet Popcorn'

TYPE/CLASS: miniature

HEIGHT: 24 inches (60cm)

BLOOM SIZE: 1 inch (2.5cm)

BLOOM TIME: repeats all summer

FRAGRANCE: none

'Gourmet Popcorn'

'Gourmet Popcorn' has been called "the most popular miniature in America," and no wonder. The flowers, carried in generous clusters, are absolutely irresistible, with a double complement of fluttery white petals centered by butter yellow stamens. The tiny buds are also yellow. So at any given time over the course of the summer, the bush is alive with fresh, spunky color—it was given the perfect name!

On the tall side for a miniature, the bush is also of high quality. The small leaves are a flattering shade of dark green, tough, and disease-resistant. The stems have a pleasant cascading habit that further showcases the wonderful blossoms. Give this plant a prominent spot, or devote an entire bed or row to it. It is sure to be a constant source of delight.

'Graham Thomas'

TYPE/CLASS: English shrub

HEIGHT: 4–6 feet (1.2–1.8m) or more

BLOOM SIZE: 3½–4 inches (8–10cm)

BLOOM TIME: repeats all summer

FRAGRANCE: strong

'Graham Thomas'

The most striking thing about this outstandingly beautiful rose is its golden yellow color, too rarely seen in old or new roses. Bred by David Austin, it is quite a tribute to the venerable English rosarian for whom it was named. The cupped flowers are very full, have a generous, tea rose scent, and bloom in clusters. Against a backdrop of matte green leaves, the blooms are completely charming. 'Graham Thomas' always puts forth a great shower of blooms in early summer.

It usually repeats well in most areas (especially those with hot summers) throughout the ensuing months.

The bush is a vigorous grower, and can become fairly tall. Some gardeners have even successfully trained it as a climber. In any event, if your taste runs to the old-fashioned, cottage-garden look, this rose is an absolute must. It is splendid among billowing perennials, especially those with blue or purple flowers.

'Granada'

TYPE/CLASS: hybrid tea

HEIGHT: 5–6 feet (1.5–1.8m)

BLOOM SIZE: 4–5 inches (10–13cm)

BLOOM TIME: repeats all season

FRAGRANCE: strong

'Granada'

There is something wonderfully festive about the deeply fragrant blossoms of this fine rose. A rich blend of dark pink, light pink, and glowing yellow, they seem to be bursting with eager energy. They are smaller than many hybrid tea flowers, but that hardly detracts from their appeal. 'Granada' is a prolific bloomer, and has long cutting stems. You'll find both single-flower stems and the occasional cluster. This rose can fit into various spots in a garden, complementing yellow flowers or contributing its multi-shaded pinks to a pastel-themed border.

The bush has nice, dark, leathery leaves, an upright habit, and is pretty thorny. It is susceptible to mildew, which is best headed off by preventative spraying. 'Granada' is not especially hardy, and does best in Zones 7 and south. It tends to bloom earlier than most roses, and may well become your season-starter.

'Handel'

TYPE/CLASS: climber

HEIGHT: 12–15 feet (3.7–4.6m)

BLOOM SIZE: 3½ inches (8cm)

BLOOM TIME: repeats all summer

FRAGRANCE: none to slight

'Handel'

A classically beautiful bicolor climber, 'Handel' has amazing flowers. Not only are they perfectly formed doubles (that is, displaying upwards of two dozen petals per bloom), but their color is flawless: pure creamy white, gently edged with rose pink. Their debut in midsummer is especially lush, but the plant always repeats on and off for the rest of the season. The fragrance, most detectable on a hot summer day, is softly fruity. Foliage is glossy and medium olive green. Blackspot can be a problem.

'Handel' is a vigorous climber, and you can count on it to cover any support you choose. Its elegant flowers look best in a formal garden setting. Try it on a fan-shaped or lattice trellis, or on a wrought-iron archway.

'Hansa'

TYPE/CLASS: rugosa hybrid

HEIGHT: 4–8 feet (1.2–2.4m)

BLOOM SIZE: 3–3½ inches (7.5–8cm)

BLOOM TIME: repeats all summer

FRAGRANCE: strong

'Hansa'

A very old rugosa hedge rose, still beloved for its rich color, 'Hansa' remains unmatched by any modern relative. The splendid purplish-crimson blooms are reminiscent of the color of a fine Zinfandel wine (though in hot weather, it subsides to lavender). Unlike some rugosas, the flowers are fluffy, full-petaled doubles. And its scent is powerfully spicy. Unfortunately, the stems are too short and weak to make good bouquets. 'Hansa' puts on a great show in spring, repeats periodically through the ensuing months, and finally yields to a full display of large, scarlet hips in autumn.

The remarkably colored blooms are well set off by dark, disease-free foliage. The plants tend to grow as wide as they are tall, a desirable quality in a hedge. If the fresh, vibrant color combination does not clash with your house color or garden scheme, 'Hansa' makes a vigorous boundary or streetside planting.

'Henry Hudson'

TYPE/CLASS: rugosa hybrid

HEIGHT: 3 feet (90cm)

BLOOM SIZE: 3–4 inches (7.5–10cm)

BLOOM TIME: repeats all summer

FRAGRANCE: medium

'Henry Hudson'

One of the newer rugosa varieties, 'Henry Hudson' is part of the Explorer series produced in Canada, so you can count on its hardiness (to Zone 4 at least). It's a dense plant and doesn't grow as tall or wide as some others, which makes it ideal for a low border or hedge in a smaller yard. If you want it to acheive its maximum height, find a spot where it gets less sun—it will grow up to a foot (30cm) taller.

The flowers are lovely. They begin as chubby, deep pink buds and burst open to almost flattened, creamy white blooms with plenty of fluffy petals and a bright center of golden stamens. Cooler temperatures cause them to flush slightly pink. The fragrance is not as overpowering as some rugosas, but still has that signature spiciness. The only shortcoming in this otherwise superb plant is that the flowers must be deadheaded; if you leave them on the rose, they shrivel up, turn brown, and detract from the plant's beauty.

'Heritage'

TYPE/CLASS: English shrub

HEIGHT: 4–6 feet (1.2–1.8m)

BLOOM SIZE: 4–5 inches (10–13cm)

BLOOM TIME: repeats all summer

FRAGRANCE: strong

'Heritage'

This perfectly gorgeous, pure pink rose is destined to become a classic. Its breeder, the esteemed David Austin, says it's his favorite—quite a statement, considering how many lovely English roses he has developed! The blooms are dense with shell pink petals, cup-shaped, and waft a seductive, lemon tea fragrance into the air. They're carried in sprays, which makes the bush's prolific performance all the more generous.

The plant is also of excellent quality. Neither too large nor too small, it has a handsome, compact habit that recommends it for single plantings as well as group shows. While not completely thornless, the canes are far less bristly than some English roses. It is also more winter-hardy than some of its relatives.

'Honor'

TYPE/CLASS: hybrid tea

HEIGHT: 5–7 feet (1.5–2m)

BLOOM SIZE: 4–5 inches (10–13cm)

BLOOM TIME: repeats all summer

FRAGRANCE: slight

'Honor'

There may be other white hybrid teas, but 'Honor' is a standout. The color is an exceptionally pure, sugared white, tending neither toward soft pink nor cream or yellow. The buds on this relentless bloomer are big and stately, and unfurl to large, double blooms that flatten out to almost a saucer shape without losing their grace. And the cutting stems are especially long. White roses aren't generally very fragrant, but you will detect a sweet, delicate scent that suits the plant's cool, soothing demeanor.

Meanwhile, the dark, glossy foliage is fairly large, in scale with the blooms. Usually quite healthy, it is occasionally troubled by mildew later in the season. The plant's habit is upright and vigorous. With these many sterling qualities, it comes as no surprise that 'Honor' is an award-winner. The All-America Rose Selections hailed it upon its introduction in 1980. If you have a white house or fence, this rose is a must.

'Iceberg'

TYPE/CLASS: floribunda

HEIGHT: 3–4 feet (90–120cm)

BLOOM SIZE: 3 inches (7.5cm)

BLOOM TIME: repeats all summer

FRAGRANCE: medium

'Iceberg'

Justly popular for almost forty years, this sweetly scented floribunda is unrivaled for its fast yet neat growth and its glorious sprays of flowers. Each spray is composed of up to a dozen blooms in various stages of opening. And at all stages, the full-petaled flowers retain their wondrous, crisp whiteness. You'll want to be out harvesting flowers for bouquets all the time, which is fine, because 'Iceberg' is an enthusiastic bloomer and will quickly replenish the supply.

A robust plant, it is enveloped in attractive, smallish light green leaves and is practically thorn-free. Admirably impervious to disease, it is vulnerable only to blackspot in areas where this disease is traditionally a problem (spraying should take care of that, though). Because 'Iceberg' is some-what taller than other floribundas, you can spotlight it as a specimen plant. Try a pair flanking a gate or doorway, where their beauty, fragrance, and near-thornlessness will be much admired.

'Ingrid Bergman'

TYPE/CLASS: hybrid tea

HEIGHT: 4 ½ feet (1.3m)

BLOOM SIZE: 4–5 inches (10–13cm)

BLOOM TIME: repeats all summer

FRAGRANCE: none

'Ingrid Bergman'

'Ingrid Bergman' is perhaps the most popular red rose in Europe, and is slowly catching on in North America. It has won numerous awards in Europe, including gold medals at competitions in Madrid and Belfast and top honors in The Hague (note the diverse climates!).

As classy as the actress it is named for, 'Ingrid Bergman' features immaculate, silky blooms of deep, dark red. These hold up remarkably well in the heat of summer, without the wilting or burned edges that some of its peers are prone to. They're carried on long cutting stems, and can last for quite a while in a vase. The dense foliage is a rich, dark green. The plant's only flaw is that it lacks fragrance. Otherwise, there is probably no finer red bedding rose anywhere.

'Intrigue'

TYPE/CLASS: floribunda

HEIGHT: 3 feet (90cm)

BLOOM SIZE: 3 inches (7.5cm)

BLOOM TIME: repeats all summer

FRAGRANCE: strong

'Intrigue'

If you adore fragrant roses, award-winning 'Intrigue' is a stunning choice. A heady, delicious, almost lemony scent literally radiates from this bush on hot summer days. And the color is a knockout: a rich, deep plum, rare in floribundas—and indeed in all roses. The petals are especially ruffled, giving the blooms an almost old-fashioned look.

Like all floribundas, this rose blooms in clusters, so the bush is frequently laden with color. Dark green, leathery leaves complete the picture. It is no wonder 'Intrigue' has many fans; its awards include the coveted Fragrance Medal at Madrid and All-America honors in 1984.

The compact bush habit makes it easy to incorporate 'Intrigue' into the garden proper, perhaps in the heart of a sunny perennial border. As for color combinations, try it with white or pale yellow flowers—in the garden and in a vase.

'Jean Kenneally'

TYPE/CLASS: miniature

HEIGHT: 1½–2 feet (45–60cm) or more

BLOOM SIZE: 1½ inches (4cm)

BLOOM TIME: repeats all summer

FRAGRANCE: slight

'Jean Kenneally'

In 1986, this superb miniature won an Award of Excellence from the American Rose Society. It's easy to see why. Not only is it of "exhibition quality" (meaning flawless form and habit), but it makes a great landscaping rose, too. When well cared for, the handsome, upright bush grows taller and wider than most miniatures.

As for the flowers, they are irresistible. They're a sweet honeyed apricot color throughout, and have a classic, hybrid tea shape (though, of course, they're much smaller). Carried in lush clusters, they cover the bush when it blooms in midseason and repeat well for many weeks to follow.

If you have a pastel flower border, 'Jean Kenneally' is an appropriate size and color for inclusion. Or use it as an edging, down a row of taller roses.

'Jeeper's Creeper'

TYPE/CLASS: groundcover

HEIGHT: 2–2½ feet (60–75cm)

BLOOM SIZE: 1½ inches (4cm)

BLOOM TIME: repeats all summer

FRAGRANCE: none

'Jeeper's Creeper'

Groundcover roses are still a relatively new introduction, but since they're long-blooming, they're bound for wide popularity. 'Jeeper's Creeper' is probably the best white to appear so far. An incredibly heavy bloomer, it smothers its low, sprawling form with crisp white blossoms. These are single, open or loosely cupped, and display a sparkling center of yellow stamens. The leaves are correspondingly small and a nice, bright green. The overall effect is both vivacious and cooling.

This plant would be ideal as a low-maintenance foundation, bank, or curbside planting. Although it doesn't grow tall, it spreads vigorously to the sides. Allow each plant about 5 feet (1.5m) of room.

'John Cabot'

TYPE/CLASS: climber (kordesii)

HEIGHT: 8–10 feet (2.4–3m)

BLOOM SIZE: 3–4 inches (7.5–10cm)

BLOOM TIME: repeats all summer

FRAGRANCE: none

'John Cabot'

Incredible as it may sound, this husky climber is hardy to Zone 3. Many years in the making, it was bred in Ottawa, Canada, and is part of the heralded Explorer series of ultra-hardy roses. The stems are long and arching, best suited to trellising, although you could also keep it in bounds as a large shrub.

The full-petaled, semidouble blooms are rich, deep pink tending toward red—sometimes they display a hint of violet. The foliage is medium green and highly resistant to disease.

A plant this tough, vigorous, and attractive is an excellent choice for anyone gardening in a harsh climate. It shouldn't need winter protection, and summer will find it showing off its lovely blooms for up to ten consecutive weeks.

'Joseph's Coat'

TYPE/CLASS: climber

HEIGHT: 8–10 feet (2.4–3m)

BLOOM SIZE: 3–4 inches (7.5–10cm)

BLOOM TIME: repeats all summer

FRAGRANCE: slight

'Joseph's Coat'

The name for this rose is truly inspired, because it is quite possibly the most multicolored or chameleonlike of all roses. To call it a "red and yellow bicolor" is an oversimplification. The large flowers open boldly yellow with red flushes; they change over a day or two to orangey red, with rose toward the outside of the petals and ivory within; finally, they become a softer rosy red and the ivory mellows to creamy yellow. Since the plant blooms in clusters, this exciting show is constantly going on in all stages. It tends to have a block-buster first round of blooms, then repeats a bit on and off for the rest of the summer. Some say 'Joseph's Coat' has no fragrance, but in fact it has quite an appealing, if gentle, somewhat fruity scent.

Although it makes a fine climber, you can also allow it to go its own way, with minimal maintenance pruning, and enjoy it as an exuberant, large shrub. Either way, it is sure to bring dynamic energy to your garden.

'Just Joey'

TYPE/CLASS: hybrid tea

HEIGHT: 3–3½ feet (90–105cm)

BLOOM SIZE: 4–5 inches (10–13cm)

BLOOM TIME: repeats all summer

FRAGRANCE: strong

'Just Joey'

Despite its large blooms, 'Just Joey' never gives the impression of being bold or aggressive. The subtle flower color has a lot to do with this—it's a gorgeous shade of coppery apricot through and through. And the foliage, which is dark green and disease-resistant, is mahogany-tinted, making for an elegant counterpart. Also, the plant itself is not especially large or spreading. The fragrance is strong, delicious, and spicy.

Before you fall in love with this rose, however, be aware of its climatic limitations. Very hot summers, as in the Deep South, tend to cause sparse growth and inhibit flowering. But it's not super-hardy, either, so gardeners north of Zone 6 will have to give it winter protection and hope for the best. That said, it is still among the loveliest and most worthwhile of all soft-colored roses.

'L. D. Braithwaite'

TYPE/CLASS: English shrub

HEIGHT: 5–6 feet (1.5–1.8m)

BLOOM SIZE: 4–4¼ inches

BLOOM TIME: repeats all summer

FRAGRANCE: strong

'L. D. Braithwaite'

Here's another triumph from English rose breeder David Austin. This one is special because the deep crimson color is outstanding, and stays fast without fading as so many other reds are prone to do. The flower is loosely packed with richly fragrant petals that are displayed in a cup shape. When it is completely open, you will detect a flash of gold from the stamens in the center.

The shrub is on the large side, and eventually grows as wide as it is tall. Its dense, emerald green foliage flatters those magnificent blooms. Whether it is placed in front of a white wall, alongside a white fence, or at the back of a classic, warm-hued perennial border, you can be sure that 'L. D. Braithwaite' will bring a touch of glory to your garden or yard.

'Louise Odier'

TYPE/CLASS: shrub (Bourbon)

HEIGHT: 4½–5½ feet (1.3–1.6m)

BLOOM SIZE: 3½ inches (8cm)

BLOOM TIME: repeats all summer

FRAGRANCE: strong

'Louise Odier'

An enduringly popular Victorian-style rose, 'Louise Odier' is a sensational, full-petaled dark pink blessed with an intoxicating scent. Its nearly thorn-free canes sometimes bow under the weight of the bloom clusters. That quality, coupled with its graceful upright, vaselike shape (most other Bourbons are large shrubs), lend the entire plant a pretty, fountain-of-blooms profile. Feature this old-fashioned classic in a prominent spot with ample elbow room so you can savor its beauty.

Unlike some other vintage roses, this rose repeat-blooms well into autumn. The plant is quite vigorous and winter hardy to Zones 4 and 5. It is also disease-resistant.

'Madame Alfred Carrière'

TYPE/CLASS: climber (noisette)

HEIGHT: 10–15 feet (3–4.6m) or more

BLOOM SIZE: 2½–3 inches (6.5–7.5cm)

BLOOM TIME: repeats all summer

FRAGRANCE: medium

'Madame Alfred Carrière'

A vigorous, old-fashioned climber that blooms in plush clusters, 'Madame Alfred Carrière' sports some of the prettiest and most fragrant blossoms to be found on a white climber. They are laden with petals, and open to a lush, loose, exuberant form. The color has a porcelain quality, opening very pale pink and maturing to a shade more cream than pure white. It repeat blooms very reliably. And the tea rose scent is quite powerful, noticeable from several feet away and dizzying if you stick your nose right into a blossom.

This rose is a good choice for a spot where you want fast and abundant cover, such as on a pillar or even a wall. Unlike some others, it will tolerate partial shade. The long, strong stems are clothed in plenty of bright green leaves. It is reasonably hardy (to Zone 6, at least).

'Madame Isaac Pereire'

TYPE/CLASS: shrub (Bourbon)

HEIGHT: 5–7 feet (1.5–2m)

BLOOM SIZE: 3½–4 inches (8–10cm)

BLOOM TIME: repeats all summer

FRAGRANCE: strong

'Madame Isaac Pereire'

It is worth noting that of all roses, both old-fashioned and new, this is the one professional rosarians frequently call "the world's most fragrant rose." The full, almost peony-shaped flowers are a splendid raspberry pink and the scent is a sure match: it's fruity and intoxicating, like sun-warmed berry jam.

Like other Bourbon roses, 'Madame Isaac Pereire' has a big, spreading, billowy form, with plenty of moderately thorny branches. The foliage is thick, dark green, and disease-resistant. You can grow it as a full shrub or train it as a climber. Either way, it will oblige with a prolific initial bloom in midsummer and continue to throw off additional blooms well into autumn.

Obviously, this is not a rose for the fainthearted. But if you have space for only one big rose, and want a showpiece, grow this one.

'Magic Carpet'

TYPE/CLASS: groundcover

HEIGHT: 18 inches (45cm)

BLOOM SIZE: 2 inches (5cm)

BLOOM TIME: repeats all summer

FRAGRANCE: medium

'Magic Carpet'

If you're seeking a fragrant groundcovering rose, look no further. Like other lavender-colored roses, 'Magic Carpet' has a pleasant spicy scent. From a distance, the blooms are a soft lilac color, but up close, you'll notice more charming details—each tiny petal has an accenting splash of white and the flower is centered with golden stamens. Blooms are semidouble, each carrying approximately fifteen petals. The foliage is a sharp, dark green.

The plant spends its vigor growing outward rather than upward. It sprawls in all directions to between 3 and 4 feet (90 and 120cm), so be sure to plan for this eventual size. No special pruning is necessary. Diligent watering and fertilizing will guarantee a lush carpet. Because of the lovely fragrance, this groundcover deserves to be sited where you can appreciate it daily, such as along the front of the house or bordering a walkway.

'Magic Carrousel'

TYPE/CLASS: miniature

HEIGHT: 15–18 inches (38–45cm)

BLOOM SIZE: 2 inches (5cm)

BLOOM TIME: repeats all summer

FRAGRANCE: none

'Magic Carrousel'

Although the semidouble blooms are small, they pack quite a punch when they're fully open. Each petal is creamy white but evenly rimmed with bright pinkish red. The overall effect is formal, which no doubt is the reason 'Magic Carrousel' is a popular choice of florists for boutonnieres. It also won an Award of Excellence from the American Rose Society in 1975.

The plant is of equally high quality. It's clothed in disease-resistant, medium-green leaves. With enough room to spread out (that is, if you plant it in the ground rather than in a pot), this vigorous miniature may reach 30 inches (75cm) tall.

To get the most out of 'Magic Carrousel', plant it where the whiteness of the inner petals becomes an accent. Try a row along a white fence or wall, or near white-barked birch trees. Just make sure it doesn't get too much shade.

'Maiden's Blush'

TYPE/CLASS: shrub (alba)

HEIGHT: 5–8 feet (1.5–2.4m)

BLOOM SIZE: 3 inches (7.5cm)

BLOOM TIME: blooms once in early summer

FRAGRANCE: strong

'Maiden's Blush'

The combination of soft pastel blooms and soft-colored leaves on this old-fashioned shrub is unique and enchanting. Although "alba" means white, the loosely double blooms open shell pink and soften over several days until the center is the darkest part remaining and the outer petals are cream-colored. This lovely sight is displayed against profuse blue-gray foliage.

The plant only blooms once a season, but it does so abundantly. Borne in sprays, the flowers seem to froth out-ward on the graceful, arching canes. The tantalizing fragrance is not overwhelming, but lingers in your memory. By all means, cut some for bouquets—and display them in your most elegant vase.

A good way to use this distinctive rose is along the rear of a pastel-themed perennial border. The flowers will enhance the display when they are in bloom, and the foliage will remain through the rest of the season as an elegant, novel backdrop.

'Mary Rose'

TYPE/CLASS: English shrub

HEIGHT: 4–6 feet (1.2–1.8m)

BLOOM SIZE: 4 inches (10cm)

BLOOM TIME: repeats all summer

FRAGRANCE: slight

'Mary Rose'

Many rosarians agree that 'Mary Rose' is one of David Austin's finest English rose introductions. The plant's habit is simply outstanding: It grows strongly into a dense, well-branched, handsome bush that responds especially well to pruning (just watch out for the thorns!). 'Mary Rose' has also shown itself to be pest- and disease-resistant.

Meanwhile, the blooms are some of the most romantic you'll find anywhere. Gorgeous, full-petaled, and cupped, they're pure peppermint pink, redolent with sweet rose perfume. The plant starts blooming early in the season, and doesn't let up until autumn, a terrific performance. If you love the look of old-fashioned roses but want a full season of bloom, look no further than this sure classic.

'Medallion'

TYPE/CLASS: hybrid tea

HEIGHT: 4½–5½ feet (1.3–1.6m)

BLOOM SIZE: 5–7 inches (13–18cm)

BLOOM TIME: repeats all summer

FRAGRANCE: strong

'Medallion'

This rose's enormous flowers are dramatic from across a yard and enchanting at close range. The classically formed pink to crimson buds unfurl to silky, rose-blushed orange blossoms that mellow to light apricot. The plant is in bloom all summer long, and the fragrance is rich and fruity, like sun-warmed nectarines. Not surprisingly, this magnificent bloomer was an All-America Rose Selection in 1973, the year it was introduced.

These flowers make fantastic bouquets not only because of the long cutting stems but also because the petals gain longevity from their heavy texture. But wait until the bud is starting to spring open before cutting, or it may not finish.

Taller and more stately than many hybrid teas, 'Medallion' offers great presence in a garden, so don't place it too far back or out of range. Instead, try to find a spot where it can solo, such as a corner or entrance. This siting will also address the plant's only flaw—its large, medium-green foliage can get mildewed, and better air circulation will help. Also, north of Zone 7, be sure to give this rose winter protection.

'Mermaid'

TYPE/CLASS: climber

HEIGHT: 15–20 feet (4.6–6m)

BLOOM SIZE: 4½–5½ inches (11–14cm)

BLOOM TIME: once in midsummer

FRAGRANCE: medium

'Mermaid'

Single, cupped flowers of a sweet canary yellow cascade from this very vigorous climber. There are only five petals per blossom, but they are flawless, and made even lovelier by a generous flush of jewellike golden stamens in their centers. The fragrance is sweetly honeyed. 'Mermaid' always has a wonderful, long-lasting debut in midsummer, and in mild climates it often reblooms repeatedly for many weeks to follow.

The plant itself is anything but delicate. The dark green leaves are admirably disease-resistant. But the long, wickedly thorny stems are lax, somewhat brittle, and difficult to prune.

Given half a chance, 'Mermaid' will grow lustily and cover a large area, so the best sites for it are probably ones where you can leave it be. Let it smother a dead or dying tree, a tall fence, or an unattractive shed or other outbuilding. Finally, be aware that this rose is rather tender, and won't thrive north of Zone 7.

'Mister Lincoln'

TYPE/CLASS: hybrid tea

HEIGHT: 4½–5½ feet (1.3–1.6m)

BLOOM SIZE: 5½ inches (14cm)

BLOOM TIME: repeats all summer

FRAGRANCE: strong

'Mister Lincoln'

A big All-America Selections award-winner in 1965, no other red rose has held rose-lovers' affections so well for so long, and perhaps none ever will. A true classic, the 'Mister Lincoln' blossom is exactly what you dream of: richly colored, powerfully perfumed, and classically formed. The cutting stems are long and strong and each one bears a single flower. You may harvest it in the bud, but wait until the lower sepals have peeled back.

The plant itself is equally elegant. It is tallish, robust, and forms a lovely urn shape. The medium-green leaves are large and significantly more mildew-resistant than those of other red roses (though they are not immune). As for the bloom period, expect a long-running performance. Rather than flagging on hot summer days, 'Mister Lincoln' is sensational.

'Morden Blush'

TYPE/CLASS: shrub

HEIGHT: 2½–4 feet (75–120cm)

BLOOM SIZE: 3–4 inches

BLOOM TIME: repeats all summer

FRAGRANCE: none

'Morden Blush'

The surprising thing about this low-growing shrub is that it possesses such delicate beauty, yet is such a tough plant. Each picture-perfect, double blossom has lightly scalloped petals of softest peachy pink; these are carried in lush sprays. They're set against splendid, glossy, dark green foliage. A single bush would bring character to a flower border of comparable-size perennials, while a whole row would make a lovely hedge.

As for hardiness, 'Morden Blush' is hard to beat. Its Canadian breeders have found that it sails through Zone 3 winters. It also tolerates summer heat very well. And if all that wasn't enough, this excellent plant is also a workhorse of a bloomer. It's been known to bloom nonstop for three solid months.

'Morden Fireglow'

TYPECLASS: shrub

HEIGHT: 3–5 feet (1–1.5m)

BLOOM SIZE: 3 inches (7.5cm)

BLOOM TIME: repeats all summer

FRAGRANCE: none

'Morden Fireglow'

The aptly named 'Morden Fireglow' is another exceptionally hardy shrub rose (to Zone 3, at least) from the famous Canadian breeding program. The fully double blossoms are brilliantly colored—rich scarlet underlaid with a coral-orange glow, and are produced in sprays of up to five blossoms. The thick-textured petals stand up well to wind and weather, and last for a long time in flower arrangements.

Best of all, the blossoms are produced constantly for many weeks running.

Upright and full in habit, the shrub is covered in forest green, durable leaves. It's a vigorous grower, so if you're seeking an especially tough hedge or border rose in this color, you won't do any better than 'Morden Fireglow'.

'Nevada'

TYPE/CLASS: shrub

HEIGHT: 6–8 feet (1.8–2.4m)

BLOOM SIZE: 4 inches (10cm)

BLOOM TIME: repeats all summer

FRAGRANCE: none

'Nevada'

The single flowers of this graceful shrub look almost like Japanese anemone blossoms: they're saucer-shaped, rich, creamy white, and centered by a small spray of yellow stamens. In cool weather, they often develop a light pink tinge. Unusual for a shrub rose, but quite attractive, is the disease-resistant, small, light lime green foliage. The plant is an especially prolific bloomer, covering itself in blooms from head to toe for weeks on end. The flowers are followed in autumn by a scattering of orange hips.

Other good qualities of this unique rose are its low thorn count and handsome, arching red canes. 'Nevada' tends to grow as tall as it is wide, so be sure to allot it enough space. It would be a wonderful choice for a property-line hedge because no neighbor could ever fault its performance or agreeable color.

'New Dawn'

TYPE/CLASS: climber

HEIGHT: 12–20 feet (3.7–6m)

BLOOM SIZE: 3–3½ inches (7.5–8cm)

BLOOM TIME: repeats all summer

FRAGRANCE: medium

'New Dawn'

A sport, or mutant, of the famed 'Dr. W. Van Fleet', this splendid climber is deservedly popular. Starting out in a soft, cool, almost silvery shade of pink, the fluffy, cupped blossoms of 'New Dawn' gradually age to cream without losing their silky texture. They're centered with bright gold stamens. The sweet and fruity scent is especially enticing on hot summer afternoons. And you'll find that the glossy leaves are disease-resistant, especially to blackspot.

Not only is 'New Dawn' beautiful, it has all the qualities you could wish for in a climber. It blooms along its entire length, extravagantly at first, and persistently, on and off, for the rest of the season. The long canes are flexible and agreeable to training, whether you choose a pillar or wall. It is hardy to Zone 4. And the plant is vigorous, so you don't have to pamper it. The only strike against it is its notoriously sharp and plentiful thorns.

'Olympiad'

TYPE/CLASS: hybrid tea

HEIGHT: 4–5 feet (1.2–1.5m)

BLOOM SIZE: 4–4½ inches (10–11cm)

BLOOM TIME: repeats all summer

FRAGRANCE: none

'Olympiad'

For almost twenty years, no red rose was good enough to rival the wildly popular 'Mister Lincoln'. But in 1984, 'Olympiad' (named in honor of the Los Angeles Olympics) captured the All-America Selections award. It is prize-worthy for a few reasons. The blooms are as close to perfect as hybrid tea blooms get: they begin as elegant, pointed buds and spiral open to a clear, velvety scarlet that tends neither toward yellow nor lavender. And the color really holds—both on the bush, and in the vase. Most of the blooms are one-to-a-stem, and the stems (though fairly thorny) are admirably long and straight.

Another great feature of this rose is its exceptional mildew-resistance, which is good news for gardeners in areas with damp weather. The leaves are big, semiglossy, and medium green, and cover the plant well. As the great rosarian Peter Schneider laments, "if only it were fragrant, this might be the perfect rose."

'Party Girl'

TYPE/CLASS: miniature

HEIGHT: 12–16 inches (30–40cm)

BLOOM SIZE: 1¼ (3.5cm)

BLOOM TIME: repeats all summer

FRAGRANCE: medium

'Party Girl'

There are a number of perky yellow miniature roses around, but 'Party Girl' offers a softer, subtler alternative. Its blooms are light yellow-apricot, barely flushed with pink. They exhibit a double load of petals, but the form is not at all cluttered; the flowers open gracefully to a tiny version of a perfect hybrid tea. Unlike some minis, 'Party Girl' boasts blooms that are fragrant—the scent is warm and spicy. These enchanting flowers appear in clusters by the dozens at first flush, and continue on and off until the cold weather comes.

Rather than mounding, the small, vigorous plant develops an upright profile, so it would be ideal for disguising the bare knees of taller roses or other flowering shrubs. 'Party Girl' is also lovely in a pot. Either way, you should place it where its beauty can be appreciated at close range. It won an Award of Excellence from the American Rose Society in 1981.

'Pascali'

TYPE/CLASS: hybrid tea

HEIGHT: 3½–4 feet (105–120cm)

BLOOM SIZE: 4–4½ inches (10–11cm)

BLOOM TIME: repeats all summer

FRAGRANCE: slight

'Pascali'

An extraordinarily adaptable and beautiful white rose, 'Pascali' was voted The World's Favorite Rose at the 1991 World Federation of Rose Societies. Actually, it has quite a long and distinguished history of awards; among them a gold medal at The Hague in 1963, another gold medal at Portland in 1967, plus it was the All-America Selection winner in 1969. It is greatly valued for its ability to perform well in diverse climates, holding up to rain and hot sun with equal grace. The upright-growing, glossy-leaved plant is also winter-hardy, to Zone 5, at least.

But the flowers of 'Pascali' are what everyone raves about. Unlike some whites, these blooms are pure creamy white, untouched by pink or yellow hues. The petals are silky and substantial, and resist the rainspotting that mars other whites. The matter of fragrance has been debated— some claim it's sweet and delicious, others can detect no scent at all—so it is probably a matter of climate or other variable factors.

'Peace'

TYPE/CLASS: hybrid tea

HEIGHT: 5–6 feet (1.5–1.8m)

BLOOM SIZE: 6 inches (15cm)

BLOOM TIME: repeats all summer

FRAGRANCE: slight

'Peace'

The most cherished hybrid tea in the world created a sensation when it was introduced near the end of World War II. Its often-told story is certainly romantic: a rose-fancying U.S. embassy official smuggled budwood out of France just hours ahead of the invading German armies. The truth is less exciting, but still exhibits good timing. It was indeed developed in France, but the hybridizer, Francis Meilland, was able to ship it to various growers around the world before the war actually arrived on French soil. Its value was quickly recognized, and the rose was widely propagated. By 1945, it had become the floral symbol of the newly formed United Nations, and had taken top All-America Selections honors.

The appeal of the large double blossoms lies in the fact that no two are alike and that the color varies according to sunlight intensity. The dominant color is a beautiful warm yellow, but it is always enhanced with rose pink, usually along the edges of the petals and often flushing throughout, especially as the flower matures. You have to put your nose right in it to pick up the soft fragrance. Meanwhile, the large, dark green leaves are in scale, and have a leathery texture. 'Peace' looks good in nearly any setting, thanks to its robust form and adaptable color.

'Pink Meidiland'

TYPE/CLASS: shrub

HEIGHT: 4 feet (1.2m)

BLOOM SIZE: 2½ inches (6.5cm)

BLOOM TIME: repeats all summer

FRAGRANCE: none

'Pink Meidiland'

There's a whole series of Meidiland shrub roses, bred in France but becoming popular on both sides of the ocean. Bred to be low-maintenance, they are especially disease-resistant, require little pruning other than an annual spring trim, and are hardy in Zones 4 to 9. Generally speaking, you can count on them to bloom on and off all summer, and to produce attractive hips by autumn. The habit is dense and vigorous, ideal for mass plantings such as hedges, bank covers, or foundation plantings.

So far, these husky plants come in shades of white, red, fuchsia, and pink. And sometimes the flowers, which are borne in clusters, are double. 'Pink Meidiland' may be the most elegant of the lot, with sweet, single-petaled blooms of pink centered with a substantial creamy white eye and a neat boss of yellow stamens. It has been hailed as totally mildew-free, but it may get a little blackspot from time to time.

'Playboy'

TYPE/CLASS: floribunda

HEIGHT: 3 feet (90 cm)

BLOOM SIZE: 3½ inches (8cm)

BLOOM TIME: repeats all summer

FRAGRANCE: medium

'Playboy'

This is a compact plant with beautiful, vivacious blossoms. Cherry red petals are underlaid with glowing, coppery gold and centered with golden stamens. (The color holds for days on end, in the garden or in a bouquet.) Because the petal count is not high and the blooms are carried in great sprays, the overall effect is ruffly and fancy. And the scent is captivating—it's fresh and sweet, like ripe, crisp apples.

All this excitement is displayed on a dense, healthy-leaved bush that is lower growing than some floribundas. So even if you have a small garden, you can fit it in. A group planting would be sensational, or you can use 'Playboy' in a hot-colored border or as a container specimen.

'Pristine'

TYPE/CLASS: hybrid tea

HEIGHT: 4–7 feet (1.2–2m)

BLOOM SIZE: 5–6 inches (13–15cm)

BLOOM TIME: repeats all summer

FRAGRANCE: slight

'Pristine'

The name 'Pristine' certainly suits this pretty rose, which has an almost pearllike purity. The pink buds open to full-petaled blossoms that are ivory in the center, gradually yielding to a soft, sweet lavender-pink on the outer petals. As with many hybrid teas, the blossoms emerge from classic, urn-shaped buds, but these have a form so perfectly balanced that 'Pristine' has become a popular exhibition rose. They also have the unique and valuable quality of remaining poised in the attractive half-open stage for several days. As for fragrance, it seems to vary according to growing conditions and climate, but when present, is light and perfumey.

The foliage is also especially good. It's dark and glossy, rather large, and quite disease-resistant. Truly an elegant plant, 'Pristine' deserves a starring role and is well suited to formal-style gardens.

'Queen Elizabeth'

TYPE/CLASS: grandiflora

HEIGHT: 5–7 feet (1.5–2m)

BLOOM SIZE: 3–4 inches (7.5–10cm)

BLOOM TIME: repeats all summer

FRAGRANCE: medium

'Queen Elizabeth'

The tall, regal 'Queen Elizabeth' is in a class by itself—literally. She made her debut in 1955, and was to be the first of a glorious new class of taller, hardier roses—the grandifloras. But her triumph has never really been repeated (other so-called "grandifloras" lack her many distinctive virtues), and there are rose experts who scoff at the entire category. But nobody scoffs at her superb quality. Indeed, this rose has won more awards than perhaps any other, both in North America and abroad.

Like the best hybrid teas, 'Queen Elizabeth' has flawlessly formed blooms. They are a lovely medium to dark, watercolor-wash pink that in some climates is enriched with a touch of coral. Like the best floribundas, these are (usually) carried in great sprays. They have very long cutting stems, sometimes up to 3 feet (90cm) long!

'Queen Elizabeth' is also hardy and easy to grow. Tough and vigorous, it buoys the confidence of beginning gardeners and spares them the trouble of constant spraying. It shouldn't be pruned too much—it likes to be free to grow to its natural lofty heights. The best spot would be along a back fence or as a backdrop to a rose or mixed flower border.

'Rainbow's End'

TYPE/CLASS: miniature

HEIGHT: 10–14 inches (25–35cm)

BLOOM SIZE: 1½ inches (4cm)

BLOOM TIME: repeats all summer

FRAGRANCE: none

'Rainbow's End'

A lively, hot-colored flower, 'Rainbow's End' created a sensation when it was introduced by the great miniature rose breeder Harmon Saville in 1984. In 1986 it won an American Rose Society Award of Excellence; it has so many terrific qualities that it has continued to play a prominent role in miniature rose breeding ever since.

The blossoms are bright lemony yellow edged with scarlet (the amount of scarlet varies depending on exposure to sunlight). Each flower is a tiny replica of a hybrid tea bloom—high-centered and symmetrical. The plant is compact, healthy, and easy to grow. If you want bold, invigorating color and truly enchanting blooms but have limited space, 'Rainbow's End' could be the perfect solution. It can be overwintered in pots indoors.

'Rio Samba'

TYPE/CLASS: hybrid tea

HEIGHT: 5 feet (1.5m)

BLOOM SIZE: 5 inches (13cm)

BLOOM TIME: repeats all summer

FRAGRANCE: slight

'Rio Samba'

No doubt about it, there is something exotic about this rose, which won an All-America Rose Selections award in 1993. Each blossom is a spirited combination of hot yellow and fiery orange-scarlet. Unlike other color-blended roses, which gradually change from one color to another over a period of days, 'Rio Samba' displays its exciting mix from the moment the petals unfurl. Sturdy, long cutting stems will inspire you to cut bouquet after bouquet. Experiment with different color combinations; try building arrangements that include red roses or blazing yellow ones.

You might think that such a bright flower would be difficult to incorporate into the garden. And perhaps the most logical plan is to plant a group of three or more 'Rio Samba' bushes on their own. But the color really is more playful than strident, and you can certainly place a plant in the company of hot-colored perennials.

'Rise 'n' Shine'

TYPE/CLASS: miniature

HEIGHT: 14–18 inches (35–45cm)

BLOOM SIZE: 1½–1¾ inches (4–4.5cm)

BLOOM TIME: repeats all summer

FRAGRANCE: none

'Rise 'n' Shine'

This prolific plant is considered to be the best yellow miniature rose going. The plush little flowers are a sunny, pure yellow. They have no red or orange touches, nor do they fade out to a sickly pale near-white. And the show is non-stop, commencing in midsummer and continuing until cool weather arrives. It was given an American Rose Society Award of Excellence in 1978, and has not yet been topped.

The compact, rounded bush is liberally covered with medium green, disease-resistant leaves. Both the habit and the superior flowers mean you can rely on this plant to bring consistent, well-behaved color to your garden. 'Rise 'n' Shine' planted in quantity promises to bring a beam of cheer wherever you place it—whether it's along a walkway, lining a bed, or gracing a sunny corner.

Rosa banksiae var. *lutea*

(Yellow Lady Banks' rose)

TYPE/CLASS: climber (rambler)

HEIGHT: 20–30 feet (6–9m)

BLOOM SIZE: 1 inch (2.5cm)

BLOOM TIME: once in early summer

FRAGRANCE: slight

Rosa banksiae var. *lutea*

Sure, the yellow Lady Banks' rose has been described as a "house-eater," but if you want a big, billowing climber that's practically thorn-free, it will fit the bill perfectly. This glorious rose has been around for well over a century, and is commonly seen draping over old homes, arbors, porches, and even trees in the South. It also thrives in the West. Unfortunately, it is not hardy north of Zone 7.

The flowers appear in early summer, and while they don't repeat, they certainly earn their keep by lasting a long time, sometimes up to six weeks. They're petite, soft to deep yellow, laden with tiny petals, and carried in great sprays. The mild scent is reminiscent of violets. The foliage, meanwhile, is green and shiny, and the smooth canes have a naturally vertical habit that climbs eagerly. Anecdotal evidence suggests that deer don't like to nibble on this rose, so if you live in deer country, this feature is certainly an added attraction.

'Rosa Mundi'
(Rosa gallica var. versicolor)

TYPE/CLASS: shrub (gallica)

HEIGHT: 3–4 feet (90–120cm)

BLOOM SIZE: 3–3½ inches (7.5–8cm)

BLOOM TIME: blooms once in midsummer

FRAGRANCE: medium

'Rosa Mundi'

Once you see this intriguingly beautiful old-fashioned rose, you can never forget it. The semidouble blossoms, no two alike, sport cream to pale pink petals that are randomly striped, streaked with bright crimson, and centered by a bright spot of golden stamens. The effect is fresh and lively, and will make you think of a peppermint candy or a whimsical petticoat. The blossoms are also fragrant, wafting a sweet sachet scent into the air. In fact, both fragrance and color hold up well in potpourri.

For such a spunky, unusual flower, the plant is surprisingly tidy. However, like other gallicas, suckering may be a problem, and pruners should be kept close at hand just in case. The sage green foliage clothes the upright stems well. It is frequently used as a novel low hedge, which suits it.

Legend has it that it was named for "Fair Rosamund" Clifford, the mistress of Henry II of England. It's a charming thought but, alas, unlikely; the rose was first recorded around 1580, and Henry II lived from 1154 to 1189.

'Rose de Rescht'

TYPE/CLASS: shrub (damask)

HEIGHT: 2½–3½ feet (75–105cm)

BLOOM SIZE: 2–2½ inches (5–6.5cm)

BLOOM TIME: repeats all summer

FRAGRANCE: strong

'Rose de Rescht'

Sometimes wonderful things come in small packages. The blossoms of 'Rose de Rescht' aren't big and dramatic, but they are wonderfully lush and full (with up to one hundred petals!), almost like chrysanthemums. The color is vibrant, a rich, fuchsia-red with hints of royal purple. And the fragrance is completely ravishing. The blossoms begin appearing in early to midsummer and continue until autumn, when they are replaced by distinctive, tubular hips.

Even the plant is rather small, certainly for an antique shrub variety. It grows a little taller than wide, and is densely covered with medium green foliage. When young, the leaves are rimmed in red, making a pleasant counterpart to the early blooms. This rose is ideal if you have limited space and want old-fashioned looks and fragrance—with the bonus of repeat bloom.

'Rotes Meer'

TYPE/CLASS: rugosa hybrid

HEIGHT: 3 feet (90cm)

BLOOM SIZE: 3–4 inches (8–10cm)

BLOOM TIME: repeats all summer

FRAGRANCE: strong

'Rotes Meer'

There is no other crimson rose quite like this one. The color is amazingly pure, almost burgundy in its richness. Although the flowers are called double, the petals are arrayed in an elegant and neat cupped form. Golden stamens flash from the center. The long, unopened buds are a darker, wine red. Both flowers and buds are held well above the leaves so you can't miss them. And, like all rugosa roses, the flowers are clove-scented.

Another feature that sets this rugosa apart from the crowd is its compact size—most of its peers are big bushes.

Yet the leaves are not correspondingly small. They're still large, forest green, and crinkled (and durable, and highly disease-resistant). Imagine what a terrific low hedge it will make! You could certainly invite it into the heart of a perennial border, something you would never do with another rugosa.

Autumn color is also worth mentioning. The foliage of 'Rotes Meer' turns a soft gold and is accompanied by scarlet hips.

'Sea Pearl'

TYPE/CLASS: floribunda

HEIGHT: 3–5 feet (1–1.5m)

BLOOM SIZE: 4½ inches (11cm)

BLOOM TIME: repeats all summer

FRAGRANCE: medium

'Sea Pearl'

There's a lot of warmth in this long-blooming rose. The buds are pink and the first impression is pink, but its secret is that it does not stay a pure pink. Each petal on the bloom is gently underlaid with a soft glow of apricot-yellow. The fragrance is sweet, but you have to get up close to appreciate it. You'll also be pleased to discover long cutting stems.

The bush is tall for a floribunda, and has a sweeping, upright profile. Often the blooms are carried on the top of the plant (it blooms singly and in clusters). For these reasons, you can safely place this rose behind other ones or toward the rear of a flower border.

You can also count on this rose to be disease-resistant. The semiglossy leaves are dark green and lightly crinkled, and provide a handsome backdrop for the lovely blossoms.

'Sexy Rexy'

TYPE/CLASS: floribunda

HEIGHT: 3–5 feet (1–1.5m)

BLOOM SIZE: 3 inches (7.5cm)

BLOOM TIME: repeats all summer

FRAGRANCE: slight

'Sexy Rexy'

Admittedly, this rose is a bit of a novelty, and not just because of its name. The official explanation for the name is that it has proven to be a wonderful parent plant in hybridizing. Once you've grown it, you might also credit the incredibly generous, candelabralike flower clusters. Up to a hundred blooms per cluster prompted one nursery catalog to comment whimsically, "for which a vase has not yet been designed." Its 1984 introduction by renowned New Zealand breeder Sam McCredy inspired a flurry of lively publicity in that country, including the bumper sticker "Have you Sexy Rexy in your rose bed?"

Be all that as it may, there's no denying it's a wonderful plant. The color is a splendid pastel pink, and the full-petaled form has an unexpected old-fashioned charm (many other modern floribundas have classic, hybrid tea–shaped blooms). The fact that it blooms readily all season long is also endearing, though you ought to deadhead for best results. The plant is on the tall side and has plenty of glossy green foliage.

'Simplicity'

TYPE/CLASS: shrub

HEIGHT: 4–5 feet (1.2–1.5m)

BLOOM SIZE: 3–4 inches (7.5–10cm)

BLOOM TIME: repeats all summer

FRAGRANCE: slight

'Simplicity'

Accurately named 'Simplicity', this is the original low-maintenance hedge rose, and probably still the best. Developed by the award-winning rose breeder Bill Warriner of Jackson & Perkins about fifteen years ago, it has proven immensely popular. And why not? It grows quickly and densely, is not fussy about soil, rarely requires spraying, and pumps out extraordinary numbers of blooms all summer long. The plants are also hardy, and because they're grown on their own roots rather than grafted, they're often able to repair winter damage with a spurt of new growth.

The medium pink flowers have a slightly cupped form and appear in clusters. It is also available in red, white, and only recently, yellow and purple. Flowers in the Simplicity series are handsome, if not particularly elegant, and generally offer a slight, pleasant fragrance.

The intended, and best, use of 'Simplicity' and its kin is as a "living fence." Plant in a long row at the base of a porch or along a property line, and savor the easy, dependable, colorful show.

'Sombreuil'

TYPE/CLASS: climber

HEIGHT: 8–15 feet (2.4–4.6m)

BLOOM SIZE: 3½–4 inches (8–10cm)

BLOOM TIME: repeats all summer

FRAGRANCE: medium

'Sombreuil'

A naturally graceful habit and long-blooming, old-fashioned flowers make an irresistible combination. The height varies according to where you grow it and how you prune it. 'Sombreuil' will take to a pillar as easily as a pergola. Its stems are pliable, though moderately thorny.

The exquisite blooms cover the entire length of the plant. The color is a heavy cream, sometimes blushed slightly with pink. There are loads of petals, but they're arranged (when the flower is fully open) in lush, symmetrical form. A rich, tea rose fragrance wafts into the air. And unlike some vintage roses, this one blooms repeatedly for the whole season.

Lovely 'Sombreuil' has only one major drawback. It's not very hardy, thriving mainly in warmer areas (Zones 7 and south). Northern gardeners who've lost their heart to her, however, can certainly try heroic winter-protection measures.

'Souvenir de la Malmaison'

TYPE/CLASS: shrub (Bourbon)

HEIGHT: 2–3 feet (60–90cm); 6–8 feet (1.8–2.4m) as
a climber

BLOOM SIZE: 5 inches (13cm)

BLOOM TIME: once in midsummer

FRAGRANCE: strong

'Souvenir de la Malmaison'

Named after Empress Josephine's renowned rose garden on the outskirts of Paris, 'Souvenir de la Malmaison' is utterly magnificent when grown under optimum conditions. It requires warm, sunny, dry weather to thrive and bloom to its full potential. Rain completely dampens its spirits!

Note that this rose comes in two forms. Both bush and climber are comparatively short, and either one would be a suitable choice for a tight space or a smaller garden.

However, like other Bourbons, the blossoms are big and full. A soft, baby pink at every stage, they're deliciously scented. They start out cupped but eventually splay out to a flat form that reveals the generous load of petals. The plant tends to bloom later than most roses, and not very lushly. But it is so beautiful, you quickly forgive the limited performance.

'Starina'

TYPE/CLASS: miniature

HEIGHT: 12 inches (30cm)

BLOOM SIZE: 1½ inches (4cm)

BLOOM TIME: repeats all summer

FRAGRANCE: none

'Starina'

Although it made its debut more than thirty years ago, 'Starina' remains a star in the miniature rose world to this day, and is widely available. It is credited with being the first miniature to have blossoms that truly mimicked the elegant form of classic hybrid tea roses, a form it displays with perfect grace from bud to fully open bloom.

The semiglossy, dark green foliage makes a handsome stage for the warm and inviting orange-red blooms. With an agreeable, slightly spreading habit, the plant is as wide as it is tall. One plant in a pot on a patio or deck will be much admired. But a miniature of this quality could also line a path to a door or garden gate in great style.

'Sunsprite'

TYPE/CLASS: floribunda

HEIGHT: 3 feet (90cm)

BLOOM SIZE: 3 inches (7.5cm)

BLOOM TIME: repeats all summer

FRAGRANCE: strong

'Sunsprite'

This terrific bloomer may very well be the best yellow floribunda. It has everything going for it: high-quality blooms, fragrance, and toughness. As is typical of floribundas, the smallish flowers are carried in clusters that display them at various stages of opening. The buds of 'Sunsprite' are a rich, buttery yellow before they unfurl to a sunny, chiffon yellow. The scent, apparent even before you get right up next to the bush, is fresh and spicy, like a sweet cinnamon coffeecake.

But what may really sell you on the plant is its durability. When other yellows flag, or fade to white in the hot summer sun, 'Sunsprite' remains sprightly. And unlike many other yellows, the bright green foliage is mildew-resistant. Last but not least, the plant is winter-hardy, and can easily be grown up to Zone 6 (north of there, be sure to shield it). Plant this one wherever your garden needs really dependable, bright color.

'Sutter's Gold'

TYPE/CLASS: hybrid tea

HEIGHT: 4–4½ feet (1.2–1.3m)

BLOOM SIZE: 4–5 inches (10–13cm)

BLOOM TIME: repeats all summer

FRAGRANCE: strong

'Sutter's Gold'

Neither pure yellow nor pure orange, but a glowing golden color somewhere in between, this magnificent rose has a haunting, summer-evening feel to it. It's an eager and prolific bloomer, starting early in the season (sometimes it's the very first rose to get going) and continuing on and off until autumn. The buds are classically shaped, but the open flower's form is looser and less formal than some hybrid teas. The fragrance is especially strong and fruity.

The bush is also super. It's an average height for hybrid teas, but it grows a little narrower than most, so you can squeeze it into a more confined spot if need be. This rose would be a good addition to a spring-flowering shrub border, bringing welcome color after those blooms have faded. Try it adjacent to anything with russet- or bronze-tinged leaves. Mercifully, thorns are rather light on 'Sutter's Gold'.

'Sweet Chariot'

TYPE/CLASS: miniature

HEIGHT: 18–24 inches (45–60cm)

BLOOM SIZE: 1½ inches (4cm)

BLOOM TIME: repeats all summer

FRAGRANCE: strong

'Sweet Chariot'

It's not often that you see a miniature in this color. 'Sweet Chariot' is not mauve or lavender, but rather a dark crimson-purple. The flowers are laden with many petals and carried in exuberant sprays. And the fragrance—unusually strong for a miniature—is rich and heady. Imagine what sweet little bouquets you can harvest!

The matte green leaves provide a nice contrast to the blooms. Although these bushy plants spread to the sides a bit more than some of their peers, you can still grow 'Sweet Chariot' in a container. Just make sure it has enough elbow room. In the garden proper, you will find it to be a steadfast performer and super-hardy. If you combine it with other flowers, choose bold companions such as a bright yellow miniature. 'Sweet Chariot' and 'Rise 'n' Shine' make a stunning combination.

'Therese Bugnet'

TYPE/CLASS: rugosa hybrid

HEIGHT: 4–6 feet (1.2–1.8m)

BLOOM SIZE: 4 inches (10cm)

BLOOM TIME: repeats all summer

FRAGRANCE: strong

'Therese Bugnet'

If a trouble-free, super-hardy, fragrant pink rose sounds like heaven to you, look no further. Bred in Canada and descended from the extraordinarily tough, disease-resistant rugosa roses, 'Therese Bugnet' is a real winner. It is hardy to Zone 2, which covers all of the United States and a good portion of Canada, so just about anyone can grow it.

It is also very pretty. The buds begin in a rich lilac to red, and burst open to big, ruffly saucers of mauve-tinged pink. A cluster that contains both stages makes a darling bouquet. You'll also savor the rich cinnamon-clove fragrance.

The plant is taller than some of its relatives, and often used as a hedge. The distinctive leaves are narrow and dark blue-green. Also, the plant's thorns, while certainly present, are not as plentiful as you might expect (new shoots are practically thornless).

'Touch of Class'

TYPE/CLASS: hybrid tea

HEIGHT: 5–6 feet (1.5–1.8m)

BLOOM SIZE: 4½–5½ inches

BLOOM TIME: repeats all summer

FRAGRANCE: none

'Touch of Class'

Hobbyists and professionals who exhibit roses competitively rave about 'Touch of Class'. And those of us who may never take our love of roses that far should certainly pay attention. Its color is obviously a factor: the blossoms are gorgeous, beginning as a warm coral and mellowing to a rich, salmon-pink, underlaid with a barely perceptible cream reverse. The form, too, is outstanding, with long, shapely buds that spiral open to high-centered blossoms with slightly ruffled petals. The petals are heavy-textured, which makes for a long life on the plant or in bouquets. As for the stems, they are a bouquet-maker's dream—long, strong, and straight.

The plant itself is less perfect. The dark green foliage looks durable, but is vulnerable to mildew and must be sprayed regularly if this disease is a problem in your area. Also, 'Touch of Class' can grow rather tall for a hybrid tea, so you'll want to place it where it won't block out other plants.

'Tropicana'

TYPE/CLASS: hybrid tea

HEIGHT: 4–5 feet (1.2–1.8m)

BLOOM SIZE: 5–6 inches (13–15cm)

BLOOM TIME: repeats all summer

FRAGRANCE: strong

'Tropicana'

It's possible that this knockout hybrid tea has suffered from too much adulation. In the thirty-five-plus years since it was introduced, it has won many coveted awards. Naturally, it is widely available, but you may notice that it is conspicuously absent from some rose catalogs and reference books, as if the pros have grown weary of its great popularity.

Nonetheless, it remains a great rose. The color is a fiery, almost fluorescent blend of orange, coral, and crimson. And the massive bloom size demands attention even from many yards away. The Jackson & Perkins catalog describes the fragrance as a "rich, fruit-filled perfume with notes of ripe raspberries and exotic citrus." Anyone who has smelled 'Tropicana' will not dismiss this as catalog hyperbole. The plant is tall and robust and boasts long cutting stems. Foliage is dark and substantial; but gardeners in humid areas find it gets mildew.

But where, oh where, are you going to place a rose like this? You might want keep it out of the traditional rose bed (where it will overwhelm almost any other color). Try it instead in the company of foliage plants, such as purple barberries or silvery artemisias, and savor the glory.

'Tuscany Superb'

TYPE/CLASS: shrub (gallica)

HEIGHT: 3–4 feet (90–120cm)

BLOOM SIZE: 3½–4 inches (8–10cm)

BLOOM TIME: once in early to midsummer

FRAGRANCE: strong

'Tuscany Superb'

Why grow a rose that only blooms once a year? A rose as beautiful and richly fragrant as 'Tuscany Superb' will certainly tempt you. The lush-petaled blossoms are truly glorious: deep crimson brushed with black, and a seductive, velvety texture to match. They're centered by a royal flash of golden stamens. The heady, almost winelike fragrance will make you swoon. (Like other gallica roses, the petals of this one hold their color and scent well in potpourris and sachets.)

This vigorous plant grows perhaps a little taller than wide, and is fairly bushy. The leaves are dark forest green, and resist pests and diseases, with the exception of occasional bouts with blackspot. The stems aren't very thorny, although you may encounter some small bristles.

One last word in favor of its blooming habit: it means you can plant 'Tuscany Superb' in a spot where later-blooming perennials that might clash with the distinctive color won't yet have made their appearance.

'William Baffin'

TYPE/CLASS: climber (kordesii)

HEIGHT: 7–10 feet (2–3m)

BLOOM SIZE: 2½ inches (6.5cm)

BLOOM TIME: repeats all summer

FRAGRANCE: none

'William Baffin'

Far northern gardeners take note: this may be the only repeat-blooming climber currently available to you. Super-hardiness (proven to Zone 3, and claimed for Zone 2 by its Canadian breeders) is not its only virtue, however.

'William Baffin' is a truly pretty rose. The plant begins blooming in early summer, when it literally cascades with bright pink flowers centered with sunny yellow stamens. In warmer areas, the petals sometimes develop a splash of white markings near the middle. The clusters may contain as many as thirty blooms apiece! The show continues steadily throughout the summer months and slows down only when autumn arrives. As an added benefit, the foliage is exceptionally disease-resistant. In fact, 'William Baffin' has never been known to have blackspot and mildew is rare.

To get the best performance out of this superior rose, grow it in full sun. There, you can count on it to be vigorous and gorgeous. Note that it may not reach its full height in colder zones, where a fence or pillar would be its best climbing surface. Otherwise, feel free to train it over any arch or trellis.

'Winsome'

TYPE/CLASS: miniature

HEIGHT: 18–24 inches (45–60cm)

BLOOM SIZE: 1½ inches (4cm)

BLOOM TIME: repeats all summer

FRAGRANCE: none

'Winsome'

A rather large and exceptionally prolific miniature, 'Winsome' sports jaunty, bright lavender to mauve (sometimes almost red) blooms of high quality. They're double, but elegantly formed in hybrid tea style. And the petals are heavy textured, which allows them to last a long time on the bush or in a flower arrangement.

The plant is quite bushy and grows taller than most of its peers, so you'll want to grow it in the ground. Its good health and sweetheart blooms would be a welcome addition to a moderate-height perennial border. 'Winsome' won an Award of Excellence from the American Rose Society in 1985.

'Zéphirine Drouhin'

TYPE/CLASS: climber (Bourbon)

HEIGHT: 8–12 feet (2.4–3.7m)

BLOOM SIZE: 3 ½–4 inches (8–10cm)

BLOOM TIME: repeats all summer

FRAGRANCE: strong

'Zéphirine Drouhin'

Introduced way back in 1868 and beloved to this day, 'Zéphirine Drouhin' is a fetchingly beautiful repeat-bloomer. Buds are long and dark pink and open to flowers in a rich, deep shade of pink. The powerful, romantic scent has a touch of raspberry to it. New growth is coppery purple, which provides a stunning contrast, but it eventually becomes a handsome and disease-resistant dark green. Even the thornless stems contribute to the show—they're burgundy.

As if she needed more selling points, 'Zéphirine Drouhin' is also shade-tolerant and handles alkaline soil and pollution better than most roses, which will entice city gardeners. Because of its medium height, this rose is ideal for training on a post or pillar. And its lack of thorns makes it a natural choice for training up and over a frequently trafficked archway or porch. Hardiness seems to be the sole concern, as the plant is rated only to Zone 6. With protection, however, it could be grown farther north.

1 0 0

*F*AVORITE

*H*ERBS

Introducing Herbs

The world of herbs is both highly intriguing and somewhat daunting to the uninitiated. Yes, it's true that most herbs are quite easy to grow. Some are fast-growing annuals; some are long-lived perennials. Yes, many are grown primarily for their foliage, which is often deliciously scented. And many, many herbs are useful in the kitchen, adding an exciting new dimension to all sorts of recipes.

But you may have your reservations. Are all herbs dry-land natives, and therefore best grown by those fortunate enough to live in a mild climate? (No, not at all, although the ones that are naturally tough can become low-maintenance stars in your garden.) Are herbs really glorified weeds that will take over your yard? (A few are rampant growers, but with wise planting and care, no herb need become a pest. Instead, you can plan for bountiful harvests.) What about safety—hasn't modern science discovered that many old herbal remedies are actually dangerous? (Many herbs have indeed been scrutinized by modern chemists and the medical world. Some are as helpful as touted; others are not. Appropriate cautions are noted in individual entries.)

Ultimately, perhaps the most common beginner's question is: just what is an herb? For the purposes of this chapter, an herb is broadly defined as a plant that not only has ornamental merits, but is also useful in some way. It may be edible—eaten fresh or dried, or added to any number of tasty recipes. It may be medicinal or have cosmetic properties. It may be useful in crafts or it may be a dye plant.

The truth is, the concerns that inexperienced herb gardeners have are unfounded. There are so many herbs that there is sure to be something for everyone, no matter what your taste or where you live. This chapter embraces a wide range of appealing herbs. Each entry should provide you with sufficient information about whether you can grow a given herb in your area and in the conditions available in your garden. (Not all herbs are simple to grow, but I have not included those with really exacting requirements.)

SHOPPING FOR HERBS

If you are lucky, you live near a garden center that has a good selection of herb plants, but you will usually only be able to find such common ones as parsley, sage, rosemary, and thyme. Some herbs enjoy a double life as perennial-garden flowers, and may be found in another part of the store or greenhouse. If you find what you are looking for, take a moment to examine the plant carefully before you buy it. Not only should it look healthy (no damaged or diseased leaves, no sign of lurking insects), it should be well rooted. Test the plant by turning it on its side or upside down and gently tapping the pot; if potting mix spills or the plant falls away, it's not a good choice. The best herbs are clearly growing vigorously, perhaps with some healthy white roots starting to quest out from the pot's bottom. These will transplant easily to your garden and grow eagerly, provided you've prepared a spot for them and care for them as they make the transition.

Another way to get good herb plants is to raise them from seed. Many grow easily and quickly in flats started indoors, and take off when you plant them outdoors after the soil has warmed up and danger of frost has passed. Some don't like to be transplanted and prefer to be sown directly in the garden. Read the seed packet carefully so you'll know best how to proceed.

If you are disappointed in the local selections, by all means shop for your herbs by mail. Perhaps even more so than for perennials, mail-order catalogs offer a huge range of herbal choices (but check their substitution policies in the event that they run out of something special you had your heart set on). And if herbs are their specialty, the catalogs often feature detailed descriptions that include cultivation information, snippets of folklore, and enticing suggestions for use. A list of mail-order companies is included at the end of this book.

PLANTING HERBS

No matter what kind of soils or sun exposures your yard offers, there's bound to be some herbs you can grow. You can always tuck a few into a flower border. For example, those with handsome foliage, like the sages, keep the display interesting when their neighbors are not in bloom; those with pretty flowers, such as calendula and nasturtium, are always welcome. Culinary herbs—especially basil and parsley—are often added to a vegetable garden.

Herbs can also be landscaping problem-solvers. If a corner has perpetually damp soil, why not plant it with mints? If you have a stone pathway or terrace, fragrant creeping thyme set in the cracks will soon scent the air and look like it has been there forever. If you'd like a pretty and low-maintenance edging plant, try lavender, germander, or rosemary.

As for planned herb gardens, there's no real secret to their design or success. You just have to prepare an area in advance by pulling out all the weeds and improving the soil if necessary. Formal layouts, like "knot gardens" or pie designs, should be planned on paper first. Use a dependable edging plant or bricks, stones, or wood to lay out the lines. As for the filler plants, just be sure you take into account their mature size so that you don't crowd them.

Some herb gardeners enjoy making "theme gardens," gardens devoted completely to one kind of herb or one concept. Popular themes include fragrance, dried flower, dye, herbal tea, medicinal, biblical, Shakespeare, and kitchen gardens. After you've carefully chosen appropriate plants, you can make the layout as artistic or informal as you wish. Just remember to allow yourself room to get in among the plants to groom, water, and harvest them.

CARING FOR HERBS

Each herb has its own cultural requirements, but some generalizations can still be made as you ponder getting started. Most herbs prefer full sun. Most prosper in good, moderately fertile soil. And most require that the soil be well drained so that they get the moisture they need to grow but don't suffer from "wet feet." If your chosen site is lacking in any of these requirements, take steps to improve it. Clip back overhanging shrubs and tree branches. Add organic matter, dampened peat moss, and/or sand to poor soil to improve its texture.

Plant your young herb plants on a cool day so that they don't have to cope with heat stress. A drizzly late-spring afternoon (after danger of frost has passed) is ideal. Pop the plant out of the pot or flat, tease loose some of the roots, and gently set the herb into an ample hole. Pat soil back in around it and water it well. Water your herb plant often in the following days and weeks until it becomes well established.

Fertilizer, on the other hand, is not often needed. Excess fertilizer may lead to lax, floppy growth that is unattractive and vulnerable to diseases and pests, and may also inhibit flowering. It's better to plant your herbs in the type of soil they are known to prefer, and leave it at that. However, an exception is made for lime lovers: if your garden soil is too acidic for an herb, a sprinkling of lime powder or chips at its base at planting time may be in order.

It's fun to raise some herbs in pots to place on a deck or patio, in a window box, or on a windowsill indoors. Some herbs are too tender to leave outdoors year-round, and must be grown indoors or in greenhouse conditions. In any event, start off with a good sterile soil mix. Sterile mixes are preferable simply because insect pests are not lurking in them, and sometimes indoor-grown herbs are vulnerable.

HARVESTING, DRYING, AND STORING HERBS

Again, every herb is different, but some generalizations can be made about harvesting your crops. Wait until a plant is growing well—late summer or, if it's a perennial, even the second season—before clipping off leaves or flowers for your own use. Otherwise, you may set the plant back considerably or even unintentionally kill it. Go for the outer leaves first, if you can, as they tend to be the youngest and most tender. Flowers are best harvested not long after they've opened. Flavor, scent, and texture are at their peak in the morning, before the heat of the day sets in.

The right timing is always key when you're harvesting flowers, flower heads, or pods for drying, either for craft projects or in order to collect edible seeds. You want the flowers to have just opened and the seeds to be ripe, so keep a sharp eye out. For seeds, the best time to intervene is late summer, just as the plant begins to go brown or yellow but before it sheds its seeds on the ground.

Clip and hang clumps upside down in a dark, dry, windless spot, such as a shed, garage, enclosed porch, cellar, or attic. If seeds are likely to fall of their own accord, place a piece of white paper or a tarp below. Otherwise, wait until everything is dry, then pluck off your harvest. In the case of flower heads that "shatter" readily, place the harvest in a paper bag so that the seeds will be easily collected. Hard seed cases may need a good whack with a plastic baseball bat or a run under a rolling pin to give up their treats.

While the gradual drying method helps herbs retain more of their color, shape, scent, and flavor, some herbs can be dried efficiently using faster modern methods. Place the leaves or seeds on a clean cookie sheet and dry them for a few hours in the oven, set on low, with the door ajar to provide a little air circulation. Or, dry them briefly on paper towels in the microwave. To avoid scorching, dry them for ten to twenty seconds at a time, on low, until you reach the desired crispness. With the oven and microwave techniques, don't overlap—let individual pieces dry separately.

In any case, when the drying process is finished, winnow out unwanted plant parts such as seed cases, stalks, twigs, and leaves.

Fresh herbs usually don't last long once they're picked, so harvest them as close to mealtime as is practical or refrigerate them separately and add them just prior to serving. To keep them longer than a day, place the stalks (not the whole herb) in an inch or two (2.5 or 5cm) of water, and cover the jar, bowl, or bottle loosely and store it in the refrigerator. Or, wash and thoroughly dry your harvest, then lay it on dry paper towels with no overlapping before rolling up the paper towels and storing in a plastic bag in the vegetable crisper.

Dried herb leaves, flowers, and seeds often contain volatile oils that give them their wonderful scent and flavor. Make the most of your homegrown harvest by preserving these qualities. Always store your harvest in airtight jars or bags, out of direct sunlight, in a cool place.

COOKING WITH HERBS

Make the most of homegrown herbs by using the flavor at its peak. Generally speaking, fresh herbs are best kept whole until just prior to being added to a recipe, when you can quickly chop or dice them with a sharp knife or even tear them into small pieces by hand. Food processors and blenders sometimes do too good a job, making tiny pieces whose flavor has literally been beaten out of them.

As for dried or powdered herbs, some give back rich, aromatic flavor when simmered with a recipe for hours, while others are at their best if added in the last few minutes before serving. Follow the recipe's recommendations, or if there are none, experiment to see what suits your taste.

Agrimony

Agrimonia eupatoria

HEIGHT/WIDTH: 2'–5' ×1½' (60–150cm × 45cm)

FLOWERS/BLOOM TIME: yellow spikes/early summer

ZONES: 3–7

RECOMMENDED USES: medicinal, dye

Agrimony

Not an especially distinctive-looking plant, agrimony has nonetheless been prized for centuries in its native Europe. The serrated, aromatic leaves have many uses, though they are not considered edible. A mild tea made from a few teaspoons of dried leaves may be used to ease a sore throat or settle an upset stomach, or you can toss some into a warm bath to soothe aching muscles. A poultice applied to cuts and sores may also bring relief and faster healing. More elaborate claims are made about agrimony's benefits, including reducing bleeding and helping to heal problems with internal organs, but you should not try these remedies without the supervision of a professional herbalist or your family doctor. Finally, a dye made from leaves and stems will be yellow; the later you wait in the season to harvest, the darker the yellow.

The plant gains a certain willowy grace when in bloom. Blooming, tapered spikes rise a foot or two (30 or 60cm) above the leaves and are composed of tiny yellow flowers that wave in the breeze. Later, they become burrs. The whole plant wafts a soft aroma that has been likened to the scent of ripe apricots. Agrimony grows best in full sun to light shade in soil that's on the dry side, and will self-seed.

Aloe vera

Aloe barbadensis

HEIGHT/WIDTH: 1′–2′ × 1′–2′ (30–60cm × 30–60cm)

FLOWERS/BLOOM TIME: not grown for flowers/rarely seen

ZONES: 10 (elsewhere, grow as a houseplant)

RECOMMENDED USES: medicinal, cosmetic

Aloe

While many herbs never receive wide use or the blessing of the medical establishment, aloe stands out as a popular and effective plant. The fact that it's simple to grow certainly helps. An aloe plant will thrive despite minimal water, gritty soil, and part-day sun on a windowsill almost anywhere. In fact, this ancient plant, said to be native to Africa, seems to prosper on neglect, developing little "pup" plants at its base in a matter of months. Dividing and repotting is simple, and the gift of an aloe plant is always welcome.

When you snap off one of aloe's fleshy leaves, both sides immediately bleed a sticky sap that brings quick relief to itchy skin, minor kitchen burns, sunburns, cuts, and abrasions. Often, once healed, no scar remains. The cosmetic industry has extracted and repackaged this healing gel in many over-the-counter treatments that ease itching and pain and keep the skin soft and supple. If you don't have this valuable plant on your kitchen sill now, you should get one.

Angelica

Angelica archangelica

HEIGHT/WIDTH: 3′–8′ × 1′–2′ (90–240cm × 30-60cm)

FLOWERS/BLOOM TIME: greenish white umbels/early to
midsummer

ZONES: 4–9

RECOMMENDED USES: medicinal, cosmetic, culinary

Angelica

An intriguing plant with a long and colorful history, angelica is not for every garden. It grows quite tall, eventually towering over its neighbors. It may not flower its first year. When in bloom, its wonderful scent—sweet and aniselike—may attract clouds of fruit flies and blackflies. And in or out of bloom, deer love to nibble it to the ground.

Having said all that, angelica's good qualities should be noted. It's a good-looking ornamental plant, sporting attractive, long-lasting flower heads and tropical-looking leaves on handsome, hollow stalks. The stalks have traditionally been harvested and sugared for use as a sweet snack, or diced and added to cakes, especially fruitcakes. Raw or sautéed, the stalks are served as a celery- or asparaguslike side dish in some countries. A soothing tea used primarily in the treatment of bronchial ailments can be made from the leaves. Angelica is also used as a flavoring in vermouth, gin, and the liqueur Chartreuse, and the entire plant is aromatic.

The plant gets its evocative name from an old legend that the archangel Michael appeared in a vision to a seventeenth-century monk, revealing angelica as a remedy against various ills, especially the Black Plague.

Angelica is best started from seed sown directly in the garden, in rich, moist soil. It will prosper beautifully in partial shade.

Anise

Pimpinella anisum

HEIGHT/WIDTH: 12″–24″ × 8″ (30–60cm × 20cm)

FLOWERS/BLOOM TIME: white umbels/mid- to late summer

ZONES: best in warmer areas (annual)

RECOMMENDED USES: culinary, medicinal

Anise

If you love the elegant flavor and aroma of licorice, this herb is the most refined source. However, you will mainly be after the seeds, and the plant takes three to four months to go to seed. So gardeners with long summers have the best luck (the rest of us can try starting plants from seed indoors in late winter). And be forewarned: what catnip is to cats, anise is to some dogs.

Anise is a pretty, lacy plant, with flattened, creamy white umbel flowers. It has heart-shaped to roundish leaves down low and more feathery ones higher on the stalk. Don't overlook using the leaves—they're nice in garden-fresh salads or minced and added to soft cheese dips or spreads. The seeds should be harvested when almost ripe (turning brown) and used whole or ground. Anise is splendid in everything from stewed fruit desserts and chutneys to soups, meat dishes, and steamed vegetables as well as breads, cakes, and cookies. It has a long history as a digestive aid, which is why it is popular in after-dinner liqueurs and teas. It also enjoys a reputation as a breath freshener and is sometimes an ingredient in cough suppressants, though more for its pleasant taste than for any remarkable expectorant qualities. Grow anise in average soil in full sun.

Anise hyssop

Agastache foeniculum

HEIGHT/WIDTH: 2'–4' × 2' (60–120cm × 60cm)

FLOWERS/BLOOM TIME: violet-purple spikes/mid- to late summer

ZONES: 4–9

RECOMMENDED USES: culinary, craft

Anise hyssop

Despite its name, this handsome herb is neither an anise nor a hyssop, but a member of the mint family. Thus it has the characteristic square stem of mints and a preference for fertile, well-drained soil. Give anise hyssop full sun or partial shade. A cool, minty flavor with anise overtones makes for a pleasantly tangy scent and taste.

The plant grows erect and has nice dark green leaves. These are joined later in the summer by lovely violet-purple spires that produce lots of nectar, attracting hummingbirds and bees. In fact, anise hyssop is sometimes grown commercially to aid honey production. For the purposes of the home gardener, however, the dried leaves can be used to make a tasty hot or iced tea. A strong brew of the liquid can also be added to favorite recipes as a sweetener. Both the leaves and the flowers hold their color and scent well in potpourris, dried bouquets, and wreaths.

Basil

Ocimum basilicum

HEIGHT/WIDTH: 2′ × 1′ (60cm × 30cm)

FLOWERS/BLOOM TIME: white whorls/late summer

ZONES: all zones (frost-sensitive annual)

RECOMMENDED USES: culinary

Basil

Few herbs are as widely used as this one—for who can resist fragrant, delicious basil? It enhances the flavor of sauces as well as many main dishes, especially in Italian and Asian cooking. Most popular is the bushy sweet basil, with its large, somewhat crinkly leaves. Plant it in full sun in fertile soil. The secret to a long and abundant harvest of leaves is to clip or pinch off the unremarkable flowers as soon as they appear. Regular harvesting of the leaves will also help keep the plant more compact.

You'll find that fresh leaves have much more flavor than dried. Roll excess leaves (cleaned and completely dry) in paper towels and freeze them in plastic bags. Basil is the major ingredient in the classic Italian pesto sauce, which doesn't freeze as well as plain basil leaves. It still tastes good once thawed, but loses its vibrant green color.

There's a broad range of related basils, available primarily from mail-order seed companies. All are worth experimenting with—they'll contribute a slightly different color or form to your garden, and there are flavor variations for all sorts of dishes. Look for lemon basil, which is a wonderful addition to fish recipes or a refreshing summer gazpacho. There are also cinnamon, licorice, and Thai basils. The pert little rounded plants of 'Spicy Globe' basil sport tiny but still flavorful leaves, and make a unique, easy-care edging plant—even in a flower garden.

Any of the basils can be grown indoors on a window sill, though they must be constantly pinched back to keep a bushy form. Full sun will also prevent the plants from becoming too rangy.

Basil thyme

Calamintha nepeta

HEIGHT/WIDTH: 12″–24″ × 8″–12″ (30–60cm × 20–30cm)

FLOWERS/BLOOM TIME: light purple/summer

ZONES: 5–9

RECOMMENDED USES: culinary

Basil thyme

This pleasant herb is not always easy to find, but it is easy to grow and easy to love (your best bet is to seek it out in specialty herb catalogs).

The emerald green leaves are ridged and have bluntly serrated edges, looking quite a bit like mint leaves. They grow in whorls around the stem like mint (in fact, it is more closely related to mint than to basil or thyme). The pretty flowers, which vary from pink to lilac, are produced over a long season, making the plant an attractive addition to an herb garden or flower border. Basil thyme is never troubled by pests or diseases. It thrives in average to damp soil and full sun. If you cut it back every month or two during the summer, it stays neat-looking. In any case, it never gets very large, making it suitable for smaller spaces.

You can use the clipped leaves to make a sweet-flavored, aromatic tea. In Europe, where it is a common weed, it has been used to sweeten preserved meats and to treat everything from colic to fever.

Bay

Laurus nobilis

HEIGHT/WIDTH: 25′–60′ × 10′–20′ (7.5–18m 3 3-6m);

   in a pot, 5′–10′ × 3′–5′ (150–300cm × 90–150cm)

FLOWERS/BLOOM TIME: small yellow clusters/early

   summer

ZONES: 8–10

RECOMMENDED USES: culinary, craft

Bay

This "herb" is actually a tree, and gardeners who must have one can always try growing it in a large pot, which will help keep the size more manageable. Just be sure to place it where it won't be tossed about by drying winds, water it regularly through the growing season, and protect it from winter cold. The potting mix can be soil-based as long as it drains well (make sure that there's a hole in the bottom of the pot).

Bay is a handsome plant, with smooth tan to gray bark, slender, pungent leaves, and inconspicuous flowers that are followed by small purple-black drupes (stone fruits, like cherries). The leaves are the main attraction, and have been prized by cooks the world over because they impart their fragrant oils to food gradually. This is why bay so enhances the flavor of slowly simmered soups, stews, and meats as well as bottled vinegars and homemade pickles. Bay is also a major ingredient in bouquet garni, a mixture that originated in France and traditionally includes thyme and parsley. Bay's sturdy dried branches make a good base for a wreath or swag, though the leaves fade somewhat.

Bee balm

Monarda didyma

HEIGHT/WIDTH: $2\frac{1}{2}'$–$4' \times 1\frac{1}{2}'$ (75–120cm $\times$ 45cm)

FLOWERS/BLOOM TIME: showy flower heads/mid- to late summer

ZONES: 4–9

RECOMMENDED USES: craft, culinary, medicinal.

Bee balm

This showy plant is popular with perennial gardeners, thanks to its large, vibrant flowers (in shades of red, pink, purple, and white), but it is also worth the notice of herb gardeners. As a member of the mint family, bee balm has the fragrant foliage you'd expect—minty, with a sunny, orange-lemon tang.

Added to summertime beverages such as iced tea, lemonade, and sangria, bee balm leaves contribute zing (steep them first for best results). Both leaves and flowers also make a nice garnish for these drinks or for fresh salads. Brewed as a hot tea, bee balm is said to ease cold symptoms, nausea, and cramps, although these uses have not been veri-

fied by scientific research. At any rate, the plant is perfectly harmless.

To grow this plant well, you must give it rich, moist soil in full sun or partial shade, and perhaps spray for mildew late in the summer (it is very susceptible). Do not eat leaves that have been sprayed.

Potpourri fanciers also enjoy adding bee balm to their mixtures. The flower heads are really clusters of small tubular flowers that, with a little encouragement, shatter when dried. They tend to lose a little bit of their color, so use the brightest cultivars such as 'Cambridge Scarlet' and 'Gardenview Scarlet' for this purpose.

Bergamot

Monarda punctata

HEIGHT/WIDTH: 12″–18″ × 8″–12″ (30–45cm × 20–30cm)

FLOWERS/BLOOM TIME: yellowish with purple spots/summer

ZONES: 4–9

RECOMMENDED USES: culinary, medicinal

Bergamot

This is the monarda sometimes seen in wild fields and meadows. It is less showy than its garden cousin, though on close inspection the spotted flowers are quite pretty. It grows best in a sandy, fast-draining soil. Overly rich soil causes it to be floppy and reduces flowering. Bergamot prefers full sun but will also do well in partial shade.

This plant was dubbed bergamot by early settlers who found its citrusy scent and taste reminiscent of old-world bergamot (an extract from a tropical tree, actually), which is used to flavor Earl Grey tea. An infusion of the leaves makes a gentle, soothing tea—add a little orange rind to bring out the natural flavor.

An oil pressed from bergamot leaves contains thymol, a substance known to help heal fungal infections when applied topically. Internal use of the oil can be dangerous, however, provoking vomiting and diarrhea. Nowadays, thymol is produced synthetically. And herb gardeners needn't fret—tea made from bergamot leaves will not have a high concentration of the oil.

Betony

Stachys officinalis

HEIGHT/WIDTH: 2'–3' × 1' (60–90cm × 30cm)

FLOWERS/BLOOM TIME: red-purple/mid- to late
summer

ZONES: 4–9

RECOMMENDED USES: medicinal, culinary

Betony

Without a doubt one of the prettiest herbs you can grow, betony is related to lamb's ears (*Stachys byzantina*), the popular perennial-garden stalwart. Like that plant, betony forms a rosette of downy leaves and features rosy purple flower spikes in the latter part of the summer, but its foliage is deep green and toothed rather than silvery gray and smooth-edged. The combination of dark foliage and rich-colored blossoms on this branching plant is irresistible. It may steal the show in your herb garden, and can certainly be added to a traditional flower border or even used as a tall edging, perhaps at the feet of some rose bushes. It will toler-

ate partial shade, but it must have fertile yet not overrich, well-drained soil—it is not a drought-tolerant plant.

Betony has enjoyed a long and colorful reputation as a healing herb. It has been credited with easing everything from headaches to hearing difficulties to problems with internal organs—and with warding off evil spirits. But its most established and reliable use, thanks to the tannin content of its dried leaves, is simply as a soothing tea to relieve sore throats or diarrhea. The tea can also be drunk just for pleasure; it has a sweet, minty flavor.

Bistort

Polygonum bistorta

HEIGHT/WIDTH: 2′–3′ × 1′ (60–90cm × 30cm)

FLOWERS/BLOOM TIME: pink spikes/late spring to summer

ZONES: 4–9

RECOMMENDED USES: culinary, medicinal

Bistort

You may start out valuing this unsung plant for its early and long-lasting blooms; the dense spikes are bright pink, especially when grown in full sun, in damp to average soil. However, you will also appreciate it throughout the summer for its handsome form and easy care. The leaves are a soft shade of blue-green and have a slightly wrinkled texture. They're edible, and taste best when eaten young. Toss a few in a salad with your first lettuce harvest.

But the plant's main attraction to herbalists over the years has been its root—more properly its chubby, creeping, reddish rhizome. Its astringent juice was used in the tanning of leather for a long time, until modern chemicals upstaged it. Herbalists also dried and powdered it for a sharp-flavored tea used in treating internal bleeding, gastronomic distress, and even diabetes. When the powder was moistened and pressed on cuts and wounds, it helped stop the bleeding and promoted faster healing. None of these applications has received the blessing of modern medicine, and you may not want to go to all the trouble, but you will always enjoy the plant as a handsome ornamental addition to your garden.

Black cumin

Nigella sativa

HEIGHT/WIDTH: 12"–18" × 8"–12" (30–45cm × 20-30cm)

FLOWERS/BLOOM TIME: light blue/midsummer

ZONES: all zones (annual)

RECOMMENDED USES: culinary

Black cumin

Not related to true cumin (*Cuminum cyminum*), this airy plant is much easier to grow. It can be direct-sown in light soil in full sun. You may be familiar with its cousin, love-in-a-mist (*Nigella damascena*), which has the same distinctive-looking flowers and is increasingly popular with gardeners who seek out unusual annuals. Black cumin's flowers are a lighter color, sometimes nearly white—and by season's end, they develop inflated seedpods that contain pungent and edible seeds.

To harvest the seeds, wait until late summer or early autumn, when the half-inch (12mm), horned seedpods turn brown and dry. Mash them open, and you'll discover several dozen black triangular seeds. Sift out the chaff and store the seeds in a cool, dry place. They have a wonderful, earthy flavor, not quite as powerful as regular cumin. Try them whole in baked goods, especially breads and rolls, or grind them into a powder and add them to soups, stews, or African and Mexican casseroles.

Bloodroot

Sanguinaria canadensis

HEIGHT/WIDTH: 6″–14″ × 6″–8″ (15–35cm × 15–20cm)

FLOWERS/BLOOM TIME: white/spring

ZONES: 3–8

RECOMMENDED USES: dye, medicinal

Bloodroot

This native North American wildflower was used by indigenous people before European settlers arrived in this country. It is still a familiar sight in early spring in wooded areas of the Northeast, where it thrives in rich, moist, acidic soil. The deeply lobed, heart-shaped leaves are very distinctive, and the creamy white blossoms are beautiful. Rock gardeners and connoisseurs of perennials often grow the showier, double-flowered variety 'Multiplex'.

Perhaps bloodroot's most notable use is as a dye. The juicy sap, which bleeds from a clipped stem or nicked root, is orange-red and colors skin and fabric easily. Be fore-warned that the fixing action of a "mordant" additive will alter the color away from orange and more toward rust or pink, depending on what you use.

Bloodroot sap's therapeutic uses are legion, but are not to be attempted at home, as the wrong dose may be toxic. The sap is a source of an alkaloid called (not surprisingly) sanguinarine, which is said to be a potent stimulant and expectorant. Some modern research has linked it to the successful treatment of certain cancers. Consult a doctor for more information if you're interested.

 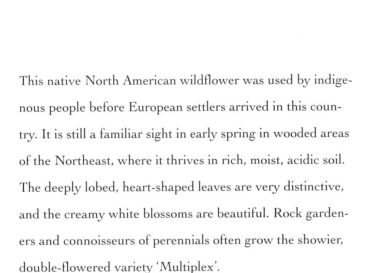

Borage

Borago officinalis

HEIGHT/WIDTH: 2′–3′ × 1′–2′ (60–90cm × 30–60cm)

FLOWERS/BLOOM TIME: blue/summer

ZONES: all zones (annual)

RECOMMENDED USES: medicinal, culinary

Borage

Borage is an eager grower, blooms heavily, and brings charm and good looks to your summer garden. The slightly furry, gray-green leaves are quickly joined by the flowers, which appear in lush, drooping clusters. Individual flowers are star-shaped and anywhere from sky blue to vivid purple. Grow the plant in full sun in moist but well-drained soil, and place it where it will have room to sprawl and where you can appreciate the flowers from the side or below—a slope or upper terrace would be perfect. You'll notice that borage attracts lots of bees, so that may also be a consideration in placement.

The entire borage plant is edible, and has a flavor that has been compared to cucumbers, making it a nice addition to fresh salads, cold soups, or iced summer beverages. The flowers are a popular choice for candying because they are both safe and pretty.

Borage is credited with many medicinal uses, including relief for bronchitis, fever, and gastronomical woes, as well as being a diuretic. The seeds contain a compound found to be useful in treating premenstrual distress. But for the average gardener, the most practical medical use is to soothe cuts or bug bites with a cooling poultice of borage leaves.

Bouncing bet

Saponaria officinalis

HEIGHT/WIDTH: 1'–2' × 1'–2' (30–60cm × 30–60cm)

FLOWERS/BLOOM TIME: pink-white/mid- to late summer

ZONES: 3–8

RECOMMENDED USES: cosmetic

Bouncing bet

When does a roadside "weed" become an herb? When the gardener discovers that it is not only easy to grow, but has intriguing virtues. Such is the case with bouncing bet, a perky little plant with delicate-looking flowers. It is related to garden dianthus and carnations, and shares with them a delicious, sweet scent with a hint of cloves. Grow bouncing bet in almost any soil, as long as it is well-drained, in full sun or partial shade. It will self-sow, so plant it where you'd like it to naturalize. If you don't want bouncing bet to spread, make certain to pick the flowers before they go to seed.

The sap of this plant is naturally soapy. This quality is most easily extracted by simmering fresh stems and leaves in a pot of rainwater, well water, or bottled water (not chemically treated tap water) for about half an hour. The mild, fragrant lather that results can be used to gently wash and revitalize delicate fabrics such as lace, old linen, wool, or kid gloves. It can also be used to wash the hands and face and soothe acne, eczema, and itchy rashes like poison oak and ivy. Warning: bouncing bet should never be ingested. Not only is its soapy flavor unpleasant, it is a strong purgative and can be dangerous.

Burnet

Poterium sanguisorba

HEIGHT/WIDTH: 8″–30″ × 12″ (20–75cm × 30cm)

FLOWERS/BLOOM TIME: tiny pink and green balls/
summer

ZONES: 4–9

RECOMMENDED USES: culinary

Burnet

The botanical name of this ancient herb reveals its long-popular use: *poterium*, from the Greek, refers to a drinking cup. Sprigs are used to garnish glasses of wine and will also bring a refreshing touch to iced teas and punches. Fresh, young leaves have a cool, cucumberlike taste. Unfortunately, when dried, they lose their flavor, so this is a plant to pick and use on the spot. Its most popular use is as a salad green (it also goes by the name salad burnet), but creative cooks mince it and add it to coleslaw, dips, herb butters, and cold summer soups.

The plant itself has a delicate, almost frail appearance that looks sweet among lacy herbs such as the silvery artemisias. But it gets overwhelmed if interplanted with huskier plants. It begins as a low clump and sends up stalks lined with rounded leaflets. Though you'll have to look closely to appreciate the detail, burnet's tiny flowers are globe-shaped and lime green with tiny, rosy pink pistils and stamens spraying out at all angles. Remove them regularly if you want a continuous harvest of fresh new leaves.

Burnet is a very hardy plant, requires little attention from the gardener, and will self-seed over the years. It prospers in full sun or light shade. Its only quirk is a preference for dryish soil that is on the sweet (alkaline) side; it does not prosper in damp or highly acidic soils.

Calamint

Calamintha grandiflora

HEIGHT/WIDTH: 12″–14″ × 8″ (30–35cm × 20cm)

FLOWERS/BLOOM TIME: pink/mid- to late summer

ZONES: 5–9

RECOMMENDED USES: culinary, medicinal, craft

Calamint

As you might guess from the name, this herb is a mint relative. The scent of the leaves has been likened to camphor and, more poetically, tangerine-mint. The leaves are toothed and blue-green and, thanks to the plant's creeping rootstock, stay fairly low to the ground. The dense whorls of flowers rise above this mound and are anywhere from lilac to bright pink.

A plant this attractive and manageable is a good citizen in a carefully laid-out herb garden, but could also be used as a groundcover or tucked into a rock garden. You might prefer the variegated version, which grows a little more compactly and features white-speckled foliage.

Dried calamint leaves make an invigorating hot or iced tea that reminds one of peppermint tea. And because their scent is persistent, they make a nice addition to potpourri. Fresh leaves have been touted as a soothing dressing for bruises.

Calendula

Calendula officinalis

HEIGHT/WIDTH: 1′–2′ × 1′–2′ (30–60cm × 30–60cm)

FLOWERS/BLOOM TIME: yellow to orange/summer

ZONES: all zones (annual)

RECOMMENDED USES: culinary, medicinal, cosmetic, dye

Calendula

It's hard to imagine a more versatile, useful plant than calendula. A native of southern and central Europe that has gained use practically worldwide, it's been in cultivation for centuries. The cheerful yellow to orange flowers appear early and repeatedly. The flower heads are up to 4 inches (10cm) across, and there are now a number of improved varieties with larger, denser (even double) heads, taller stems, and bright, consistent colors. All calendula needs is full sun and average, well-drained soil.

The flowers are the main attraction for herbal uses. Picked fresh, the petals are a pretty, if not particularly flavorful, garnish for salads and soups (the flavor is subtly sweet). For drying, petals should be pulled loose and separated to dry on a screen; they'll retain their color well.

Calendula petals have been used as a substitute for the more expensive saffron in soups, rice dishes, and sauces. Boiled in water, they yield a bright yellow liquid that has been used as a dye. And a strong infusion made from the petals has been shown to kill some bacteria and fungi, which validates the plant's folk uses as a treatment for everything from cuts, bruises, and topical infections to chicken pox and measles. Calendula is gentle enough to use on babies or others with sensitive skin and can be found as an ingredient in soothing natural lotions and creams. People with light-colored hair can use calendula-based shampoos and rinses to bring out highlights.

Caper

Capparis spinosa

HEIGHT/WIDTH: 2'–3' × 2'–3' (60–90cm × 60–90cm)

FLOWERS/BLOOM TIME: white/early summer

ZONES: 7–10

RECOMMENDED USES: culinary

Caper

A rounded, shrubby plant, caper hails from rocky, dry Mediterranean hillsides. It can certainly be grown in any similar climate, as in the South or West, or anywhere else in a pot and overwintered in a greenhouse. As you might guess, it is quite heat and drought tolerant, though it should be watered regularly until well established.

The leaves are shiny and oval, and are borne on long, arching stems. They should be trimmed back a few inches every year just to keep the plant looking tidy. The small green buds develop into lovely but frail white blossoms 2 or 3 inches (5 or 7.5cm) across and centered with showy purple- or red-tipped stamens. The petals fall off within a day, but the plant keeps pumping out more flowers all summer.

Even if you are captivated by low-maintenance caper's beauty, you should harvest the tasty, tender immature buds. Collect them when they reach the size of peas, and preserve them in a vinegar-based pickling mixture. They are wonderful with eggplant and tomato dishes, and add real zest to any number of Greek, Italian, or Spanish recipes. A small jar makes a novel gift for your favorite chef.

Caraway

Carum carvi

HEIGHT/WIDTH: 24″ × 6″–12″ (60cm × 15–30cm)

FLOWERS/BLOOM TIME: white umbels/spring

ZONES: 4–8

RECOMMENDED USES: culinary, medicinal

Caraway

Savory caraway makes you wait for its seed harvest, but the plant is easy to grow and the homegrown seeds are so delicious, it's worth the delay. All it asks is full sun and fertile, well-drained soil. A biennial, caraway spends its first year establishing a strong root system and forming a short plant of rather feathery foliage. The following summer, it adds hollow stems topped with flat umbels of white flowers.

When the umbels start to turn brown late in their second summer, they are ready to be harvested. Clip them off and hang them upside down in a cool, dark place in a paper bag. The paper bag will catch the tiny crescent-shaped seeds as they fall. Dry the seeds thoroughly (a week or two) before storing them in a jar.

Caraway seeds have many, many uses, though their most popular modern use is as a nutty-licorice flavor ingredient in breads (especially rye and Irish soda bread), cookies, crackers, and apple pie. They're also a common ingredient in sauerkraut and other cabbage dishes (perhaps due to their reputation as a digestive aid), and may be added to meats—especially pork—to good effect. When possible, add them late in the recipe, as overcooked seeds tend to become bitter.

Cardamom

Elettaria cardamomum

HEIGHT/WIDTH: 6′–12′ × 2′–4′ (180–360cm × 60–120cm)

FLOWERS/BLOOM TIME: white to yellow/spring

ZONES: 9–10 (or grow as a houseplant in other zones)

RECOMMENDED USES: culinary, medicinal

Cardamom

Also known as "cinnamon palm," this shrubby plant is related to the showy ornamental gingers popular in some southern and Gulf Coast gardens. In more northern zones, it can be grown in a container and overwintered in a warm spot indoors or in a greenhouse. In any event, this native of the tropics must have plenty of moisture and partial shade in order to prosper. It has deep green, lance-shaped leaves about a foot (30cm) long. The small flowers appear in long racemes and are followed by the prized seedpods.

If you succeed in growing this difficult plant, you'll have a real treat with the seed harvest, as store-bought cardamom rapidly loses its scent and flavor. Each pod contains three sections, or cells, and small, fragrant, mahogany-colored seeds lurk inside. Do not split open the pods until just before you are ready to use them. A couple of seeds (bruise them first) make a splendid, exotically spicy addition to mulled wine or cider, and add enchanting aroma and taste to an ordinary pot of coffee. You can chew on a few for a breath freshener and to alleviate indigestion. Ground cardamom is also used in breads, cakes, and pastries. It is a popular ingredient in many East Indian, Arabic, African, and Scandinavian recipes.

Catnip

Nepeta cataria

HEIGHT/WIDTH: $1'$–$3' \times 1'$–$2'$ (30–90cm $\times$ 30–60cm)

FLOWERS/BLOOM TIME: white with lavender/mid- to late summer

ZONES: 3–10

RECOMMENDED USES: medicinal

Catnip

Even if you're the sort of gardener who believes in sharing your garden with wildlife, your generosity may still be tested when you find this handsome herb constantly flattened by enthusiastic felines. On the other hand, perhaps you feel they should have some fun, too! Scientists who've studied this famous attraction have found that catnip's irresistible active ingredient is a volatile chemical called nepetalactone. Cats crush, bite, and chew the plant not to ingest it but to release the scent into the air. Depending on the particular plant, the dose, and the cat, it acts as a sedative or an aphrodisiac. As for its effects on humans, catnip has been shown to have no significant psychoactive properties except perhaps as a digestive aid and a mild sedative when the dried leaves are made into a rather tasty hot tea.

Catnip plants grow quickly and thickly, with soft green leaves that are soon joined by airy spires of white to lavender flowers. They must have well-drained soil, and you shouldn't pamper them too much or they'll spread rampantly, like any mint. Either full sun or partial shade will do. A more compact relative that also seems to be less of a cat magnet is *Nepeta mussinii* 'Blue Wonder'.

Chamomile

Chamaemelum nobile

HEIGHT/WIDTH: 3"–9" × 12" (7.5–22.5cm × 30cm)

FLOWERS/BLOOM TIME: tiny daisies/summer

ZONES: 3–9

RECOMMENDED USES: culinary, medicinal, cosmetic

Chamomile

This gentle herb is beloved for its sweet apple scent. It's actually a rather tough, sprawling, winter-hardy little groundcover. In fact, some gardeners like to slip it between paving stones on a path or terrace, where it will take foot traffic well and reward passersby with its enchanting aroma. (In medieval times, it was used as a strewing herb and an air freshener.) Of course, if you'd prefer, you can grow chamomile in the more congenial conditions of the garden proper, where it does best in light, dry soil. You can also grow it in a pot or window box. Full sun is best.

Chamomile's most famous use is as a soothing herbal tea. This may be brewed from the dried flowers—more properly the yellow centers, as the white "petals," or ray flowers, tend to fall off. It is credited with soothing indigestion, menstrual cramps, insomnia, and jangled nerves. (No wonder Peter Rabbit's mother gave him a cupful after his ordeal in Farmer McGregor's garden.) It is also added to hand and face lotions. As an ingredient in shampoo, it brings out blond highlights.

Chervil

Anthriscus cerefolium

HEIGHT/WIDTH: 24″ × 8″–12″ (60cm × 20–30cm)

FLOWERS/BLOOM TIME: tiny white umbels/summer

ZONES: all zones (annual)

RECOMMENDED USES: culinary

Chervil

You may never go back to parsley once you've tried the fresh yet delicate, almost aniselike, flavor of chervil, its close relative. This lovely herb looks a bit like parsley, with plenty of cut and divided leaves and leaflets, though it has a lacier, more graceful profile and it doesn't grow as wide or tall. The flowers are small white umbels that wave gently above the foliage. At season's end, chervil turns pale pink and then increasingly red, adding a nice touch of autumn color to the herb garden. It often self-sows, so you may have more plants to enjoy next year. Chervil thrives in partial shade and moist soil.

To use tasty chervil to its full potential, harvest young leaves and, if you wish, young stems. Chop them up and add generous handfuls to everything from salads to soups and sauces, or try them in egg dishes and casseroles. Wait to add chervil until late in the recipe, or the leaves will lose their flavor and texture. Small, fresh-cut sprigs also make a nice garnish. Dried chervil is not nearly as flavorful as fresh, but it is a component of fines herbes. This famous French cooking blend also includes dried parsley, thyme, and tarragon—again, this should be added to a recipe in the last few minutes for maximum effect.

Chia

Salvia columbariae

HEIGHT/WIDTH: 8″–18″ × 6″–12″ (20–45cm × 15–30cm)

FLOWERS/BLOOM TIME: blue/summer

ZONES: 8–10

RECOMMENDED USES: culinary, craft

Chia

Chia is a pretty, smallish sage from the chaparral and desert areas of the West, and as such grows best in hot, dry settings and requires well-drained soil. (And yes, it's the plant used for "chia pets.") Downy, wrinkled, dark green leaves appear first in a basal rosette, and line the erect stems at intervals, so the plant's profile is more airy than some of its relatives. The blue flowers with purple bracts stand out well in the herb garden. Wonderfully fragrant, chia can be dried and added to potpourri, and can also be used in the kitchen as you would other sages (in soups, roasted poultry and meat, stuffing, and sausage, for example).

Unlike other sages, chia has long been prized for its edible seeds. Native American tribes nibbled on them raw, and roasted and sprinkled them on many dishes. They also ground the seeds and used the flour in baking, and added it to a refreshing beverage. Those who fancy sprouts in their salads and sandwiches have discovered that chia sprouts have a pleasant, delicate flavor. (Make your own sprouts by placing ripe seeds on a damp paper towel for a few days.) The word "chia" comes from the Mayan language and means "strengthening," but knowledge of the plant's healing properties seems to be lost to history.

Chicory

Cichorium intybus

HEIGHT/WIDTH: 3'–5' × 1' (90–150cm × 30cm)

FLOWERS/BLOOM TIME: blue/summer

ZONES: 4–9

RECOMMENDED USES: culinary

Chicory

Have you ever had a cup of real New Orleans roast coffee, the kind where you keep adding milk or cream but the brew seems to stay persistently dark and powerful? Chances are you were at the mercy of chicory-enhanced coffee. Chicory is supposed to mellow coffee's flavor, and it does not contain any caffeine. But it does feature sedative, laxative, and diuretic properties. Thus chicory, while nontoxic, is not entirely innocuous.

The dark, gnarly, bittersweet root is harvested in autumn. Dried and ground, it looks a lot like coffee. In fact, in the nineteenth century, consumers complained that they were being tricked by unscrupulous merchants who sold ground chicory root as coffee or at least cut their coffee blends with it. The uproar led to the first pure-food labeling legislation.

The plant itself is a familiar roadside weed, originally from Europe but now widespread in North America. So, not surprisingly, it is an undemanding garden plant, and seems to want nothing more than a sunny spot. The jaunty blue flowers are prolific and pretty, but you'll notice that they are open only in the mornings. They close up shop by afternoon, even on sunny days.

Chives

Allium schoenoprasum

HEIGHT/WIDTH: 12″–18″ × 6″–8″ (30–45cm × 15–20cm)

FLOWERS/BLOOM TIME: bluish pink to lavender/early summer

ZONES: 3–9

RECOMMENDED USES: culinary, craft

Chives

Easy to grow and more attractive than other members of the onion and garlic family, cheery chives are a wonderful addition to any garden. The smallish, globe-shaped flowers are lovely, and the clump-forming plant doesn't grow to towering heights or flop over constantly. Some people even add chives to the flower border (beware of self-sowing, however). A lot of companion-planting lore is attached to chives, too: they're said to prevent blackspot on roses, mildew on cucumbers and squashes, scab on apples, and so on.

Chives are unique because they don't have a long natural dormant period. So if you live in a mild climate, you'll be harvesting year-round. In cold-winter areas, consider digging up some plants in late summer, potting them, and letting them die down outdoors through a frost or two. Then bring the pots inside to the kitchen windowsill, where they'll resprout. The harvest will be especially welcome on frosty nights when you're serving mashed potatoes with dinner.

The grassy, hollow leaves are, of course, a popular addition to salads, soups, and spreads. What you may not know is that the flowers are also edible and can make a pretty contribution to the same dishes. Dried-flower arrangers like the flowers because they keep their shape and color well and don't shatter.

Clary

Salvia sclarea

HEIGHT/WIDTH: 3′–5′ × 2′–3′ (90–150cm × 60–90cm)

FLOWERS/BLOOM TIME: white to lavender/summer

ZONES: 6–9

RECOMMENDED USES: medicinal, cosmetic, culinary

Clary

Apparently "clary" is a shortened version of this sage's earlier name, "clear eye," which it earned from its reputation as an eyewash. A boiled seed produced a thick mucilaginous gel that was applied to the irritated eye. The theory behind this rather farfetched process was that the offending foreign particle(s) would adhere to the gel; when everything was removed from the eye, clear sight would be restored.

It is also known as muscatel sage in Europe, where a liquid made from steeping the leaves along with some elder flowers was added to Rhine wines, mimicking the sweet flavor of muscadine grapes. Beer brewers have reportedly used clary sage in the absence of hops.

Modern gardeners in mild climates are most apt to grow this plant for its strong, appealing fragrance. More like balsam than mint, the scent is a terrific additive for homegrown cosmetics (bath mixtures, soap, lotion, etc.). A tea brewed from the dried leaves is said to settle an upset stomach. You can also use the dried leaves in any recipe that would be enhanced by other sages.

One caveat: clary is a biennial, and won't flower until its second season. The flower-and-bract colors vary quite a bit, too, from near-white to pink to lavender. Grow it in average to dry soil in full sun.

Comfrey

Symphytum officinale

HEIGHT/WIDTH: 2′–3′ × 2′–3′ (60–90cm × 60–90cm)

FLOWERS/BLOOM TIME: pink to blue/summer

ZONES: 5–9

RECOMMENDED USES: medicinal (with care), cosmetic

Comfrey

Comfrey has been cultivated and prized for many uses over the centuries, though its reputation has lost some of its luster under the scrutiny of modern science. The leaves contain calcium, phosphorus, potassium, and vitamins A, B_{12} (quite rare in plants), and C. Such a bounty made them a popular part of the vegetarian diet for many years, whether chopped fresh into salads and other dishes or cooked like spinach.

In recent years, however, several studies have called comfrey's safety into question, and until scientists sort it all out, we are advised not to ingest it. Apparently, lab rats fed on a diet that includes comfrey leaves quickly develop liver cancer, probably due to the presence of harmful alkaloids.

Comfrey is also credited with healing abilities when applied topically, and these have not been called into doubt. In fact, the leaves and the sticky root have been shown to contain soothing allantoin, a protein that helps regenerate

damaged tissue. A poultice of the leaves, or a store-bought cream containing allantoin, can ease everything from athlete's foot to burns to sores. In years past, comfrey was also prescribed for broken bones and open wounds.

As a garden plant, this herb is not for the fainthearted. It gets rather large and rangy, and its big taproot makes it difficult to move once established (plus, root fragments, given half a chance, generate new plants). The dark green, prickly leaves grow long and thick. The flowers, borne in nodding bell-like clusters, are pink and blue. Plant comfrey toward the back of your herb garden or anywhere it can spread out, in moist, fertile soil and full sun or light shade.

Coneflower

Echinacea spp.

HEIGHT/WIDTH: 1'–3' × 1–2' (30–90cm × 30–60cm)

FLOWERS/BLOOM TIME: purple daisies/summer

ZONES: 3–9

RECOMMENDED USES: medicinal

Purple coneflower

Native to North America, these handsome plants provided the indigenous people with many remedies, and some of these uses prevail to this day. You won't find them listed on the labels of products in regular drugstores, mainly because newer and apparently more effective substitutes exist. But coneflower's popularity continues unabated on the shelf in health-food stores. It is nontoxic.

Coneflower's useful part is the spindly brown root of mature plants. The Plains Indians sucked on it to treat mumps, measles, smallpox, venereal diseases, and even tumors. They also valued it for easing sore throats and toothaches. And it helped heal topical problems such as sores, wounds, insect bites, snake bites, and infections. Modern clinical studies have shown that this wide range was justified; the plant is capable of activating the body's immune system and has antiviral and antibacterial properties. For this reason, some people take coneflower tablets or drink the tea as a preventive.

Echinacea angustifolia is not as tall or showy as the more commonly grown *E. purpurea* (purple coneflower) but it is certainly attractive in its own right and perhaps better suited to today's smaller gardens. Both are very hardy perennial plants and thrive in most soils, so long as the drainage is good. They're also fairly drought tolerant. Harvest and dry the root only after the plant is three or four years old; make your move in autumn, when the plants are going dormant.

Coriander

Coriandrum sativum

HEIGHT/WIDTH: 12″–36″ × 8″–12″ (30–90cm × 20–30cm)

FLOWERS/BLOOM TIME: pink/summer

ZONES: all zones (annual)

RECOMMENDED USES: culinary, medicinal

Coriander

Although coriander can be tricky to grow, this herb rewards the diligent gardener with its many uses. An annual, it's best sown directly into the garden after the last frost. It requires well-drained soil and cannot tolerate "wet feet." Coriander grows quickly, sending up frail, slender stalks topped with tiny umbels of pinkish flowers. Until it is well established, keep the bed weeded and mulched.

Harvest the savory, lemony leaves—known as cilantro or Chinese parsley—early. You want to pick the young leaves, which look very much like parsley. Older leaves are as feathery as dill and not nearly as appealing. It is also important to harvest relatively quickly because the plant tends to go to seed early. Successive sowings will assure you a continuous harvest. Fresh-chopped leaves are a common ingredient in Asian recipes and are also used in Mexican, North African, and Caribbean dishes and sauces. Note that dried leaves are virtually flavorless.

Some cooks harvest the small, spicy seeds. Proper timing is key: use the seeds too early, and they have a distinctly unpleasant odor; too late, and they have scattered themselves on the ground. Catch the seeds as they're turning brown, and dry them further before storing. They'll become more aromatic with age. Use them whole or ground in curries, soups, cooked vegetable dishes, and fruit breads and cakes. You may also nibble on a few, or make a tea, to treat an upset stomach.

Costmary

Tanacetum (Chrysanthemum) balsamita

HEIGHT/WIDTH: 1′–3′ × 1′–2′ (30–90cm × 30–60cm)

FLOWERS/BLOOM TIME: tiny daisies/summer

ZONES: 4–9

RECOMMENDED USES: culinary, craft

Costmary

Despite the fact that it is not a very striking plant, costmary has a colorful history. The aromatic leaves, smelling of mint to some noses, balsam to others, served many uses. They were added to ale to help preserve it and to contribute a minty bitter flavor (hence the plant's other common name, alecost), used as a strewing herb, and steeped in water to make a mild infusion for washing and scenting fine linens. Nowadays, whole or chopped leaves may enhance cool summer drinks such as iced tea and lemonade. The flowers, which appear in the latter part of the summer, are very small yellow daisies.

Costmary sprigs were often pressed between the pages of the family Bible, a tradition that is traced back to the early Puritans. But they were more than a mere bookmark. Herbalists are quick to point out that costmary was also a practical choice—apparently, a drowsy parishioner could revive himself by sniffing or chewing on the bookmark if need be. Dried and crumbled leaves, flowers, and stems also make nice sachets.

Grow this herb in full sun in well-drained soil. Be forewarned that it can get leggy (so harvest leaves or sprigs regularly) and it will spread quickly via its creeping rootstock.

Cumin

Cuminum cyminum

HEIGHT/WIDTH: *6″–12″ × 3″–6″ (15-30cm × 7.5–15cm)*

FLOWERS/BLOOM TIME: white to pink/summer

ZONES: all zones (annual)

RECOMMENDED USES: culinary

Cumin

If you love to cook, growing cumin may be on your wish list. Unfortunately, it is not always an easy project. For one, the plants are small and vulnerable. They never get very large or wide, and their leaves are thin and threadlike. They sulk in soil that is too wet, die out in soil that is too dry, and languish in settings that are exposed to too much sun or wind. The good news is that some gardeners have successfully conquered these problems by growing cumin plants in small pots, placing them in a sheltered spot, and keeping a constant eye on them.

To harvest those wonderfully earthy, spicy seeds, you'll also need a long growing season—up to four months—or a good head start indoors. Like other umbel-forming herbs, you want to wait until the flower heads begin to turn brown before harvesting them. In a cool, dry place, dry them upside down in a brown paper bag, or tug off the seeds and lay them on a sheet. Later, store the precious harvest, whole or ground, in an airtight jar. Add to curries and chili powder or directly to soups, stews, or casseroles. Cumin is often found in Middle Eastern, Indian, and Mexican recipes.

Dame's rocket

Hesperis matronalis

HEIGHT/WIDTH: 1'–3' × 1'–2' (30–90cm × 30–60cm)

FLOWERS/BLOOM TIME: pink, purple, or white/summer

ZONES: 4–8

RECOMMENDED USES: culinary, craft

Dame's rocket

Looking a bit like a wild version of garden phlox (although the two are not related), dame's rocket is a delightful plant. The color varies from creamy white to softest pink to nearly magenta to purple, and the flowers are sweetly clove-scented, making them a lovely choice for summer bouquets. If you leave them be in the garden, you'll notice that their fragrance is especially strong in the evening, when they attract pollinating moths. The common name comes from the tradition of using the blooms to scent ladies' chambers.

Please note, however, that this plant is biennial, so you'll have to wait to enjoy the bounty in its second season.

Thereafter, though, dame's rocket will self-sow readily, and you'll never be without.

The spear-shaped, toothed leaves are a dark mint green, and have been used in salads. They have a sharp, tangy flavor like some of their close relatives in the mustard (arugula) family. The youngest ones are the most tender and tasty. The flowers are also edible; charm your guests by sprinkling them in a salad, atop a dip, or as a garnish for a cold soup or dessert. Dried, they retain their color and scent fairly well, so you may enjoy adding them to potpourris.

Dill

Anethum graveolens

HEIGHT/WIDTH: 2′–5′ × 2′ (60–150cm × 60cm)

FLOWERS/BLOOM TIME: yellow umbels/summer

ZONES: all zones (annual)

RECOMMENDED USES: culinary

Dill

As a culinary herb with edible leaves as well as edible seeds, lovely dill is hard to beat. It grows easily and eagerly, rewards with a delicious harvest, and self-sows. All it asks for is regular watering; it prospers in rich, well-drained soil, but will still produce in less-than-ideal conditions. About the only criticism gardeners ever have of it is that the plant is a rangy, sometimes floppy grower. However, that problem can be avoided if you grow one of the newer, more compact cultivated varieties. The best one is 18-inch (45cm) -high 'Fern Leaf', which won All-America Selections honors in 1992. Another worthy dwarf variety is 'Dukat' ('Tetra').

The best time to harvest the leaves is early in the morning, when they are full of moisture. Use them promptly for maximum flavor—in salads, in seafood and chicken dishes, and in soups of all kinds. You may freeze any excess by rolling sprigs in plastic wrap.

If you want to harvest aromatic dill seeds, read seed packet or catalog descriptions carefully. A "slow-bolting" dill may give you plenty of luscious leaves but resist going to seed. To harvest, just hang a browning flower head over a sheet or cloth. Whole or ground, the seeds make a tasty addition to apple pie, herb butter, breads, cookies, and cakes. And of course, where would pickles be without dill seeds? (Some home canners also tuck in a few immature flower heads.) By the way, dill seeds are rich in mineral salts, so people on salt-free diets may want to try them.

Dittany of Crete

Origanum dictamnus

HEIGHT/WIDTH: 12″ × 8″–12″ (30cm × 20–30cm)

FLOWERS/BLOOM TIME: pink with purple bracts/ summer

ZONES: 8–10 (elsewhere, grow in pots)

RECOMMENDED USES: medicinal

Dittany of Crete

Something of a novelty among herb fanciers, Dittany of Crete is related to the familiar oregano. As its name suggests, this small, shrubby, compact plant originally hails from Greece. As such, it is not a hardy plant, and must have protection from freezing. It is also a drought-tolerant sun lover and, in mild climates, makes a nice edging or rock-garden plant. In most of North America, however, it is grown in a hanging basket or in a pot on a windowsill.

Dittany of Crete has beautiful, thick, rounded, furry silver leaves that are crowned in summer with pretty blossoms of pink with darker, purple bracts. These are fatter than regular oregano flowers, and remind some people of hops blossoms. Collected and dried, they've been used to make a mild-flavored digestive tea. In centuries past, the plant was also reputed to have remarkable wound-healing abilities, but the methods have been lost to history.

Epazote

Chenopodium ambrosioides

HEIGHT/WIDTH: 2′–4′ × 1′–2′ (60–120cm × 30–60cm)

FLOWERS/BLOOM TIME: tiny, green/summer

ZONES: 5–10

RECOMMENDED USES: culinary

Epazote

Too often dismissed as a roadside weed, epazote is currently enjoying renewed interest thanks to the popularity of authentic Mexican cooking. Epazote is related to the valuable Andean grain plant quinoa (*C. quinoa*) and the spinach-like lambs' quarters (*C. album*), but is valued more for its ability to reduce flatulence than for any spectacular nutritional benefits.

The edible part of this plant is the leaves, and the young, smaller ones are best for cooking. They have a wild, powerful aroma that, while not offensive, takes some getting used to. Deeply cut or toothed, up to 5 inches (12.5cm) long, epazote leaves may be minced and added fresh to soups and stews, particularly ones that contain beans. It is also found in green mole and pipián sauces, where it contributes to the green color as well.

Grow this herb in full sun and well-drained soil. Beware, though: epazote is an enthusiastic grower and self-seeder, and can take over large areas in short order. You might be better off growing a few plants in pots.

Fennel

Foeniculum vulgare

HEIGHT/WIDTH: 3′–5′ × 2′–4′ (90–150cm × 60–120cm)

FLOWERS/BLOOM TIME: large yellow umbels/mid- to
late summer

ZONES: 6–9

RECOMMENDED USES: culinary, dye, cosmetic

Fennel

This big, bold herb radiates a sweet, warm licorice smell that's a bit more nutty than that of anise. In average but well-drained soil, it can soar up to 5 feet (1.5m) tall in a single season, topped with broad yellow umbels of flowers. You may wish to seek out the alternative variety known as bronze fennel, which is similar in every way except coloring. The contrast of its bronze stems and tinted foliage with the golden flower heads is a beautiful sight.

Fennel doubles as a vegetable and a spice. The sweet-flavored stalks, which resemble celery stalks, are tasty to nibble on raw, and can be diced into soups and salads or served steamed. The curved, greenish brown seeds are also prized. Watch the plant carefully late in the season and clip off the flower heads the moment you spot them going brown (turning ripe). Otherwise, even a slight breeze will spill your eagerly awaited harvest—and then you'll have more fennel plants in your garden in the coming years than you ever bargained for! Pop the harvested head in a paper bag, wait a week or two, and then collect your bounty and store it in an airtight jar. Use the seeds in bread baking, fish dishes, homemade sausages, and tomato-based sauces.

Fennel tea is a pleasant breath freshener and also enjoys a reputation as a diuretic (high doses can overstimulate the nervous system and should be avoided). The flowers and leaves have been used to make yellow and brown dyes for wool. Fennel is also used to scent soap as well as in steam facials as a pore cleanser.

Fenugreek

Trigonella foenum-graecum

HEIGHT/WIDTH: 1'–2' × 1'–2' (30–60cm × 30–60cm)

FLOWERS/BLOOM TIME: white, pealike/summer

ZONES: all zones (annual)

RECOMMENDED USES: culinary, medicinal

Fenugreek

You have to wonder how fenugreek's wonderful culinary properties were discovered in the first place. The plant, a member of the pea family, is somewhat lax and rangy, and looks a lot like ordinary clover. Native to the Mediterranean, it remains popular in that area as a fodder and agricultural cover crop. The small white flowers are practically lost in all the herbage, and the brown seedpods that follow (about 6 inches [15cm] long) don't stand out much either.

Even after you harvest those seedpods and extract the oblong, honey-colored seeds within, you won't find them very appealing. They have little scent and a bitter taste, and must be roasted carefully to bring out the splendid, spicy, maplelike flavor coveted by cooks the world over. Once the seeds are dried and ground, their scent and flavor reach their full potential. Fenugreek is a common ingredient in Indian curries and chutneys as well as many North African dishes. It is also used in halvah, the Middle Eastern sweet treat.

Modern science has discovered or verified from folk remedies some amazing properties in fenugreek seed—everything from lowering blood sugar in diabetics and easing gastronomic woes to treating impotence in men and easing both nursing and menopausal problems in women.

Feverfew

Tanacetum (Chrysanthemum) parthenium

HEIGHT/WIDTH: 2′–3′ × 2′–3′ (60–90cm × 60–90cm)

FLOWERS/BLOOM TIME: small daisies/summer

ZONES: 5–9

RECOMMENDED USES: medicinal

Feverfew

This pretty plant has a lot going for it. Easy to grow in almost any soil, it flowers profusely, is rarely troubled by pests or diseases, and makes a fairly tidy appearance. For this reason, it is often incorporated into regular flower gardens, used as an edging plant, and tucked into charming window box schemes.

But some gardeners have noticed an odd quirk: bees avoid feverfew, perhaps because of its strong, bitter smell (most noticeable to humans when plant parts are touched or crushed). So if you have a vegetable garden or other plants in your garden that rely on bee pollination, you might want to think twice about planting feverfew. It also likes to self-sow, but you may consider that a virtue.

Feverfew gets its common name from its long-standing reputation as a fever reducer. It is no longer credited with this ability, but researchers have verified another valuable quality lurking in its leaves: it has anti-inflammatory properties similar to that of aspirin. It is now being touted as a relief or even cure for headaches, including debilitating migraines. You'll find over-the-counter feverfew preparations on the shelves of many health-food stores. Eating the leaves fresh out of your garden is not recommended without the supervision of a qualified doctor or herbalist. In any event, the sharp, bitter flavor may put you off.

Flax

Linum usitatissimum

HEIGHT/WIDTH: 2'–4' × 1'–2' (60–120cm × 30–60cm)

FLOWERS/BLOOM TIME: blue/summer

ZONES: all zones (annual)

RECOMMENDED USES: craft

Flax

True flax, the flax that has been used for centuries to make linen, is an annual plant, not to be confused with the similar but shorter perennial *L. perenne*, but it is just as easy to grow. Sow seeds directly into your garden after the soil has warmed up and danger of frost has passed. Note that the plant is shallow-rooted, so choose a spot where your seedlings won't be disturbed by hoeing or foot traffic.

In bloom, flax is a pretty sight. Clouds of delicate, soft blue, half-inch (12mm) flowers cover the plant. Individual flowers wither and drop their petals quickly, but are just as quickly replaced. However, it is the stems that are most valued. The fibers that can be woven into linen cloth are inside; extracting them involves soaking the plants in water, scraping off the outer stem, and combing out the fine but strong fibers. They are at their best (soft yet tough) when harvested after the plant has bloomed, just as the stalks begin to dry and turn yellow.

This plant is also known as linseed, and a yellowish oil extracted from the brown seeds was used in times past as a cough medicine and laxative. It is not used today because scientists have identified a number of toxic chemicals, particularly in the immature seeds. Overdoses can lead to hyperventilating and even paralysis. Linseed oil is an ingredient in printing ink, paint, and varnish.

Garlic

Allium sativum

HEIGHT/WIDTH: $2' \times 1'$ (60cm $\times$ 30cm)

FLOWERS/BLOOM TIME: white/summer

ZONES: 3–9

RECOMMENDED USES: culinary, medicinal

Garlic

If you love garlic, you owe it to yourself to raise it in your garden. Not only is it easy to grow, but you'll discover that the flavor is richer and more pungent than anything you've ever bought in the store. Garlic plants don't take up a lot of space, so you can plant a whole bed of them or just tuck a few behind some of your other herb plants. They do best in full sun in soil that is reasonably fertile and drains well.

The secret to growing good garlic is planting ahead of time—the previous autumn. But don't plant too late in the season; get the little cloves in the ground a month or more before you expect the ground to freeze. (You can plant grocery-store cloves, but mail-order companies offer a wider range of choices.)

They'll start forming roots, and when spring comes, the plants will burst into vigorous growth. Encourage them with a dose of fertilizer, if you wish. Snap off the odd-looking flowerstalks so that the plant's energy will be directed toward root development (these stalks, and the "bulbils" they are topped with, are edible—try them in salads). Around midsummer, you'll notice growth slowing down. Reduce watering, wait for the leaves to wither, then harvest what should be big, fat, juicy bulbs with the leaves still attached. Air dry for a few weeks, then braid them or store in a cool, dry place (never in the refrigerator).

As for garlic's culinary uses, entire cookbooks are devoted to the subject. Its medicinal uses are also legendary, and many have been verified by modern science. It is an antiseptic, brings relief to cold symptoms, lowers blood pressure, and is more effective than penicillin against typhus!

Garlic chives

Allium tuberosum

HEIGHT/WIDTH: 2′–3′ × 1′–2′ (60–90cm × 30–60cm)

FLOWERS/BLOOM TIME: white/late summer

ZONES: 3–9

RECOMMENDED USES: culinary

Garlic chives

Unlike some of its garlicky, oniony relatives, garlic chives' flowers are sweetly fragrant—the scent has even been compared to that of a rose. Shaped like starry tufts, the creamy white flowers are also pretty. They're edible, and make a nice seasoning or striking garnish.

But the real reason to grow this plant is for its foliage. Long, flat, and thin, it resembles chives but is taller. The subtle, garliclike flavor makes it ideal for mincing into salads, soups, and savory dips. Other names for this plant—

Chinese chives, Chinese leeks, Oriental garlic, gow choy, chung fa, and yuen sai—reveal its importance in Asian cuisine. It is a common ingredient in stir-fries.

This perky little plant is a perennial, plus it self-sows with abandon, so unless you want an ever-burgeoning harvest you'll have to keep an eye on it. Like garlic, it wants decently well drained soil and a spot in full sun. Clip flowerstalks before they go to seed, and pull out unwanted plants as they appear.

Geranium

Pelargonium spp.

HEIGHT/WIDTH: 6"–36" × 6"–36" (15–90cm × 15–90cm)

FLOWERS/BLOOM TIME: not generally grown for flowers

ZONES: 9–10 (elsewhere, grow in pots)

RECOMMENDED USES: culinary, craft

Geranium

If fragrance is your goal in growing herbs, you must have some scented geraniums in your collection. They resemble the familiar window box geraniums, but the flowers are not nearly as showy. The leaves, especially when brushed against, radiate scent—everything from apple (*P. odoratissimum*) to chocolate peppermint (a hybrid) to lemon (*P. crispum*) to true rose (*P. graveolens*). You'll also appreciate the great variation in leaf shapes and textures. Some are broad, some are lacy; some are velvety soft, and some are crisp and smooth. Color may also vary, from dark emerald green to lime green with splashes or touches of black, darker green, cream, or yellow.

The only drawback to scented geraniums is that they are tender plants. However, they are charming in pots and window boxes, and you can overwinter them indoors. If that's too much trouble, simply take cuttings from your favorites toward the end of the summer and start new plants. In any case, they should be grown in a good, well-drained potting mix and watered regularly. Warm temperatures and good air circulation keep them healthy.

All scented geraniums make nice additions to potpourris and sachets. For best results, snip off leaves in the morning of a dry, sunny day and lay them to dry flat in the shade. Fresh-picked rose-scented leaves are a popular addition to apple jelly (just lay a leaf or two on top before sealing the jar). They'll also contribute their soft, sweet scent to a canister of white sugar, enhancing all sorts of baked goodies.

Germander

Teucrium chamaedrys

HEIGHT/WIDTH: 6″–18″ × 12″–18″ (15–45cm ×
30–45cm)

FLOWERS/BLOOM TIME: pink to purple/summer

ZONES: 5–9

RECOMMENDED USES: medicinal

Germander

Germander is a handsome, fast-growing, shrubby mint relative. Its most popular use is as an edging plant in designed
herb gardens (knot gardens, mazes, etc.). Indeed, it has
sometimes been referred to as "the poor man's boxwood."
More winter-hardy than boxwood, gardeners in more
northern limits would still be wise to mulch it for the winter,
just in case. Like boxwood, it responds well to shaping and
pruning, filling in gaps quickly with fresh new growth. The
tiny, half-inch (12mm) green leaves are small, stiff, and scalloped. Plant germander in full sun, in average, well-drained
soil. Keep plants lush with a good pruning each spring.

Germander flowers may not be welcome in your hedging
or edging scheme and can be clipped off as they appear. But,
like all mint-family flowers, they are rather pretty—borne on
upright stems, they vary from pink to purple.

As for uses, germander's main claim to fame is as a treatment for gout. Tea brewed from its leaves was credited with
curing the sixteenth-century German emperor Charles V of
gout. Germander was also employed in soothing cold symptoms and jaundice and reducing fever. Nowadays, other
herbs can do a better job of treating the same ills, but germander's ornamental grace and beauty continue to be valued.

Ginger

Zingiber officinale

HEIGHT/WIDTH: 2'–4' × 1'–2' (60–120cm × 30–60cm)

FLOWERS/BLOOM TIME: greenish spikes/summer

ZONES: 9–10 (elsewhere, grow as a houseplant)

RECOMMENDED USES: culinary, medicinal

Ginger

Ah, ginger—so pungent, so spicy, so warming. And although it is a tropical plant, many gardeners have had good luck raising it at home from ordinary grocery-store rhizomes. All it needs is an ample pot of fertile, well-drained soil and a warm, sheltered spot out of direct sunlight. It appreciates extra humidity, which is easily provided by setting the pot on a tray of water and pebbles and by misting it occasionally. It will produce long, lance-shaped leaves and occasionally a flower that resembles a tiny pineapple.

But of course it is the root you are after, and the good news is that you can harvest after a year or less. Freshly harvested, your homegrown ginger root will have several branches and be plump and juicy, ready to add to stir-fries and marinades. Or, let it dry out and grate it into all sorts of dishes, from meats to vegetables to baked goods. Dried chunks may be candied for a delicious snack eaten straight or added to cookies or cakes.

Ginger also offers useful medicinal benefits. It eases indigestion, morning sickness, and motion sickness, and it has been found to be a stimulant that promotes circulation and the absorption of other medications. Ginger liniments are used to relax sore muscles.

Goldenseal

Hydrastis canadensis

HEIGHT/WIDTH: 6″–12″ × 6″–8″ (15–30cm × 15–20cm)

FLOWERS/BLOOM TIME: greenish/spring

ZONES: 5–9

RECOMMENDED USES: medicinal, with caution; dye

Goldenseal

A native American wildflower, goldenseal (its yellowish root, to be exact) is credited with all sorts of healing properties. And while it has been shown that many of these claims are inaccurate and that certain uses are in fact dangerous, its great popularity hasn't waned. The result is that wild stands are rapidly disappearing and the price is going up, up, up. It seems only logical, then, to try to grow your own.

Unfortunately, it is not easy to grow. Goldenseal is a woodland plant and needs similar conditions in cultivation: filtered shade, humid air, and soil that is rich, moist, and light. Best raised from pieces of sprouted root, a mature, usable harvest may be several years away. The plant itself is attractive but not especially unusual-looking. The leaves are light green and deeply lobed, the stems are erect and fuzzy, and the flowers are small and inconspicuous.

The active ingredient in the root is an alkaloid called hydrastine. In large doses, it adversely affects the nervous system and may lead to severe vomiting, respiratory failure, convulsions, paralysis, and death. Also, it lingers in your system and accumulates, so current conventional wisdom counsels against taking goldenseal internally. Apparently safe topical uses include using it to treat conjunctivitis, herpes, and canker sores. But as with some other potentially harmful herbs, it is best to check with your doctor or a professional herbalist before you use it. The belief that it masks the positive results of urine tests for drug users has been debunked. Also, dyes can be made from infusing the roots.

Good King Henry

Chenopodium bonus-henricus

HEIGHT/WIDTH: 1'–3' × 1'–2' (30–90cm × 30–60cm)

FLOWERS/BLOOM TIME: yellow/summer

ZONES: 5–8

RECOMMENDED USES: culinary

Good King Henry

Who was "Good King Henry," and how did his name become attached to this leafy European herb? The plant was not named for England's Henry VIII, whose reputation is not especially good anyway. Rather, the name appears to come from a German folk tale about a virtuous goblin named Henry who helped women with their household chores (which, presumably, included harvesting greens from the garden) in exchange for a saucer of milk.

This compact-growing plant is a pleasant addition to any garden, and brings broad-leaved texture to an herb-garden scheme that might otherwise be dominated by lacy foliage. The leaves, which have a distinctive arrow shape, are glossy and dark green. Eat them raw or cooked, alone or in salads, casseroles, and soups. Keep in mind that the younger leaves taste best, much like a mild, tangy version of spinach. Their iron content is even higher than that of spinach.

Good King Henry grows best in deep, rich soil, and can be slow to get established. Depending on how it does for you, you might be wise to let it grow for a year and begin harvesting in the second summer. In any event, keep it well watered so that the leaves are at their succulent best. Trimming off the imconspicuous yellow flower spikes will keep the plant in production.

Horehound

Marrubium vulgare

HEIGHT/WIDTH: 1'–2' (30–60cm) × 1'–2' (30–60cm)

FLOWERS/BLOOM TIME: white/mid- to late summer

ZONES: 4–9

RECOMMENDED USES: medicinal

Horehound

Justly famous as a sore-throat and cough remedy, horehound has been prized since the days of ancient Egypt and Greece. In fact, its common name is believed to have been derived from Horus, the Egyptian god of the sky and light. The "hound" part may have to do with the old belief that it cures the bite of a mad dog.

The plant has a wonderful, distinctively menthollike scent with a touch of woodsiness. An extract from the leaves is used to this day in throat lozenges, cough drops, cough syrups, and sometimes savory candies. Apparently the plant's high concentration of mucilage gets the credit, but it also contains soothing volatile compounds and even some vitamin C.

Horehound is a bushy, branching plant, and the stems and leaves are extremely woolly and soft. The color is light green, but thanks to its overall furriness, horehound sometimes looks almost white. The small white flowers, which make their debut in the second season, don't stand out much to our eyes but are a magnet for bees.

Grow horehound in full sun in well-drained soil (even sandy soil is okay). Harvest the leaves early in the day and immediately dice them into small pieces and seal in an airtight jar (dried leaves quickly lose their potency). Brew in a soothing tea or make your own lozenges by boiling them with sugar, then cooling and cutting into small chunks.

Horseradish

Armoracia rusticana

HEIGHT/WIDTH: 2'–3' × 1' (60–90cm × 30cm)

FLOWERS/BLOOM TIME: small, white/early summer

ZONES: 5–8

RECOMMENDED USES: culinary, medicinal

Horseradish

The fresh root of this otherwise undistinguished-looking plant has a powerful flavor, unrivaled in the herb and vegetable world. Grow your own, and you will enjoy it at its full potency. But before you plant, pick the site with care. Horseradish will conquer the area in which it is planted in short order and is practically impossible to eradicate. Consign it to an out-of-the-way spot, or put it in a wide but bottomless container. Or, grow it as some people grow potatoes—in mounds—or in its own raised bed. Once you've taken care of that problem, devote some effort to soil preparation. The best horseradish roots—as with any root crop—are grown in rich, well-drained soil that is well sifted (free of rocks and clumps) and weed-free.

Harvest in autumn, after the floppy, oblong leaves begin to yellow. Clean off the roots and store them in the refrigerator, where they'll keep for up to three months. (They may also be stored in dry sand in a cool basement or garage.) The sooner you eat them, the more pungent the flavor will be. Note that the flavor does not survive cooking. A popular use for horseradish is to mince it, add it to mayonnaise or mustard, and serve with roast beef. It's also good with baked or cold fish and in fish salads. You may want to grate it into vinegar or lemon juice, which keeps the flavor intact while preventing discoloration.

Although it isn't used much as a remedy anymore, in times past horseradish was valued as a digestive aid and, not surprisingly, a way to clear the sinuses.

Hummingbird sage

Salvia leucantha

HEIGHT/WIDTH: 3′–5′ × 3′–5′ (90–150cm × 90–150cm)

FLOWERS/BLOOM TIME: lavender/late summer to fall

ZONES: 7–10

RECOMMENDED USES: craft

Hummingbird sage

Also known as Mexican bush sage, this attractive dry-climate plant forms a dense, shrubby mound of rough-textured gray-green leaves. Late in the season, the leaves are joined by masses of spectacular flowers. Borne in velvety spikes up to 8 inches (20cm) long, these are lavender to dark purple and accented by white or purple protruding "tongues" (corollas). Crowds of bees, butterflies, and, of course, hummingbirds flock to them. They're wonderful in bouquets and also dry well, so they are a nice addition to dried arrangements, wreaths, and swags.

There are a few cultivated varieties of hummingbird sage. 'All Purple' has rich, two-tone purple flowers.

'Emerald' flowers are lavender-purple accented with white, plus the foliage is a darker green than the species. 'Emeralds 'n' Cream' has the same flowers as 'Emerald', but with lovely variegated foliage.

Gardeners in mild climates should have no trouble growing this plant. But even if you're north of its hardiness range, you may want to give it a try; it's a fast grower and can reach a substantial size and flower in just one season. In any event, be sure to give it a spot with plenty of sun and decent, well-drained soil. Don't overwater, or it may languish. You may fertilize lightly to encourage flowering.

Hyssop

Hyssopus officinalis

HEIGHT/WIDTH: 2′–3′ × 1′–2′ (60–90cm × 30–60cm)

FLOWERS/BLOOM TIME: blue to purple/summer

ZONES: 4–8

RECOMMENDED USES: medicinal, culinary

Hyssop

Related to both the mints and the sages, easy-going hyssop is a bit like each of them. Along with the characteristic square stems of mint, it also has the powerful scent you'd expect (almost too powerful for some tastes, and more camphorlike than mint-sweet). Like sage, it grows well in soil that is on the dry side, and it has a shrubby profile that, with age, gains a semiwoody base. The flowers, carried in loose whorls, are very pretty, usually a vibrant shade of deep purple, though lighter ones often appear. You can also find hyssop flowers in white and pink. They make a lovely contribution to any herb garden, and attract bees and butterflies.

Hyssop has been in cultivation a long, long time. Though it is mentioned by name in the Bible, experts agree that marjoram or a similar plant was probably meant instead, as hyssop doesn't grow wild in the Middle East. In years past, hyssop was often used as a strewing herb. Its pungency also made for good, strong teas administered to people suffering from a sore throat, bronchitis, or even asthma. These days, you occasionally find it in natural cold remedies. You may also see it as an ingredient in the aromatic liqueurs Benedictine and Chartreuse. And modern science has found that the plant has antiviral properties—in fact, AIDS researchers are taking a closer look at it.

Jerusalem sage

Phlomis fruticosa

HEIGHT/WIDTH: 2′–4′ × 1′–3′ (60–120cm × 30–90cm)

FLOWERS/BLOOM TIME: yellow/early summer

ZONES: 5–10

RECOMMENDED USES: craft

Jerusalem sage

A lovely, low-maintenance choice for the herb or flower garden, Jerusalem sage grows into a pleasantly scented, much-branched plant. The gray leaves are large (up to 4 inches [10cm] long), lance-shaped, wrinkled, and velvety to the touch. Unlike those of many of its relatives, Jerusalem sage's flowers are not in the blue and purple range, but rather a sunny lemon yellow. They're borne in whorls along the erect stems and are about an inch (2.5cm) across. They dry beautifully, which endears them to makers of wreaths, dried bouquets, and potpourris.

Grow this handsome plant in full sun or partial shade in well-drained soil that is on the dry side; a slope is an excellent setting. Don't neglect it completely, though—a little supplementary water inspires robust flowering. In mild climates, Jerusalem sage remains evergreen over the winter; to keep it from becoming scraggly, cut it back by one-third to one-half each autumn. In other climes, it dies back to the ground but returns with gusto the following spring.

Johnny jump-up

Viola tricolor

HEIGHT/WIDTH: 6″–12″ × 4″–8″ (15–30cm × 10–20cm)

FLOWERS/BLOOM TIME: purple and yellow or white/summer

ZONES: all zones (annual)

RECOMMENDED USES: culinary, craft

Johnny jump-up

The common name for this sweet, tufted little plant comes from its ability to catapult seeds every which way when its ripe pod bursts open. This enthusiastic shower of seeds leads to new plants "jumping up" in unexpected places around the yard.

In rich, moist soil, you are sure to have plenty of plants, and may adopt a rather indulgent attitude toward them, as they are so small and charming. The flowers, generally no more than an inch (2.5cm) across, are usually of three colors: petals of purple, blue, and creamy white are accented with tiny "whisker" markings radiating from a yellow center. The leaves become heart-shaped as they mature.

The pansylike flowers are edible, and are pretty in salads or as a garnish for dips, soups, or omelets. Pinch one out and taste it alone and you will detect a bubble-gum flavor. Johnny jump-up flowers also candy well and make lovely decorations for special cakes. (Gingerly brush freshly harvested blossoms with a water/egg white mixture, then sprinkle with white sugar and allow to dry.)

Another common name for this violet is hearts-ease, which refers to its long-ago reputation as a heart stimulant. The preparation and techniques have not survived to this day, and it may have been purely folklore, as other related violets were never touted for this ability.

Lady's mantle

Alchemilla vulgaris

HEIGHT/WIDTH: 1'–2' × 1½' (30–60cm × 45cm)

FLOWERS/BLOOM TIME: chartreuse/spring

ZONES: 4–7

RECOMMENDED USES: medicinal, dye

Lady's mantle

Alchemilla translates from the Latin as "little magical one," an indication of this long-popular plant's reputation. The broad lime green leaves are soft to the touch. When rain or early-morning dew gathers on them, the water beads up like quicksilver and sparkles—a unique and enchanting sight.

But the magic may also refer to the plant's medicinal uses. Infusions made from the leaves have been used to treat a wide range of female problems, from reducing heavy menstrual flows to easing cramping to regulating fluctuating hormone levels just after childbirth or during menopause. The leaves also yield a green dye for wool. And the fresh root, pressed against a cut, has been used to halt bleeding.

Even if you never avail yourself of these interesting uses, you will cherish the plant for the soft yet elegant beauty it brings to your herb garden. The scalloped leaves (up to 4 inches [10cm] across) are wide as herb leaves go, adding nice contrast. The frothy flowers, in a sharp, clear shade of yellow-green, appear in profusion each spring on short stalks that hold them slightly away from the leaves. Try lady's mantle as an edging plant to soften the straight lines of the garden's layout or to skirt a central birdbath or sundial.

This plant is easy to grow and adapts well to sun and partial shade alike, provided it gets well-drained but moist soil. If your summers are hot and dry, coddle it with fertile soil, some shade, and extra water.

Lavender, English

Lavandula angustifolia

HEIGHT/WIDTH: 2′–3′ × 2′–3′ (60–90cm × 60–90cm)

FLOWERS/BLOOM TIME: purple/summer

ZONES: 5–9

RECOMMENDED USES: cosmetic, craft, medicinal,
repellent

'Dutch' lavender

Beloved the world over for its delightful, penetrating fragrance, lavender surely is an herb-garden classic. There are several species and many cultivars, including ones with rosy flowers and white flowers, ones with foliage that is more green than gray, and especially compact or dwarf ones. But the quintessential hardy lavender, the one that has the strongest scent and makes the finest dried flowers and oil, remains good old English lavender. It grows best in light, well-drained soil with a higher pH. (If your soil is acidic, try adding lime dust or chips to the planting area.)

Many gardeners like to grow lavender as an edging plant or as a low hedge, uses that suit it very well. Even when it matures and develops a somewhat woody base, it retains a tidy, even graceful appearance. Shearing or clipping is a pleasant chore and one from which the plant recov-

ers quickly. If you want to use the harvest, prune either just as the flowers are opening or when they are completely full. Dry them in a hot, dark place such as a garage or attic.

You may already be thinking of lavender for homemade potpourris and sachets, but it has many other uses. The leaves really do repel insects and moths, which is why sprigs are tucked into linen closets and chests. The yellowish oil, which is collected by boiling the flowers, can be added to baths to soothe dry skin and sore muscles. A few drops in hot tea act as a sedative. Both the dried flowers and the oil continue to be popular ingredients in all sorts of soaps, creams, and perfumes.

Lemon balm

Melissa officinalis

HEIGHT/WIDTH: 2′–3′ × 1′–2′ (60–90cm × 30–60cm)

FLOWERS/BLOOM TIME: pale yellow/summer

ZONES: 5–9

RECOMMENDED USES: medicinal, culinary

Lemon balm

Not an especially interesting-looking plant, lemon balm nonetheless distinguishes itself with other praiseworthy qualities. It is perhaps the most lemony of all the plants in the mint family and isn't nearly as invasive as its relatives. It spreads sideways, with a trailing habit. The plant does self-sow, so keep after it if you don't want an ever-expanding crop. Grow it in rich, moist—but very well drained— soil. And if you're able to provide partial shade, the plant will be more lush. You'll notice that bees adore the flowers, small and inconspicuous as they are.

Lemon balm is at its strongest when picked just as the tiny flowers begin to open. Chopped into green or fruit salads, it adds a welcome tang. Some chefs also prize it for baked or broiled fish dishes. A tasty yet mild tea brewed from lemon balm calms cold and flu symptoms, fevers, and tension headaches. (It is said that a thirteenth-century English nobleman who lived to be 108 had a cup of lemon balm tea nearly every day of his life. This story has almost certainly helped popularize the tea.) In any event, always use lemon balm fresh—dried leaves lose their flavor.

Lemongrass

Cymbopogon citratus

HEIGHT/WIDTH: 4′–6′ × 2′ (120–180cm × 60cm)

FLOWERS/BLOOM TIME: greenish clusters/summer

ZONES: 8–10

RECOMMENDED USES: culinary, medicinal, insect repellent

Lemongrass

Lemongrass is a true grass, though it grows taller and denser than many of the ornamental grasses we are used to inviting into our gardens. It is native to the hot, humid tropics of southern India, Sri Lanka, and Ceylon, where it is known as serah. It rarely flowers or sets seed, so it is raised from divisions, which come with a small bulbous root. Gardeners in the Deep South or West ought to be able to raise it; the rest of us can bring it into a warm greenhouse for the winter or try it as a houseplant (it will grow smaller when confined to a pot). In any event, keep it well watered.

The broad blades emit a strong lemon scent when cut or broken. In fact, lemongrass is related to citronella and also repels mosquitoes, flies, and fleas. But it is best known as an essential ingredient in Indonesian and Thai cuisine, where it enhances everything from coconut milk–based soups to stir-fries. Your homegrown lemongrass will certainly add splendor to such dishes.

Lemongrass also makes a pleasant, soothing tea. It has been used to treat all sorts of disorders, including indigestion, fever, colds, and headaches. The oil has been shown to lower high blood pressure as well as inhibit blood coagulation, so look for this herb to be of continued interest to the medical world.

Lemon verbena

Aloysia triphylla

HEIGHT/WIDTH: 6′–10′ × 3′–6′ (180–300cm × 90–180cm)

FLOWERS/BLOOM TIME: white spikes/summer

ZONES: 8–10

RECOMMENDED USES: culinary, cosmetic

Lemon verbena

Not a leafy herb at all but rather a robust shrub, lemon verbena holds an important place in the worlds of herbal cosmetics and cooking. The useful part is the lime green leaves, which sport a delicate lemon aroma when touched. Cooks like to add the fresh or dried leaves to all sorts of recipes, from fish and chicken to desserts. As you might guess, the leaves are also great for a sweet tea. It used to be a tradition to place a sprig next to finger bowls at fancy meals. Lemon verbena is also an ingredient in some citrusy colognes; you may wish to steep sprigs in a hot bath.

Native to South America, this tender shrub is not very hardy up north. However, gardeners in mild areas of North America have succeeded in growing it, with winter protection when warranted. It also takes well to life in a tub, so gardeners in other areas can grow it if they don't mind haul-ing it indoors each autumn. It will drop its leaves, but then rebound the following spring.

Lemon verbena needs full sun, does best in rich, moist soil, and should never be overwatered. With age, the plant becomes leggy, so underplant it with something shorter and unscented (so that there'll be no competition for your nose). Some gardeners have had fun capitalizing on this tendency towards legginess by pruning their plant to look like a big lollipop. The plant is vulnerable to spider mites and white-flies, so keep it in good health as a preventative measure, and go to battle against the pests quickly should they appear.

Licorice

Glycyrrhiza glabra

HEIGHT/WIDTH: 3′–7′ × 2′–4′ (90–210cm × 60–120cm)

FLOWERS/BLOOM TIME: purple spikes/midsummer

ZONES: 8–10

RECOMMENDED USES: culinary, medicinal, cosmetic

Licorice

If you are a fan of licorice candy, you may be surprised to learn that you have not been enjoying the real thing. The little black candies and ropy twists are actually flavored with milder anise. Most true licorice—derived from the pungent root of a rangy member of the pea family—is imported into North America to enhance the flavor of tobacco products, including chew, cigarettes, and snuff.

In its native Mediterranean and Asia, sticks of licorice root continue to be popular as a sweet snack food and to slake thirst. Over the centuries, the plant has been employed in a wide range of remedies, but recent studies of some of these uses have raised red flags. In particular, the active ingredient glycyrrhizin has been implicated in causing high blood pressure, salt and water retention, cardiac arrest, kidney failure, and paralysis. In small doses in over-the-counter treatments, though, licorice is still considered safe and effective in cough syrups and lozenges and as a digestive aid that limits acid production. It's also an effective shampoo additive for those with oily hair.

Should you wish to try your hand at growing it, be sure to give it an out-of-the-way spot where it can spread, partly because it isn't especially attractive, but also because once planted it's hard to eradicate. It needs rich, well-drained, deep soil in full or partial shade. Generally raised from cuttings, it takes up to four years to develop a mature, usable root.

Lovage

Levisticum officinale

HEIGHT/WIDTH: 4'–6' × 2'–3' (120–180cm × 6090cm)

FLOWERS/BLOOM TIME: tiny yellow umbels/summer

ZONES: 4–9

RECOMMENDED USES: culinary, medicinal

Lovage

Although not directly related to celery, lovage looks and tastes a bit like it—but best of all, it's much easier to grow. Lovage is a tall and vigorous perennial, so plan on giving it the elbow room it needs toward the back of your garden. It is tricky to raise from seeds (they sprout slowly and irregularly), so buy young plants instead. Plant them in a site with full sun. The soil should be rich and well drained, especially if you are planning to harvest the tasty roots; it should also be on the sweet side. Mulch the area to conserve moisture and keep weeds at bay. By the second season, your lovage will be ready to supply you with a hearty harvest.

All parts of the lovage plant are edible. The flavor is hard to describe. It resembles celery but is stronger and, to some palates, "warmer." For this reason, it's a better choice for adding to stocks, soups, stews, and casseroles. It's a favorite for potato dishes, from basic mashed to cold potato salad. Experiment to see which parts you find tastiest—the tender young leaves, the mature stems, the stout root, or the savory seeds.

The one medicinal use that has stood the test of time is using the fresh or dried root to brew a diuretic tea (though pregnant women and people with kidney problems should not use it).

Lungwort

Pulmonaria officinalis

HEIGHT/WIDTH: 1′ × 1′–2′ (30cm × 30–60cm)

FLOWERS/BLOOM TIME: pink to blue/spring

ZONES: 3–9

RECOMMENDED USES: medicinal

'Bertram Anderson' lungwort

According to medieval doctrine, plants or plant parts that resembled body parts had a connection with those body parts. Thus the pretty, oval-shaped, cream-dappled leaves of this plant were associated with the lungs. Lungwort was used in folk medicine in Europe and Russia to treat minor bronchial congestion as well as bronchitis and even tuberculosis. These days, the evidence in its favor is weak. But the plant has been found to contain allantoin, a protein also found in comfrey that helps regenerate damaged tissue. Products containing allantoin are used to ease everything from athlete's foot to sores and burns. Lungwort's astringent properties are also used to treat diarrhea and hemorrhoids.

But for most herb gardeners, the real reason to grow this plant—and any of its charming relatives, especially Bethlehem sage (*P. saccharata*)—is its beauty. It grows well in partial shade and the leaf markings help it to stand out. The small, tubular flowers are also lovely, starting out rosy pink and opening to violet-blue. Because lungwort blooms in spring, it is a nice addition to a bulb garden, or it can be among the first signs of life each year in your herb garden.

Marjoram, sweet

Origanum majorana

HEIGHT/WIDTH: 1′–2′ × 1′–2′ (30–60cm × 30–60cm)

FLOWERS/BLOOM TIME: white or pink/midsummer

ZONES: 6–9

RECOMMENDED USES: culinary

Marjoram

Marjoram is not oregano, but because they are related and resemble each other, people continue to confuse the two herbs. The main differences are in the flavor (marjoram is sweeter and more balsamlike) and the hardiness (marjoram is a more tender plant). It originally hails from the Mediterranean.

No matter where you live, though, you are bound to notice that it grows slowly and is not a large plant. For these reasons, you ought to start the tiny seeds indoors early or buy small plants when getting started. Marjoram likes full sun and decent, well-drained soil that is on the alkaline side. It can easily be overwhelmed by more vigorous plants, including weeds, so coddle it until it hits its stride. If you live in a mild climate, bring it through the winter outdoors by mulching it, or just start over each year.

The best time to harvest the delicious leaves is just as the small flowers appear. If you cut the plant back to within an inch (2.5cm) or so of the ground, expect a second, lusher crop later in the season. Marjoram, unlike some herbs, keeps its full flavor even after it has been dried.

Cooks prize marjoram for all sorts of recipes. Try it in Italian dishes where you would usually use oregano. It is also a better choice for meat dishes (especially lamb) and a favorite in omelettes and homemade sausages.

Mexican lemon hyssop

Agastache mexicana

HEIGHT/WIDTH: 2′ × 1′–2′ (60cm × 30–60cm)

FLOWERS/BLOOM TIME: purple spikes/late summer

ZONES: 9–10

RECOMMENDED USES: culinary

'Giant Lemon' Mexican lemon hyssop

Not a hyssop at all but rather a member of the mint family and a close relative of anise hyssop, Mexican lemon hyssop has a bold mint-lemon scent and taste. A bushy plant that branches at the top, Mexican lemon hyssop sports fragrant, smooth, lance-shaped leaves. The appealing flowers, carried in spikes, are about 4 inches (10cm) long, tubular, and rosy pink to reddish purple.

As the name suggests, it is a native of Mexico, and thus it is not very hardy. However, it grows readily from seed and flowers its first summer, so gardeners in more northern zones can still enjoy it. They'll just need to treat it like an annual or dig it up each autumn to overwinter indoors. It does best in full sun and is not fussy about soil.

Use Mexican lemon hyssop leaves fresh or dried in hot or iced tea, summer drinks, sangria, and festive punches. The leaves also add an exotic, savory flavor to lamb dishes. You'll find that the flowers are just as tasty, and make a nice addition to salads and cold soups or as garnishes.

Mexican mint marigold

Tagetes lucida

HEIGHT/WIDTH: $2'$–$3' \times 1'$–$2'$ (60–90cm $\times$ 30–60cm)

FLOWERS/BLOOM TIME: gold/autumn to winter

ZONES: 7–10

RECOMMENDED USES: culinary, craft, medicinal

Mexican mint marigold

Gardeners in areas with hot summers will cherish this perky little plant, not just for its beauty but also for its scented and tasty foliage, which is often likened to tarragon. And unlike French tarragon, Mexican mint marigold can take the heat. A rather small, clump-forming plant, this Mexican native blooms late in the season and continues until cool weather slows it down. It may bloom too sparsely or too late for gardeners in the North, but those with mild autumns and winters appreciate its cheerful and bountiful color. It's at its best when grown in full sun and moist but well-drained soil.

The flowers are not large—only about half an inch (12mm) across—but their warm golden orange color really stands out. They can be collected, dried, and brewed for a sweet-scented hot tea that eases cold symptoms and stomach woes. Known for retaining their color fairly well, the flowers are often included in dried wreaths, bouquets, and potpourris. If you let the flowers go to seed, you'll have many more plants next year—but you may appreciate this in case winter kills your original plants.

As for the lance-shaped leaves, they are dark green and bluntly toothed, and have a sweet, almost aniselike fragrance. Fresh leaves are wonderful in any recipe that calls for tarragon, including chicken, seafood, and veal dishes. They are sweet enough to be used in cool summer drinks and desserts (try them in fruit salad and sorbet).

Mexican oregano

Poliomintha longiflora

HEIGHT/WIDTH: 4'–6' × 3'–4' (120–180cm × 90–120cm)

FLOWERS/BLOOM TIME: pink-lavender, tubular/summer

ZONES: 8–10

RECOMMENDED USES: culinary

Mexican oregano

A handsome shrub that is sometimes used as a landscape hedge or foundation plant, Mexican oregano is also edible and makes a worthy substitute for regular oregano. It thrives in full sun and adapts to rich and dry soils alike. The glossy, oblong leaves are rather small—only about half an inch (12mm) long—and have a spicy, pungent scent much like oregano, though a bit sharper. They're delicious fresh or dried. Many cooks use them in tomato-based sauces and chili and they also make a wonderful contribution to stewed or roasted meats and marinated vegetables.

As an ornamental, the plant is quite pretty. It blooms prolifically once established, literally covering itself with small, tubular blossoms that vary from pink to lavender. In fact, sometimes the show is so heavy that the branches bend or sag under the weight. The flowers also attract a steady stream of bees, hummingbirds, and butterflies.

Mexican oregano prefers full sun and average soil. It can take a frost, but if grown north of Zone 9 it may not stay evergreen over the winter, and will appreciate a protective mulch. You can certainly cut it back, right to ground level, and watch for it to revive the following spring. If it is tender in your area, try digging up the plant and overwintering it indoors or taking stem cuttings in late summer.

Mint

Mentha spp.

HEIGHT/WIDTH: 1'–3' × 1'–3' (30–90cm × 30–90cm)

FLOWERS/BLOOM TIME: white, pink, or lavender
  spikes/midsummer

ZONES: 5–9

RECOMMENDED USES: culinary, medicinal

Spearmint

Refreshing mint is wonderful in all seasons—in summer, the fresh leaves are terrific in everything from mint juleps and iced tea to tabouli salad; in winter, the dried leaves make a warming tea (just for the pleasure of sipping or to treat sore throats and colds) and enhance lamb dishes and steamed vegetables. And creative cooks have come up with dozens of other ideas.

Mint's popularity is not just due to its flavor. It is also adaptable and extremely easy to grow. All it really needs is adequate water. Yes, its reputation for invasiveness is well earned. In fact, if mint has plenty of water—say, in a spot by a pond or stream—it will spread frighteningly fast. But its eager growth is a virtue if you plan to harvest often. Contain it by sinking a barrier around the outer limits of where you want it to stay (try bricks or metal edging), or plant it in a pot and plunge that into the ground. The flowers, borne in clusters to form small spikes, vary in color from white to light purple; you can trim them off if you don't care for their looks.

There are literally hundreds of different mints, some of which are hard to distinguish from one another. The two most widely grown are, of course, peppermint (*M.* × *piperita*) and the shorter, somewhat sweeter spearmint (*M. spicata*). There are varieties of these, including variegated selections, as well as many closely related species. Shop around and try whatever appeals to you.

Mountain mint

Pycnanthemum muticum

HEIGHT/WIDTH: 2′–3′ × 1′–2′ (60–90cm × 30–60cm)

FLOWERS/BLOOM TIME: silvery pink/summer

ZONES: 5–9

RECOMMENDED USES: culinary

Mountain mint

This species—not a true mint—is native to eastern North America and enjoyed wide popularity until *Mentha* was introduced and overtook it. However, it is not nearly as aggressive and will grow well in drier soil. Also, the habit is more upright than spreading; over the years, it will form a handsome, multistemmed clump. So you can rest easy if you invite mountain mint into the herb garden proper.

The leaves radiate a fresh, minty scent that makes them suitable substitutes for true mint. Carried close to the plant on short stems, they're 2½ inches (6cm) long and medium green. The long-lasting pompon flowers are especially pretty—light pink to white, in a ruff of silvery bracts.

In the West, another plant goes by this name and shares the same qualities of easy growth and handsome appearance. Western mountain mint (*Agastache urticifolia*) is not a true mint, either. Related to anise and lemon hyssop, it grows 3 feet (90cm) tall and sports large, pink, fragrant blooms and minty foliage. Brewed hot, it makes a splendid, aromatic after-dinner tea.

Mugwort

Artemisia vulgaris

HEIGHT/WIDTH: 5′–6′ × 1′–2′ (150–180cm × 30–60cm)

FLOWERS/BLOOM TIME: tiny, reddish brown/ midsummer

ZONES: 4–9

RECOMMENDED USES: culinary, medicinal, craft

Mugwort

Slender, unprepossessing mugwort may not look special, but a great deal of folklore swirls around it. In the Middle Ages, people believed that wearing a wreath of it would protect them from evil spirits. In China, swags were hung over doorways for the same reason. The common name's origins are muddled; "wort" means plant, but the "mug" part is a mystery. It has been attributed to everything from midge or maggot (the plant does have insect-repelling abilities) to the cup that holds beer (it has been used in brewing in England and Ireland). And to this day, some acupuncturists use little wads of the leaf to burn a small spot on their patients' skin before inserting the needles.

From a modern gardener's point of view, however, mugwort is simply a graceful, easy to grow, sage-scented herb. It likes full sun and grows in most soils (though in damp soil it will spread rapidly). The leaves, up to 4 inches (10cm) long, are gray-green on top, cottony white below. They are perhaps too bitter for some palates, although European cooks have used small amounts in stuffings and sausages. Teas are not recommended for consumption because the plant contains the same toxins found in its notorious cousin wormwood or absinthe (*A. absinthum*).

A poultice made from the leaves, however, is effective in reducing inflammation, including a flare-up of poison oak or ivy. The leaves may also be dried and used to stuff a soothing sleep pillow.

Mullein

Verbascum thapsus

HEIGHT/WIDTH: 6′–8′ × 2′–3′ (180–240cm × 60–90cm)

FLOWERS/BLOOM TIME: yellow spikes/late summer

ZONES: 3–8

RECOMMENDED USES: medicinal

Mullein

Probably just about the tallest herb in the garden, stately mullein is easy to grow and softens its imposing appearance with broad, woolly leaves. Many people think it is a native roadside weed, but it is actually an ancient plant native to Europe and Asia that has escaped in North America. In a garden, you may want only one or two plants, but with a little attention to siting (a focal point in the middle of a sunny area, or a backdrop for a wall or hedge) and minimal care, mullein will provide great drama.

The plant is a biennial, which means that you get only foliage the first year, which is then joined the next year by that great, yellow flower-studded stalk. Let it shed its seeds if you want mullein beyond that point; otherwise, it will have exhausted itself and won't return the third year.

The leaves are a great attraction with mullein. They are large, sage-green, and fuzzy to the touch. As they ascend, they get smaller—apparently this design enables the plant to spill rain down to its lower levels and eventually to its roots.

Mullein has been used to treat respiratory problems, as a diuretic, and to ease gastronomic distress. However, the topical uses are more commonly employed these days. An extract of the flowers, mixed with oil, reduces the inflammation and pain of insect bites, earaches, and bruises.

Musk mallow

Malva moschata

HEIGHT/WIDTH: 2′–4′ × 2′–3′ (60–120cm × 60–90cm)

FLOWERS/BLOOM TIME: pale pink or white/summer

ZONES: 3–10

RECOMMENDED USES: medicinal

Musk mallow

Like its cousin hollyhock, musk mallow has simple, finely veined, five-petaled flowers (in softest pink to almost transparent white). But unlike hollyhock, this plant is compact and bushy. It gets the "musk" part of its name from the pleasant fragrance emitted when you rub or crush the light green leaves. An old-world plant, it was brought over by the earliest colonists, who cherished it for its prettiness, its long blooming period, and a number of folk remedies, most of which have been forgotten.

All of the plant parts contain a sap that produces a soothing mucilage, so like many other herbs, it makes a comforting tea. A poultice made from the leaves and stems was used to treat inflammations and insect bites.

Musk mallow asks little of the gardener, save well-drained soil. It grows well in full sun or partial shade and gets by with minimal maintenance. However, if you cut it back after it flowers, it will quickly rebloom. It also will self-sow.

Mustard

Brassica spp.

HEIGHT/WIDTH: 3'–6' × 2'–4' (90–180cm × 60–120cm)

FLOWERS/BLOOM TIME: yellow/summer

ZONES: all zones (annual)

RECOMMENDED USES: culinary, medicinal

'Giant Red' brown mustard

When you grow your own mustard seed, you are in for a special treat. Your harvest will have a fresh tang quite unlike the musty seeds you find in jars on store shelves. And, happily, mustard is very easy and fast-growing. It likes full sun and fertile soil, but will still produce a good crop in less-than-ideal conditions. Sow the previous autumn for an early summer harvest; sow in early spring for a mid-summer harvest. Cut down the stalks as soon as you notice the pods turning from green to brown, and lay them to dry so that you can collect their bounty. Be forewarned: plants left in the garden will self-sow.

There are three basic kinds of mustard in cultivation. The most familiar is white, or tan, mustard (*B. hirta*). It has light cream-colored, mild seeds that are used straight, for mustard powder, and for making yellow mustard (which actually gets its color from the addition of turmeric). The flavor of brown mustard (*B. juncea*) is stronger and is released when the seeds are ground and mixed with a liquid, such as oil or wine. Black mustard (*B. nigra*) seeds are tiny, making them difficult to harvest. They have the most pungent flavor of the three.

You may have heard of "mustard plasters," the time-honored remedy for treating congestion. Powdered seed is mixed with water, oil, or even egg whites and then applied as a poultice to the chest. The paste literally heats up due to the active ingredients in the seeds. It should be applied through a cloth and should not be left on too long because it can eventually cause blistering.

Nasturtium

Tropaeolum majus

HEIGHT/WIDTH: 1′ × 2′ (30cm × 60cm)

FLOWERS/BLOOM TIME: orange, red, or yellow/summer

ZONES: all zones (annual)

RECOMMENDED USES: culinary

'Empress of India' nasturtium

The bright, cheerful flowers of nasturtiums are always welcome. They bloom continually all summer and they do especially well in dry, poor soil—a real boon for some gardeners! Not surprisingly, a plant this agreeable and charming is available in many forms. Look for climbing nasturtiums (which can either ascend a support or trail down from a deck or window box), ones with dappled (variegated) foliage, dwarf varieties, and pastel colors. Somewhere along the way, certain nasturtiums lost the spur in their flowers, which takes away some of the old-fashioned appeal.

Creative cooks prize nasturtiums. The large, roundish leaves, often used in salads, have a crunchy texture and boast ten times the vitamin C of lettuce! Their peppery taste reminds some people of watercress. The flowers (with the bitter pistils removed) have a similar flavor. You can also use the flowers as a pretty garnish, float some in a big bowl of party punch, or stuff them with cream cheese or tuna salad. Add the stems to simmering soups. The buds, pickled in vinegar, have been used as a piquant substitute for capers. Dried seeds can be ground and used as a pepper substitute.

Oregano

Origanum vulgare

HEIGHT/WIDTH: 1′–3′ × 1′–3′ (30–90cm × 30–90cm)

FLOWERS/BLOOM TIME: pink/midsummer

ZONES: 5–9

RECOMMENDED USES: culinary

'Aureum' and common oregano

Originally from the dry, sun-washed hillsides of Greece and Turkey, true oregano, when grown well, produces a richly fragrant, almost peppery crop unlike any other herb. The secret to success is to select your initial plants with care (raising from seed is risky because the plant is naturally variable). There are other species and many cultivars out there, plus a long-standing confusion with the similar-looking but milder-tasting marjoram. Some enthusiasts swear by *O. vulgare* ssp. *hirtum*, also known as *O. heracleoticum*; the cultivar 'Viride' has received a lot of praise as well. Whether you find these or not, let your nose be the judge—rub the leaves between your fingers and sniff as you hunt for the oregano of your dreams. Once you get it home, plant your oregano in conditions similar to its native habitat: warm, friable soil that is on the dry side. Hot weather increases the oil content, leading to a superb harvest.

To harvest, snip young leaves. The plant will generate more and, indeed, grow bushier. Although it dries and freezes well, use fresh oregano in your favorite recipes whenever possible.

Orris root

Iris × germanica var. florentina

HEIGHT/WIDTH: 1½′–2½′ × 1′–2′ (45–75cm × 30–60cm)

FLOWERS/BLOOM TIME: white/early summer

ZONES: 3–10

RECOMMENDED USES: cosmetic, craft

Orris root

It looks like a regular bearded iris, with its creamy white petals, purple-tinted falls, and golden beard, but this beauty is no ordinary iris. The difference is in the root, which was long ago discovered to harbor a unique, heady scent that has been likened to sweet violets. Not evident immediately upon harvesting, the fragrance becomes more potent the longer the root has been dried—and it may take up to two years to reach its finest potential.

At any rate, the dried root is pulverized to a powder, which is used in a variety of ways. It is mixed into perfumes and powders, and has been added to a shampoo that is supposed to be especially effective on oily hair. It is an ingredient in the famous Italian fragrance mixture frangipani.

Orris root powder also lends a wonderful, romantic quality to sachets and sleep pillows. In potpourris, it has the added quality of acting as a fixative.

Grow orris root as you would any other iris, in well-drained soil that is rich in organic matter and toward the alkaline side. Plant in late summer or autumn, placing the rhizome only halfway into the soil (otherwise it is likely to rot). When it flowers, cut the blooms for bouquets or promptly deadhead so that the plant puts maximum energy into root development. Harvest on a dry autumn day: dig up the roots, trim away the stems, scrub off all dirt, and lay them out to dry in a cool, dark, but ventilated location.

Parsley

Petroselinum crispum

HEIGHT/WIDTH: 1′–3′ × 1′–3′ (30–90cm × 30–90cm)

FLOWERS/BLOOM TIME: tiny greenish yellow

umbels/summer

ZONES: 4–9

RECOMMENDED USES: culinary, medicinal

Parsley

When you look out over your garden on a dreary winter day, you may be surprised to see one bright green spot—the parsley plant, lingering on. This herb is especially hardy and also a cinch to grow, thriving in full sun and average soil. But unless you have a lot of patience, you'd better raise it from small plants; the seeds are notoriously slow starters. Also, parsley is technically a biennial, which means that the survivor out there will still be there next spring and summer, though its second year is never as good as its first. In fact, it usually goes to seed and dies back. So easygoing is this herb, it has become popular with windowsill gardeners. Give it sun, as big a pot as practical, and regular water.

There are two popular kinds of parsley. The species is curly leaf; flat leaf is *P. crispum* var. *neapolitanum*. Experienced cooks will tell you that the latter has a stronger, richer flavor. (As a result, it dries better, although fresh parsley is generally preferable to dried.) Too often dismissed as a mere garnish, parsley is actually vitamin-packed and deserves to be eaten for that reason alone. It is rich in vitamins A and C, certain B vitamins, iron, and calcium. Use it to enrich many recipes, including stocks, soups, grilled meats, stuffings, casseroles, and vegetable dishes.

Parsley's most famous folk use is as a natural breath freshener, diminishing even the power of garlic. At one time, parsley brewed in a mild tea was considered to be an appetite stimulant. That may be true, but too much can damage the kidneys, so this use has fallen out of favor.

Patchouli

Pogostemon spp.

HEIGHT/WIDTH: 2'–4' × 2'–3' (60–120cm × 60–90cm)

FLOWERS/BLOOM TIME: White to pale purple/summer

ZONES: 9–10

RECOMMENDED USES: cosmetics, medicinal, insect repellent

Patchouli

This attractive tropical plant, related to mint and native to India and the Philippines, is easily grown as a houseplant. It thrives in hot weather, so put it outside during the summer. In mild climates, it can be grown right in the ground in well-drained soil and will survive the winter with a light mulch. In any case, water patchouli regularly, and protect it from midday sun if the leaves show signs of sunburn. Two very similar species are available: *P. cablin*, which is up to 4 feet (1.2m) tall, and the more compact *P. heyneanus*, which is a little trickier to grow and must not be allowed to dry out.

Patchouli is grown for its glossy, slightly scalloped leaves. When rubbed, they release a spicy, incenselike scent. They retain their fragrance well when dried. Patchouli is a popular component of incense sticks, cones, and candles as well as potpourri blends. It has been used by Indian rug merchants to protect their products from moth damage. An oil derived from the leaves makes an earthy, penetrating perfume. The oil has also been used medicinally as an antiseptic. In larger doses, it is a sedative.

Pennyroyal, English

Mentha pulegium

HEIGHT/WIDTH: *4"–16" × 8"–18" (10–40cm ×*
20–45cm)

FLOWERS/BLOOM TIME: blue/summer

ZONES: 6–10

RECOMMENDED USES: insect repellent

Pennyroyal

If you're looking for a scented, mat-forming groundcover, perhaps in a sunny rock garden or as an edging for your herb beds, pennyroyal just may be your plant. A low-growing, many-branched mint, it creeps with lax runners that send down roots wherever they touch the soil. The foliage is dark green and sports an especially strong minty fragrance.

Unlike other mints, however, this one should never be ingested. In days gone by, it was used to induce vomiting, to treat fevers, and even to induce menstruation and abortion, but the dangers have proven to outweigh the benefits. It contains chemicals that are highly toxic, even in small doses—as little as an ounce (29.5ml) of the oil can bring on convulsions and even a coma!

Pennyroyal's claim to fame is that it repels insects—mosquitoes, fleas, ticks, chiggers, gnats, and biting flies, among others. Indeed, many bug sprays, lotions, and pet flea collars list it as a main ingredient. Leaves clipped from your homegrown plants can be rubbed on your skin before you go on a hike or picnic.

Pineapple sage

Salvia elegans

HEIGHT/WIDTH: 2'–4' × 2'–3' (60–120cm × 60–90cm)

FLOWERS/BLOOM TIME: red/late summer

ZONES: 7–10

RECOMMENDED USES: culinary

'Americana' pineapple sage

There are many, many sages, of course, but this one is unique for its sweet, inviting, ripe-pineapple scent. It's a bushy plant, and tends to require more water than some of its relatives. Although it's not very hardy, gardeners north of its range can still enjoy it as an annual or in a pot.

Pineapple sage also looks different from other sages, with softly hairy lime green leaves that are lightly toothed and rimmed in red, and often reddish stems. In late summer and autumn, it envelops itself in gorgeous, ruby red flowers. A wonderful cultivar now available, 'Frieda Dixon', has dusty, coral-red blooms. The flowers attract bees, butterflies, and hummingbirds.

The delicious scent and flavor make this plant suitable for all sorts of uses in the kitchen. Use both leaves and flowers in teas, green salads, and fruit salads, or add them to iced summer drinks (imagine pineapple sage sprigs as garnish for homemade piña coladas!). The dried leaves, which retain the distinctive scent well, make a novel addition to pork recipes and rice dishes.

Plantain

Plantago major

HEIGHT/WIDTH: 6″–12″ × 6″–12″ (15–30cm × 15–30cm)

FLOWERS/BLOOM TIME: tiny greenish spikes/summer

ZONES: 3–10

RECOMMENDED USES: medicinal

'Atropurpurea' plantain

In all truth, you are unlikely to plant plantain, but you should stop thinking of it as a nuisance weed when you encounter it in your lawn. An old-world import that has dispersed throughout North America, this super-hardy herb actually has a number of handy and verified medicinal uses.

Plantain, like dandelion, forms a ground-hugging rosette early in the season. The flower spikes appear later and aren't much to write home about—they look a bit like tiny cattails. They produce seeds quickly and spread them liberally, so here is your control measure if you don't want too much plantain: chop or mow off the spikes as soon as they appear.

The tough, fibrous, wide, oval-shaped leaves are the useful part of the plant and are easily distinguished from similar plants by their parallel veins. Their antiseptic properties have been valued for centuries. Crushed, they emit a pleasant, grassy scent and provide quick and soothing relief for insect bites and bee stings. Salves and poultices (sterilize the leaves first by dipping them briefly in boiling water) have been used to treat sores, wounds, and all sorts of dermatis, from heat rash to poison oak and ivy. In India, southeast Asia, and Russia, plantain has a long history of other uses, especially in the treatment of coughs, colds, bronchitis, and even asthma.

Rosemary

Rosmarinus officinalis

HEIGHT/WIDTH: 5′–6′ × 3′–6′ (150–180cm × 90–180cm); in a container, 1′–2′ × 1′–2′ (30–60cm × 30–60cm)

FLOWERS/BLOOM TIME: blue or pink/summer

ZONES: 8–10

RECOMMENDED USES: culinary, medicinal, cosmetic

Rosemary

On a long, hot summer afternoon, one herb plant still looks crisp and graceful and radiates a drowsy, piney scent as you brush by—that's rosemary. Because it hails from the dry hillsides and valleys of the Mediterranean, it is a sun lover, drought tolerant and adaptable to nearly any soil (though in an acidic soil, a little counteracting lime powder or wood ash is recommended). In mild climates, depending on the cultivar, it will grow slowly and spread over the years as a groundcover or semiwoody shrub. Try it as a foundation planting, trailing over a wall, or as a low hedge. In cooler climates, protect it from winter's cold with a mulch, or dig it up and overwinter it indoors. In a container, rosemary appreciates a light, sandy soil so that it can avoid root rot.

Harvest rosemary any time during the growing season (but if possible, pick before the plant flowers). The newest, youngest stems have the most fragrant and flavorful leaves. You'll find that rosemary dries and freezes well. Fresh or dried, it is a splendid addition to roasted meats and poultry, and dishes that feature tomatoes, squash, beans, or peas.

Potions derived from the leaves have been used for treating all sorts of ills, including headaches, infections, poor circulation, and poor digestion. Topically, an ointment is said to soothe the pain of rheumatism. You can toss some sprigs in a hot bath to soothe aching muscles. Shampoo with rosemary in it brings a fresh luster to dark hair.

Rue

Ruta graveolens

HEIGHT/WIDTH: 1′–3′ × 1′–2′ (30–90cm × 30–60cm)

FLOWERS/BLOOM TIME: tiny yellow clusters/summer

ZONES: 4–9

RECOMMENDED USES: medicinal ornamental

Rue

If your herb garden is turning into a sea of green, try adding this lovely, true-blue-leaved herb. A mound-forming plant, it has small, somewhat spoon-shaped leaves, borne in symmetrical, much-divided leaflets that give the plant an almost fernlike delicacy. If the small, mustard yellow flowers don't appeal to you, you can easily remove them.

Rue is simple to grow. It likes sandy or loamy soil best and is drought tolerant. Pests and diseases never bother it. The only thing to watch out for is possible dermatitis when handling the plants—some people develop a rash. Each spring, remember to chop it down to ground level so that the new growth will be more compact.

No doubt the unusual-looking and pungent leaves have added to the many beliefs and uses surrounding rue. It was used to ward off witches, evil spirits, and sinfulness, not to mention the Black Plague and epileptic seizures. Less colorful uses included treating digestion problems and promoting menstruation; recent studies have shown, however, that large doses of rue can be very dangerous, inducing vomiting, convulsions, and abortion. You are best off appreciating rue for its ornamental beauty, regaling garden visitors with these stories, and using it only as a striking addition to flower arrangements.

Safflower

Carthamus tinctorius

HEIGHT/WIDTH: 2′–3′ × 1′–2′ (60–90cm × 30–60cm)

FLOWERS/BLOOM TIME: orange-yellow puffs/mid-summer to autumn

ZONES: all zones (annual)

RECOMMENDED USES: craft, dye, culinary

Safflower

This plant looks a bit like a thistle, with bristly leaves, spiny stems, and compact, round flowers. But what flowers! Their thin, tubular petals are electric orange-yellow. Not surprisingly, enterprising gardeners have found good uses for such bright color. They're terrific in potpourris, dried-flower arrangements, and wreaths. They also yield dyes in shades from scarlet to rose to yellow.

But perhaps the most intriguing use of the flowers is as a saffron substitute. As you may know, saffron is a small bulb plant whose harvest is quite small and therefore expensive. Dried and used as is or infused to make a concentrate, safflower can give cream sauces, soups, curries, rice dishes, and salad dressings that desirable reddish hue. The flavor, alas, is much weaker than saffron, so add extra if you're aiming for more than just the coloring effect. This is also the same plant that yields a quality low-cholesterol oil, though extracting it from the ripe seeds may be too ambitious a project for a home gardener.

To grow safflower, direct-sow the seeds in the garden in late spring in a spot that receives full sun. Average, well-drained soil is fine. You might want to place your crop out of the way a bit because of the prickles.

Sage

Salvia officinalis

HEIGHT/WIDTH: 1′–3′ × 1′–3′ (30–90cm × 30–90cm)

FLOWERS/BLOOM TIME: purple, pink, or white/summer

ZONES: 4–8

RECOMMENDED USES: culinary, medicinal

'Aurea' sage

Usually gray-green and always aromatic, sage is deservedly popular. And growing your own is especially satisfying because the plants are so easy to raise and the harvest is always pretty and delicious. They thrive in full sun and well-drained soil, are drought tolerant, and require little care once established. They should, however, be pruned back hard each spring to keep the plant's habit neat and manageable. Expect to replace them every few years, because with age they do tend to become woody and ragged-looking. Also, thanks to their handsome flower spikes (colors vary), you'll welcome plenty of butterflies and hummingbirds to your garden.

You can certainly remain with the plain old species, *S. officinalis*, but it has a number of appealing cultivars that will add to the beauty of your herb garden. There are also many worthy related species.

Sages of this species, however, are not strictly decorative and will do double duty in the kitchen. Fresh leaves can be used in stuffings, vegetable dishes, casseroles, egg dishes, soups, and sausages. Both flowers and leaves can be used as garnishes, fresh or candied. The leaves dry well, though the flavor loses some of its subtlety. Store dried sage leaves in a dry, airtight container out of sunlight and away from heat.

Medicinal uses abound, from drinking the soothing tea at bedtime or to ease a sore throat to making a salve for treating sores, cuts, and bruises. Apparently, sage is also useful as an antiperspirant and has been proven to lower blood sugar in diabetics.

Savory, Summer

Satureja hortensis

HEIGHT/WIDTH: 12″–18″ × 12″–18″ (30–45cm × 30–45cm)

FLOWERS/BLOOM TIME: white to pale pink/summer

ZONES: all zones (annual)

RECOMMENDED USES: culinary

Savory

What would homemade potato salad or freshly steamed green beans be without a fresh sprinkling of minced summer savory leaves? This herb has a wonderful, peppery tang that adds a finishing touch to so many dishes. When you harvest often, the plant is prevented from flowering (which slows growth) and continues to pump out a great supply of lanky stems lined with tiny, 1-inch (2.5cm) -long leaves all summer long.

Summer savory is easy to raise from seed, germinating quickly and growing eagerly. In the garden, all it requires is full sun, occasional water, and well-drained soil. In a container garden or window box, don't neglect watering, and clip often so that the plant's floppy stems remain within bounds.

If you enjoy summer savory, you might also try its close relative, winter savory (*S. montana*). This is a short-lived perennial plant, hardy to Zone 6. It grows shorter and yields similar but stronger-flavored leaves.

To dry summer or winter savory leaves, lay them on a screen or paper in a warm, shaded location. When they're ready, zip them off the stems and store in an airtight jar. Bring them out to dress up soups and stews containing beans and lentils or to mix into an herb butter. They're also great with roasts and in all sorts of vegetable dishes.

Self-heal

Prunella vulgaris

HEIGHT/WIDTH: 12″–18″ × 8″–12″ (30–45cm × 20–30cm)

FLOWERS/BLOOM TIME: purple/summer

ZONES: 4–9

RECOMMENDED USES: medicinal, dye

Self-heal

A plant with a name like this must have a great reputation as a healing herb, and so it does—or did in times gone by. Also known as all-heal, this mint relative has been used for a wide range of treatments. Topically, a salve or poultice was used on cuts, burns, rashes, and bleeding hemorrhoids. Taken internally, it was used to reduce high fevers and as a diuretic. A gentle tea brewed from the leaves was also touted as a soothing gargle for gum inflammations or a sore throat, to ease laryngitis, and as a mouthwash. None of these uses for self-heal has been studied carefully in modern times, though they remain popular folk remedies. Another use for self-heal is as a dye plant. Depending on the strength of the infusion, the leaves produce a soft yellow to golden color in various fabrics.

Self-heal is an agreeable garden plant. A creeping mat-former, it is not terribly invasive. It does best in full sun, becoming raggedy and leggy in partial or full shade, and it grows more vigorously in damp soil. It makes a good groundcover. The flowers, like most members of the mint family, are purplish and not showy.

Sesame

Sesamum indicum

HEIGHT/WIDTH: 2′–3′ × 1′–2′ (60–90cm × 30–60cm)

FLOWERS/BLOOM TIME: white to purple/summer

ZONES: 8–10 (annual in other zones)

RECOMMENDED USES: culinary

Sesame

Grow your own sesame seeds? Why not? This handsome, easygoing plant is a tropical native and looks like it, with ample, lance-shaped 5-inch (12.5cm) leaves and showy, drooping 1-inch (2.5cm) -long flowers in shades of purple to pink to white. It can be grown outdoors in warm climates, such as the South and Gulf Coast, and as an annual in more northern zones. Sesame's main requirement is sufficient water, so don't allow it to dry out.

The flowers, if given a long enough season, fade away to 1-inch (2.5cm) -long brown capsules that contain those tasty, nutty, flat seeds in abundance—about a tablespoon per pod. The seeds are an excellent source of protein and carbohydrates as well as phosphorus, niacin, and sulfur. They can be ground up into a paste called tahini, a popular condiment or cooking ingredient in Middle Eastern cuisine. Of course, fresh or lightly toasted, the seeds are also a great addition to breads, rolls, and bagels, and can be tossed over fresh salads or used to flavor soups and casseroles.

Sesame seeds also provide an edible oil, called sesame or "gingelly" oil, that is valued for its rich flavor.

Shiso

Perilla frutescens

HEIGHT/WIDTH: 1′–3′ × 1′–3′ (30–90cm × 30–90cm)

FLOWERS/BLOOM TIME: pinkish spikes/summer

ZONES: all zones (annual)

RECOMMENDED USES: culinary

'Crispa' shiso

Although this plant resembles the ordinary houseplant or edging plant coleus, shiso is not to be underestimated. Long a staple of Asian cookery, it is versatile, has wonderful flavor, and is quite attractive in its own right. The glossy leaves, which have a distinctively spicy taste and crunchy texture, may be added to fresh salads, marinated salads, and tempura. The leaves are not used dried. The flower spikes flavor cold and hot soups. The seeds are salted and added to vinegar, dressings, pickles, and tempura. They're also sometimes served as a meal-ending savory.

Shiso comes in two forms. The green form, called 'Crispa', is a bright spring green with ruffled edges. The red, or purple, form, called 'Atropurpurea', has a nearly metallic sheen. Both are beautiful in the garden and are sure to excite comments from visitors. Both forms grow best in rich, well-drained soil, and although they are annuals, they'll self-sow. During the growing season, harvest the leaves often and remove the flowerstalks as they appear; this pruning will keep the plants fuller and bushier.

Sorrel, French

Rumex acetosa

HEIGHT/WIDTH: 12″–36″ × 8″–24″ (30–90cm ×
20–60cm)

FLOWERS/BLOOM TIME: reddish-green spikes/summer

ZONES: 5–9

RECOMMENDED USES: culinary

Sorrel

One of the quintessential treats of summer is savory, lemony cream-of-sorrel soup, served cold outdoors on the back porch. Its main ingredient is an undistinguished, weedy-looking perennial plant with broad, arrow-shaped, bright green leaves clustered at the base and ascending a crisp, juicy, reddish stalk. The leaves get their sharp flavor principally from the presence of oxalic acid and vitamin C.

The best harvest comes when summer is well under way—immature leaves don't have the tangy flavor. Harvest in the morning when the plants are at their most succulent, and puree for soup or other dishes. The leaves are also wonderful diced into salads and cheese omelettes and added to fish recipes. Some people like to steam them like spinach.

Growing sorrel is not difficult. It does best in fertile, moist soil and appreciates a sheltered spot so that the wind doesn't batter the leaves. Sorrel is appealing to slugs, so if these pests are a problem in your yard, take steps to protect your crop (set out bait, copper strips, or wood ash).

Sweet Annie

Artemisia annua

HEIGHT/WIDTH: 5'–10' × 3'–5' (150–300cm × 90–150cm)

FLOWERS/BLOOM TIME: tiny pale yellow balls/summer

ZONES: all zones (annual)

RECOMMENDED USES: craft

Sweet Annie

A lovely, feathery, many-branched plant, sweet Annie smells just like ripe, sweet apples. Individual leaves, a soft shade of gray-green, are about 4 inches (10cm) long at most, but are much-divided and carried in such density on the plant that the effect is always lush. Later in the summer, they are joined by loose, nodding panicles of tiny flowers.

Sweet Annie grows quickly and does best in full sun and average soil. Because of its height and texture, it makes a wonderful backdrop or screen for other herbs or flowers. It is too graceful and fragrant to be considered a weed!

Cut the stems toward the end of the summer, before the plant goes to seed, and hang them upside down to dry in a cool, dark place. The leaves and tiny flowers will turn golden brown but retain that wonderful scent. Crafters like to fashion the long, flexible dried stems into a base for a delicate scented wreath or include short pieces in mixed wreaths. Of course, sweet Annie also makes a wonderful addition to dried-flower arrangements.

Sweet cicely

Myrrhis odorata

HEIGHT/WIDTH: $2'–3' \times 1'–2'$ (60–90cm $\times$ 30–60cm)

FLOWERS/BLOOM TIME: white umbels/spring

ZONES: 3–8

RECOMMENDED USES: culinary

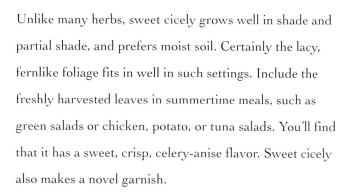

Sweet cicely

Unlike many herbs, sweet cicely grows well in shade and partial shade, and prefers moist soil. Certainly the lacy, fernlike foliage fits in well in such settings. Include the freshly harvested leaves in summertime meals, such as green salads or chicken, potato, or tuna salads. You'll find that it has a sweet, crisp, celery-anise flavor. Sweet cicely also makes a novel garnish.

The broad white flowers look like those of many other herbs. But they bloom in less than full sun and appear in the spring rather than the summer, attracting the early attention of foraging bees. The thin, ridged, ¾-inch (2cm) seeds are edible and may be eaten unripe or ripe. Unripe seeds are green and have a sweet, nutty flavor. They can be enjoyed on the spot or tossed into fruit salad or other desserts. Ripe ones are dark brown and glossy; used whole, they add great character to apple pie or pear tarts. They can also be crushed or powdered and stored in an airtight jar to be used later to sweeten baked goods such as sweet holiday breads and muffins.

The plant is best raised from store-bought seedlings or divisions donated by another gardener, as the seeds germinate slowly and erratically. It forms a thick, gnarled taproot, so plant it where you want it to stay.

Sweet woodruff

Galium odoratum

HEIGHT/WIDTH: 6″–12″ × 12″ (15–30cm × 30cm)

FLOWERS/BLOOM TIME: white stars/spring

ZONES: 3–9

RECOMMENDED USES: culinary, craft

Sweet woodruff

This enchanting plant makes a wonderful groundcover for full- to partial-shade areas in damp or dry soil. The long, thin, apple-green leaves occur in whorls and spread slowly but surely over the years. They are joined each spring by tiny, dainty flowers (only ¼ inch [6mm] across and white- to cream-colored). Both the leaves and flowers exude a sweet, grassy scent; when dried, the fragrance becomes noticeably more vanillalike.

Not surprisingly, there are many uses for this charmer. In Germany, it flavors May wine (*Mai Bowle*), a beverage that has been used for centuries in May Day celebrations.

To taste something similar to this treat, try immersing a few sprigs in a bottle of sweet white wine a day before you plan to serve it. At one time, sweet woodruff was also used to makes a scented hot tea intended to soothe upset stomachs. Recent studies have shown, alas, that this herb's active ingredient coumarin is dangerous in large quantities and is safe to consume only in the wine, not straight up. Sweet woodruff is also a natural addition to potpourris, and some craftspeople like to add clumps to the stuffing in pillows and mattresses.

Tansy

Tanacetum vulgare

HEIGHT/WIDTH: 3'–4' × 2'–3' (90–120cm × 60–90cm)

FLOWERS/BLOOM TIME: small yellow buttons/mid- to late summer

ZONES: 4–9

RECOMMENDED USES: insect repellent, craft

Tansy

Here is a plant with a long and fascinating history. Often associated with royalty in the past, nowadays it's relegated to the status of an ornamental herb. The oldest story about it goes back to the Greek legends: lore has it that a drink made from tansy conferred immortality on a handsome young man named Ganymede so that he could serve as Zeus' cup bearer. Tansy was often used as a strewing herb; King James II had it spread along the road to his coronation ceremony.

No doubt about it—tansy has a strong personality. The pungent peppery pine scent is released when you brush past the plant or if you crush the leaves between your fingers. It has been employed, often with success, as an insect repellent—in particular, it is said to keep away ants and flies. Organic gardeners find it useful, too, especially in warding off the Colorado potato beetle.

The plant is an aggressive grower in full sun and average soil. It spreads quickly by means of underground rhizomes, so site it where you won't have to be constantly trying to rein it in. The flowers are a bright mustard yellow that stands out well in the garden. They dry fairly well and for this reason are used in dried wreathes, swags, and arrangements.

As for tansy's medicinal and culinary uses, these have fallen out of favor since the essential oil thujone was identified as a component of all the plant parts. Thujone damages the central nervous system and can cause seizures; it is potentially fatal to pregnant women.

Tarragon

Artemisia dracunculus

HEIGHT/WIDTH: 2' × 1'–2' (60cm × 30–60cm)

FLOWERS/BLOOM TIME: tiny pale yellow panicles/
summer

ZONES: 4–9

RECOMMENDED USES: culinary

Tarragon

Beloved particularly by French chefs, this sharp, tangy herb is an essential ingredient in many recipes. It appears in the popular mixture known as *fines herbes*, along with parsley and chervil. Tarragon is also used in many delicious sauces, including béarnaise, hollandaise, and tartar, and is frequently added to mayonnaise, herb butter, and salad dressings. You'll want to try it in egg and vegetable dishes as well as with veal and poultry.

There are a few tricks to growing tarragon well. Begin with a seedling or cutting, as seeds are usually the similar-looking but coarser-flavored *A. dracunculus* var. *sativa* (Russian tarragon). Plant it in decent, well-drained soil, as it often struggles in damp sites and ground that is too acidic. If flowers appear, and they may not, clip them off to keep leaf production going. Tarragon has a tangled—to some eyes, "dragonlike" (hence the Latin name)—root system that requires division every couple of years to keep the plant vital. Mulch it to help it through cold winters.

The leaves are much tastier fresh than dried. Harvest them carefully so that you don't bruise them, and use them the same day if possible. You can also preserve them in white vinegar or freeze them. Dried sprigs lose their color and should be stored in an airtight jar to retain what flavor they do have.

Thyme

Thymus vulgaris

HEIGHT/WIDTH: 6″–12″ × 6″–12″ (15–30cm × 15–30cm)

FLOWERS/BLOOM TIME: tiny, tubular, lavender to pink/summer

ZONES: 5–9

RECOMMENDED USES: culinary

'Argenteus' thyme

Thyme is an absolutely charming plant, both for its history and for its beauty. It is also, of course, a great boon to cooks. There are many sorts of thyme, but the species remains the easiest to grow and the most popular. If you're curious, though, you might seek out lemon thyme (*T. × citriodorus*), caraway thyme (*T. herba-barona*), or creeping thyme (*T. praecox* ssp. *arcticus*). Also check the tantalizing cultivars in the catalogs of herb specialists (see Sources).

Perhaps because its leaves and pretty, fragrant flowers are so tiny, thyme was once associated with fairies. In the Middle Ages, it was believed that if you ate certain dishes that featured thyme you would then be able to see the little folk. Gardeners also believed that fairies lived in thyme, and planted patches to provide shelter for them.

Modern-day gardeners may not reap these benefits but will nonetheless enjoy growing this useful herb. Its only requirement is well-drained soil, as the plant is vulnerable to root rot. However, thyme tends to become woody and raggedy-looking after a few seasons, and should be replaced with new plants. Provide winter protection, especially if your ground freezes.

Fresh or dried, thyme leaves are a wonderful asset to meats, poultry, game, shellfish, sausages, and vegetables, soups, and casseroles. The oil, once extracted, is called thymol and is found in cough medicines, mouthwashes, and other remedies, but can be dangerous in large quantities.

Turmeric

Curcuma domestica

HEIGHT/WIDTH: 12″–24″ × 6″–8″ (30–60cm × 15–20cm)

FLOWERS/BLOOM TIME: pale yellow spikes/summer

ZONES: 9–10

RECOMMENDED USES: culinary, dye

Turmeric

A dramatic tropical plant best grown as a houseplant or in a greenhouse, turmeric is prized for its fleshy root, or rhizome. Until it is ready to harvest (at least several seasons), you will enjoy its beauty. Turmeric has large, lance-shaped leaves, up to 18 inches (45cm) long and 8 inches (20cm) wide. The flowers appear densely on spikes, and are a soft yellow with a tuft of white bracts at the tips.

To get this display, pot the plant in rich, moist soil and keep its atmosphere humid, either by raising it in a humid greenhouse or placing it on a tray of water and pebbles and misting it. Feed it occasionally during the growing season with a balanced houseplant fertilizer, and let it slow down in the winter months.

The root is yellow to deep orange and pleasantly fragrant. Dried and ground, it yields a bright powder that is used as a food coloring—most notably in common hot dog mustard and commercial curry powder. The root can also be soaked in water and the resulting liquid used to dye various fabrics yellow.

Valerian

Valeriana officinalis

HEIGHT/WIDTH: 2′–5′ × 1′–2′ (60–150cm × 30–60cm)

FLOWERS/BLOOM TIME: pale pink clusters/early
summer

ZONES: 4–8

RECOMMENDED USES: medicinal

Valerian

Looks are deceiving with this pretty, clump-forming plant. The tall, graceful stems are lined with small, divided leaflets of toothed leaves, and are topped for weeks in the first part of the summer with dense little clusters of lovely white or lilac-pink blossoms that sway in the breeze. But be warned: its scent is, to some noses, unpleasant. The good news is that the strongest source is the root, so unless you dig up the plant, the scent may not trouble you. You should also know that while humans may not relish valerian's aroma, cats adore it, as do rats. In fact, legend has it that the Pied Piper of Hamelin lured the rats out of town by stuffing valerian in his pockets—the music was just for show.

The offending root, however, is also the plant's useful part. Valerian has a long history, and was used to treat everything from fevers to gastronomic distress. But its most famous uses are as a tranquilizer, depressant, and insomnia treatment for both humans and animals. These uses have been asserted as safe and effective by modern European researchers. You won't find it in medicines in the United States, however, because no drug company has yet put valerian through the paces that the FDA requires. Prolonged use or large doses have been reported to cause headaches, muscle spasms, and heart palpitations.

The plant will do well in full sun or partial shade, and prefers rich, moist, fertile soil. Harvest the roots in the autumn and use them in a cold or hot tea (one teaspoon to one pint [473ml] of water). Or dry the roots thoroughly and store in a moisture-free spot.

Wintergreen

Gaultheria procumbens

HEIGHT/WIDTH: 4″–6″ × 4″–6″ (10–15cm × 10–15cm)

FLOWERS/BLOOM TIME: small white bells/summer

ZONES: 4–8

RECOMMENDED USES: medicinal, culinary

Wintergreen

Here's the source of that invigorating, penetrating scent we associate with cough and cold remedies, chewing gum, salves for sore muscles, and even real root beer. In recent times, true wintergreen has been replaced by synthetic imitations or the more easily extracted oil from black birch trees (*Betula lenta*). But for centuries, this little native North American plant was widely used.

Wintergreen is a hardy, creeping, groundcovering plant. The leaves are small, roundish, and glossy, and emit that wonderful menthol smell when broken or chewed. The equally fragrant roots may also be used and are best when freshly harvested. Extracting the oil from either is a long process that requires lots of plant parts, which is probably why it has been replaced by alternatives. For home use,

though, you can simply chop up some leaves as needed for a refreshing tea. In addition to relieving cold symptoms, the tea soothes an upset stomach and freshens your breath. A poultice makes a wonderful liniment or skin softener.

In nature, this plant thrives in moist soil on the forest floor under the dappled shade of high trees. So if you have an area in your yard with similar conditions, wintergreen will make a good groundcover. In addition to the glossy leaves, you can enjoy the appearance of small nodding white bell flowers that later yield round, bright red berries. Both the leaves and the berries remain over the winter months in many areas, and are a pretty and welcome sight.

Yarrow

Achillea millefolium

HEIGHT/WIDTH: 1½′–4′ × 1′–2′ (45–120cm × 30–60cm)

FLOWERS/BLOOM TIME: white, flat-topped/summer

ZONES: 3–10

RECOMMENDED USES: medicinal, craft, dye

Yarrow

Lacy-topped yarrow, with its thin, feathery, sage-green foliage, is an herb garden classic. Not only is it easy to grow—asking only full sun and fertile, well-drained soil—it is both pretty and useful. The species is white-flowered but is also available in pink, red, and violet, as well as mixes. Related species, such as *A. filipendulina* and *A. tomentosa*, extend the range into yellow, from pale pastel yellow to bold gold. All yarrows are long-blooming, so you can count on color from their corner of the garden all summer long. Plus, the flowers dry well, making them popular with flower arrangers and wreath makers. Harvest them at their peak and dry them upside down in a dark place. (Steeped in water, they'll yield a yellow dye.) The plants will often rebloom after an initial shearing.

As for medicinal uses, yarrow has been employed in a wide range of remedies. Perhaps its most enduring use has been as a poultice for wounds. (It allegedly gets its botanical name from the legend of the battle of Troy; apparently the hero Achilles used it to treat the injuries of his fallen comrades.) The modern-day discovery of various compounds in the plant that encourage blood clotting and act as anti-inflammatories validates this folk use. Other uses, such as treating fevers, acting as a diuretic, and easing indigestion, though not yet validated, continue to be practiced by some.

1 0 0

Favorite

Flowering

Shrubs

Introducing Flowering Shrubs

Flowering shrubs play an ever-increasing role in today's landscapes, whether you garden on a large country estate, a suburban yard, a compact patio space, or even a balcony. Plant suppliers and professional hybridizers are working continuously to provide a plant for every niche, from the tiniest woody shrub to a towering vision. Shrubs offer a diversity of seasonal color, shelter for wild animals, food for birds, pollen for honeybees, and fresh and dried flowers for home decoration. They help conceal unattractive areas, and represent a friendly way to mark boundary lines; dense and thorny hedges can even be used to deter trespassers. Shrubs, like other plants, are also essential in creating a clean living environment for all creatures roaming the earth.

WHAT IS A SHRUB?

Confusion exists about the difference between a shrub and a tree. Shrubs usually have several woody stems that branch from the base; rather than a main trunk, like trees, shrubs have multiple branches at the base. Also, shrubs—ranging in size from about 8 inches (20cm) to 15 feet (4.5m) tall—are generally shorter than trees. There are borderline

species, however, sometimes called "treelike shrubs" or "shrublike trees," which may grow taller. Some species may be pruned to a single trunk like a tree or let alone to develop the characteristic shrublike branching stem. With today's less spacious garden sites, a shrub trained as a small tree may be ideal for your garden.

Each entry denotes the plant size, but because so many new cultivars and varieties are available today, make sure to check with the nursery about the ultimate size of the spe-

cific plant you are purchasing. This is especially important if you need a shrub of a specific height or width.

TIME TO PLANT

Deciduous shrubs, those that lose their leaves in autumn, should be planted after leaf fall and before spring leaf appearance. In general, shrubs planted in early to mid-autumn make better new growth and produce more flowers than shrubs planted in spring. Winter planting is impossible in areas that receive snow, since frost in the soil will cause the shrub to wilt and die, but many warm-winter regions allow for easy winter planting.

Evergreen shrubs are best planted in early spring, late summer, or early autumn. While planting can be done in late autumn, the shrub doesn't have time to get established before growth ceases for the winter.

PURCHASING SHRUBS

Deciduous shrubs are often sold bareroot, that is, loosely surrounded by some type of biodegradable packing material. Later in the season, shrubs may appear in earth-filled containers, which somewhat increases the cost.

Evergreen shrubs should not be purchased bareroot, but rather should be "balled and burlapped" (B&B), which means that their roots are surrounded by soil, then tightly wrapped in burlap or other protective material. In many garden shops, evergreens are always sold in containers. Shrubs

purchased through the mail are nearly always sold bareroot, as shipping the relatively heavy soil necessary for container-ized or B & B plants adds much to the cost of the shrub.

PLANTING

While preparing the planting hole, newly purchased shrubs should be kept in a wind-free, shaded area. Some people like to soak the plant roots of both bareroot and container-ized plants before planting. All wrapping materials should be removed immediately before planting. Metal containers should be cut away without damaging plant roots. You can ask the nursery to do this for you. Some small shrubs are now available in biodegradable containers that may be placed directly into the ground. One important caution: do not let plants in a container dry out in the interim between purchase and planting.

Dig a hole at least 12 inches (30cm) deeper and wider than the estimated root spread. Place at least 8 inches (20 cm) of good topsoil nearby. If this is not available in your garden, purchase it in advance of planting. Putting a shrub in nutritionally deficient, rocky, salty, or otherwise incompatible soil is dooming it to slow growth or possible death. Those shrubs that do well in difficult soil situations are specifically noted in the text.

Place a layer of topsoil at the bottom of the planting hole and firm it down. Gently spread the roots out on this topsoil layer. Put topsoil over the roots a little at a time, firming down each layer. When the hole is two-thirds full, add water. This eliminates small air pockets and provides moisture for the roots.

After the water has settled, fill the planting hole with soil to about an inch below regular ground level. This small basin helps prevent water runoff. Use good organic soil as the remaining backfill whenever possible, although ordinary garden soil will suffice. When finished, the shrub base should be at about the same level as it was in the nursery. You can determine this by noting the bark discoloration at its base. Most shrubs do not need staking. If you choose to stake your shrub, place the stake firmly in the hole before planting the shrub.

Planting Tips

The following hints will help you purchase and care for your new shrubs properly:

• Do not purchase shrubs that have visible girdling roots or shrubs that have become rootbound (the roots have completely filled the container and are pushing out the container holes). It is difficult for these roots to grow correctly into the soil and they dry out easily.

• Shrubs planted in the vicinity of the wide-spreading, shallow roots of such trees as maple, chestnut, birch, and alder may fail to thrive because the trees extract much of the water and nutrients from the soil.

• Under deep-rooted trees such as pine, larch, ash, and oak, make certain to plant shrubs that do well in shade.

• If you are growing shrubs in decorative pots, always use pots with drainage holes. Soggy soil will kill a plant quickly.

• In difficult planting areas, or if you prefer not to spend a lot of time in the garden, use native plants. There may be a native plant society in your area that can advise you about the best choices for your region, or you can find information at the local library.

• Shrubs chosen because of their colorful flowers or berries are more effective in groups of three, five, or seven.

CARE AND MAINTENANCE

It is extremely important that you water the shrub thoroughly around its entire root area for the first few days after planting, and every few days thereafter until the leaves no longer wilt. The existing roots of a newly planted shrub are not immediately capable of moving into the soil for water, and they will die if deprived. After the initial settling-in period, you may water less frequently, according to the plant's needs as noted in its description. However, even shrubs touted as drought-tolerant must be watered initially so that the soil does not dry out. Drought-tolerant shrubs must first develop a sturdy root system, and this takes at least one season. About 4 inches (10cm) of mulch around the base of newly planted shrubs reduces water evaporation and keeps down weeds.

Some shrubs need or benefit from regular pruning, and these species are noted in the individual entries. All shrubs should be checked periodically for dead and decaying branches, and these branches should be removed before decay has a chance to spread to other parts of the shrub.

PESTS AND DISEASES

Common-sense care diminishes possible pest and disease problems. Wise shrub selection, proper light, adequate water, good soil, shelter from the elements where necessary, and regular fertilizer allow plants to resist many pest depredations. Do not purchase sickly looking plants. Watch out for discolored or spotty leaves, tiny bumps on trunk or branches, wilting leaves, and, of course, visible insects of any kind that appear to be feasting on the plant. Common sap-feeding insects include aphids, scale, thrips, and whiteflies. Minute mites are especially attracted to water-stressed and dusty plants. Try hosing tiny pests off or use an insecticidal soap spray.

Abelia grandiflora

Glossy abelia

BLOOM TIME: summer–autumn

HEIGHT/WIDTH: 6' × 5' (1.8 × 1.5m)

LIGHT: full sun–partial shade

ZONES: 6–9

OTHER: attracts butterflies, honeybees

Glossy abelia

This vigorous abelia provides tubular flowers in white to soft lilac-pink from June through first frost. The delicate flowers cluster at branch ends. A stunning cultivar called 'Edward Goucher' has dark green leaves that turn bronze to purplish in autumn and winter. The compact 'Frances Mason' has variegated foliage, while 'Golden Glow' has leaves of sunny yellow.

In mild climates, the shrub's small, glossy leaves are retained throughout the year, though it will drop its leaves in cooler regions. In all climates, shelter glossy abelia from wind. Often planted for its graceful, arching branches, a pleasing shape is achieved through precise pruning in winter and early spring. Even when winters are not that severe, expect some winterkill and be sure to remove deadwood in early spring. Abelia prefers well-drained acidic soil, although it will generally tolerate any reasonably good soil. Glossy abelia makes an excellent garden space divider or foundation planting.

Abutilon spp.

Flowering maple, Chinese lantern

BLOOM TIME: spring–autumn

HEIGHT/WIDTH: 8' × 8' (2.5 × 2.5m)

LIGHT: full sun

ZONES: 9–10

OTHER: possible indoor plant

Flowering maple

The eye-catching dangling bell- or cup-shaped flowers quite resemble Chinese lanterns (hence one of the shrub's common names), and in some areas may bloom almost continuously. Just looking at a photograph will make you want at least one of the hundred and fifty *Abutilon* species. The cultivar 'Canary Bird' has lemon yellow flowers that grow to almost 3 inches (8cm) long. 'Kentish Belle' boasts flowers with apricot-yellow petals, red calyxes, and purple stamens. There are also reds, whites, oranges, and a plethora of purples, from the palest lilac to a dark, saucer-flowered cultivar called 'Violetta'.

While this plant grows as a garden shrub only in very warm regions, hybrid flowering maple is often used as a border plant in cooler areas, where it will grow only 12 to 18 inches (30 to 45cm) tall. It can be moved indoors for the winter, as it is not hardy enough to survive outdoors.

Give this rapidly growing, somewhat rangy shrub a wind-free, well-drained, warm growing site with moist soil. Flowering maple is also a decorative patio shrub when grown in a container, and is easily pruned to size.

Aesculus parviflora

Bottlebrush buckeye

BLOOM TIME: midsummer

HEIGHT/WIDTH: 12' × 12' (3.5 × 3.5m)

LIGHT: sun with afternoon shade–partial shade–full shade

ZONES: 5–9

OTHER: attracts butterflies

Bottlebrush buckeye

If you have a problem growing anything substantial under a large shade tree, this wide-spreading, hardy, deciduous shrub may amply fill the space. Small white flowers with red anthers appear in 8- to 12-inch (20–30cm) -long, narrow, upright clusters showing well above dark green, coarse-textured foliage. Leaves turn yellow in autumn, providing late-season interest. Ovoid, smooth-skinned fruits containing one or more large blackish brown seeds (which are poisonous if eaten) follow the flowers; stems bearing the seeds are popular in flower arrangements.

The best soil for growing bottlebrush buckeye is moist, well-drained, and improved only with organic amendments. Although not truly invasive, this rangy shrub, also called "horse chestnut," does sucker. Prune suckers off and use them to propagate new shrubs. If you prefer a suckerless variety, be sure to purchase *Aesculus parviflora* 'Roger's', which has even longer white flower clusters.

Amelanchier laevis

Allegheny serviceberry, shadblow

BLOOM TIME: spring

HEIGHT/WIDTH: 25' × 18' (7.5 × 5.5m)

LIGHT: partial sun

ZONES: 5–9

OTHER: attracts birds, honeybees

Allegheny serviceberry

Covered with profuse clusters of white flowers in early spring when, theoretically, the shad are running, this graceful shrub is native to coastal areas and wetlands of eastern North America. Black, sweet, summer berries were prized by Native Americans long before colonists arrived to share the crops. Birds are also fans of the fruit, so the berries rarely stay around for long. Dark green leaves turn a lovely orange in autumn.

Deciduous serviceberry thrives best in moist, acidic, organic soils with good drainage. No pruning is necessary, except for occasional suckers. Because of its upright growth with spreading branches, this shrub can also be trained as a small tree. Watch out for fireblight, borers, various mites, and powdery mildew.

Plant Allegheny serviceberry by a pond, in a seaside garden, or at the edge of a woodland. They especially complement other native shrubs. There are many other worthy *Amelanchier* species, including *A. alnifolia* and *A. grandiflora*.

Aronia arbutifolia

Red chokeberry

BLOOM TIME: spring

HEIGHT/WIDTH: 7' × 7' (2 × 2m)

LIGHT: full sun–partial shade

ZONES: 5–9

OTHER: attracts birds

Red chokeberry

Bright red, pea-size berries appear in late summer and persevere through winter, a hallmark of this deciduous shrub. Berries are framed by 3-inch (7cm) leaves that turn from dark green to bright reddish purple in early autumn if the shrub receives enough sun. Small white flowers that resemble apple blossoms appear in late spring. For prime flowering and fruiting, give this tolerant plant full sun, although it does nicely in partial shade.

This versatile shrub thrives in moist soil, though it will tolerate soil that is slightly dry. Chokeberry's suckering habit dictates that it is best placed at the back of a border rather than used as a specimen shrub. But the suckers make it easy to propagate the plant, since they root readily if taken in springtime. There is also a black chokeberry, *A. melanocarpa*, which is somewhat shorter and bears shiny black fruits in autumn.

Berberis spp.

Barberry

BLOOM TIME: early spring

HEIGHT/WIDTH: 3'–8' × 3'–8' (1–2.4m × 1–2.4m)

LIGHT: full sun–partial shade

ZONES: 4–7, depending on species

OTHER: attracts birds, honeybees; good cut flower

'Boughton's Gold' barberry

There are many barberries, both deciduous and evergreen, to choose from, and all are useful, easy-to-grow garden shrubs. Small, handsome leaves cover thorny branches, which make barberry a formidable barrier hedge. Many species display autumn foliage color, and in spring pretty yellow flowers accent barberry. These blooms are followed by oval red or purple berries.

Barberries perform quite well in average soil and need minimal watering. They are generally pest- and disease-free, though some species, particularly *B. vulgaris*, are hosts to black stem rust, which can be transmitted to wheat. Some wheat-growing states have banned the planting of certain barberry species, so be sure to check with your local agricultural extension office before installing any new barberries.

Popular barberries include the deciduous Japanese barberry (*B. thunbergii*), a widely adaptable upright-growing shrub that is hardy to Zone 5; wintergreen barberry (*B. julianae*), a hardy (to Zone 5) evergreen shrub; and Korean barberry (*B. koreana*), a deciduous shrub that can be grown as far north as Zone 4.

Bruckenthalia spiculifolia

Spike heath

BLOOM TIME: late spring–early summer

HEIGHT/WIDTH: 8" × 12" (20 × 30cm)

LIGHT: full sun

ZONES: 6–8

Spike heath

If you need a shrub groundcover and like the appearance of heather, consider spike heath. Low-growing and somewhat sprawling, its ½-inch (1cm) -long, needlelike, dark green leaves densely cover shoots and persist all year long. In late spring or early summer, very small, clustered, rosy pink bell-shaped flowers seem to almost cover the plant in long racemes. Another bonus is that the flowers are sweetly fragrant. And even past their prime, the flower heads are quite attractive, though deadheading faded flowers will result in lusher foliage.

Like heathers, heaths prefer moist, lime-free, peaty soil in full sun. Spike heath is an excellent choice for rocky ground; its roots penetrate deeply, and once the plant is established it is tolerant of drought. In cold-winter regions, the shrubs will benefit from a cover of pine boughs. Some aficionados create a special mixed species garden just for heaths and heathers.

Brunfelsia pauciflora
(B. calycina)

Yesterday, today, and tomorrow

BLOOM TIME: spring–early summer

HEIGHT/WIDTH: 3' × 3' (1 × 1m)

LIGHT: partial shade

ZONES: 7–10

Yesterday, today, and tomorrow

You'll have to fuss a bit with yesterday, today, and tomorrow in order to enjoy the clustered, pansylike, 2-inch (5cm)-wide flowers. The blooms are also pleasantly fragrant. This shrub takes its rather unwieldy name from its changing appearance: flowers appear on the first day as white-centered, intensely dark purple blooms then pale to lavender and finally change to white within two days. While the most active flowering takes place in spring and early summer, this unusual shrub may flower almost constantly in frost-free regions.

Rich, lime-free, well-drained soil is just one of this shrub's many requirements. Determined watering and regular fertilization are also mandatory. Occasionally pinching off the ends of stems will keep the shrub attractively bushy. Some gardeners grow yesterday, today, and tomorrow in a greenhouse in order to best meet all its needs, but others place this evergreen in containers on a sheltered patio or near an entranceway, where they will be constantly reminded to offer tender loving care. Yesterday, today, and tomorrow can also be grown as a flowering houseplant.

Buddleia alternifolia

Fountain butterfly bush

BLOOM TIME: early summer

HEIGHT/WIDTH: 12' × 12' (3.5 × 3.5m)

LIGHT: full sun

ZONES: 5–9

OTHER: attracts butterflies; good cut flower

Fountain butterfly bush

In spring, butterflies decorate the lightly fragrant lilac waterfall that nearly blankets the small, fine-textured, forest green leaves of fountain butterfly bush. The gracefully arching branches of deciduous *Buddleia alternifolia* also make it an excellent small willowlike tree if trained to shape.

Initially discovered in China in 1875, the *Buddleia* genus was named after the Reverend Adam Buddle, a noted amateur English botanist. New *Buddleia* shrub varieties appear all the time, all carrying the signature trait of attracting butterflies.

A related species, *B. davidii*, blooms throughout the summer, and allows you to select for color as well as scent.

'Royal Red', 'Pink Pearl', 'Empire Blue', 'Burgundy', and 'Black Knight' are among the multiple selections, which grow from 10 to 15 feet (3 to 4.5m) tall.

All butterfly bushes are easy to grow, thriving in most well-drained soils if given sufficient sun and regular watering. They even do well near the sea, and tolerate pollution. The bush will often die to the ground with the winter, but will generally return in spring; *B. alternifolia* is the hardiest butterfly bush but may lose a season of bloom due to heavy winterkill.

Caesalpnia pulcherrima
(Poinciana pulcherrima)

Pride of Barbados

BLOOM TIME: late spring to early autumn

HEIGHT/WIDTH: 10' × 10' (3 × 3m)

LIGHT: full sun

ZONES: 9–11

OTHER: attracts hummingbirds

Pride of Barbados

Pride of Barbados is the island of Barbados' national flower. Each fiery red or yellow five-petaled flower has ten conspicuously long red stamens. Flowers, which are 1½ inches (3.5 cm) wide, are grouped on 12-inch (30cm) -long erect racemes. The attractive leaves are fernlike and dark green. Note that the pods, which contain seeds, can cause serious illness if ingested.

If your growing area suffers a cold spell, this semitropical plant may freeze to the ground, but it very well may come back quickly in spring. Pride of Barbados is also amenable to heavy pruning, if you want to control the shrub's size and shape. Grow this fine screening shrub in hot sun, in good, well-drained soil. Infrequent, deep watering is usually sufficient.

Callistemon citrinus

Lemon bottlebrush

BLOOM TIME: summer (spring–autumn in warm
climates)

HEIGHT/WIDTH: 15' × 7' (4.5 × 2m)

LIGHT: full sun

ZONES: 9–11

Lemon bottlebrush

Although most often called lemon bottlebrush, the less commonly used name crimson bottlebrush better suits this evergreen shrub, since its flowers are bright scarlet. Blooms, which are large and fuzzy, are clustered in profuse 4-inch (10cm) groups. The leaves, when crushed, emit a lemony scent, hence the species name "citrinus." Foliage starts off a reddish color but turns to green as the leaves mature.

Scarlet flowers are also the hallmark of the related species *Callistemon linearis*, but if you want yellow flower groups, look for *C. pallidus*, which is often recommended as a windbreak. The vigorous *C. salignus* has creamy yellow flowers.

Bottlebrushes are Australian natives, which means that they love strong sun, but adjust to cold spells with a sturdy mien. Poor soils, even those with some lime or salt, don't traumatize bottlebrush, and they thrive in semidry surroundings once they become established.

Hummingbirds fixate on the flowers, and small birds use the shrub as shelter. Lemon bottlebrush can be easily pruned to tree shape as it matures; simply prune side branches so that a single trunk remains.

Calluna vulgaris

Scotch heather

BLOOM TIME: midsummer to late autumn

HEIGHT/WIDTH: 4'–24' (10–60cm)

LIGHT: full sun

ZONES: 4–7

OTHER: attracts honeybees; flowers good for cutting
and drying

Mixed cultivars of Scotch heather

This is the moorland plant of Europe, where lime-free, moist, peaty soil is the natural growing medium. In other regions you will have to re-create these conditions, but if you can do so successfully, heathers will grow quite vigorously.

Small, bell-shaped flowers grouped on spikes are long-lasting. Some cultivars are excellent for drying too, such as the double white 'Alba Plena', the double silvery pink 'Elsie Purnell', and the deep pink 'Peter Sparkes'. Overlapping, scale-like leaves provide a gray-green backdrop for the bright flowers. Leaves develop a purple tinge in winter.

Heathers, as a group, are low-growing plants, ranging in height from 4 inches (10cm) to about 3 feet (90cm), depending on the variety. You may consider the smaller heathers for groundcover use as well as for edging sub-shrubs. All heathers make excellent additions to a rock garden. Heathers and heaths (*Erica* spp.) are often grown together, and many aficionados create special gardens for these lovely plants.

Calycanthus floridus

Sweetshrub

BLOOM TIME: spring–summer

HEIGHT/WIDTH: 8' × 8' (2.5 × 2.5m)

LIGHT: light shade–partial shade–full shade

ZONES: 5–9

OTHER: good cut branches

'Athens' sweetshrub

Strawberry-scented, burgundy-red, 2-inch (5cm) -wide flowers that appear in midsummer are the chief attraction of this hardy deciduous shrub. The flowers are most fragrant on warm days, and were once commonly used as potpourri to freshen homes. Shiny, dark green, 5-inch (12cm) -long leaves turn yellow in autumn.

Native to eastern North America, and often found along stream banks, sweetshrub grows best in moist, well-drained, loam augmented by leaf mold or peat moss. Pruning is largely unnecessary except for removal of dead wood in spring and a bit of thinning if branches become crowded.

Plant this shrub near a porch, patio, or window so that you can best enjoy its unusual fragrance and to offer it some protection. Make note that its seeds, if ingested in large quantities, can cause illness, but the pods are only produced every couple of years.

Sweetshrub has several other common names, including "sweet-scented shrub," "strawberry shrub," "sweet bubby bush," and "Carolina allspice." For variety, try *C. floridus* 'Athens', which bears fragrant yellow flowers, or *C. floridus* 'Edith Wilder', which has wine-scented flowers.

Camellia japonica

Common camellia

BLOOM TIME: late winter–spring

HEIGHT/WIDTH: 7'–10' × 5'–7' (2–3 × 1.5–2m)

LIGHT: light shade

ZONES: 7–8

OTHER: good cut flower

'Admiral Nimitz' common camellia

If their growing conditions are well met, these lovely shrubs can be quite long-lived; one of the oldest camellias in the United States, planted in 1786, still grows in a specialty garden near Charleston, South Carolina. Once confined to the greenhouses of wealthy eighteenth-century plant collectors, camellias later became the darlings of Victorian gardeners and are now an integral part of modern horticulture.

The common camellia bears large, delicate flowers of white, pink, or red, and is covered in shiny dark green leaves.

This tender evergreen performs best when shaded from strong direct sunlight, and may be placed under the protec-tion of tall trees. Note, though, that too much shade will inhibit flowering. Moist, well-drained, somewhat acidic organic soil and regular fertilizing are additional growing requirements of the common camellia. A deep mulch may also be helpful. If their needs are well met, camellias belie their delicate appearance.

Popular *Camellia japonica* cultivars available include 'Bob Hope', which bears dark red flowers; 'Elegans Supreme', which has salmon-pink flowers, and 'Lavinia Maggi', with double flowers striped red, pink, and white.

Carissa grandiflora

Natal plum

BLOOM TIME: all year

HEIGHT/WIDTH: $7' \times 7'$ (2 × 2m)

LIGHT: full sun

ZONES: 9–11

Natal plum

Natal plum is unusual in that its white, star-shaped, 2-inch (5cm) -wide, fragrant flowers appear throughout the year. The flowers are followed by bright red, 2-inch (5cm) -long, plum-shaped fruit. While the fruit is edible, its seeds are poisonous. Because flowering occurs all year long, both flowers and ripe fruit often appear on the shrubs at the same time. Natal plum's attractive oval leaves are a shiny medium green.

The taller versions of this thorny evergreen South African native make a good screen when pruned lightly and a barrier hedge when pruned heavily. Shorter cultivars, such as *C. grandiflora* 'Tuttlei' do well in containers. Spreading dwarf cultivars 'Nana' and 'Boxwood Beauty' will grow to a height of only 18 inches (45cm) if they are pruned regularly.

Natal plums should not be placed near walkways because of the thorns. This semihardy shrub requires only ordinary well-drained garden soil and regular watering, but is susceptible to spider mites. Seaside conditions are tolerated.

Caryopteris × clandonensis

Blue spirea

BLOOM TIME: late summer–early autumn

HEIGHT/WIDTH: 2' × 2' (.6 × .6m)

LIGHT: full sun–light shade

ZONES: 6–9

OTHER: attracts butterflies, honeybees

'Longwood Blue' blue spirea

It isn't always easy to bring shades of blue into the garden, but this low-growing deciduous shrub accomplishes this goal quite effectively with the small-clustered flowers of cultivars such as 'Azure', 'Blue Mist', 'Kew Blue', 'Longwood Blue', 'Arthur Simmonds', and 'Heavenly Blue', among others. The foliage, which has a spicy aroma when crushed, is usually silvery green, although 'Worcester Gold' has bright yellow to chartreuse leaves.

Moderately hardy, blue spirea, nicknamed "bluebeard" in some growing areas, will sometimes die to the ground in colder regions, but most likely will resurrect itself in the spring. Hard pruning stimulates fresh growth and a pleasing shape.

Blue spirea is a good border plant in very well-drained garden sites; it seems to thrive in dry surroundings. Cutting back growth after each wave of blooms results in even more flowers. Complement the vibrant blue of this handsome shrub with yellow tones in other shrubs or perennials planted nearby.

Ceanothus americanus

New Jersey tea

BLOOM TIME: midsummer

HEIGHT/WIDTH: 3' × 3' (1 × 1m)

LIGHT: full sun

ZONES: 4–8

OTHER: attracts honeybees

New Jersey tea

The dense white flower clusters of New Jersey tea display themselves at the tips of the branches in high summer. Glossy dark green leaves grow up to 2 inches (5cm) long; in autumn interesting reddish fruits appear.

Intriguing as a single specimen within a bed of perennials or when planted in groups of varying sizes, New Jersey tea performs best in garden conditions similar to those of the Eastern forests where it grows wild. Give New Jersey tea a warm, dry site with light, humus-rich soil containing lime. Waterlogged soil is not tolerated. The shrub may die to the ground in winter, but will usually grow back full force in the spring. The blooms are carried on new wood, so dieback does not affect flowering.

Many gardeners use this hardy deciduous shrub for banks and semi-wild areas, since it adapts readily to poor growing conditions and needs no care. New Jersey tea has many regional names, including redroot, mountain sweet, and wild snowball.

Chaenomeles japonica

Japanese flowering quince

BLOOM TIME: spring

HEIGHT/WIDTH: 4' × 8' (1.2 × 2.5m)

LIGHT: full sun

ZONES: 5–9

OTHER: attracts birds

'Texas Scarlet' Japanese flowering quince

Japanese flowering quince, an undemanding woody plant, is equally at home in suburban backyards or in expansive country gardens. Low-growing varieties, such as reddish orange–flowering 'Orange Delight', are sometimes used as groundcover, to add dimension to a rock garden, or to balance a background of taller woody plants. Taller varieties, such as red flowering 'Minerva', find use as individual specimens, in grouped shrub plantings, or as thorny hedges.

The blooms of Japanese flowering quince are surrounded by 2-inch (5cm) -long shiny green leaves.

Yellowish fruits, which are many-seeded, round, sweet-smelling and 1-inch (2.5cm) long, follow the flowers. Unless eaten by birds, the fruits may remain on the shrub through the middle of winter, extending seasonal interest.

Tolerant of pollution and city sites, these sturdy shrubs need only ordinary well-drained garden soil and regular watering. If you like bonsai, consider growing the delicate cultivar 'Pygmaea', which bears beautiful double apricot-pink flowers.

Clethra alnifolia

Summersweet

BLOOM TIME: midsummer

HEIGHT/WIDTH: $7' \times 7'$ (2 $\times$ 2m)

LIGHT: full sun–partial shade

ZONES: 3–9

OTHER: attracts honeybees

Summersweet

Native to swamps and woodlands, this slow-growing deciduous shrub naturally prefers moist, or even wet, growing conditions. While this shrub (which is sometimes listed as *Clethra paniculata* in catalogs) is not easy to establish, the long-lasting, exquisite spicy scent of its pink to white, 4-inch (10cm) -long flower clusters make summersweet worth a little extra effort. The dark green shiny leaves are attractive even when the shrub is not in bloom; expect the foliage to turn golden yellow in autumn.

Plant summersweet in early spring, give it quite ample water the first year, and make sure to mulch heavily to improve your odds of success.

There's a useful compact cultivar of summersweet called 'Hummingbird'; another good one is known as 'Ruby Spice', which boasts dark pink flowers, adapts well to salty winds and seacoast life. Summersweet was nicknamed "Sailor's Delight" by those who enjoyed its fragrance wafting on the breeze as ships pulled out to sea.

Cornus mas

Cornelian cherry

BLOOM TIME: late winter

HEIGHT/WIDTH: 15' × 10' (3 × 3m)

LIGHT: full sun

ZONES: 5–8

OTHER: attracts birds; good cut flowering branches

Cornelian cherry

Cornelian cherry, a welcome harbinger of spring, is one of the earliest of the flowering shrubs, and boasts masses of petite yellow blossoms that decorate bare branches in late winter. Leaves are shiny, green, 3-inch (7cm) ovals that turn yellow in autumn, with the cultivar 'Elegantissima' sporting gold-edged leaves flushed with pink. This fine cultivar is harder to find but worth looking for. Carmine-red, barrel shaped, 1-inch (2.5cm) fruits provide startling autumn color, and become edible after first frost—that is, if the birds permit leftovers.

'Golden Glory' is a more columnar version of cornelian cherry, and grows to 20 feet (6m) tall. 'Rosea', a pink-flowered cultivar, blooms a bit later than the species.

This warmth-loving shrub needs regular watering, but it's just about pest-free. Cornelian cherry can also be pruned into a small, spreading, and rather open specimen tree. In winter, gray and tan flaking bark helps provide year-round interest.

Cotinus coggygria

Smoke bush

BLOOM TIME: spring

HEIGHT/WIDTH: 10' × 10' (3 × 3m)

LIGHT: full sun

ZONES: 5–8

OTHER: good branches for arrangements

'Royal Purple' smoke bush

Royal purple foliage gives a stunning look all summer to many varieties of this large multistemmed shrub. Native to southern Europe and central China, smoke bush has long been a favorite of gardeners and remains exceedingly popular today. The yellow flowers aren't particularly noticeable, the common name "smoke bush" being earned because of the multiple smoky pink, fuzzy, fading flower stalks that persist until early autumn, providing welcome garden interest. Note that only female plants produce the "smoke," so if you are interested in the smoky effect, be sure to purchase a female shrub.

Grow this regal plant in any well-drained garden soil, including poor or rocky ground. To avoid mildew, give smoke bush full sun. Water regularly when the shrub is young, then cut back older stems in spring to encourage vigorous new growth.

Commonly found purple-leafed varieties include the attractive and hardy 'Royal Purple', 'Velvet Cloak', and 'Purpureus'. Leaf color changes to a beautiful red-purple in autumn, an extra bonus.

Cotoneaster apiculatus

Cranberry cotoneaster

BLOOM TIME: midsummer

HEIGHT/WIDTH: 3' × 8' (1 × 2.5m)

LIGHT: full sun

ZONES: 5–7

OTHER: attracts birds, honeybees; bonsai

Cranberry cotoneaster

Small, round, red fruit practically covers this low-growing, vigorous, cotoneaster in early autumn. Fruit persists for a long period if birds or chipmunks don't get to it first, though they probably will. The fruits are a bit larger than those of other cotoneasters, about the size of cranberries, which earned this species its common name.

Framing the fruit are small, dark green, glossy leaves that turn reddish purple in late autumn. The following summer, petite red-tinged flowers appear. Cranberry cotoneaster has a spreading habit, and when the growing branches reach a flat surface such as the ground or a wall they will spread along it in an attractive fan shape.

Give this deciduous shrub average, well-drained soil that is slightly on the dry side. This is a low-maintenance shrub once it gets started, however, you must plant it where it is to grow as it doesn't transplant well. If you have very limited garden space but want bright green leaves, red autumn color, and red berries, consider the dwarf cultivar 'Tom Thumb' for container use.

Cotoneaster divaricatus

Spreading cotoneaster

BLOOM TIME: midsummer

HEIGHT/WIDTH: 6' × 6' (1.8 × 1.8m)

LIGHT: full sun

ZONES: 5–7

OTHER: attracts birds, honeybees

Spreading cotoneaster

Profuse rose-tinged white flowers, each ½-inch (12mm) wide, bloom in spring, but spreading cotoneaster's main attraction is its small, conspicuous, ⅜-inch (10mm) coral red berries, which appear in autumn. This wide-spreading, medium-height deciduous shrub grows wild in central and western China. Dark green shiny leaves on arching branches turn scarlet-red in autumn.

Like most cotoneasters, this species does well in average, well-drained soil that is allowed to become somewhat dry between regular waterings. If given a good start, spreading cotoneaster will thrive in poor soil too. While some gardeners like this as an individual plant across from a view window so they can watch birds enjoy the berries, the prime use of spreading cotoneaster is as a picturesque informal hedge.

Cytisus × praecox

Warminster broom

BLOOM TIME: spring

HEIGHT/WIDTH: 6' × 6' (1.8 × 1.8m)

LIGHT: full sun

ZONES: 6–9

'Moonlight' Warminster broom

In springtime, the arching branchlets of Warminster broom are completely covered with ½-inch (1cm) -wide, creamy yellow flowers that resemble those of pea plants, to which they are related. The scent is considered by many to be unpleasant, so you may wish to plant Warminster broom away from the house.

Hairy 1-inch (2.5cm) seedpods, which may cause mild stomach upset if ingested, follow bloom. Small medium green leaves tend to drop early. To keep this semihardy Mediterranean native content, give it dryish, mostly lime-free, well-drained soil in sun.

Plant warmth-loving Warminster broom in the company of compatible heathers, heaths, junipers, and birches, where it makes an excellent specimen shrub. Warminster broom also performs well as a hedge.

The cultivar 'Allgold' has cascades of soft golden yellow flowers, while the bicolored 'Hollandia' has pale pink to cerise flower centers, with the rest of the petals in the same shade as the species. 'Gold Spear', which reaches only 3 feet (90cm) in height, displays golden flowers; 'Moonlight' has flowers in a pale silvery yellow.

Daboecia cantabrica

(also D. polifolia)

Irish heath

BLOOM TIME: late spring–early summer

HEIGHT/WIDTH: 2' × 2' (.6 × .6m)

LIGHT: full sun

ZONES: 6–8

Irish heath

Delicate, pink, white, or purple bell-shaped flowers held in racemes 3 to 6 inches (7 to 15cm) long dangle from the branches of this charming dwarf evergreen shrub. Irish heath is not actually a heath (*Erica* spp.) or a heather (*Calluna* spp.), but rather a low-growing shrub that resembles heaths.

This semihardy plant is sure to thrive if you are able to create its preferred conditions, which include regular watering, excellent drainage, and acidic soil mixed with an equal amount of peat moss. Use a permanent protective mulch of ground bark or chunky peat moss. Nourish Irish heath in spring with a light application of azalea fertilizer.

Irish heath is a good choice for a rock garden, where it will receive the sharp drainage it requires. Or you may wish to plant it among azaleas and rhododendrons (*Rhododendron* spp.), which share a need for the same growing conditions.

If you can meet the cultural requirements of Irish heath, consider several excellent cultivars, including 'W. Buchanan' and 'Atropurpurea', both with rose-purple flowers, or 'Alba' and 'David Moss', which bear white flowers. 'David Moss' is especially good for cut flowers, either arranged fresh or dried.

Daphne × burkwoodii

Burkwood daphne

BLOOM TIME: spring–early summer

HEIGHT/WIDTH: 3'–4' × 4'–5' (1–1.2 × 1.2–1.5m)

LIGHT: full sun–partial shade

ZONES: 5–8

'Carol Mackie' Burkwood daphne

Daphnes in general are inclined to be temperamental, but if you simply must have that delectable fragrance in your garden, Burkwood daphne is among the easiest of the forty species to grow. Pale pink flowers grow in 2-inch (5cm)-wide clusters among narrow, pale green leaves. Foliage may be variegated on some cultivars, including the popular 'Carol Mackie'. Small, reddish fruits follow the flowers.

Burkwood daphne requires a well-drained, neutral soil, and is improved by mulching. It does best in full sun, but will tolerate some shade during the day. Water the shrubs sparingly, as they don't adapt well to wet soils. Feed Burkwood daphne each spring with a fertilizer appropriate for rhododendrons.

Fruits, flowers, leaves, and bark are highly toxic if ingested, and contact with sap may irritate skin. Since daphnes resent transplanting, make sure to place them where they will remain permanently. Note that Burkwood daphne is also an excellent daphne for containers, where its scent can be appreciated from nearby sitting areas.

Daphne odora

Winter daphne

BLOOM TIME: early spring

HEIGHT/WIDTH: 6' × 6' (1.8 × 1.8m)

LIGHT: partial shade

ZONES: 7–9

OTHER: attracts birds

'Marginata' winter daphne

In its native China, this incredibly sweet-scented daphne has been cultivated since A.D. 960. Petite, rosy-purple, star-shaped flowers form ball-like clusters in March, even before the 3-inch (7cm) -long, dark green, narrow leaves have fully unfolded.

Purchase daphne in containers, and plant it in early spring or autumn in the spot it is to remain, as moving this evergreen seldom succeeds. Slow to get started, and a sometimes a finicky grower, winter daphne may reach a rounded 6 feet (1.8m) in height and width. Its natural globe shape may be helped along by judicious pruning. Best adapted to partial shade, winter daphne requires very well-drained soil rich in organic matter, and does best with a leaf mulch.

All parts of the plant are poisonous, especially the berries, so it is probably best to avoid planting this shrub if children are often about. Otherwise, place winter daphne where you can enjoy its strikingly delicious fragrance. The cultivar 'Marginata' offers distinctive leaves with cream-colored margins.

Deutzia gracilis

Slender deutzia

BLOOM TIME: spring

HEIGHT/WIDTH: 4'–6' × 4'–6' (1.2–1.8 × 1.2–1.8m)

LIGHT: full sun–light shade

ZONES: 5–8

OTHER: good branches for cutting

Slender deutzia

Named after J.D. van der Deutz, a Dutch alderman and supporter of horticultural adventures, this very old garden favorite is amazingly easy to grow: any reasonably good garden soil is fine as long as the shrub receives regular watering.

Glorious clusters of pure white, fragrant flowers on slender stems cover this mounding deutzia like snow in springtime for as long as two weeks. While the blooms are spectacular and prolific, they are scentless, which is actually a plus for some gardeners but a big minus for others. Attractive, bright green, 2-inch (5cm) -long leaves appear after the flowers. For an additional eye-catcher, look for the cultivar 'Variegata', which has green and yellow variegated leaves.

Since this shrub tends toward the inconspicuous after spring bombastics, place slender deutzia among other shrubs where it will peacefully blend in. Occasionally, depending on weather, winter dieback does occur. Prune the dead wood out in spring for the best plant appearance. While slender deutzia prefers full sun, it will happily tolerate light shade.

Elaeagnus pungens

Thorny eleagnus, silverberry

BLOOM TIME: autumn

HEIGHT/WIDTH: 10' × 10' (3 × 3m)

LIGHT: full sun–partial shade

ZONES: 7–9

'Fruitlandii' thorny eleagnus

For a thorny boundary hedge or an impenetrable screen, consider thorny eleagnus, which offers small, silvery, gardenia-scented flowers as an additional bonus. The blooms appear in autumn, somewhat unusual in itself, and are followed by red fruits in spring. Leaves are about 4 inches (10cm) long, and are gray-green with rust-colored dots, so the shrub blends easily into the overall landscape.

This fast-growing evergreen thrives in just about any garden soil, including that oceanfront yard corner that seems to mean certain death for other plants. Wind doesn't bother thorny eleagnus; nor does heat or intermittent drought.

It's best to prune this shrub heavily in midsummer for size control and to encourage dense foliage, particularly if used as a hedge windbreak. Thorny eleagnus may be either sheared for use as a formal hedge or clipped with garden shears for a more natural shape.

The cultivar 'Maculata' has green leaves with a gold mark in the center, while 'Variegata' offers leaves with cream-colored edges.

Erica carnea
(E. herbacea)

Spring heath

BLOOM TIME: midwinter–early spring

HEIGHT/WIDTH: 6'–12' × 16"–24" (15–30 × 40–60cm)

LIGHT: full sun (except in very hot areas)

ZONES: 5–7

OTHER: attracts butterflies; good cut flowers

Spring heath

Related to heathers (*Calluna* spp.), heaths require similar cultural conditions. If you have heavy clay soil, you will need to do quite a bit of improvement before you put in any heath, as lime kills special root bacteria that help transfer nutrients from the soil to the plant. Although spring heath is more tolerant than most other species, to forestall starvation provide a bedding of peat moss, compost, and sand, accompanied by superb drainage. Regular watering is necessary.

Planted in the soil they prefer, cared for well, and mulched regularly, these compact evergreen shrubs will reward you handsomely with rosy red, purple, rich pink, or white bell-shaped flowers. The blooms appear in profusion amidst needlelike, dense, pale or dark green foliage. While most spring heaths bloom in late winter and spring, the aptly named cultivar 'Winter Beauty' may be more suitable as a Christmas present.

Most heaths are sure butterfly beckoners. Plant spring heath in groups of five or more for a taller, shrubby groundcover. Cutting spent flowers will help keep the shrub in good shape.

Euonymus alatus

Winged euonymus, burning bush

BLOOM TIME: late spring–summer

HEIGHT/WIDTH: 8' × 10' (2.5 × 3m)

LIGHT: full sun–partial shade

ZONES: 4–9

'Compacta' winged euonymus

Almost unrivaled for its spectacular crimson red autumn leaf color, this ultra-hardy deciduous shrub needs ample space in the garden. While winged euonymus does bear flowers, they are rather insignificant, and the shrub's other virtues are the main reasons for growing it. Use several winged euonymus as a background hedge, and admire the seasonal changes: blue-green, 3-inch (7cm) -long leaves and small yellowish flowers in summer; reddish purple, pea-sized fruit and brilliant, long-term color in autumn; and branches that usually exhibit prominent corky wings in winter. If you want to be certain to have these corky wings for use in floral arrangements, seek out the cultivar 'Monstrosus'.

Spreading by nature, slow-growing winged euonymus is easily trimmed to satisfaction. Adaptable to all but wet soils, there are no serious pest or disease annoyances. Happy in sun or partial shade, the main difference between the two situations is some color variation in the leaves. 'Compacta' is a dwarf cultivar, as is the new 'Rudy Haag', which is even smaller. Both are just as autumn-bright, though they lack the corky "wings" on the branches.

Exochorda × macrantha

Pearlbush

BLOOM TIME: spring

HEIGHT/WIDTH: 4' × 7' (1.2 × 2m)

LIGHT: full sun

ZONES: 5–9

OTHER: attracts butterflies

'The Bride' pearlbush

The strings of pearly buds on this small, white-flowering shrub have lent it the common name "pearlbush." If you are a somewhat intermittent gardener, pearlbush might suit, since it tolerates some neglect. Well-drained soil, not overly alkaline, regular water, and full sun are its only requests.

Plant pearlbush in a mixed border with brightly colored perennials and annuals, as this shrub can be rather demure except when displaying its multitude of 1-inch (2.5cm) flowers.

Pearlbush has no objection to having its medium green foliage pruned for shape, and in fact, a good pruning will help the shrub maintain its shape. Cut out weak branches after the pretty flowers have faded to promote a fuller shape, as pearlbush has a tendency to get somewhat leggy, especially when it is young.

Pearlbush is best planted in spring, as a container-grown or balled and burlapped species, since bareroot plants have a tougher time getting established.

If you have a small garden space and require a more compact shrub, look for the cultivar 'The Bride', which grows only 3 feet (1m) tall and as wide.

Feijoa sellowiana

Pineapple guava

BLOOM TIME: spring

HEIGHT/WIDTH: 15' × 15' (4.5 × 4.5m)

LIGHT: full sun

ZONES: 8–10

Pineapple guava

If you want a fruit tree in the South, and nothing else will tolerate that hot, sunny garden spot, pineapple guava just might do the trick. It is the hardiest of the subtropical fruits, and grows as a large multistemmed shrub unless pruned.

In springtime, white, thick-petaled, 1-inch (2.5cm) -wide flowers with startling crimson stamen tufts attract both birds and bees. Oval leaves, about 3 inches (7cm) long, are glossy green with silvery backing. If you have another plant to cross-pollinate, about five to seven months after bloom (as long as the shrub is given regular watering) you'll have ripe 2-inch-long, oval, gray-green fruit with whitish pineapple-flavored pulp. The fruit is good eaten fresh, and delicious in jellies and preserves.

Pineapple guava may also be pruned in late spring to create a small tree, hedge, or espalier. Pruning will also keep it to a manageable size, if you are gardening in a small space.

Varieties such as 'Coolidge', 'Beechwood', and 'Nazemete', are self-fertile, however cross-pollination improves the fruit crop.

Forsythia × intermedia

Golden bell, border forsythia

BLOOM TIME: early spring

HEIGHT/WIDTH: varies

LIGHT: full sun

ZONES: 6–9

OTHER: good for forcing indoors

Golden bell

In Southern regions, forsythias bloom as early as February, and have become a golden harbinger of springtime. Even in more northerly areas, forsythia is among the earliest flowering shrubs. To enjoy even earlier flowers, bring budded branches indoors and place them on a sunny windowsill in a vase of lukewarm water, where they will burst into glorious bloom.

There are many cultivars of border forsythia available, all hardy and all with profuse lemon yellow to bright gold flowers. Choose for size among the cultivars 'Fiesta' at 3 feet (1m) high, 'Minigold' at 5 feet (1.5m) high, or 'Variegeta' which grows to 6 feet (1.8m) and has foliage splashed with white.

Forsythia, named after English horticulturist William Forsythe, does well in a wide range of soils, but must have regular watering. Forsythia does well in full sun or partial shade; while it will grow in deep shade it will not flower to any significant degree. It is surprisingly effective against an evergreen background. Prune after flowering, following the natural habit of the shrub and removing old or dead wood.

Fothergilla major

Large fothergilla

BLOOM TIME: spring

HEIGHT/WIDTH: 6'–10' × 7' (1.8–3 × 2m)

LIGHT: full sun–partial shade

ZONES: 5–8

Large fothergilla

A favorite among gardeners who plant for autumn color, large fothergilla has leaves that turn yellow, then orange, and finally purple-red. Note, though, that autumn color may be inhibited if the shrub is grown in too much shade. Native to the rich moist woods of southeastern North America, this medium-sized deciduous shrub also bears small white, honey-scented, brushlike flowers in spring.

Pest-free, large fothergilla prefers moist, well-drained, acidic soil, but is adaptable to varying soil types as long as they are not alkaline. Plant this attractive shrub in spring or autumn, preferably on a sunny site. Where summers get quite hot, though, partial shade is best. Because large fothergilla is slow-growing, it will need only occasional pruning, which should be done after flowering.

A favorite specimen plant, large fothergilla is also eye-catching in groups. There are also dwarf fothergillas available, including *Fothergilla gardenii* 'Mt. Airy', which, like its bigger cousin, provides reliable, brilliant autumn color.

Gardenia augusta
(G. jasminoides)

Common gardenia

BLOOM TIME: late spring–autumn

HEIGHT/WIDTH: 2'–8' × 2'–8' (.6–2.5m × .6–2.5m)

LIGHT: full sun (light shade in hot climates)

ZONES: vary by cultivar

OTHER: very fragrant cut flower

Common gardenia

Sentimentalists who have fond memories of their fragrant white prom corsages will want to plant an evergreen gardenia near an entryway or potted up on a patio. Large, lush flowers with white waxy petals bloom among shiny dark green leaves.

Native to China and Japan, gardenia is available in many beautiful cultivars. 'White Gem' is the classic container gardenia, and grows only 2 feet (60cm) tall. For narrow entryways try 'Veitchii' or 'Kimura Shikazaki', which reach only 4 feet (1.2m) in height. There is also a plethora of taller hedge gardenias, the size of which can be easily controlled by pruning.

While most gardenias are hardy only in zones 8 to 10, 'Klein's Hardy' was specifically created for cold-winter climates and is supposed to withstand temperatures down to 0°F(17.78°C). Full sun is best in all but very hot climates, but light shade is tolerated.

Gardenias require very well-drained soil high in organic matter, and regular fertilizing with acid plant food or fish emulsion. Cut faded flowers to encourage new blooms and prune the shrub to promote a bushier habit. Plants may be visited by pesky whiteflies and aphids, but a strong water stream usually takes care of minor infestations.

Hamamelis mollis

Chinese witch hazel

BLOOM TIME: late winter–early spring

HEIGHT/WIDTH: 8' × 8' (2.5 × 2.5m)

LIGHT: full sun–light shade

ZONES: 5–9

OTHER: good cut branches

Chinese witch hazel

Almost unrivaled for dependable winter or early spring flowering, Chinese witch hazel bears 1½-inch (3.5cm) -wide, rich yellow, spidery flowers in February and March. The blooms, cradled in a red-brown base, bring summer glory far in advance of the season to bare stems. Better yet, the flowers are sweetly fragrant. In autumn, dark green woolly leaves change to a clear charming yellow.

For the best display, place this slow-growing, disease-resistant, deciduous shrub to highlight a dark backdrop.

With its tall and spreading, yet neat, habit, many gardeners like to use it as a specimen plant; it may also be grown as a small tree. Set witch hazel where it is to grow, since it dislikes transplanting. Slightly acid soil is best, with organic matter added. Witch hazels are popular shrubs for spacious city gardens, as they tolerate pollution and dry, gritty air. Water well until the shrub is established, but do not fertilize.

The cultivar 'Pallida' has sulfur yellow flowers and a slightly sweeter fragrance.

Hebe speciosa

Showy hebe

BLOOM TIME: late summer

HEIGHT/WIDTH: 2'–5' × 2'–5' (.6–1.5m × .6–1.5m)

LIGHT: full sun–partial shade

ZONES: 10–11

Showy hebe

Glossy evergreen leaves are a hallmark of this New Zealand native. In summer, deep reddish purple or bluish flowers are carried proudly on multiple dense 3-inch (7cm) -long racemes.

At its best in the seaside garden, showy hebe is also a city garden favorite, as it is tolerant of dust and pollution if watered regularly. Inland, in hot areas, showy hebe appreciates some light shade, but in a coastal location it fares quite well in full sun. Poor, light soil is its friend, which makes hebe very useful as an edging, groundcover, hedge, or shrub for the mixed border. But make certain drainage is good, as root rot can sneak into perpetually soggy soils.

For a change of pace, the cultivar 'Variegata' has leaves splashed with cream, while 'Imperialis' has magenta flowers accompanied by reddish leaves. Showy hebe also makes a nice, unfussy container plant for the patio.

Hibiscus syriacus

Rose of Sharon

BLOOM TIME: midsummer–autumn

HEIGHT/WIDTH: 6'–10' × 4' – 6' (1.8–3 × 1.2–1.8m)

LIGHT: full sun

ZONES: 5–9

OTHER: attracts butterflies, birds

Rose of Sharon

Native to China, this free-flowering deciduous shrub is quite hardy in warm gardens, and can be grown in colder areas against a reflecting wall. Exotic, trumpet-shaped flowers, 3 to 5 inches (7 to 12cm) in diameter, evoke reveries of tropical climes and a leisurely lifestyle. Whether the variety is pink, blue, or white, rose of Sharon provides color when many other flowers are finished for the season, although it does come into bloom later than most.

While the single-flowered varieties are the hardiest, nurseries often carry double-flowered types, such as 'Blushing Bride', which has bright pink blossoms, and 'Violaceus Plenus', which bears blue-purple blossoms.

Deep, well-drained, easily worked soil provides the best growing conditions. Make sure to move these plants only in spring, as they take some time to get established. A layer of mulch through the winter for the first few years will offer additional protection until rose of Sharon matures somewhat. Prune in spring to shape the shrub and fertilize monthly from April through August. Regular watering is a must.

Hippophae rhamnoides

Sea buckthorn

BLOOM TIME: spring

HEIGHT/WIDTH: 15' × 15' (4.5 × 4.5m)

LIGHT: full sun–light shade

ZONES: 3–8

Sea buckthorn

This common deciduous plant of seacoasts and river banks tolerates salty soils and actually prefers a sandy home, making it a gem for those living near waterfront sites. Suckers spread underground, preventing sandy dunes from shifting, so sea buckthorn is especially valuable for seaside gardeners. The shrub does, however, have long fierce spines on its branches, so set it back a distance from pathways.

Young shoots are glossy yellow-brown, and become dark brown with age. Small, dullish, yellow flowers appear before the leaves. However, the narrow, 2-inch (5cm) -long, silvery green leaves unfold from attractive golden brown leaf buds. Both male and female plants are needed to form the persistent and plentiful ½-inch (1cm) -wide, yellow-orange fruits, which appear in autumn. The berries are not appreciated by birds, so they stay on the shrubs, adding color to the winter landscape through the winter. For large-acreage screening, five females to one male plant works well with wind-blown pollination.

Hydrangea macrophylla

Big-leaved hydrangea

BLOOM TIME: summer

HEIGHT/WIDTH: 3'–6' × 3'–6' (1–1.8 × 1–1.8m)

LIGHT: full sun

ZONES: 6–9

'Nikko Blue' big-leaved hydrangea

In its native surroundings—Southern China, Japan, and the Himalayas—this deciduous hydrangea will grow to 10 feet (3m) in height. But in most gardens, about half that height is usual. Puffed "snowballs" of flowers appear in summer, when few other shrubs are in bloom.

Hydrangeas are especially fun for the chemically oriented, as the flowers may change color according to soil conditions. Pink-flowering varieties produce blue flowers when in acidic soils and red flowers when in alkaline soils. Because the soil's pH can be altered with fertilizer and additives, a pleasing array can be arranged in varying garden sections. Note, though, that white cultivars will not change flower color.

Moderately hardy, big-leaved hydrangea needs rich, moist soil and a sheltered site, and does best with a spring mulch. Many varieties are available, most of which give a clue as to their color: 'White Swan', 'Amethyst', 'Pink Monarch', 'Blue Wave', and so on. The cultivar 'Nikko Blue' is somewhat hardier in colder areas; it blooms on new wood, so that some winter dieback does not interfere with flowering.

Hydrangea paniculata 'Grandiflora'

PeeGee hydrangea

BLOOM TIME: summer–autumn

HEIGHT/WIDTH: 12' × 12' (3.5 × 3.5m)

LIGHT: full sun–partial shade

ZONES: 4–8

OTHER: dried flowers

PeeGee hydrangea

So common in rural North America that it almost seems a native, PeeGee hydrangea actually hails from Asia. A vigorous, late-blooming deciduous shrub, this hydrangea is often trained to tree form, that is, with a single trunk. Large, coarsely toothed leaves add impact to fluffy, white, pyramidal, flower clusters, each an immense 12 by 12 inches (30 by 30cm). The flowers, which start off a greenish white, turn first a purple-pink, then bronzy green with age. The exact flower color depends both on the pH, which should be slightly acid, and the soil's aluminum content.

PeeGee hydrangea makes a fine specimen shrub in a slightly sheltered position. You can remove lower branches to encourage a cascading form. Grow this lovely shrub in rich, moist soil. While it tolerates light shade, it prospers best in full sun. Mulch PeeGee hydrangea in winter, prune it in early spring, and fertilize after pruning. The dried flowers are stunning when gathered in easy winter bouquets (make sure to use garden gloves if you are possibly allergic to the foliage).

Hydrangea quercifolia

Oakleaf hydrangea

BLOOM TIME: spring–summer

HEIGHT/WIDTH: 3'–6' × 4'–6' (1–1.8 × 1.2–1.8m)

LIGHT: full sun–partial shade

ZONES: 5–9

OTHER: good cut flower

Oakleaf hydrangea

This rounded shrub has garden gifts for all seasons. As its botanical name indicates (*quercus* is the genus name of oak trees), the deeply lobed, 8-inch (20cm) leaves resemble those of oaks. The leaves, which are green in spring and summer, turn crimson, purple, or deep bronze in autumn. In winter, stems are a pleasing brown and exfoliate with age to display a darker, reddish brown interior.

When spring arrives, 10-inch (25cm) -long, pyramidal flower clusters appear. The flowers, fragrant and white, last for several weeks, turning pinkish purple as spring moves into summer.

This deciduous shrub is fast-growing and quite hardy when grown in a protected location in the northern reaches of its zone. It needs well-drained, richly organic, moist soil, regular watering, and some shade if you live in a truly hot area. In fact, this is the hydrangea species best suited to shade, so if you have your heart set on a hydrangea and have a shady yard, this is most likely your best bet. The cultivar 'Sikes Dwarf' makes a good shrub for a container.

Hypericum frondosum

Golden St. John's wort

BLOOM TIME: midsummer–autumn

HEIGHT/WIDTH: 3' × 3' (1 × 1m)

LIGHT: full sun–partial shade

ZONES: 6–8

'Sunburst' Golden St. John's wort

Quite a bit of superstition, folklore, and poetry cluster about the multiple varieties of St. John's wort. One species of *Hypericum*, *H. perforatum*, is currently popular for treating anxiety and emotional disturbances, and the legends regarding this shrubby herb go back to the Greeks. Note that the garden shrub discussed here, *H. frondosum*, is in fact listed as a poisonous plant and should never be ingested.

The bright golden yellow, 2-inch (5cm) flowers of this deciduous shrub bring cheery color from midsummer to early autumn. The genus' common name derives from the fact that the flowers are traditionally gathered on June 24th, St. John's Day, but the flowers of golden St. John's wort tend to begin blooming a bit later. Bark is reddish and peeling, ornamented with long, blue-green leaves.

Golden St. John's wort is very easy to grow in most garden soils, including heavy, sometimes dryish, soil with a pH range from 5.0 to 7.5. This shrub will fare well in light shade, though it prefers full sun.

Ilex verticillata

Winterberry

BLOOM TIME: winter–early spring (berries)

HEIGHT/WIDTH: varies 4'–20' × 4'–20' (1.2–6 ×
1.2–6m)

LIGHT: full sun–light shade

ZONES: 4–8

OTHER: attracts birds

Winterberry

Birds flock to the winter and spring red fruit of this deciduous hardy native holly, an ideal shrub for wet, almost swampy gardens. In dryer soils, the shrub will still perform well, but will never grow as tall, often a plus in normal garden situations.

You'll want to use the taller varieties, such as the 20-foot (6m) high 'Emily Brunner', if you are planting winterberry as a background; make sure it is accompanied by its pollinator 'James Swan'. For fruit production, all winterberries require both male and female plants to be present. Be clear about this when purchasing, and make sure you get some of each.

Though winterberry drops its deep green leaves in autumn, the smooth, dark branches and bright red berries remain attractive throughout the winter. The branches are often cut and brought indoors for Christmas decorations.

There are at least four hundred species of holly trees, and many more named cultivars. Don't eat any of the berries, which may cause illness. Christmas lore about hollies is plentiful, including the belief that if "He Holly" (from a male plant) is clipped and brought into the house, the husband will be boss for the next year, while if "She Holly" is used for ornament, the wife will rule until the next Christmas. Decorate with a tad of both.

Indigofera kirilowii

Kirilow indigo

BLOOM TIME: summer–autumn

HEIGHT/WIDTH: 5' × 5' (1.5 × 1.5m)

LIGHT: full sun

ZONES: 4–8

Kirilow indigo

If summers are hot where you live, Kirilow indigo proves to be a quite long-flowering shrub, blooming with small, sweet-smelling, pink flowers held in erect racemes from summer through early autumn. The foliage is bright green and the small, fine leaves are somewhat fernlike.

While 5-foot (1.5m) heights are standard, this shrub may grow taller against a warm wall or sunlit fence. Particularly suited for well-drained garden areas that get semiregular watering, Kirilow indigo may be planted either in spring or in autumn. You can multiply Kirilow indigo via root or semi-ripe cuttings.

You may want to shape your shrub, but pruning is generally not necessary. Some gardeners cut it back sharply in spring or autumn when the shrub is dormant in order to produce a bushier growth.

The related species *Indigo amblyantha*, which bears rose or deep pink flowers, is especially hardy. While *I. heterantha* or "false indigo" is less hardy, it does have darker rosy purple flowers. If you need a nitrogen-fixing plant, indigo meets the requirement.

Ixora coccinea

Flame-of-the-woods

BLOOM TIME: late spring–autumn

HEIGHT/WIDTH: 8' × 6' (2.5 × 2m)

LIGHT: full sun

ZONES: 9-10

Flame-of-the-woods

Flame-of-the-woods hails from tropical climes, where its fragrant, bouquet-style, yellow, orange, pink, white, or red flower groupings are almost taken for granted in the consistently warm, humid weather. It's true that this shrub may be a smidge fussy about its growing medium and location, but its blooms are quite spectacular. It requires well-drained, amply organic soil tending toward acidic. Regular watering is an absolute must.

Except for southern Florida and similar climates, flame-of-the-woods is most successfully grown in a greenhouse. If the temperature drops below 59°F (15°C), this warm-climate plant may promptly die back. But don't give up hope too quickly, as it often returns.

Keep a watchful eye out for scale insects and aphids, which will make the leathery, dark green leaves start to yellow. Is flame-of-the-woods really worth all the effort? Yes!

Jasminum nudiflorum

Winter jasmine

BLOOM TIME: midwinter–early spring

HEIGHT/WIDTH: $3' \times 5'$ (1×1.5m)

LIGHT: full sun–partial shade

ZONES: 6–9

Winter jasmine

A native of China, winter jasmine needs fertile, well-drained soil, but does well in northern gardens, where other jasmines may prove difficult. Do not anticipate the renowned jasmine fragrance, as the 1-inch (2.5cm) -wide, bright yellow flowers are definitely unscented. Nonetheless, they're a welcome sight in midwinter when any color is a joyful harbinger of the coming warm weather. In really cold weather, the flowers may even freeze. Trifoliate leaves a deep glossy green appear after the flowers on year-old willowy stems. Among the leaves are tiny black berries.

Used as a medium-height shrub or 15-foot (4.5m) -high vine, this rapidly growing jasmine also makes a good deciduous bank cover, rooting wherever draping stems touch soil. Prune winter jasmine occasionally to keep its size and shape appropriate to its site, but make sure to prune after flowering. If old branches seem to have stopped flowering, cut them back severely to assure new growth.

Kalmia latifolia

Mountain laurel

BLOOM TIME: spring

HEIGHT/WIDTH: 10' × 8' (3 × 2.5m)

LIGHT: partial shade

ZONES: 5–8

OTHER: decorative branches

Mountain laurel

Growing primarily in the woodlands of the East, mountain laurel has glorious white, pink, or red bell-shaped flowers appearing in abundant 6-inch (15cm) -wide clusters. Like azaleas, mountain laurel needs cool, moist, acidic, well-drained soil in order to flourish. As their native habitat would indicate, mountain laurel does well, and looks completely natural, at the edge of a woodland garden. It is also a welcome addition to the shrub border or as part of a foundation planting.

Seed capsules are produced after the flowers pass, but if you want to ensure generous flowering the next season, it is best to remove these capsules. Be aware that leaves and flower nectar are poisonous if ingested. Mountain laurel does grow slowly, but feeding it an azalea-rhododendron fertilizer abets progress. Proper conditions, including a deep mulch, help to ward off occasional localized leaf spot fungus problems.

As a gnarled senior plant, mountain laurel becomes quite picturesque. Native Americans once made spoons from its hard wood; early colonists used it to make weaver's shuttles.

The cultivar 'Heart of Fire' is more adaptable than other cultivars.

Kerria japonica

Japanese kerria

BLOOM TIME: spring–summer, possibly autumn

HEIGHT/WIDTH: 5' × 6' (1.5 × 1.8m)

LIGHT: full sun–partial shade

ZONES: 4–9

'Pleniflora' Japanese kerria

Kerrias tolerate air pollution, and so make excellent plants for industrialized areas. Site these upright-growing shrubs singly or in groups, perhaps mixed with other shrubs for color contrast. Single or double bright golden yellow flowers resembling small wild roses appear on Japanese kerria between May and June, but may make a second showing in autumn. While the single-flowered forms are less hardy than the double-flowered ones, the single will flower quite happily in deep shade. Bright green glossy leaves also turn golden yellow in autumn, prolonging sunny color in the garden.

Flowers are followed by hard, black-brown, inedible fruits, each about 4 inches (10cm) long. Fruits, each containing four to six brownish yellow seeds, ripen in September. Not a fussy shrub, Japanese kerria does well with regular watering and ordinary garden soil. Cut off suckers as necessary.

Several good cultivars offer more options: 'Aureo-vittata' has arching branches that are striped yellow and green, a lively sight in winter; 'Pleniflora' has fully double flowers and is more likely to survive the cold than some other forms.

Kolkwitzia amablis

Beauty bush

BLOOM TIME: late spring–midsummer

HEIGHT/WIDTH: 10' × 8' (3 × 2.5m)

LIGHT: full sun–light shade

ZONES: 5–9

Beauty bush

An abundance of small, bell-shaped flowers carried in 3-inch (7cm) -wide clusters covers this large shrub in early summer. The pale pink flowers have yellow centers, though occasionally the flowers can be found in white or dark pink. Bristly pinkish brown seedpods appear in summer after the flowers, providing interest for an additional few weeks.

Native to China and virtually care-free, this deciduous, hardy plant adapts to many soil types, including lime, and survives a large climate variation. If you place beauty bush in the sun, the dark, gray-green foliage becomes denser and the shrub grows in a more compact shape. Give it semi-shade, and beauty bush's growth is taller and arching, making its delicate, brown, flaking bark more visible in winter.

Wood from the prior year carries the spring flowers, so be judicious when pruning to shape. Occasionally suckers may appear; take them out unless you want the shrub to spread.

Good cultivars to look for include the rosy red 'Rosea' and the deep pink 'Pink Cloud'.

Lagerstroemia indica

Crape myrtle

BLOOM TIME: summer–autumn

HEIGHT/WIDTH: 20' × 10' (6 × 3m)

LIGHT: full sun

ZONES: 7–10

OTHER: attracts birds

Crape myrtle

Crape myrtle's fantastic exfoliating bark is a visual delight, so make sure to place it in the garden where it can be easily appreciated. In fact, horticultural experts consider this deciduous shrub a must for the complete Southern garden.

But there are rewards other than the peeling brown-gray bark, such as dark green leaves that turn to bronze, russet, or red in autumn and an array of flower hues. The flowers of crape myrtle arrive in small, crinkled-petal clusters and they may be as long as 8 inches (20cm). Popular hybrid varieties include the coral-pink 'Comanche', lavender 'Lipan', and dwarf 'Victor', which has bright red flowers and is perfect for the patio pot or border.

Not fussy as to soil type or pH, crape myrtle does need good drainage. Mulching is beneficial. Plant only container-grown or balled and burlapped plants, as crape myrtle may have some difficulty establishing if planted as a bareroot. This shrub can also be pruned into a small tree. Prune in late winter; flowers are carried on new wood, so pruning will not interfere with bloom.

Lavandula angustifolia

English lavender

BLOOM TIME: summer

HEIGHT/WIDTH: 3' × 3'–4' (1 × 1–1.2m)

LIGHT: full sun

ZONES: 5–8

OTHER: attracts honeybees; good for drying

English lavender

Back when good folk thought baths weren't healthy, something was needed to mask unpleasant body aromas. Evergreen lavender, quite commonly grown, proved to be one solution, as it could be used to make an inexpensive perfume. It is still used in perfume today, as well as in potpourri, soaps, sachets, candles, and as dried scented flower wands.

A favorite for perennial and herb gardens, English lavender has small flowers that appear on long, wiry stems. Often planted along paths, where its glorious scent will be truly appreciated, lavender also makes a good low hedge.

Grow this hardiest of shrubby herbs in dryish, rather limey soil and bright sunshine. It's fine in coastal areas, but absolutely won't tolerate humidity. Deadheading the faded flowers will help assure vigorous new growth.

Varieties include the white-flowered 'Alba', at 3 -feet (30cm) tall; 'Twickel Purple', at 18 inches (45cm) tall, with light purple flowers; and 'Irene Doyle' with lavender-blue flowers. For patio or balcony, try the compact 'Rosea' or 'Jean Davis', both with pink flowers. All have serene gray or gray-green leaves.

Lespedeza spp.

Bush clover

BLOOM TIME: early autumn

HEIGHT/WIDTH: 4'–8' × 10' (1.2–2.5 × 3m)

LIGHT: full sun

ZONES: 4–8

Bush clover

Silky, ½-inch (1cm) flowers similar to those of the pea plant create seemingly endless wands of rose-purple on this deciduous shrub. Thriving in areas ranging from rocky outcrops to meadows, this Asian native needs only well-drained, fertile, light soil and full sun.

It's not always easy to find late-flowering, medium-sized shrubs to balance out the garden, but two species of bush clover fit the bill. Shrub bush clover (*Lespedeza bicolor*) has mid- to dark green oval leaves and is somewhat hardier (to Zone 4), while purple bush clover (*L. thunbergii*) has blue-green leaves and is hardy to Zone 5; both have rose-purple flower clusters that reach 6 inches (15cm) or longer. There is also a slightly shorter bush clover cultivar, *L. bicolor* 'Gibralter' with rose-pink flowers, ideal for today's often smaller garden.

Some pests and diseases may annoy this shrub—mainly rust, powdery mildew, and leafhoppers—but good care keeps these to a minimum.

Leucothoe fontanesiana
(*L. catasbaei*)

Drooping leucothoe

BLOOM TIME: early summer

HEIGHT/WIDTH: 6' × 4' (1.8 × 1.2m)

LIGHT: partial shade–full shade

ZONES: 5–8

'Rainbow' drooping leucothoe

Native to the Southern mountain streamsides of North America, drooping leucothoe demands the same type of conditions when planted elsewhere; it requires acidic, moist, well-drained soil high in organic matter, along with ample protection from the wind. Provide the proper environment and this graceful, fountainlike evergreen augments the spring wildflower or woodland garden with pendulous clusters of fragrant, white flowers.

Come autumn and winter, dark green, leathery, lance-shaped, 5-inch (12cm) -long leaves turn red or bronze-purple. The cultivar 'Scarletta', unsurprisingly, has scarlet foliage in spring, which gradually turns dark green over the summer, then burgundy in autumn. While the shrub retains it foliage in mild winters, the leaves may drop if the cold is severe.

Because leucothoe spreads by means of underground runners, it may form a clump if its conditions are good. Suitable companion plants for leucothoe include mountain laurel, azaleas, and rhododendrons.

There's also a dwarf variety, at 3 feet (1m) high, called 'Rainbow' (also sometimes called 'Girard's Rainbow'), which has red, yellow, and cream variegated foliage.

Ligustrum spp.

Privet

BLOOM TIME: midsummer

HEIGHT/WIDTH: 10' (3m) × varies widely

LIGHT: full sun–partial shade

ZONES: 4–9

OTHER: attracts birds, honeybees, butterflies

English privet

All privets are used extensively as clipped or unclipped hedging shrubs, and make worthy specimens as well. When the shrubs are clipped they do not produce flowers or berries, but left to their natural shape the plants produce small but attractive white flowers in midsummer. Very hard, shiny, black berries appear after flowers have passed.

Privets—grown mainly for their green, glossy, oval leaves—are admired as tough, quick-growing shrubs. They are tolerant of a wide range of conditions, including the challenges of city gardens. Except for English, or common,

privet, which is subject to blight in some areas, they are generally free of pests and diseases. Note that ingestion of any part of the privet plant will cause serious illness.

English privet (*L. vulgare*), is a wide-growing shrub that is usually deciduous but may remain semievergreen in the South. Ibolium privet (*L. × ibolium*), an upright-growing deciduous shrub, is one of the prettiest privets for more northern climes (to Zone 5), and closely resembles California privet (*L. ovalifolium*), a beautiful choice for Zone 6 and southward.

Lindera benzoin

Spice bush

BLOOM TIME: spring

HEIGHT/WIDTH: 10' × 6' (3 × 1.8m)

LIGHT: partial shade

ZONES: 5–9

OTHER: attracts honeybees, birds

Spice bush

Spice is nice, especially when it occurs in fragrant flowers, twigs, and foliage. In fact, the twigs and leaves were once used to flavor food and teas. This eastern North American native develops masses of small yellow flowers that appear while branches are still bare. Large medium green leaves cover the shrub when flowers have finished. In autumn, the leaves turn yellow and frame ½-inch (1cm) red fruits. Early American colonists sometimes dried the fruits, then ground them into a powder as a substitute for allspice. Fruiting occurs on female plants only if there's a male spice bush in the vicinity, so keep this in mind when planning your garden.

Make sure to buy container-grown or balled and burlapped shrubs, as bareroot spice bush is difficult to get established. Plant spice bush in acidic, moist, well-drained soil, and don't plan on moving it. Transplanting can be difficult due to an extended, deep, root system. You'll want to encourage a profusion of wildflowers in the vicinity, as they bloom just about the same time as spice bush, a double treat.

Lonicera fragrantissima

Fragrant honeysuckle

Fragrant honeysuckle

BLOOM TIME: late winter–early spring

HEIGHT/WIDTH: 6' × 6' (1.8 × 1.8m)

LIGHT: full sun–partial shade

ZONES: 5–8

OTHER: attracts honeybees, hummingbirds, birds

To recall soft memories of childhood spring evenings, cradle a honeysuckle blossom in your hand and inhale deeply. Even just one creamy-white, ½-inch (1cm) flower is a fragrant gem—an entire shrub can be nostalgic nirvana. Leaves are bluish green and delicate red berries succeed flowers, though they are often stolen by birds as soon as they ripen. Note that the berries are not edible by humans, and can cause illness.

Named after a German physician, Adam Lonicer, this hearty shrub may even be trained as a multistemmed small tree. Tolerating a variety of soils, fragrant honeysuckle requires only moderate water. Site this semievergreen winner where its glorious scent can be best enjoyed, but note that it is wide-spreading, and may have to be constantly pruned if not given enough room. Make sure to prune after flowering, as blooms are carried on the previous year's wood. Full sun is best, but fragrant honeysuckle will tolerate some shade, while continuing to flower.

There are many honeysuckle species and cultivars, and not all are fragrant. Scented shrub alternatives are *Lonicera syringantha*, which bears lilac flowers, and *L. standishii*, which has white flowers.

Magnolia stellata

Star magnolia

BLOOM TIME: late winter–early spring

HEIGHT/WIDTH: 8' × 8' (2.5 × 2.5m)

LIGHT: full sun–light shade

ZONES: 5–9

OTHER: good cut flowers for fragrance

Star magnolia

Many think sweet-scented magnolias exist solely in huge tree form, but deciduous shrub forms abound, including the 8-foot (2.4m) -tall *Magnolia stellata* 'Royal Star' and *M. stellata* 'Waterlily', as well as *M. sieboldii* 'Siebold', and *M.* 'Jane', which may grow to 15 feet (4.5m) tall. Many magnolias may be grown either as multistemmed shrubs or as single-stem small trees.

Flower colors may vary: 'Jane' bears 3-inch (7cm) flowers that are reddish purple outside and white inside; 'Waterlily' has pink buds and white flowers tinged with pink; and 'Siebold' has brilliant red stamens that ornament white, cup-shaped flowers. Most magnolias are fairly hardy, but do need moist, organic, well-drained, lime-free soil in order to thrive. Just place them in an uncrowded site where they are to remain, then enjoy ample flowers in early spring. When planted in a sheltered spot, magnolias may bloom earlier than they otherwise would, star magnolia being among the earliest to bloom. Cut flowers, placed in ornamental bowls, both perfume and decorate a room.

Mahonia aquifolium

Oregon grapeholly

BLOOM TIME: spring

HEIGHT/WIDTH: 3' × 5' (1 × 1.5m)

LIGHT: partial shade–shade

ZONES: 5–9

OTHER: attracts birds

Oregon grapeholly

Native to North America, Oregon grapeholly's common name derives from its region of origin, its grapelike clusters of dark blue berries, and its shiny, green, hollylike leaves. Seasonal changes serve Oregon grapeholly well. In spring, small, golden-yellow flowers are carried in dense, upright, 3-inch (8cm) -long racemes. The glaucous berries ripen in autumn, and the stiff glossy leaves turn reddish bronze in winter.

This evergreen shrub thrives in moist, well-drained, slightly acidic soil that is high in organic matter. Generally hardy, it requires protection from both wind and very hot sun. Oregon grapeholly combines well with conifers, makes a fine low hedge, and does well as an underplanting beneath large trees. The shrub spreads by underground stems, and may form large clumps over time.

There is a shorter version, 'Compacta', which reaches to only 3 feet (90cm) in height; it has yellow flowers but bears few fruits.

Malus sargentii

Sargent crabapple

BLOOM TIME: late spring

HEIGHT/WIDTH: 6' × 12' (1.8 × 3.5m)

LIGHT: full sun

ZONES: 4–8

OTHER: attracts birds

Sargent crabapple

Most of the twenty-five crabapple species are trees, but a few have the compact, mounding habit that qualifies them as shrubs. Native to Asia, Sargent crabapple grows wider than it does tall, and has a horizontal branching habit. Sargent crabapple wins accolades not only for its musky-sweet scent, showy white flower clusters, profuse dark red fruits, and leaves that turn orange and yellow in autumn, but also for its superb disease resistance. Unlike most other crabapples, Sargent crabapple is not susceptible to cedar-apple rust.

Like all crabapples, it requires regular watering and tolerates most soils, as long as they are well-drained. It does not tolerate shade, however. Remember that for this species, sun equals flowers. The flowers are followed by pea-sized fruits, which will display through most of the winter if not eaten by birds.

The cultivar 'Rosea' has pink flowers; 'Candymint' bears lovely pink flowers with red borders.

Myrtus communis

Common myrtle

BLOOM TIME: spring–autumn

HEIGHT/WIDTH: 3' × 3' (1 × 1m)

LIGHT: full sun

ZONES: 8–9

OTHER: bonsai

Common myrtle

In European folklore, myrtle brings happiness to the house it surrounds. Bridal bouquets often contained fragrant myrtle sprigs, which were later planted close to the door of a new home, and it was one of the plants the ancient Greeks used to make crowns for celebrated figures. Cultivated for its aromatic, glossy, green leaves as well as its sweet-smelling, cream-colored flowers, this evergreen needs well-drained soil, but tolerates both heat and occasional drought.

White berries follow the fragrant flowers. While *Myrtus communis*, common myrtle, gets rather tall, there are multi-ple shorter varieties: *M. communis* 'Compacta' stays at 3 feet (90cm) tall and makes a good low hedging shrub, as do the slightly taller cultivars 'Jenny Reitenbach' and 'Nana'.

While myrtle will not survive the winter in regions above Zone 8, it is perfect for growing in containers and moving indoors for the winter. All myrtles make fine topiary plants for yard or patio, and the smaller ones can be trained for bonsai.

Nandina domestica

Heavenly bamboo

BLOOM TIME: midsummer

HEIGHT/WIDTH: 6' × 3' (1.8 × 1m)

LIGHT: full sun–partial shade

ZONES: 6–9

Heavenly bamboo

The word "bamboo" may conjure in the minds of gardeners images of underground rhizomes taking over a yard. But don't let this nickname, a misnomer, scare you away from the self-contained, beautifully textured *Nandina*, actually not a bamboo at all. Heavenly bamboo is not particular about soil, though semimoist soil is best; the plant is practically pest-free.

In midsummer, small, clustered, white flowers appear in profusion. Throughout the year, heavenly bamboo's fine foliage is a beautiful asset, but it really shines in autumn, when the leaves turn brilliant red and bronze. Large clusters of dark orange-red fruit in autumn create a festive holiday garden appearance.

In the northern reaches of its zone, heavenly bamboo will benefit from some winter protection, and even then may succumb to severe winters.

A favorite in Japanese gardens, heavenly bamboo may also be planted in hedges or as a graceful specimen planting.

For even more color, try the cultivar 'Yellow Fruited'. Patio varieties, such as the 2-foot (60cm) -high 'Fire Power', are also available.

Nerium oleander

Oleander

BLOOM TIME: late spring–autumn

HEIGHT/WIDTH: varies widely

LIGHT: full sun

ZONES: 8-9

Oleander

This shrub is so durable and easy to grow, it is planted along freeways in several states. In the garden, it does require caution, since all parts are poisonous if ingested. In fact, wood must not be used for barbecue or other food skewers, or burnt where smoke can be inhaled. Yet for tough garden sections, oleander survives where other plants fail. In addition to tolerating auto exhaust fumes, the shrub withstands somewhat salty soil and partial drought.

Beautifully ornamental, this warm-climate shrub produces clusters of red, pink, or white flowers from spring until autumn. The foliage, too, is attractive, and remains green throughout the seasons.

Oleander's size varies widely, from 'Petite Pink', which reaches only 3 feet (1m) in height, to the white-flowered 'Sister Agnes', which can grow moderately quickly to 20 feet (6m) tall. Make certain to ask the nursery about the ultimate size of the cultivar you wish to purchase. Since there are multiple color choices, including apricot, lilac, yellow, and several reds, seeing this evergreen shrub in bloom before purchasing is a good idea.

Osmanthus heterophyllus

Holly osmanthus

BLOOM TIME: autumn

HEIGHT/WIDTH: $10' \times 10'$ (3×3m)

LIGHT: full sun–partial shade

ZONES: 6–9

'Goshiki' holly osmanthus

Autumn bloom makes this an excellent shrub for the year-round garden. While the quite small, white, tubular flower clusters aren't easily visible among the dark, glossy, holly-like, evergreen leaves, their presence becomes obvious once you sniff the extremely sweet fragrance. Specimen planting is always recommended near a window where the fragrance can be thoroughly enjoyed. Holly osmanthus is also quite useful as a dense barrier hedge.

Moderately hardy, holly osmanthus needs moist, well-drained, somewhat acidic soil, and protection from cold, strong winds. Purple-black fruits appear only in warm areas. This useful shrub performs quite well both in sun and shade, which makes it a versatile plant for foundation plantings or for hedging. Hard pruning won't harm the shrub; prune in early spring.

There are several good cultivars available, including 'Goshiki', which has bronze-tinted leaves in spring, later splashed with yellow; 'Variegatus', which has cream-edged leaves; and 'Purpureus', which has unusual, deep purple new leaves in spring.

Paeonia suffruticosa

Tree peony

BLOOM TIME: spring

HEIGHT/WIDTH: 6' × 6' (1.8 × 1.8m)

LIGHT: mild sun–partial shade

ZONES: 4–8

Tree peony

Regarded as the "King of Flowers" by the Chinese, the tree peony's extraordinarily showy, fragrant, large flowers have made this plant prized in horticultural circles for centuries. Chinese writings more than eight hundred years old record peony collections, one enthusiast growing as many as sixty thousand peonies. While most people are familiar with the popular herbaceous peonies (*Paeonia lactiflora*), not all are aware of the deciduous shrubs discussed here.

If given a satisfactory environment, the beautiful tree peony is not difficult to grow. It needs rich, somewhat moist, well-drained soil with morning sun and afternoon shade. It does not tolerate soggy soil, strong winds, or being disturbed. Prune tree peony in spring, after it flowers. Container-grown or balled and burlapped plants may be set out at any time during the year. Bareroot tree peonies must be planted in autumn.

Gorgeous new color selections are available each year. 'Karmada Fuji' is a semidouble lavender pink. 'Demetra' is a double yellow-gold, with petals edged in burgundy. 'Hyphestos' is a double-flowered dark red with pointed, ruffled petals.

Philadelphus coronarius

Fragrant mock orange

BLOOM TIME: early summer

HEIGHT/WIDTH: 8' × 7' (2.5 × 2m)

LIGHT: full sun–partial shade

ZONES: 5–8

OTHER: attracts butterflies, honeybees

Fragrant mock orange

The enchanting orange blossom fragrance of this serene shrub transforms it from Cinderella plainness into a garden princess. It almost seems a miracle that such ordinary green leaves and unprepossessing white flowers can scent the air with romance on a fine spring day.

The upright-growing deciduous mock orange accomplishes all this without requiring much effort from the gardener. It grows in any garden soil, seldom gets serious pests or diseases, and you won't have to worry about constant watering, as mock orange tolerates occasional drought.

Mock orange grows well in full sun or in light shade. Fragrant mock orange is among the hardiest of the mock oranges, and when in a sheltered spot may survive winters even in the southern ranges of Zone 4, though it is reliably hardy to Zone 5. Select your specimens when they are in bloom, as some plants have the mock orange label, but lack the fragrance.

If you are planting for porch or patio, look for the cultivar 'Dwarf Snowflake', which reaches only 3 feet (1m) in height.

Photonia fraseri

Fraser photonia

BLOOM TIME: spring

HEIGHT/WIDTH: 15' × 15' (4.5 × 4.5m)

LIGHT: full sun

ZONES: 7–9

OTHER: branches good for arranging

Fraser photonia

A good accent plant because of its bright, bronze-red, springtime foliage, Fraser photinia's leaves mature to a deep green. Small, ivory-colored flower clusters that appear in midspring, followed by red berries, complete the show.

Vigorous and fast-growing photonia requires full sun and a well-drained soil with ample organic matter. The soil should be improved with peat moss or leaf mold when the shrubs are planted and on a continuing basis. Water Fraser photinia profusely, aiming at roots rather than leaves, to forestall fireblight problems. In the northern parts of

photonia's hardiness range, cut back watering in autumn to allow the leaves to mature before winter sets in. Aphids and scale insects can also present problems.

Fraser photonia does well in containers, so consider it for patio use. It also makes an unusual espalier, an eye-catching hedge, and a tidy small tree. Pruning is the key to getting the desired shape.

Popular cultivars available include 'Red Robin', 'Birmingham', and the very vigorous 'Robusta'.

Pieris floribunda

Mountain andromeda, mountain pieris

BLOOM TIME: spring

HEIGHT/WIDTH: 6' × 6' (1.8 × 1.8m)

LIGHT: partial shade

ZONES: 5–8

Mountain andromeda

While less widely available than *Pieris japonica*, this broad-leaved evergreen pieris has a better resistance to lacebug and a higher pH tolerance, so it's worth checking specialty nurseries and mail-order sources to find this species. Upright 5-inch (13cm) -long clusters of tiny, fragrant, white flowers display themselves in spring among fine-textured, deep green leaves that make their initial appearance with red-bronze coloration. If ingested, leaves may cause severe discomfort. In late summer, buds form for the following year's flowers, and remain decorative through the autumn and winter.

Native to southeastern North America's damp mountain slopes, mountain andromeda prefers cool, moist, somewhat acidic soil, plus shelter from wind, cold, and harsh winter sun. A sheltered situation, perhaps against the wall of a house, is especially important in the northern reaches of the shrub's hardiness range. Once established and given a mulch, mountain andromeda is drought-tolerant, barring extremely hot weather. A slow-grower, this gracefully arching shrub is ideal for smaller gardens and looks particularly beautiful when combined with needleleaf evergreens.

Pittosporum tobira

Japanese pittosporum

BLOOM TIME: spring

HEIGHT/WIDTH: 15' × 12' (4.5 × 3.5m)

LIGHT: full sun–partial shade

ZONES: 9–10

'Variegata' Japanese pittosporum

Flowers with the fragrance of orange blossoms make Japanese pittosporum a prized addition to the scented garden. Pittosporum's small, creamy white flowers appear in multiple clusters among dark green, leathery leaves. Leaves are spaced quite close together on the stems, and appear to grow in whorls. Flowers are followed by pear-shaped, yellow-brown seed capsules that split open in autumn, displaying red-orange seeds. The vigorous growing habit, mild watering needs, and low maintenance of this popular ever-green shrub make it useful for foundation plantings, screens, and borders. Prune lightly only as necessary. Japanese pittosporum will grow in nearly any soil, and adapts to heat and to the windy conditions of the coast. The species will also tolerate some shade. For the patio garden, Japanese pittosporum does well in containers, and can be trained as a small, crooked-stemmed tree.

The cultivar 'Variegata' has gray-green leaves edged with white.

Plumbago auriculata

Cape plumbago

BLOOM TIME: spring–autumn

HEIGHT/WIDTH: 10'–20' × 3'–10' (3–6 × 1–3m)

LIGHT: full sun

ZONES: 9–10

Cape plumbago

Grow cape plumbago as a shrub or as a vine, and enjoy pale blue or white (*Plumbago auriculata* var. *alba*), 1-inch (2.5cm) -wide flowers grouped in clusters up to 4 inches (10cm) wide. Flowers, which are surrounded by light green leaves, may continue to bloom throughout the year in climates that get no frost. Persuade free-flowering bloom by giving cape plumbago a sheltered position in full sun and fertile soil.

This South African native semievergreen has many roles, including a drought-tolerant one. Give it well-drained soil and only occasional water once established. A feisty sprawler, cape plumbago takes its time at the starting gate, but once it gets going, it will cover a fence or an otherwise dismal hillock. Fertilize cape plumbago in early spring and again in midsummer to stimulate growth. Pinch off the tips of long young canes to encourage branching. Unless you desire a very large shrub, cut old canes back to the ground each spring. Make sure to use gloves, as handling the plant may cause severe skin irritation.

Potentilla fruticosa

Bush cinquefoil

BLOOM TIME: late spring–autumn

HEIGHT/WIDTH: 4' × 4' (1.2 × 1.2m)

LIGHT: full sun

ZONES: 2–7

Bush cinquefoil

The fine-textured, grayish green foliage on this dense, bushy shrub makes a complementary backdrop for colorful annuals and perennials. The common name "cinquefoil" derives from the shrub's five-fingered leaf, a popular emblem of long-ago heraldry; it symbolized the five senses and fivefold victory. Single yellow flowers, about 1 inch (2.5cm) wide, appear profusely in midsummer and may continue until frost.

Incredibly easy to grow, bush cinquefoil needs only a sunny spot in well-drained soil. This upright-growing shrub is bothered by no pests or diseases and needs no pruning. Use bush cinquefoil in hedges, as specimens, or in a shrub border.

Good cultivars of bush cinquefoil abound, with many different color selections, including 'Tangerine', with copper-colored flowers; 'Abbotswood' with white blooms; 'Day Dawn', which bears pale pink flowers; 'Red Ace', a red with yellow centers; and the new double-flowered 'Yellowbird'. Note that with brighter red, orange, or yellow flowers fading from the sun may occur.

Prunus glandulosa

Chinese bush cherry

BLOOM TIME: April

HEIGHT/WIDTH: 4' × 5' (1.2 × 1.5m)

LIGHT: full sun

ZONES: 5–8

OTHER: attracts honeybees

Chinese bush cherry

If you need a small shrub, this hardy ornamental cherry is among the most widely cultivated of the two hundred *Prunus* species due to its profuse early bloom. Slender bare branches are almost completely covered by clusters of splendidly small blooms in white or pink. The flowers, which may come in both single and double forms, are soon joined by ovoid, medium green leaves. Tiny, dark red berries appear on single-flowered forms only, after flowers have passed. Ingestion of either leaves or fruit causes severe discomfort.

All *Prunus* species thrive in ordinary garden soil, doing best in a reasonably wind-free site. They also need full sun. Regular, modest fertilization is beneficial.

For those interested in re-creating a Victorian or Edwardian garden of ages past, consider *Prunus glandulosa* 'Sinensis'. Its bright pink double flowers made this shrub very popular during those decorative days, and it appeared in thousands of gardens across England and North America.

Prunus triloba

Flowering almond

BLOOM TIME: early spring

HEIGHT/WIDTH: 8' × 8' (2.5 × 2.5m)

LIGHT: full sun

ZONES: 6–8

OTHER: attracts honeybees

Flowering almond

Flowering almond is a delightful ornamental rather than a delicious almond-provider, and can be pruned to make a small tree as well as left to form a substantial dense shrub. Peach-pink, many-petaled double flowers, each about 1½ inches (3.5cm) across, resemble small rose. There is also a single-flowered form. The blooms herald springtime along the length of long, narrow branches. Round red fruits, which may cause severe discomfort if eaten, follow the flowers.

Use this shrub in hedges, in a shrub border, or against a wall. The darker the wall, the better the pink blossoms dis-play. While hedges need to be trimmed after flowering, this very durable deciduous shrub doesn't otherwise require a lot of care if sited in a sunny, well-drained area.

Note that the name *Prunus triloba plena* appears in many catalogs to distinguish the double-flowered forms from the single-flowered ones, but this designation has no botanical standing. The shrub is in fact the same species as *Prunus triloba*. The cultivar 'Multiplex' flowers in midspring.

Punica granatum

Pomegranate

BLOOM TIME: summer–early autumn

HEIGHT/WIDTH: 10' × 7' (3 × 2m)

LIGHT: full sun

ZONES: 8–10

Pomegranate

Julia Child, empress of delectable cuisine, mentions rolling pomegranate seeds into small cream cheese balls or cooking them to make a delicious jelly. These are just a few ideas in addition to eating them scooped directly from the 3-inch (7cm) -wide red fruit picked right off the tree in autumn. 'Wonderful' is the best fruit-bearing cultivar now available. Fruit follows funnel-shaped, bright orange-red flowers, each over 3 inches (7cm) wide. Double-flowered forms are available, and bloom for several months in summer but do not bear fruit.

In the open garden, pomegranate can be grown as a deciduous shrub or small tree. Plant it in well-drained, average soil, and water regularly. A sunny location is mandatory for fruiting and plant survival, and a hotter, drier climate will stimulate the shrub to produce more fruit. In slow-sun climates, up the odds by placing pomegranate near a heat-reflecting wall. A dwarf variety, 'Nana', which has scarlet flowers, is available, but fruits are small and dry. Make certain the *Punica* you purchase bears edible fruit, if that's your garden hope.

Pyracantha coccinea

Scarlet firethorn

BLOOM TIME: early summer

HEIGHT/WIDTH: 8' × 8' (2.5 × 2.5m)

LIGHT: full sun–light shade

ZONES: 6–9

OTHER: attracts honeybees, birds

Scarlet firethorn

The botanical name of this popular shrub comes from the Greek words *pyr*, meaning fire, and *akanthos*, meaning thorn—an apt name. Long thorns are piercing and plentiful, so place this shrub away from pathways and make sure it has ample space to spread. Pruning is beneficial, but use long cutting tools or protective garden gloves. Dryish soil and full sun are best for this thorny shrub.

Small, creamy white flowers precede ample clusters of bright scarlet, pea-sized berries. Berries appear in autumn and would probably persist into midwinter except that birds eat them with a voracious appetite.

Evergreen firethorn is occasionally afflicted with fireblight, which causes blackened leaves almost overnight, although many plants regrow. Otherwise, the shrub is fairly durable. *Pyracantha coccinea* is less affected by fireblight than some other species, and the cultivar 'Mohave' has been bred for resistance to both scab and fireblight.

The cultivar 'Lalandii', with orange berries, is more cold-tolerant than the species; 'Harlequin' has variegated leaves rather than the usual dark green.

Rhamnus frangula

Alder buckthorn

BLOOM TIME: summer

HEIGHT/WIDTH: 15' × 12' (4.5 × 3.5m)

LIGHT: full sun

ZONES: 2–8

OTHER: attracts honeybees

Alder buckthorn

This is the only buckthorn with autumn color, its dark green glossy leaves turning bright red or yellow in autumn. Despite its name, this large shrub has no thorns.

Flowers are tiny, whitish green, and appear in clusters. Small berries follow the flowers, and ripen from green to yellow to red to black. Ingestion of leaves, bark, or fruit causes severe discomfort. Give this very hardy shrub moist, organic, slightly acidic soil and full sun. It is tolerant of air pollution, and will grown even in very wet soils. If pruning is necessary to shape or to curtail size, clip the shrub in early spring.

While not an otherwise demonstrative shrub, the cultivar 'Columnaris' has ample virtue as a hedging or screening plant, making a dense barrier that requires minimal trimming. 'Aspenifolia', otherwise known as fern-leaf buckthorn, doesn't have the red-to-black small berries of the species and 'Columnaris', however it does have very long, narrow, glossy leaves that give it a lacy demeanor.

Rhaphiolepis umbellata

Yeddo hawthorn

BLOOM TIME: summer (cool climates); winter–late spring (hot climates)

HEIGHT/WIDTH: 4' × 5' (1.2 × 1.5m)

LIGHT: full sun–partial shade

ZONES: 8–10

Yeddo hawthorn

This vigorous white-flowering shrub can be planted as a specimen, as a formal or informal low hedge, or in mixed borders for flower diversity. It can even be potted up in a container for the patio or balcony. Purple-black berries appear in spring, along with new leaves shaded bronze. Mature leaves, 3 inches (7cm) long, are dark green and rounded, with a glossy, leathery texture.

Evergreen Yeddo hawthorn does best in full sun, but tolerates light shade as well. It adapts to a variety of soils, including ocean coast, but requires regular watering in very dry soils, though it will tolerate brief periods of drought. Pests are minimal, but watch out for leaf spot fungi. Plant this shrub in spring or in autumn, and make sure to water well until established.

If you like Yeddo hawthorn, but want a truly compact variety, consider the cultivar called 'Minor'.

Rhododendron calendulaceum

Flame azalea

BLOOM TIME: late spring–early summer

HEIGHT/WIDTH: 10' × 8' (3 × 2.5m)

LIGHT: partial shade

ZONES: 5–9

Flame azalea

Two hundred years ago, a horticultural writer proclaimed flame azalea as "certainly the most gay and brilliant flowering shrub yet known." Azaleas are among the most free-flowering of all deciduous shrubs. Not only are the large, trumpet-shaped flowers vivid shades of red, orange, and yellow, but the autumn leaves often take on the same hues. The blooms last for several weeks, and during that time the woods seem to be on fire with color. While pretty, the leaves are poisonous if ingested.

Less demanding than evergreen rhododendrons, flame azaleas still need moist, well-drained soil with a pH of 5.0 to 6.0. If you live in an area with acidic soil, your flame azaleas will thrive, but if you live in a region with alkaline soil, you will most likely have to treat the soil with an acidifier or replace the soil in which you are to plant your azaleas. In clay soils, it is best to plant in raised beds, where good drainage can be assured. Use a special azalea fertilizer regularly. Plant flame azaleas in late spring or early autumn, and give them a site with some relief from the hot sun—a lightly shaded spot like the edge of a woodland garden is ideal. Native to Eastern North America, flame azaleas should be a definite part of any heirloom garden.

Rhododendron schlippenbachii

Royal azalea

BLOOM TIME: late spring

HEIGHT/WIDTH: 6'–8' × 6'–8' (1.8–2.5 × 1.8–2.5m)

LIGHT: partial shade

ZONES: 5–8

Royal azalea

Buy this deciduous shrub while it is in bloom to find the most satisfying hue for your garden, as it has some color variation, from white to pale pink to deep rose. Trumpet-shaped, 3-inch (7cm) -wide flowers are quite fragrant and are surrounded by dark green leaves, creating small, natural bouquets. Royal azalea's leaves turn a multitude of colors in autumn: red, orange, and yellow. Delightful to look at, ingestion of plant parts can cause serious illness.

Unlike most other rhododendrons, royal azalea does not require highly acidic soil, performing well with a soil pH of about 6.5. However it does demand excellent drainage, as well as protection from wind and high summer heat. A site under a high-branched tree may work well, though you must remember that rhododendrons like ample water and tree roots can be competitive. Don't forget to mulch, which will help the roots stay cool and the soil retain water.

Rhodotypos scandens

Jetbead

BLOOM TIME: late spring–summer

HEIGHT/WIDTH: 5' × 7' (1.5 × 2m)

LIGHT: full sun–partial shade

ZONES: 5–8

Jetbead

Shiny, black, pea-sized fruits arranged in groups of four, ornament this adaptable shrub throughout otherwise drab winter months, giving added interest and depth to the garden scene. In spring 1¼-inch (3cm) -wide, papery white flowers display a clean-cut demeanor amongst dark green 4-inch (10cm) -long, toothed leaves. The flowers persist into midsummer, and are followed by the fruits.

Jetbead, also called "black jetbead," "jetberry bush," and "white kerria" adjusts to just about any garden soil, wet or dry. Not only does it disregard insect pests but it doesn't flinch a bit at air pollution. If pruning is required, clip this shrub in spring. The only cause for hesitation in planting this adaptable flowering shrub are its fruits, which are highly poisonous if eaten. Otherwise, jetbead is an ideal deciduous shrub for small urban or suburban gardens, since it thrives both in sun or partial shade, and stays under 6 feet (1.8m) tall.

Ribes aureum

Golden currant

BLOOM TIME: spring–summer

HEIGHT/WIDTH: 7' × 5' (2 × 1.5m)

LIGHT: full sun

ZONES: 3–8

Golden currant

Drooping clusters of small, tubular, yellow flowers give off a delicious spicy fragrance, and are followed by red, orange, or black fruits. But this medium-sized, leathery-leafed flowering shrub is grown for its ornamental value rather than its fruits. Like the other one hundred and fifty species of *Ribes*, golden currant is usually planted in groups and is used to cover slopes and fill odd spaces in the garden. It also makes a good hedging shrub, either clipped or unclipped.

Of all the currants, hardy golden currants are the best for the novice gardener, as they are forgiving of a number of adverse conditions. Not overly particular as to soil, as long as it's well-drained, deciduous golden currant will succeed in both sandy and gravelly soils as well as good loam. The better the soil, the more the shrub will sucker. Air pollution doesn't affect growth. Cut back old shoots after flowering to stimulate new growth.

Note that currants may carry a fungus, called white pine blister rust, that affects white pines trees; *Ribes* species are therefore prohibited in certain regions. Check with your local agricultural extension office to be sure that any currant you are planning to include in your garden is safe for your area.

Ribes odoratum

Clove currant, buffalo currant

BLOOM TIME: late spring

HEIGHT/WIDTH: 7' × 5' (2 × 1.5m)

LIGHT: partial shade

ZONES: 5–8

OTHER: attracts birds; fruit for preserves

Clove currant

If you make preserves and want to experiment with a scintilla of clove, place clove currant near your kitchen door, where you can garner a few small black fruits with just a step or two outside. The clovelike aroma from sunny yellow flowers is so delightful that you should be certain to site this shrub near a porch, patio, or window if the backdoor entry spot won't do. Just make certain that clove currant's situation is quite dry and somewhat shady, as this deciduous Great Plains native thrives best in its traditional environment. Meet this shrub's needs and you'll get not only edible fruit, perky flowers, and spicy scent, but also pale green leaves that turn a lovely scarlet in autumn. Note that you'll need a plant of each sex in order to produce fruit. Clove currant spreads by means of underground suckers, so make sure to allow it plenty of space.

Like golden currant and other *Ribes* species, clove currant may act as a host for white pine blister rust, a fungus that decimates white pine trees. For this reason, currants' use is restricted in certain regions, so make sure to check with your local agricultural extension agent before planting.

The cultivar 'Crandall' has extra-large fruits, tart and sweet.

Robinia hispida

Rose acacia, bristly locust

BLOOM TIME: late spring–early summer

HEIGHT/WIDTH: 8' × 6' (2.5 × 1.8m)

LIGHT: full sun

ZONES: 6–10

OTHER: attracts honeybees

'Rosea' rose acacia

Pollution- and drought-tolerant, this very tough, thornless, deciduous shrub fits well in semi-wild areas, where its suckering tendencies won't be a nuisance to smaller plants. Small, rose pink flowers similar to those of the pea plant hang in loose clusters about 6 inches (15 cm) long. The large clusters mean that the flowers can be appreciated from some distance, a decided benefit. Blooms are sometimes followed by bristly, brown seedpods. Soft, fine, red bristles cover the stems.

Not at all particular as to soil, rose acacia even tolerates stony and sandy ground, but make sure to plant it in full sun. This vigorous shrub grows at a rate of 12 inches (30cm) or more per year. Young shrubs must be staked, as branches are brittle and will break in the wind. Regular pruning is necessary.

A less commonly seen variety is *Robinia hispida* var. *fertilis*, which has narrower leaves that feature downy undersides.

Rosa rugosa

Japanese rose, sea tomato

BLOOM TIME: spring–autumn

HEIGHT/WIDTH: 6' × 5' (1.8 × 1.5m)

LIGHT: full sun

ZONES: 2–9

OTHER: attracts birds

Japanese rose

Prickly stems make Japanese rose a good barrier shrub as well as a formidable groundcover designed to keep off wanderers. Among the hardiest of roses, this gorgeous wild rose needs little care. Aside from good drainage and lots of sun, its has virtually no requirements. Single, 2-inch (5 cm) -wide, dark green leaves change to orange in autumn, and orange-red fruits, called hips, form. These hips are rich in vitamin C, and have been used to make jellies and herbal teas. They are also a notorious favorite of birds.

In some areas Japanese rose is used as a roadside plant, and it has no problems adapting to ocean salt spray, wind, or hard frosts.

Three of the many excellent cultivars are 'Fru Dagmar Hastrup', which has clove-scented, rose-pink flowers followed by crimson rosehips; 'Blanc Double de Coubert', which bears large, semidouble, fragrant, white flowers and intermittent red rosehips; and 'Roseraie de l'Hay, with double, strongly fragrant, wine-red flowers.

Rosmarinus officinalis

Rosemary

BLOOM TIME: winter–spring

HEIGHT/WIDTH: 2'–6' × 8' (.6–1.8 × 2.5m)

LIGHT: full sun

ZONES: 8–10

OTHER: attracts honeybees

'Blue Spire' rosemary

Bouquets of rosemary were once brought to bridegrooms on a wedding morning, in the hope of assuring a happy marriage. Plant of legend, perfumery, culinary, and medicinal use, the easygoing rosemary does well in poor, albeit well-drained soils. It is most cheerful in sunny areas, but will survive even in ones where light reflects off a wall. Water-thrifty once established, rosemary doesn't have any serious pests, and requires no fertilizer.

Tiny, lavender-blue flowers appear in clusters during winter, a welcome sight, as well as in spring. Needlelike leaves are pungently fragrant when rolled between fingers. These leaves can be harvested at any time for culinary use, and make a perfect seasoning for chicken, lamb, or potatoes.

While rosemary will not winter outdoors above Zone 8, it is commonly grown in cooler climates in pots and wintered in a sunny spot indoors. The pots can then be moved outside in summer. Rosemary can also be grown as a standard and is a favorite subject for small topiaries.

Choose from a variety of cultivars, including trailing 'Irene'; 2-foot (60cm) -tall and spreading silvery green 'Lockwood'; 'Golden Rain', which has gold-striped needles in spring; and brightly flowered 'Tuscan Blue'.

Rubus odoratus

Flowering raspberry, thimbleberry

BLOOM TIME: summer

HEIGHT/WIDTH: 8' × 10' (2.5 × 3m)

LIGHT: partial shade

ZONES: 7–9

OTHER: attracts birds

Flowering raspberry

This ultra-tough, fast-growing, thornless shrub—native to the eastern part of North America—makes a good thicket in a wild or woodland garden, particularly if allowed to enjoy its suckering habit. Raspberry-scented, rose-purple flowers, up to 2 inches (5cm) wide, appear during the summer and are followed by red, raspberrylike fruits in long-summer zones. Dark to light green leaves are attractive and unusual, being maple-shaped with a velvety texture.

This *Rubus* is grown as an ornamental shrub and does not have edible fruit. If you want the fresh raspberries or blackberries, there are other, equally hardy *Rubus* varieties to choose from. Check a specialty book on growing fruits and berries or ask at your local nursery, as good fruit production requires certain care of the bushes.

Grow flowering raspberry in well-drained, average soil in partial shade. If you must put it in a spot with lots of sun, make sure to keep the soil evenly moist. Note that flowering raspberry spreads aggressively by way of suckers, so don't plant it unless you have the space to give it. Prune hard to promote flowering.

There are several good cultivars of flowering raspberry: 'Albus' has white flowers; 'Pink-Flowered Thimbleberry' has pink flowers.

Salix discolor

Pussy willow

BLOOM TIME: late winter

HEIGHT/WIDTH: 10'–18' × 5'–8' (3–5.5 × 1.5–2.5m)

LIGHT: full sun

ZONES: 4–8

OTHER: catkins for cutting

Pussy willow

For many, the sight of pussy willow catkins announcing winter's close are the quintessence of childhood memories. The soft gray 2-inch (5cm) -long catkins on slender red-brown stems invite you to touch them, and look supremely artistic in a vase of any kind. *Salix discolor* has leaves that are colored blue-green on the undersides.

Native to North America, this pussy willow is generally found in the wild along streambanks and in wetlands. Easy enough to trim into small tree form, the deciduous pussy willow requires full sun and ample water. Otherwise, it is not fussy, adapting to any soil and even to poor drainage, so it's the perfect plant for that swampy spot. Be warned, however, that pest insects may visit, tree diseases can take hold, and a shallow, somewhat invasive rooting system deters underplanting. Pussy willow's hardy rooting system does have one advantage: it makes this fast-growing shrub excellent for erosion control.

Salvia leucantha

Mexican bush sage

BLOOM TIME: winter–spring

HEIGHT/WIDTH: 4' × 3' (1.2 × 1m)

LIGHT: full sun

ZONES: 10–11

OTHER: attracts hummingbirds, butterflies

Mexican bush sage

All the salvias seem to beckon to hummingbirds, and connoisseurs have entire gardens consisting of nothing but different types of salvias: shrub, subshrub, perennial, and annual. Mexican bush sage has long, velvety, rose-purple or lavender-purple spikes inset with small white flowers. There are also all-purple and all-pink varieties available from some specialty nurseries.

This sturdy salvia is native to Mexico and tropical Central America, and likes to stay on the slightly dry side once established. Like most herbs, Mexican bush sage demands a very sunny site and soil with excellent drainage. While blooms usually appear on the bush from winter to spring, in some growing areas flowers are seen throughout the year. Attractive, lance-shaped, grayish green leaves have the typical sage aroma when rubbed between the fingers.

Other shrub sages include autumn sage (*S. greggi*), purple sage (*S. leucophylla*), *S. microphylla*, *S. muelleri*, and *S. regla*.

Sambucus canadensis

American elderberry

BLOOM TIME: early summer

HEIGHT/WIDTH: 10' × 10' (3 × 3m)

LIGHT: full sun

ZONES: 4–9

OTHER: attracts birds

American elderberry

If you need a fast-growing, quick-spreading shrub and like the "wild" look (or are willing to prune regularly), this native North American might work well in your large garden. A truly rampant grower, American elderberry grows best in moist, well-drained, organic soil and full sun.

Creamy white, flat-topped flower clusters, about 8 inches (20cm) wide are followed by profuse clusters of fruits that are much enjoyed by birds. The purple-black fruits of selected forms of American elderberries are good baked in pies or made into jellies, and the really ambitious gardener can make old-time elderberry wine from the purple-black fruits. Two fruiting varieties are needed for pollination. No elderberry fruit should be eaten uncooked, and red fruits are never edible.

American elderberry can be left unpruned, or it can be pruned hard if you want to cut back its growth. Prune early in spring, while the bush is still dormant, so that the new growth can bear flowers and berries.

There is also another ornamental elderberry, called golden elder (*Sambucus canadensis* 'Aurea'), with bright yellow to yellow-green foliage.

Spiraea prunifolia

Bridal wreath

BLOOM TIME: midspring

HEIGHT/WIDTH: 6' × 8' (1.8 × 2.5m)

LIGHT: full sun

ZONES: 4–10

OTHER: attracts butterflies; good cutting branches

Bridal wreath

The arching bare branches of this deciduous shrub are covered in spring with rounded bouquets of small, white, double flowers, each resembling a tiny rose. Spirea is among the most popular of garden shrubs, and bridal wreath is at the top of the popularity poll. Other than the shrub's sheer beauty, gardeners list bridal wreath's very easy culture as the chief reason to grow it—truly an amateur's delight.

Spirea will thrive almost anywhere as long as it receives moderate water. It grows best in full sun but will tolerate some light shade. In addition to its lovely spring flowers, bridal wreath features handsome dark green leaves that turn orange or red in autumn.

Prune bridal wreath just after it flowers, as blooms are carried on the previous year's wood. In China, where this spirea has been a favorite garden plant for many hundreds of years, its name translates as "smile-laugh-flowers."

Symphoricarpos orbiculatus

Coralberry

BLOOM TIME: spring

HEIGHT/WIDTH: 5' × 4' (1.5 × 1.2m)

LIGHT: full sun–medium shade

ZONES: 2–9

OTHER: attracts honeybees, birds

'Variegatus' coralberry

Wind, poor soil, sites under trees, and pollution don't faze this aptly named native North American shrub. Dense and bushy, it sports dark coral-red, inedible, pea-sized fruit along bare stems in autumn and winter. Fruit may cause stomach upset or skin irritation. Racemes consisting of many small, pinkish green flowers precede berries.

Because deciduous coralberry is so cold-tolerant and tough, and tends to naturalize via suckers, this shrub makes a great bank and waterside cover where you have only natural rainfall, and it can be grown in the North. Woolly gray-green leaves may turn orange-red in autumn. Long ago, coralberry branches were used to make baskets.

'Variegatus Coralberry' is a potentially lower-growing, sun-only version, with leaves edged and veined in yellow. Note that many catalogs list the species *Symphoricarpos orbiculatus* as *S. vulgaris*, so if you can't find coralberry under the name listed above, try the synonym.

Syringa vulgaris

Common lilac

BLOOM TIME: late spring

HEIGHT/WIDTH: 12' × 10' (3.5 × 3m)

LIGHT: full sun

ZONES: 4–8

OTHER: attracts butterflies; cut flower; forcing indoors

Common lilac

Pioneers traveling westward purchased lilacs from plant peddlers and placed these nostalgic fragrant shrubs near the entrances of their new wilderness homes. In spring, lilacs are festooned with blossoms in shades of pink, blue, purple, mauve, and white. While lilac flowers symbolize modesty, the purple ones signify the romances of youth.

Grow lilacs in rich, moist, well-drained soil that is neutral or slightly alkaline. A sunny site is perfect, but hot, humid conditions are not tolerated. Deciduous common lilac can be trimmed into tree shape. Lilacs are often bothered by lilac scale and borers.

Common lilacs have been widely hybridized, most famously by the French nurseryman Victor Lemoine, and these hybrids are known as French lilacs. The individual names seem to span not only several countries, but several continents: 'Alphonse Lavallee', 'Congo', 'Jan van Tol' 'Charles X', 'Krasavitsa Moskvy', and 'Yankee Doodle'. There are more than fifty different types of French lilacs to choose from, all quite durable. Most fragrance lovers put several in the garden, choosing cultivars that bloom at different times to extend the season.

Vaccinium corymbosum

Highbush blueberry

BLOOM TIME: spring

HEIGHT/WIDTH: 6' × 8' (1.8 × 2.5m)

LIGHT: full sun

ZONES: 3–8

OTHER: attracts birds; edible berries

Highbush blueberry

If you can grow your own blueberries, do. Not only are the shrubs highly ornamental, but the freshly picked fruits are indescribably better than any found on the grocery produce shelf. Northern highbush blueberries require true winter cold, and ripen between June and August. For mild-winter areas, the newer Southern highbush blueberries ripen in April and May. There are multiple varieties available, and the best choice will depend on your growing area and particular tastes.

Blueberry flowers are tiny and whitish; the leaves are blue-green but with beautiful autumn color variation. All blueberries require cool, moist, well-drained, acidic soil.

They thrive in a soil with a pH of between 4.5 and 5.5, so if your soil is neutral or alkaline you may need to add an acidifier or to replace the soil around the shrub altogether.

Mulch the blueberries to conserve water and to protect fine roots that stay near the soil surface. Pruning is not usually necessary, but you may want to cut out old canes to improve flowering and berry production. You'll most likely want to plant several types, both for pollination advantages and to gain a long fruiting season. Birds love blueberries, so you may have to protect the tasty fruits with netting if you want a reasonable harvest.

Viburnum carlcephalum

Fragrant snowball

BLOOM TIME: spring

HEIGHT/WIDTH: 8' × 8' (2.5 × 2.5m)

LIGHT: full sun–partial shade

ZONES: 6–8

OTHER: attracts birds

Fragrant snowball

The bright red fruit of fragrant snowball, which ripen to black, act as a veritable magnet for birds. Small, waxy, white, tubular flowers are supremely fragrant, and they burst forth from pink buds into multiple 6-inch (15cm) -wide globular clusters. Heart-shaped, toothed leaves, 5 inches (13cm) wide, turn a lively reddish purple in autumn.

Fragrant snowball is a deciduous shrub with loose, open, wide-spreading branches. It looks best planted as a specimen, as its large flower clusters and spreading habit do not mix well in a shrub border.

Viburnums, as a group, prefer moist, well-drained, slightly acidic soil, although they can tolerate some deviation. Give them regular water and fertilizer for best flowering and general vigor. Fragrant snowball sometimes has trouble getting established after transplanting, but once the roots are established it is quite low maintenance. Fruiting improves if several viburnums of the same species are planted near each other so that cross-pollination can occur.

Viburnum plicatum var. tomentosum

Doublefile viburnum

BLOOM TIME: late spring–early summer

HEIGHT/WIDTH: 10' × 10' (3 × 3m)

LIGHT: full sun–partial shade

ZONES: 4–8

OTHER: good cutting branches

'Shoshoni' doublefile viburnum

A somewhat ordinary shrub when not in bloom, this doublefile viburnum's miniature bouquets are so gorgeous that they make it worth including in the garden. Tiers of horizontal branches are laden with deliciously fragrant white flower clusters, each 4 inches (10cm) wide. The clusters are carried above the foliage on either side of the branches, giving the shrub its common name "doublefile." Following the flowers are red fruits that usually ripen to black. Leaves, a yellow-green throughout most of the growing season, turn purple-red in autumn.

Deciduous viburnums tolerate a wide range of soil conditions, although they prefer moist, well-drained, organic soil and will not tolerate drought. You'll need to prune only dead wood; prune in early summer, after flowering. Viburnums will grow in either sun or partial shade, which makes them particularly versatile shrubs.

Cultivars include 'Japanese Snowball', 'Shasta Snowball', 'Shoshoni', and 'Summer Snowflake'. There's also a compact 'Pink Snowball', with fragrant flowers that open white, then fade to a deep pink.

Viburnum trilobum

American cranberry bush

BLOOM TIME: late spring

HEIGHT/WIDTH: 12' × 12' (3.5 × 3.5m)

LIGHT: full sun–partial shade

ZONES: 2–7

OTHER: attracts birds; berries for fruit jelly

American cranberry bush

Yellow and red fruits ripen to scarlet in late summer and persist through winter, that is, if the birds leave any left-overs. You might also want to rob the shrub of its fruit to make homemade cranberry jelly.

Small, pinwheel-shaped, pleasantly scented, white flowers cover American cranberry bush with 3-inch (7cm) bouquets in spring. The shrub's maplelike leaves turn flaming red in autumn.

This deciduous eastern North American native is partic-ularly fond of moist soil rich in humus and lime. American cranberry bush does best in full sun but will tolerate some shade. Sited properly it is quite tough, although aphids may turn up for an occasional meal. Pruning isn't necessary except for the removal of dead branches. Planted in groups and allowed to grow to full size, American cranberry bushes make attractive shelter for birds.

In addition to the medium-height version, there's a smaller, 4-foot (1.2m) -tall cultivar, 'Compactum', which provides an excellent choice for small yards and patios.

Vitex agnus-castus

Chaste tree

BLOOM TIME: summer–autumn

HEIGHT/WIDTH: 10' × 12' (3 × 3.5m)

LIGHT: full sun

ZONES: 6–9

OTHER: attracts butterflies, honeybees

Chaste tree

This handsome shrub got its name from the alleged ability of its flowers and foliage to tame lust; it was widely planted in England in centuries past, presumably for this talent. Today not grown as often as it should be, this tolerant shrub is a fine addition to those often difficult seaside gardens, as well as other garden sections. Requiring little care, it prefers a medium-dry situation. Small, quite fragrant, lilac-blue flowers charm on 6- to 8-inch (15 to 20cm) panicles at branch ends, and last from late summer through autumn. Long narrow leaflets are gray-green above, gray beneath.

If you live in a warm climate, expect chaste tree to grow rapidly to 25 feet (7.5m) tall. But if you reside in a cooler climate, it may reach 10 feet (3m), and in even colder areas, grow to just 3 feet (1m) in height. This is because even relatively mild winters will cause dieback. Simply prune the dead branches to the ground; the shrub will grow back quickly, and since flowers are borne on the current season's growth, there is no loss of bloom. Protect newly planted chaste trees through their first winter by placing a cold frame over them. The cultivar 'Alba' has white flowers.

Weigela florida

Rose weigela, cardinal shrub

BLOOM TIME: late spring–early summer

HEIGHT/WIDTH: 6' × 6' (1.8 × 1.8m)

LIGHT: full sun–light shade

ZONES: 5–8

OTHER: attracts hummingbirds, birds; flowering branches good for arrangements

'Rubridor' rose weigela

Take your pick of foliage colors—red, brown-red, purple-green, green, green and white, gold, or yellow-green trimmed in red—when you go to select one or more of the modern cardinal shrub cultivars for your autumn-color garden. This practically pest-free, disease-resistant, and pollution-tolerant shrub is almost guaranteed to bring courting hummingbirds into your yard. Ample nectar comes from profuse, clustered, 1-inch (2.5cm) -wide tubular flowers colored rosy pink, crimson-red, wine red with golden centers, or dwarf lilac-purple with yellow center.

Give this shrub regular watering and well-drained soil, but it does tolerate nearly any soil type. Weigela will get quite large, so make sure to give it plenty of garden space. It grows best when sited in full sun, but will still thrive under light shade. Prune only lightly, to get rid of dead branches and to thin out canes.

Try the smaller weigela cultivars, 'Bristol Ruby' and 'Bristol Snowflake' for example, as potted plants for patio gardens. Some cultivars, such as 'Red Prince' and 'Evita', may even rebloom reliably.

Xanthorhiza simplicissima

Yellowroot

BLOOM TIME: spring

HEIGHT/WIDTH: 2'–3' × 3' (.6–1 × 1m)

LIGHT: partial shade–full shade

ZONES: 3–9

Yellowroot

This small deciduous shrub is grown primarily for its attractive 2- to 4-inch (5 to 10cm) -long, shiny green, deeply toothed leaves. The foliage turns a handsome bronze-purple in autumn, giving a long display. Inner bark is yellow, as are the roots. Small, purplish, grouped flowers are rather inconspicuous.

At an almost uniform 24 to 36 inches (60 to 90cm) tall, depending on location, a common alternate use for yellowroot is as a very cold-hardy, shrubby groundcover.

Yellowroot will spread rapidly by suckers, making large patches if given a wind-free, moist, mostly shady growing site. It is excellent for the areas beneath trees or for edging a shrub border, and can be a perfect solution for that damp, shady site where little else will grow. Often seen growing along streambanks, yellowroot is native to the wet woods of eastern North America.

1 0 0

Favorite

Garden

Wildflowers

Introducing Garden Wildflowers

If you enjoy taking walks or hikes in the woods or mountains, you've probably seen lots of different wildflowers, and likely have thought to yourself, "Oh, I wish I could grow that in my yard." Perhaps you've given in to impulse and dug up a few, wrapped them in a piece of tissue or a plastic bag, and transported them home. Even if you got them into the ground right away, however, chances are they died.

This experience does not mean that you cannot grow wildflowers in your garden. It just shows that transplanting from the wild is tricky. Plants growing in the wild are adapted to wild conditions. Their roots wend their way around natural obstacles, such as other roots, rocks, and fallen trees, and even if you succeed in the difficult task of extracting most or all of a root system without damaging it, a mature plant separated from its natural soil is probably doomed. If the soil in your garden is not similar, the plant may perish on those grounds alone. In the case of pink lady's slipper, for example, transplanting is an even greater risk, because the roots of these wild orchids depend on a delicate relationship with naturally occurring soil fungi. Also, few plants, even the most durable-looking wildflowers, appreciate being moved when they are in bloom.

To get a spectacular wildflower display at home, begin with nursery-raised plants. When purchased from reputable sources, they are young, well-rooted plants (raised from seeds, cuttings, or divisions), which transplant best. And because they have not been subjected to the stress of life in the woods or fields, their foliage is healthy and uniform. Before long, they will bring all the color and beauty to your garden that you dreamed of.

You will be delighted to discover that wildflowers tend to be tougher than other garden plants. If they hail from your area, they are already adapted to local climate and soils, as well as area pests and diseases. If they are not, well, you may still be able to grow them, as long as you can meet their needs. Prairie plants, for instance, are not just for residents of the Midwest; those in the East or West may well succeed with them, too.

Note that some wildflowers are short-lived, while others will be with you forever. Some will stay put, some will spread or self-sow. So read carefully the descriptions here, and do further research in more specialized books if you have lingering questions.

SHOPPING FOR WILDFLOWERS

As with any other new garden acquisition, you need to be a wise consumer. Will the wildflower that has captured your fancy grow in the soil or light or moisture conditions found in your yard? The ones described in the following pages were selected because they are good garden subjects; if your wildflower is not here, it may be too difficult to domesticate.

Next, be savvy about your source: you don't want to dig up plants in the wild, or buy ones that someone else has plundered. In years past, the biggest offenders were wholesale suppliers to retail nurseries, and gardeners sometimes ended up with plants that died soon after coming home. Ethical nurseries and concerned botanists spread the word to gardeners and put pressure on the culprits. These days, the chances of finding wild-collected wildflowers for sale are diminished. Be suspicious, though, if the plants look irregular or are not well rooted in their pots, or if your source cannot say whether they were nursery-propagated ("nursery grown" is not necessarily the same thing). Another clue is price. Nursery-propagated trout lilies will never sell ten for five dollars.

Fortunately, you can get garden-ready wildflowers from

well-stocked nurseries and from a number of mail-order nurseries that specialize in native plants (these are listed in the Sources section at the back of this book). If you shop locally, examine your choices carefully to make sure they look healthy and are well rooted. If you shop by mail, open the box immediately upon arrival, remove the packing material, and examine your purchases for the same qualities. Remember, in either case, that a good, strong root system is more important than a lot of green foliage and flowers on top—those will come once your wildflowers are in the ground.

What about growing wildflowers from seed? Certain ones are so quick and easy that it seems silly to buy them as potted plants—for example, columbines and California poppy. On the other hand, there are many wildflowers that are slow or difficult to sprout, such as trilliums and bloodroot. In these cases, you are better off letting the nursery do the work for you and paying the extra charge for their time and expertise. Of course, as you gain experience and confidence, you may become interested in learning all the special germinating techniques and doing this work yourself; there are a number of good books that can help guide you on this journey.

One final note: think twice before you buy a "wildflower meadow in a can." These mixes are frequently designed for quick color the first year and seldom live up to their promise in ensuing years. Others are poorly balanced, meaning that in time more vigorous plants overwhelm their fellows. Also, read the label! Many of these mixes contain aggressive grasses as filler. This does not mean you should never buy a mix. Just shop with care, looking for one that is adapted to your region or conditions (and one that contains no grass seed).

PLANTING WILDFLOWERS

Whether native or slightly out of its range, a wildflower brought into the garden appreciates a little soil preparation. If grass or weeds have been growing in the chosen spot, dig them out. Young wildflowers are no different from other young plants in that they need a chance to get started without being crowded out. Adding organic matter to the soil is often a good idea. It will increase the moisture-holding capacity of dry or sandy soil and lighten compacted or clay-laden soil.

Autumn is a good time to plant wildflowers in all but the harshest climates. The soaking rains this time of year help plant root systems get established. Wildflowers planted in the spring should be sheltered from hot sun and stiff breezes, and watered often until they are well established. In either case, mulching lightly around the base of the plant is generally wise—the mulch will help conserve water, moderate soil-temperature fluctuations, and prevent frost-heaving over the winter.

Remember as you plant to take into account your wildflower's mature size. This is listed at the top of each page (of course, actual dimensions in your garden may vary). Some wildflowers get quite large and sprawling, and while you can cut them back if need be, it is easier to site and space them well at the outset. If you are aiming for a groundcovering effect, or a carpet of color, closer spacing is, of course, the way to go. For wildflowers that self-sow or spread by creeping roots, if you have the patience, you may simply plant a few at wide intervals and let them fill in over the years.

WILDFLOWER GARDEN DESIGN

There are whole books devoted to this fascinating topic, but you should be aware of a few issues at the outset. First, bear in mind that all the flowers we now cherish in our gardens have their origins in the wild. The ones that have been most successfully domesticated are predictable in performance and uniform in appearance. This cannot always be said of wildflowers. So you need to expect variability—not just in your garden's particular conditions, but within a plant grouping, and even in individual plants. What this means in terms of garden design is a looser, informal look. If that appeals to you, you will be happy with your wildflowers.

This does not mean you have to be bound to a casual-looking garden. Many wildflowers combine very well with the most domesticated flowers—threadleaf coreopsis is wonderful among the highly mannered lavenders, for instance; Virginia bluebells are enchanting among traditional spring bulbs like daffodils; and blazing star is a good companion for some roses. Do what you like. If you need ideas, study garden-design books, browse magazine articles, or visit a botanical garden that displays wildflowers.

Another thing you should be aware of is that some wildflowers can grow aggressively. Each autumn, unless you intervene and deadhead beforehand, they will shed their seeds, and the following spring you will have many more than you started with, sometimes in unexpected nooks and crannies. Or your wildflowers may spread by underground runners, poking up volunteers nearby as well as many feet away. Plan for this tendency and you will end up pleased with great swaths of foliage and carpets of color, or with plants you enjoy digging up and giving away or selling. The alternative is to fight a constant battle, which takes the joy out of gardening.

The unpredictable nature of wildflowers also means that your garden will look different from one year to the next. One summer the bachelor's buttons or California poppies, annuals that often self-sow, will be spectacular; the next year they may not return in glory, but the biennial mulleins and evening primroses will have come into their own.

CARING FOR WILDFLOWERS

Don't assume that just because it's a wild species a wildflower doesn't need any care. Nurture the seedlings just as you would with any prized garden plants. Water them when they need it. And keep their sites well weeded—just a month or two of neglect, and they may get swallowed up by a jungle of aggressive grasses and invasive weeds. Generally, wildflowers do not need to be fertilized, however. Fertilizer tends to cause lush vegetative growth at the expense of flowers.

As the years go by, your wildflowers will require less and less care. The effort you put into their debut in your garden will be repaid in lovely flowering plants, perhaps now spread out in drifts like you originally imagined. If you're like me, you'll be peering over them carefully to monitor their progress. You may be gratified to notice details about your garden-grown wildflowers that you never noticed in the woods or mountain meadows, where you were just passing through.

Achillea millefolium

Yarrow

BLOOM TIME: summer

HEIGHT/WIDTH: 1'–3' × 1' (30–90cm × 30cm)

LIGHT: full sun

ZONES: 4–8

Yarrow

Too often maligned as a weed, common yarrow has in recent times been rediscovered by horticulturists who admired its good qualities and made selections that broadened the color choices. The plant is a trooper, blooming all summer, even in hot and dry ones, and weathering cold winters. If yarrow is given the full sun and well-drained soil that it favors, it becomes invasive and/or self-sows in unexpected places unless you keep after it — or unless you make sure to plant it in a spot where you are happy to see it naturalize.

The species has flat white flower heads and aromatic, finely dissected gray-green leaves, making it an agreeable companion to other herbs or a filler among colorful sun-loving perennials and annuals. You can grow a colorful cultivar, such as the vibrant cherry red 'Cerise Queen', the deep pink 'Rosea', or a host of other possibilities, including the obvious — sowing a mix (available from many seed companies). All of these are great for bouquets, fresh or dried, thanks to their erect stems and ability to hold their color well past harvest.

Allium cernuum

Nodding onion

BLOOM TIME: summer

HEIGHT/WIDTH: 8"–2' × 6" (20–60cm × 15cm)

LIGHT: full sun

ZONES: 4–8

Nodding onion

In recent years, species onions have come into vogue as ornamental plants. These are related to the ones you grow in the vegetable garden, but some are smaller and less pungent, and have downright pretty, lilylike flowers. And they are simple to grow, particularly when you are not as concerned about developing perfect roots. A sunny setting in decent soil is all they ask. One of the best is a native North American plant called nodding onion.

As the name says, it has flower heads that bend over modestly at the top. They are a loose mop of soft pink,

attractive as solo performers here and there in a rock garden but also nice for mingling with pastel perennials or old-fashioned roses. A few variations are to be found at specialty nurseries and bulb suppliers, among them the soft white *A. cernuum* 'Album'.

Just one caveat: like its kin, this onion sheds its seeds liberally each autumn, leading to great numbers of volunteers the following spring. To discourage such behavior, simply remove (deadhead) the spent blossoms before they go to seed.

Amsonia tabernaemontana

Bluestar

BLOOM TIME: spring–early summer

HEIGHT/WIDTH: 2'–3' × 2'–3' (60–90cm × 60–90cm)

LIGHT: full sun–partial shade

ZONES: 3–9

Bluestar

It's hard to find true-blue flowers, in the wild or in fancy garden settings (rose breeders have still had no luck producing a blue rose, for instance). But here is the genuine article. Bluestar's blossoms are about a half-inch across and star-shaped, and appear in domed clusters at the tops of the stems. The tidy foliage, between 3 inches (7cm) and 6 inches (15cm) long, is narrow and willowy and encircles the stems.

Despite these seemingly delicate qualities, the plant is strong and tough, standing erect and thriving in moderately fertile soil. (It can be grown in some shade and in richer soil but will become leggy and need to be trimmed back

occasionally to keep growth dense.) Bluestar is also usually free of disease and pest problems. Autumn foliage is a real plus: instead of fading away, the leaves turn a vibrant shade of gold that looks wonderful in the company of autumn bloomers like asters and mums.

Bluestar is probably best grown in groups or sweeps, so its fine texture won't be lost and the wonderful shade of blue has a chance to really stand out. It's also a striking companion for orange- or red-flowered deciduous azaleas, which generally bloom at the same time.

Anaphalis margaritacea

Pearly everlasting

BLOOM TIME: late summer

HEIGHT/WIDTH: 1'–3' × 1'–2' (30–90cm × 30–60cm)

LIGHT: full sun

ZONES: 3–8

Pearly everlasting

The name of this sturdy plant is ideal: the white flower heads have a pearly hue (and, one could say of the individual flowers, a pearly shape), and they preserve so well that they are highly esteemed by dried flower arrangers and wreath-makers. If you wish to grow everlastings and want guaranteed success, start here. Note that the foliage is silvery, and the sturdy yet flexible stems are woolly and white, so you can feature the entire plant in your craft projects. Begin harvesting shortly after the flowers appear.

A true drought-buster that can become invasive, pearly everlasting would be a good candidate for a spot that you have otherwise given up on as productive garden space, such as a curb strip or side yard. Its neutral appearance also makes it a nice backdrop or foil for more vivid flowers, especially pink or purple ones.

Note that this is a perennial plant, usually sold as seed (it grows quickly). Male and female flowers appear on separate plants; but if you sow the better part of a packet, you'll have plenty of both, and the differences between the two will strike you as minor.

Anemone pulsatilla

(Pulsatilla vulgaris)

Pasque-flower

BLOOM TIME: spring

HEIGHT/WIDTH: 8"–10" × 6"–9" (20–25cm × 15–23cm)

LIGHT: full sun

ZONES: 3–7

Pasque-flower

Pasque-flower is one of the earliest perennials to bloom, and what a welcome sight it is. Furry buds spring open to display big yet delicate blooms in softest purple, with golden stamens in the center. (A selection called 'Budapest' has pale blue flowers.) The stems are also furry. When the entire plant is backlit by the pale sunlight of early spring, the sight is truly enchanting.

The common name refers to the fact that these blooms often appear right around the Easter and Passover holidays (in fact, "pasque" comes from the Hebrew word "pesakh," which means "a passing over"). When the flowers fade, puffs of similar-hued silky plumes take over and hang on for many weeks. Sometimes, blooming flowers and these graceful plumes are on the same plant at the same time—an intriguing sight. The leaves, by the way, are also attractive; they are reminiscent of small, furry carrot foliage.

In the wild, this plant favors dry soil that drains well, such as banks, roadsides, and ridges, so it is a natural for a dry rock garden, where it will establish itself and carry on for many years. Some gardeners also have had good luck growing it, because of its small stature, at the front of a flower border or along a path.

Anemonella thalictroides

Rue anemone

BLOOM TIME: spring

HEIGHT/WIDTH: 6"–10" × 4"–6" (15–25cm × 10–15cm)

LIGHT: partial shade

ZONES: 5–8

Rue anemone

Many spring wildflowers have a brief show; this one keeps on blooming for up to six weeks. If you have a semishady, somewhat sheltered area and are seeking a delicately beautiful groundcover that you can get a surprising amount of mileage out of, look no further. All rue anemone requires is organically rich soil. It grows from a tuberous root, best planted in autumn when you're doing your bulb plantings.

The flowers are sweet little things, with frail petals and a tiny spray of jaunty stamens. They are usually creamy white, but occasionally soft pink. If you especially like the pink, you might want to seek out the selection 'Schoaf's Double Pink'.

Rue anemone foliage is equally dainty. As the *"thalictroides"* part of the botanical name suggests, it resembles that of meadow rue (*Thalictrum*), just, of course, much smaller and shorter. It precedes the blooms and remains for a while after they pass, but eventually, long about midsummer, the plant goes dormant.

Aquilegia canadensis

Columbine

BLOOM TIME: spring–early summer

HEIGHT/WIDTH: 1'–3' × 1'–2' (30–90cm × 30–60cm)

LIGHT: full sun–partial shade

ZONES: 3–9

Columbine

If you are new to wildflower gardening, and want sure success, grow this charmer. Columbine takes quickly and easily to garden conditions and has unusually pretty flowers, and its handsome, lacy foliage is an asset long after blooming is over.

The nodding, upside-down blossoms make it worth getting down on your hands and knees for a closer look. Generally, the spurred outer petals are red and the fluted inner ones are bright yellow. Golden-tipped stamens hang down like bell clappers. Nectar is located in the spurs, and hummingbirds, with their long tongues, will sometimes visit. Bees cannot reach in that far, but have been observed landing on top and poking a hole in to feed.

If you enjoy this species, wonderful variations await you. Another wild species carried by some seed companies is the state flower of Colorado, *A. caerulea*, with blue and white flowers. And there are many larger-flowered garden hybrids, some solid colors, many bicolors, and some with fluffy "double" forms.

Columbine's only flaw is that its lacy foliage is prone to leaf miners, which weave their trails inside the leaves until little green is left. The flowers keep on blooming, though, seemingly unaffected. Remove all affected foliage, or wait until flowering is over and cut the entire plant down. A fresh flush of new foliage will appear shortly after.

Arctostaphylos uva-ursi

Bearberry, kinnikinick

BLOOM TIME: spring

HEIGHT/WIDTH: 6" × 8"–20" (15cm × 20–51cm)

LIGHT: full sun–partial shade

ZONES: 2–7

'Massachusetts' bearberry

This trailing plant may be one of nature's favorite ground-covers—and, if you have the right conditions in your yard, it could become one of yours. In spring, it sports tiny, nodding pinkish or white bells (if you definitely want pink blooms, plant its near its cousin, *A. nevadensis*). A cultivar, 'Massachusetts', flowers more heavily and has denser, darker foliage than the species. From spring through summer, the neat little glossy green leaves form a dense mat. In autumn, the bright red berries appear and the foliage often acquires a bronze hue. The berries are too mealy to be tasty to people and most birds, so the autumn show—which persists into early winter in milder areas—looks downright Christmassy (though picked sprigs, unfortunately, shrivel and wilt indoors).

Bearberry is related to heaths and heathers and, like those stalwarts, tolerates bitterly cold winters and dry summers. It performs best in sunny spots in acidic soil. Boggy conditions lead to its demise—instead, plant it in well-drained, even sandy, soil. This combination of requirements, plus its tough constitution, means bearberry might be just the plant for an otherwise inhospitable bank or streetside area—over the years, it will carpet an increasingly large area. Bearberry will also do well under the high shade of evergreens, where few other plants grow.

Argemone mexicana

✿

Prickly poppy

BLOOM TIME: spring–autumn

HEIGHT/WIDTH: 1'–3' × 1'–2' (30–90cm × 30–60cm)

LIGHT: full sun

ZONES: 7–9

✿

Prickly poppy

Sure, it's got bristly stems, spiny-edged leaves that remind you of thistles, and prickly seed capsules, but, ah, those gorgeous golden flowers! And they literally cover the plant from spring to first frost—an irresistible performance.

A wild relative of the more familiar garden Oriental poppies, this species has the same sort of flower: large, crinkly petals centered by a fluffy boss of stamens. Prickly poppy is a bit of a novelty because it is yellow through and through (or, sometimes, orange). A near relative is the white-flowered, yellow-centered *A. platyceras*. These plants are not long-lived, alas, but they do self-sow well. They look best in a wild garden, perhaps with some grasses (they'll hold their own in the company of aggressive growers). For a patch of glowing color, sow them with California poppy.

Native to dry grasslands and desert areas, prickly poppies are just as tough and drought-tolerant as you might expect. Once a colony gets established, they are practically no-maintenance. Just remember that good drainage is a must.

Arisaema triphyllum

Jack-in-the-pulpit

BLOOM TIME: spring

HEIGHT/WIDTH: 2'–3' × 1' (60–90cm × 30cm)

LIGHT: partial–full shade

ZONES: 4–8

Jack-in-the-pulpit

Arguably not an especially beautiful wildflower, at least not in the traditional sense, this woodland North American native has an eccentrically elegant look. Each plant grows two stalks; one bears a pair of leaf-topped stems, the other bears the odd-looking flowering structure. A green-and-maroon-striped hood that curves over at the top, the "pulpit" shields "Jack," a slender, dark red-brown and white spadix. The true flowers lurk at the bottom of the spadix and are very tiny. Through it all, the broad leaves, borne in leaflets of three, form a canopy over the show.

In autumn, if the plant is growing in rich, moist soil and prospering, a cluster of oval red berries appears, sheathed in a papery cylinder. They are not edible. Unless you plan to collect one and sow the seed, however, for the good of the plants long-term vigor, you should remove the berries.

Those gardeners with woodland conditions will find Jack-in-the-pulpit easy to grow. Moist soil is essential. The plant is tedious to grow from seed, taking up to four years to reach blooming size. Better to start with a seedling that has already developed its corm (a bulblike root).

You will be intrigued to learn that this plant's Asian relatives are now making it into specialty catalogs. Some have textured or marbled foliage and stems, dramatic colors, and a few have orange autumn berries.

Asarum canadense

Wild ginger

BLOOM TIME: spring

HEIGHT/WIDTH: 4"–12" × 4"–6" (10–30cm × 10–15cm)

LIGHT: shade

ZONES: 5–8

Wild ginger

If your shady garden needs a dense, dependable ground-cover, look no further. The lustrous green, heart-shaped leaves of wild ginger are handsome, and over the years the plant forms broad, thick patches. The leaves look like they should be evergreen, but they are not; however, the plants return with gusto each spring. The only threat to their well-being is slugs, so be on the lookout.

Wild ginger's flowers are not a reason to grow the plant, for they are hidden under the leaf cover at the base; but they are fascinating. They are tiny things, reddish inside, gray-green outside; one botanist aptly likened them to "little brown stone crocks." They last for many weeks, and when they pass, the seeds are carried off by small creatures.

The plant gets its name from its root, which has an appealing, gingerlike scent and flavor. Native Americans used it in cooking and medicinally. It is not related to commercial ginger root.

Asclepias tuberosa

Butterfly weed

BLOOM TIME: summer

HEIGHT/WIDTH: 1'–3' × 1'–2' (30–90cm × 30–60cm)

LIGHT: full sun–partial shade

ZONES: 3–9

Butterfly weed

An orange this vivid is not often seen in gardens. Adventurous garden colorists, though, absolutely should not be without butterfly weed. It will set your summer borders afire. Pair it with the long-blooming golden daylily 'Stella d'Oro' or yellow coreopsis or brilliant purple blooms such as veronica. If you want its glow, but not as the center of attention, grow it with white or blue flowers. Butterfly weed is also excellent in a vase, with erect stems and durable blossoms that last a week or more.

Humans aren't the only ones drawn to this wildflower. Monarch and swallowtail butterflies, bumblebees, and even hummingbirds hover around it. Part of the satisfaction of growing butterfly weed is knowing that your garden welcomes such visitors.

A drought-tolerant plant, butterfly weed develops a thick taproot, so put it where you want it to stay. It survives best on benign neglect; don't coddle it with rich soil, mulch, extra water, or fertilizer. Once it is several years old, you may mow it down after it blooms to inspire a second round of blooms in late summer or early autumn.

Aster nova-angliae

New England aster, Michaelmas daisy

BLOOM TIME: late summer–autumn

HEIGHT/WIDTH: 3'–4' × 2'–3' (90cm–1.2m × 60–90cm)

LIGHT: full sun

ZONES: 4–8

New England aster

Here's a wildflower that had to travel overseas, and back, before Americans would take it seriously as a garden plant. It has many natural virtues, including abundant color for many weeks late in the season, robust growth, and reliable winter-hardiness. The species is a hearty plant covered with clouds of small, light purple daisies. European plant breeders renamed this wildflower Michaelmas daisy (because it blooms around that autumn holiday), and worked with it and some closely related varieties to create a range of fabulous cultivars. Among their triumphs is the popular, large-flowered, electric pink 'Alma Potschke'. A more recent introduction is the mounding, bloom-laden 'Purple Dome'.

As they grow, New England asters form clumps, develop woody stems, and may require staking to support upright growth. The leaves are lance-shaped, and the lower ones tend to drop, leaving the plants bare-kneed (if this bothers you, plant something shorter in front of them).

Balsamorhiza sagittata

Arrowleaf balsamroot

BLOOM TIME: spring

HEIGHT/WIDTH: 1'–3' × 1'–2' (30–90cm × 30–60cm)

LIGHT: full sun

ZONES: 4–7

Arrowleaf balsamroot

If you live in the Mountain West, or have traveled there, perhaps you've admired this bright, daisylike wildflower. It puts on quite a show for many weeks in spring, sporting large, cheerful yellow, 2- to 4-inch (5 to 10cm) flowers that surge above big, arrowhead-shaped leaves.

To grow it in your garden, you need fertile, well-drained soil that is slightly alkaline, like the hillsides from which it comes. If you start from seed, you also need patience; arrowleaf balsamroot takes a few years to reach blooming size. By that time, it will have developed a strong, deep root system that ensures its long-term survival. Just be sure to sow it where you want it to stay, because it is a notoriously poor transplanter.

This is not a plant that needs coddling. Your best bet is to mimic the conditions it enjoys in nature: keep it watered in the spring if rainfall seems sparse, then let it dry out as summer hits its stride.

Baptisia australis

False blue indigo

BLOOM TIME: early summer

HEIGHT/WIDTH: 3'–6' × 3' (90cm–1.8m × 90cm)

LIGHT: full sun–partial shade

ZONES: 3–9

False blue indigo

A picture in blue, this shrubby perennial wildflower has blue-green foliage and 10-inch (25cm) spikes of lavender-blue flowers that stay in bloom for up to a month. It is a member of the pea family, which also includes sweet peas and lupines, and you can easily see the resemblance both in the leaflets and in the classic flower form.

Simple to grow, false blue indigo requires only well-drained soil. As in its wild habitat, it does fine in poor to average soil. Just be sure to place it where you want it to stay, because it forms a deep taproot that makes later transplanting an ordeal. It is disease- and pest-free. False blue indigo is at home in a casual, cottage garden setting, or you could devote a slope or curbside planting to it.

When the flowers fade, they are replaced by brown, pendulous pods that some people enjoy harvesting for dried-flower arrangements or as a rattling toy for a child or cat. But if you cut off the blooms before they go to seed, you can also coax the plant into blooming longer.

Baptisia pendula

White indigo

BLOOM TIME: spring

HEIGHT/WIDTH: 2'–4' × 2'–3' (60cm–1.2m × 60–90cm)

LIGHT: full sun–partial shade

ZONES: 5–9

White indigo

Tall and regal, white indigo is certain to elicit admiration from everyone who visits your garden. It begins as a modest clump of sage green foliage; in late spring, once it is established, expect 3- to 4-foot panicles of soft white, pealike flowers. The stems (and older flower buds) are charcoal gray, making a dramatic contrast with the purity of the flowers. It's quite a sight.

White indigo is also a cinch to grow. Average soil in sun or a bit of shade suits it just fine. Give it extra water and perhaps some mulch the first year or two, and it will form a large, deep root system that will stand it in good stead through future periods of drought. Thereafter, white indigo will take care of itself and bloom more profusely with each passing year.

Because of its stature and somewhat shrubby habit, white indigo is a good choice for the back of a flower border. It is equally at home among roses and cottage garden flowers, and other wildflowers. A natural combination is interplanting it with false blue indigo (*Baptisia australis*).

Belamcanda chinensis

Blackberry lily

BLOOM TIME: midsummer

HEIGHT/WIDTH: 1'–3' × 8"–12" (30–90cm × 20–30cm)

LIGHT: full sun

ZONES: 5–10

Blackberry lily

This unusual, easygoing plant gets its name not from its flower, but from the contents of its autumn pod, which splits open to reveal a seed cluster that looks just like a ripe, succulent blackberry. Unfortunately, it doesn't taste anything like one and in fact is rarely nibbled on by any creature. Some gardeners enjoy harvesting the "berries" to include in wreaths or dried-flower arrangements.

The 2- to 3-inch, star-shaped flower that precedes this interesting seedpod stands out in the garden, bright orange with reddish-purple speckles (some books and catalogs therefore call it the leopard lily). The plant forms clumps and produces long, flat leaves that look like iris foliage (it is actually in the iris, not the lily, family). Like irises, blackberry lily grows from a rhizome that should be planted shallowly and divided every few years to keep the show going.

Blackberry lily asks only for adequate sun and average soil. Those needs met, you can look forward to it providing two seasons of intrigue.

Apparently it came over with early American colonists and eventually escaped the bounds of their gardens. It has jumped back over the garden fence in the past decade or so and is not hard to find in well-stocked garden centers and nursery catalogs.

Boltonia asteroides

Boltonia

BLOOM TIME: late summer–autumn

HEIGHT/WIDTH: 4'–6' × 2'–4' (1.2–1.8m × 60cm–1.2m)

LIGHT: full sun

ZONES: 4–9

'Snowbank' boltonia

An exuberant plant, boltonia has become the darling of gardeners who want weeks of showy color in late summer and autumn. It literally billows with hundreds of small 1-inch (2.5cm) daisies, white with yellow centers, that look perky all day and really light up the garden in the evening hours. They are carried on strong stems on a casual mound of thin, willowy, gray-green foliage. The plant can get quite large, to 6 feet (1.8m) tall, and may require staking to keep it from flopping over. You can also seek out the more modest-size cultivars. The popular 'Snowbank' grows to between 3 and 4 feet (90cm–1.2m). There is also a pink-flowered one of about the same size called 'Pink Beauty'.

An easy plant to grow, boltonia asks only for plenty of sun. If the soil is naturally moist and fertile, the plant will prosper for years with little attention from you. Even in drier soils, it does well, though it may not grow as tall or as lushly. Grow it with other daisylike wildflowers—it looks wonderful among asters, both the species ones and the cultivated varieties. Another idea is interplanting boltonia with goldenrod so that the golden spikes shoot up and around boltonia's more mounding shape.

Callirhoe involucrata

Wine cups

BLOOM TIME: spring–summer

HEIGHT/WIDTH: 8"–12" × 1'–3' (20–30cm × 30–90cm)

LIGHT: full sun

ZONES: 4–8

Wine cups

Among the many plants often recommended for dry, sunny spots in poor to average soil, including boring junipers and overused dusty millers and artemisias, wine cups is rarely mentioned. Perhaps this is because this native of the Midwestern prairies hasn't been sufficiently publicized. Too bad. It's a terrific choice for such trying conditions, bringing stunning color and plenty of it. Once it's established, its deep taproot prohibits transplanting but assures long-term survival, especially during periods of drought or neglect.

Wine cups is aptly named. The 2-inch (5cm), cup-shaped blooms are somewhat variable, but generally a lovely, vivid magenta—zinfandel red, you might say—with a contrasting white center. The sprawling plant generates loads of these in late spring, and continues to pump them out all summer long, stopping only when frost hits. Now your dry bank, curb strip, or front walk can be full of color.

You also can invite this appealing plant into the garden proper, bearing in mind its low, spreading growth habit. It's pretty with lamb's ears (if you're the sort of gardener who always clips off the rosy flower stalks, you may wish to leave them for contrast, both in form and color). Blue flowers with similarly shaped blooms also make nice companions; try it with mounding *Campanula carpatica* or at the feet of blue flax.

Calochortus spp.

Mariposa lily

BLOOM TIME: late spring–early summer

HEIGHT/WIDTH: 1'–2' × 1' (30–60cm × 30cm)

LIGHT: full sun–partial shade

ZONES: 5–9

Mariposa lily

Visitors to the dry mountains and meadows of western North America in late spring never fail to be captivated by these beautiful wildflowers. With their large, goblet-shaped blooms, they superficially resemble poppies, though they are more closely related to tulips. The color of the silky petals varies from one species to the next: *C. clavatus* has yellow flowers with chocolate markings, the flowers of *C. catalinae* are porcelain white–pink, those of *C. nitidis* are creamy white, *C. splendens* is lavender, and the highly variable *C. venustus* may be anywhere from creamy white to dark red, with contrasting blotches and eye. The name

"mariposa" means "butterfly" in Spanish, a likeness no one who has seen a patch in full bloom can deny.

Mariposa lilies have erect branching stems and thin grassy leaves. They grow very slowly from seed, eventually forming a small bulb (which, by the way, is edible). They do go dormant in midsummer, and should be allowed to dry out then, as they would in nature. They tend to bloom fabulously one year and then take a year or two off to regroup. They need conditions similar to what they favor in the wild, and, yes, they require patience. But once established, they take care of themselves, and win your heart all over again.

Caltha palustris

Marsh marigold

BLOOM TIME: spring

HEIGHT/WIDTH: 12"–18" × 9"–12" (30–45cm × 23–30cm)

LIGHT: full sun–partial shade

ZONES: 4–10

Marsh marigold

This sunny-flowered buttercup relative is ideal for wet sites. If you grow it in damp garden soil, it tends to have a short but exuberant period of glory each spring. Consider interplanting it among, or providing a backdrop for, bulbs that don't mind similar conditions, like camas or winter aconite.

After the flowers finally go by, if your soil begins to dry out as summer advances, the foliage of marsh marigold gradually dies down and fades from view and the plant goes dormant (not unlike the behavior of your bulbs, come to think of it). If this leaves you with a bare area, be sure to plant marsh marigold in the company of other bog-loving plants that continue the show, like cardinal flower or irises.

Gardeners with water gardens also value this plant. It will wade right into the shallow water near the edge (up to 6 feet [1.8m] deep). Since it makes runners, the plant is best confined to a large pot. After the flowers fade, the succulent, cabbagelike leaves will remain, particularly if you keep after it with fertilizer.

Marsh marigold flowers really are sensational. They are bright, about 2 inches (5cm) across, and carried in clusters. A cultivar, 'Plena', has double flowers.

Camassia spp.

Camas

BLOOM TIME: early summer

HEIGHT/WIDTH: 1'–2' × 8"–12" (30–60cm × 20–30cm)

LIGHT: full sun

ZONES: 3–8

Camas

Like the buffalo, this gorgeous plant used to be plentiful in the great meadows of the West and its decline can be blamed on the encroachment of European settlers. For centuries, Native American tribes, among them the Bannocks and the Nez Perce, valued camas as a food plant (the small onionlike bulb is edible, raw or roasted) and even fought battles to retain their claims. To this day, springtime visitors to central California, Washington, Idaho, and Utah are awestruck when they happen upon remaining drifts in full bloom, which have been likened to lakes of clear blue water.

The good news is that camas is available to gardeners (generally from nurseries in the West but also from specialty bulb catalogs) and easy to grow. As with other bulbs, you should plant them in autumn; camas is also easy to grow from spring-sown seed. In any case, the plants may not bloom their first year, but the flowers are worth waiting for. Tall spikes bear starry, long-lasting blooms. *C. quamash* (*C. esculenta*) is a brilliant blue; *C. cusickii* is light blue; and *C. leichtlinii* ssp. *suksdorfi* 'Alba' is white. They make a fascinating addition to your bulb beds, and are stunning planted among traditional favorites like late-blooming tulips. To emulate their glory in the wild, however, you'll need a damp location in full sun, such as the edge of a pond or a semiwild wet area.

Castilleja spp.

Indian paintbrush

BLOOM TIME: summer

HEIGHT/WIDTH: 1'–2' × 8"–12" (30–60cm × 20–30cm)

LIGHT: full sun

ZONES: 4–9

Indian paintbrush

You may have heard this famous Native American legend. A young boy finds he has a talent for painting but he is continually frustrated in his wish to paint the colors of the sunset, until one night he is directed by a dream-vision to take a canvas up to a nearby hillside. There, he finds fiery red and orange brushes, paints quickly while the light fades, and returns in triumph to his village. In the morning, the hills are abloom with the "paintbrushes" he left behind.

Gardeners often find their pursuit of the Indian paintbrush equally frustrating. The seeds germinate very slowly; they can take at least a year to sprout. Transplants are slow to get established, or don't make it. It turns out that this wildflower's roots have suckers on them that (partially) parasitize the root systems of other plants. Obviously, this characteristic is a tricky situation to re-create at home, though some gardeners have had spectacular success. Your best bet is to start with young plants and tuck them in with companions that they might have had in the wild—other wildflowers, grasses, sages.

The "paintbrush" flowers are technically bracts, and the color varies depending on the species and, sometimes, the setting. *C. linariaefolia* is orange-red; *C. angustifolia* is soft pink; *C. coccinea, C. miniata,* and *C. hispida* are scarlet, and *C. unakaschcensis* is yellow.

Centaurea cyanus

Bachelor's button, cornflower

BLOOM TIME: summer

HEIGHT/WIDTH: 1'–3' × 4"–8" (30–90cm × 10–20cm)

LIGHT: full sun

ZONES: annual, all zones

Bachelor's button

Some gardeners grow this beauty solo, but perhaps its best and most popular use is as an ingredient in a mixed wildflower planting. (This is why it is often a component in wildflower meadow mixes. For more information on those, please refer to page 471.) It is also a pretty candidate for a cottage garden scheme. Bachelor's button comes in various shades of blue and purple as well as pink and white. The plants bloom eagerly and dependably for the better part of the summer.

It is an easygoing annual plant, not particular about soil or water, though extremes of any kind may do it in. Sow it in full sun, lightly covered (and expect its progeny to self-sow over the ensuing years). If you live in a mild climate, try autumn sowing for a late winter or early spring show; everyone else should sow in spring. It tolerates autumn frosts with admirable perkiness.

The ability of bachelor's button to keep its bright color in the garden holds over in harvest. It is wonderful in casual bouquets, thanks also to its wiry stems. The petals are slow to shatter and are more likely to simply, finally, fade. And as the name suggests, it certainly makes an ideal boutonniere. Wreath-makers and dried-flower arrangers also cherish the blooms because they provide a welcome spot of bright color.

Chasmanthium latifolium

Sea oats

BLOOM TIME: midsummer

HEIGHT/WIDTH: 3'–4' × 2' (1–1.2m × 60cm)

LIGHT: full sun–partial shade

ZONES: 4–9

Sea oats

Ornamental grasses have been all the rage in naturalistic gardens in recent years. While some are admittedly pretty fabulous of leaf or plume, nothing quite matches the shimmering beauty of this native, clump-forming grass.

The bladelike foliage is attractive, particularly early in the season when it has a bluish purple hue. But the "flower" panicles, composed of little spikelets, are the real draw. These come out after summer is well under way, but linger into autumn. As the weather cools, they change from green to maroon to copper before drying out to brown. At any time, they enchant the eye and ear as they rattle and flitter in the breeze. They also make a wonderful contribution to flower arrangements, whether you pick them green or in their autumn splendor. (Do remove them if you don't want the plant to self-sow.)

The fact that this grass tolerates shade well suggests nontraditional uses. It offers a quick screen for the dying-down foliage of spring bulbs, for instance. It would be a novel choice for a solo planting in a container, sited on a deck or porch where no visitor could miss its charms. But perhaps it will get the most attention when you mass it along a fence, walkway, or foundation.

Chelone lyonii

Turtlehead

BLOOM TIME: late summer

HEIGHT/WIDTH: 2'–4' × 1'–2' (60cm–1.2m × 30–60cm)

LIGHT: full sun–partial shade

ZONES: 5–7

Turtlehead

In late summer, there's not much going on in the semishady garden. These lusty pink to reddish purple blooms, then, are a welcome sight. They look somewhat like snapdragons, to which they are distantly related. To say the puffy, lipped flowers resemble the head of a turtle, however, is a bit of a stretch.

Like its namesake, though, turtlehead loves wet places. This plant will thrive in shallow water, a low, muddy spot, or naturally moist soil with the additional insurance of a mulch laid at the plant's base. The exposure is less critical. When it is happy, it will increase quickly. So if you have a good spot, there's no need to start with a lot of plants.

As far as companions go, ferns are always a safe bet. Their dark foliage will set off the colorful flowers to good advantage. If you want to dress up your damp site with additional color, though, consider great blue lobelia or pink obedient plant.

Chrysanthemum leucanthemum

Oxeye daisy

BLOOM TIME: summer

HEIGHT/WIDTH: 1'–3' × 8"–15" (30–90cm × 20–38cm)

LIGHT: full sun

ZONES: 3–9

Oxeye daisy

There are plenty of fancier, cultivated daisies, but this old faithful of field and meadow has enduring appeal. Unlike some other daisies, it carries its blooms on sturdy, unbranched stems—this quality, plus its tendency to bloom profusely, makes it a constant supply of cheery bouquets.

As you might expect, oxeye daisy is no trouble to grow, tolerating all sorts of soils and less than full sun if need be. Its only flaw is its enthusiasm for life; it spreads by rootstock as well as seed. One rhizome can pump out quite a few new little rosettes each season. And one flower head (the center, yellow part, which is where the true, minute flowers reside) can generate upward of three hundred seeds—multiply that by the number of flowers on a single plant, and you see the problem! So be sure to remove fading flowers promptly, and dig under unwanted seedlings. Unless, of course, you want an impromptu meadow in your yard or curb strip.

Occasionally, you will observe a frothy mass along some of the stems. This is the work of the spittlebug, who can suck enough fluid out of the stems to make them bend or become deformed. If this becomes a problem, simply spray it off the stem with the hose or wipe it off with your gloves.

Chrysogonum virginianum

Goldenstar

BLOOM TIME: summer

HEIGHT/WIDTH: 4"–12" × 1'–2' (10–30cm × 30–60cm)

LIGHT: full sun–partial shade

ZONES: 5–9

Goldenstar

For a spot that needs brightening, little goldenstar is unbeatable. A low, spreading (but not aggressive) plant, it has dark green leaves and bears marvelous, glowing yellow, 1½-inch (4cm) daisylike blooms on short stalks. If you grow it in soil that is neither boggy nor dry, it will bloom generously, perhaps even for the whole summer—a claim few other traditional groundcovers can rival.

This wildflower is native to the area from the Appalachians down south to Florida, and will surely thrive in gardens in that part of the country. But goldenstar also does just fine further north, provided you give it a good winter mulch.

Mass plantings, as along a woodland walkway or bordering a line of shrubs, always look great and call attention to the vivacious though small flowers. But you can successfully combine goldenstar with other perennial wildflowers—try it with alumroot, columbine, or Virginia bluebells.

Cimicifuga racemosa

Bugbane

BLOOM TIME: midsummer

HEIGHT/WIDTH: 3'–6' × 3' (1–1.8m × 1m)

LIGHT: full sun–partial shade

ZONES: 3–8

Bugbane

This is a tall, full plant, not for every garden, but spectacular in the right setting. It is best employed in back of shorter plants, where its imposing presence enhances rather than overwhelms; some gardeners like to place it in the middle of an "island bed," where it can be admired from all sides. It is also a bold choice for an area of filtered shade.

Dark green, much-divided foliage creates a bushlike form up to about 3 feet (90m) tall and wide. The creamy white flower plumes, 6 inches (15cm) or more long, rise up an additional 2 or 3 feet (60 to 90cm) above the foliage and

are a sight to behold: they are branched, rather than individual spires, so the effect is like candelabras. Bugbane puts on a regal show for several weeks in midsummer, and never needs propping up. Some nurseries don't mention the scent, while others tell you it's "rank," but the truth is that it's not very obtrusive.

Bugbane is long-lived and trouble-free, unfussy about soil and asking only for sufficient moisture. In hot climates, or if you want extra drama from those remarkable flower plumes, grow it in partial shade.

Coreopsis verticillata

Threadleaf coreopsis

BLOOM TIME: summer

HEIGHT/WIDTH: 1'–3' × 2'–3' (30–90cm × 60–90cm)

LIGHT: full sun

ZONES: 5–9

Threadleaf coreopsis

Unlike some other wildflowers, this one looks like a cultivated flower already, without any intervention from plant hybridizers. Its naturally sunny yellow blooms generally cover the plant for most, if not all, of the summer months.

Threadleaf coreopsis brings with it a natural toughness, too. It thrives in a wide range of soils, and adapts easily to drought once established. It does best in full sun.

One unique feature of this particular species—and the reason for its common name—is its thin, needlelike leaves.

The result is an airy plant that weaves its way among taller or more substantial perennials with ease and grace. Because the flowers of threadleaf coreopsis are not large and bold, they flatter their companions while providing dependable color.

If you want a softer hue, look for the cultivar 'Moonbeam', which billows with lovely, pale yellow flowers.

Cornus canadensis

Bunchberry

BLOOM TIME: spring

HEIGHT/WIDTH: 3"–9" (7–23cm)/spreading habit

LIGHT: shade

ZONES: 2–6

Bunchberry

Here is a splendid groundcover for shade. In its native woods, it grows in broad colonies, lighting up the gloom with its large (for its size) white flowers—a sight you may wish to imitate in your garden. It must have humus-rich, moist, well-drained soil to do well, however, so it is happier under deciduous trees or a combination of deciduous and evergreen ones (the ground under a grove of shallow-rooted evergreens is often too dry and infertile). It is also nice at the feet of rhododendrons and azaleas.

Bunchberry flowers look just like those of dogwood trees, which is no surprise, as they are in the same genus. The orange-red berries that follow by autumn are also char-acteristic and, while pulpy to our taste, are beloved by birds. As for the leaves, they grow in a loose whorl around the stem and are a nice, shiny green. In sheltered locations, they may last all winter.

Your best bet is to start with young seedlings; although bunchberry can be grown from seed, this is a tedious process best left to the nursery. Also, older plants tend to be woodier and to resent transplanting. Keep your bunchberry crop well-watered its first season, and add a moisture-retaining mulch. If your plants are happy, they will slowly spread far and wide throughout your shade garden; extras are easily removed.

Cypripedium spp.

Lady's slipper

BLOOM TIME: spring

HEIGHT/WIDTH: 1' × 8" (30cm × 20cm)

LIGHT: partial–full shade

ZONES: 5–8

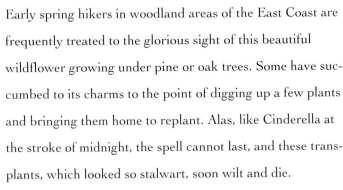

Lady's slipper

Early spring hikers in woodland areas of the East Coast are frequently treated to the glorious sight of this beautiful wildflower growing under pine or oak trees. Some have succumbed to its charms to the point of digging up a few plants and bringing them home to replant. Alas, like Cinderella at the stroke of midnight, the spell cannot last, and these transplants, which looked so stalwart, soon wilt and die.

If you do the politically and horticulturally correct thing and turn to specialty catalogs that sell nursery-propagated wildflowers, you may again be disappointed. Ethical nurseries don't dig up plants in the wild, knowing the plants won't survive in their customers' gardens. Nor will they buy plants from "freelance poachers," who sometimes offer the plants cheaply and in quantity (and often looking very much worse for wear).

That leaves seed-raised lady's slippers. Those who have tried this report that it takes patience and greenhouse conditions, and that even then the little seedlings sometimes expire when finally transplanted outdoors. Some gardeners have had limited success broadcasting ripe seeds in autumn in a suitable spot (a humusy woodland area).

Otherwise, I'm afraid you'll have to be content with paying an annual visit to your favorite wild patch to admire lady's slippers in situ.

Daucus carota

Queen Anne's lace

BLOOM TIME: summer

HEIGHT/WIDTH: 3'–5' × 1'–3' (1–1.5cm × 30–90cm)

LIGHT: full sun

ZONES: 3–9

Queen Anne's lace

If you think of Queen Anne's lace as a weed, think again. It is a tough, attractive plant that can contribute great beauty to flower beds, herb gardens, and meadow plantings. Because it forms a taproot (as the botanical name suggests, it is related to our cultivated carrot), it is drought-tolerant, making it a good choice for sunny spots in ordinary soil.

Queen Anne's lace is a biennial, which means that it blooms in its second season—and should probably be pulled out after that. If it is surrounded by other plants, it is unlikely to spread much, and you may find yourself in the position of collecting and sowing the seeds to get more plants. The flat-topped, lacy flower heads are fascinating. The outer florets are larger, the inner ones smaller, and in the very center is a lone purple one—botanists have suggested that this arrangement looks like a bullseye to pollinators, which should get their attention! It has also been observed that, in rainy weather, the stem right below the flower head becomes soft enough to nod down, thus shielding its pollen (older flowers that have already lost their pollen don't bend).

As for the charming name, one legend has it that the fourteenth-century English queen, then a young girl, copied the flower form when she learned to tat. A variation says that the queen pricked her finger while making lace, and the tiny purple center floret represents the droplet of her blood.

Dicentra eximia

Wild bleeding heart

BLOOM TIME: spring–summer

HEIGHT/WIDTH: 1'–2' × 1'–3' (30–60cm × 30–90cm)

LIGHT: partial shade

ZONES: 2–9

Wild bleeding heart

Everyone has seen this native wildflower's showy Japanese relative, *Dicentra spectabilis*, with its bold foliage and plump, locket-shaped flowers in white and pink. Where that plant shouts, this one whispers. Wild bleeding heart takes up just as much space but with more grace and subtlety. Its softer-textured, fernlike foliage carries slender, arching wands laden with inch-long (2.5cm) flowers in a soft shade of pink or mauve. Generally a very agreeable plant, this species does best in rich soil. Exposure is key—too much sun causes the leaves to yellow.

One important quality in which wild bleeding heart excels over its showier cousin is its especially long blooming period. In fact, it is one of the few plants, wild or cultivated, that can be relied upon to remain in bloom from early spring to autumn frost.

Gardeners who have discovered the charms of wild bleeding heart like to plant it in masses. With its mounding, broad habit, it is perhaps too large to be called a ground-cover, but groupings emphasize its airy quality. Try a sweep of it under tall deciduous trees, along a woodland path, at the foot of a rock wall, or in any shaded spot that would benefit from prolific and continual color. Of course, individual plants are welcome in a shady rock garden or shady perennial border.

Diphylleia cymosa

Umbrella-leaf

BLOOM TIME: spring

HEIGHT/WIDTH: 1'–3' × 1'–4' (30–90cm × 30cm–1.2m)

LIGHT: partial–full shade

ZONES: 6–9

Umbrella-leaf

This aptly named woodlander is an adventurous choice for a shade garden. The lobed leaves, carried in pairs, can grow impressively large, up to 20 inches (51cm) across. The flowers, which appear in early spring, are completely upstaged; they are a small cluster of white blooms that don't tend to last very long. However, splendid dark blue berries follow in late summer. Borne aloft on reddish stems, they make a dramatic sight.

Umbrella-leaf has only one stringent requirement—it must have moist soil. The wetter it is, the faster the plant will grow, so site it with care, depending on your plans. It makes nice colonies in humusy soil under the high shade of deciduous trees. For a textured green carpet, intersperse it among ferns or astilbes. You may grow it with other wildflowers, but choose ones that won't be hidden by it. An appropriate big companion is bugbane (*Cimicifuga*).

Dodecatheon meadia

Shooting star

BLOOM TIME: spring

HEIGHT/WIDTH: 6"–20" × 8"–12" (15–51cm × 20–30cm)

LIGHT: full sun–partial shade

ZONES: 4–9

Shooting star

This spring bloomer can travel in two worlds: it is a fine addition to an informal garden along with other wildflowers, but is also at ease in the company of formal tulips, hyacinths, and so forth. In either case, though, the moments of pleasure are to be savored, because shooting star dies back and goes dormant come summer.

The rosettes, composed of light green, paddle-shaped leaves, have a tidy appearance. A slender, leafless stalk rises up from the middle and bears a cluster of dangling little "stars." It is an unusual flower, with swept-back petals and a tiny, pointed, banded cone in the middle. The color varies from purple to lavender to white, and you may have some of each if you plant in quantity.

Shooting star performs well in light shade or even full sun. Its main requirement is for ample soil moisture, at least while it is in bloom. It is appealing in great sweeps—which you'll get over the years as it gradually self-sows. If you manage to match its bloom time with other spring favorites, you are in for a treat.

Echinacea purpurea

Purple coneflower

BLOOM TIME: summer

HEIGHT/WIDTH: 2'–4' × 1'–2' (60cm–1.2m × 30–60cm)

LIGHT: full sun

ZONES: 3–8

Purple coneflower

This native of the North American prairies is widely popular: perennial gardeners prize its good looks and easy care, and herbalists value it for its medicinal qualities (it has a reputation for boosting the immune system, to fight the common cold).

Its big, splendid blooms have especially long petals, up to 2½ inches (6cm), and are generally light purple; the orange to bronze "cone" in the center of each is symmetrical and very prominent. Often the petals droop downward from the cone, giving the plants a whimsical appearance and providing a welcoming stage for visiting butterflies. Carried in great numbers on a coarse, well-branched plant, these blooms make for wonderful bouquets, and flower arrangers love to collect and dry them for the central cones alone—though if you leave them be, the plant tends to self-sow and add to your display with each passing year.

All this hardy plant requires is conditions that match what it thrives on in nature: full sun and average, not overly rich, soil. Purple coneflower develops a substantial root system and deep taproot, so moving and dividing is not recommended. However, this means it will weather periods of drought well and contribute many years of beauty to your garden.

Epilobium angustifolium

Fireweed

BLOOM TIME: summer

HEIGHT/WIDTH: 2'–6' × 2'–3' (60cm–1.8m × 60–90cm)

LIGHT: full sun

ZONES: 3–8

Fireweed

After the great fires in Yellowstone National Park several years ago, this plucky, beautiful wildflower was one of the first plants to begin growing on the ravaged ground. It also grows wild in Europe—it appeared in great numbers around London after the bombings of World War II. In any event, it gets its name from this ability, which advertises its preference for open ground in full sun.

A tall plant, fireweed has striking purple or rosy pink flowers that line the upper portion of the graceful, unbranched stems, the lower ones opening first. They are centered prettily by white stamens and produce lots of nectar for visiting bees (the resulting honey is excellent). When the flowers pass, fluffy seeds gather, then blow away. If you don't want the plant to spread, be sure to deadhead!

Plant fireweed at the back of your borders or along a fence, where it can gain a little support from adjacent plants while interjecting its pretty blooms. If you have the space, try combining it with plants of similar habit, such as *Crocosmia* 'Lucifer', gaura, or dierama.

Eryngium yuccifolium

Rattlesnake master

BLOOM TIME: summer

HEIGHT/WIDTH: 1'–6' × 1'–3' (30cm–1.8m × 30–90cm)

LIGHT: full sun

ZONES: 5–8

Rattlesnake master

Gardeners in mild climates, with dry, infertile soil, may find this to be an intriguing alternative to the ubiquitous yucca. Like yucca, rattlesnake master forms a clump of long, sharp-pointed, and parallel-veined leaves. But the plant generally is not as large as the yucca. Still, you may fool your neighbors until the plant blooms.

A tall flowering stem emerges from the center of the plant, just as it does with the yucca, but the blooms could not be more different. They appear in a small cluster, each button-shaped bloom less than an inch (2.5cm) in diameter.

The flowers are pale green at first, but over time they take on a bluish tinge. The texture is hard and spiny. Be sure to cut them off before they go to seed, or you may have more than you bargained for the next year. Better yet, pick them when they are fully open and they will dry well (retaining their color) for use in dried flower arrangements.

The odd name comes from an old medicinal use. It was believed that a tea made from the root was an effective antidote to rattlesnake bites.

Erythronium spp.

Trout lily

BLOOM TIME: spring

HEIGHT/WIDTH: 5"–12" × 5"–12" (12–30cm × 12–30cm)

LIGHT: partial shade

ZONES: 4–8

Trout lily

Trout lilies probably get their whimsical name from their distinctive foliage; each plant sports just two simple, lance-shaped leaves, mottled or speckled with brown, purple, or even cream markings. One botanist suggests that the other common name, "fawn lily," is inspired by their resemblance to the perked-up ears of a young deer.

The bloom rises above the pair of leaves on slender, wiry stems. It's a pretty thing, between 1 and 3 inches (2.5–7cm) across and looking very much like a nodding, slightly flared lily flower (the plant is in the same family as cultivated lilies). The flowers of *E. americanum* are chiffon yellow brushed with chocolate brown marks. Because those

of the enchanting *E. revolutum* vary from rosy pink to soft pink to white, selections were inevitable. 'Rose Beauty' and 'White Beauty' are available from bulb suppliers and specialty nurseries. But perhaps the most popular cultivar, apparently derived from *E. tuolumnense*, is the sunny yellow 'Pagoda'. Its flowers and leaves are much larger than those of the others, and it is an eager, robust grower.

The best place for trout lilies is high, open shade under deciduous trees. The soil should be organically rich and well drained. Because they go dormant after blooming, you may wish to overplant with other shade-tolerant plants.

Eschscholzia californica

California poppy

BLOOM TIME: summer

HEIGHT/WIDTH: 6"–12" × 6"–12" (15–30cm × 15–30cm)

LIGHT: full sun

ZONES: all zones (annual)

California poppy

Anyone who has seen a California hillside or meadow strewn with these deep orange flowers never forgets it. Up close, the flowers look a bit frail; they are composed of four silky petals that splay outward (and drop not long after being picked). They do fold up each evening, a habit that led early Spanish explorers to dub it "dormidera," the drowsy one.

California poppy is an annual, a cinch to raise from seeds sown each spring (in milder climates, it will self-sow for you in subsequent years). As its native habitat suggests, it prospers in lean soil in full sun. In recent years, seed catalogs have been offering alternative colors, including lemon yellow, crimson, bicolors, and mixes. 'Apricot Flambeau' is exotic-looking, with fluted petals and semidouble form.

The foliage deserves praise, too. It is a wonderful shade of gray-green, ferny and lacy, and almost succulent in texture. It can be a bit sprawling, especially late in the season, but this is a virtue if you are growing the plants among other flowers as a "weaver."

Eupatorium fistulosum

Joe-Pye weed

BLOOM TIME: summer–autumn

HEIGHT/WIDTH: 4'–8' × 2'–4' (1.2–2.4m × 60cm–1.2m)

LIGHT: full sun–partial shade

ZONES: 4–8

Joe-Pye weed

Here is another North American wildflower that has gained appreciation in the gardens of Europe but is still underused in its native land. It's a shame, because, in the right spot, Joe-Pye weed is both magnificent and utterly dependable.

This is a large, imposing plant, best used in informal groups at the back of the border or as a perennial screen. It does well in sun and part shade alike, prefers damp soil, and blooms best when it gets enough moisture. The flowers appear later in the summer, and they are worth the wait: they foam forth in clusters of rose-pink to light purple, waft a sweet, enticing fragrance, and draw butterflies.

The erect but hollow stems are wine-red and very robust—they remain standing after late-summer storms while other garden plants are smashed down. They are clothed in handsome, toothed leaves that may be as long as a foot (30cm).

Joe-Pye weed is also available in other sizes and colors. The most popular is 'Gateway', a handsome hybrid between this species and the similar *E. maculatum*; it features darker, reddish purple blooms and is not as tall.

Filipendula rubra

Queen-of-the-prairie

BLOOM TIME: summer

HEIGHT/WIDTH: 6'–8' × 3'–4' (1.8–2.4m × 1–1.2m)

LIGHT: full sun–partial shade

ZONES: 3–9

Queen-of-the-prairie

A towering, bushy beauty, this plant has elegant flower plumes up to 9 inches (23cm) long. They're composed of myriad tiny pink flowers. Deadheading will prolong the already generous blooming period. (Alas, the flowers don't hold up well in a vase, but they can be dried for use in wreaths and swags.) The flowers are joined by jagged, forest-green leaves that clothe especially strong stems; the plant stands up well to wind and weather.

Queen-of-the-prairie is not a dryland plant, despite what the name may suggest. In nature, it grows in damp or even wet soil in meadows and wetlands, and you must give it the same if you want it to thrive. Try it in a poorly drained spot such as along a back stone wall or fence. Sometimes water gardeners border the far side of their pools with it, with spectacular results.

A wildflower this handsome and long-blooming has not escaped the notice of nurserymen. You can find 'Venusta', with deep rose-pink blooms, the related *F. ulmaria* 'Variegata', with white flowers and yellow-dappled leaves, and—if the species is just too big for your garden—a dwarf one called 'Nana', which grows to only 15 inches (38cm) tall.

Gaillardia pulchella

Indian blanket, blanket flower

BLOOM TIME: summer

HEIGHT/WIDTH: 1'–2' × 1'–2' (30–60cm × 30–60cm)

LIGHT: full sun

ZONES: all zones (annual)

Indian blanket

You probably know this bright wildflower's perennial cousin, which also goes by the name of Indian blanket, *Gaillardia* × *grandiflora*. That species has a number of popular cultivars, most notably the red-and-yellow 'Goblin'. *G. pulchella* also has seen the hand of the horticulturist—the cultivar 'Red Plume' was an All-America selections winner back in 1991. 'Red Plume' is a fabulous wine-red through and through, and so full of petals that to call it "double" would be an understatement. In fact, the flower looks a bit like a mum. It does not look much like its parent, though.

Let's not forget the original Indian blanket, which is a worthy garden subject in its own right. Although it is native to fields and roadsides of the southeastern United States, it can be grown almost anywhere. As you might expect from its native habitat, it is sun-loving and drought-tolerant. Best of all, as an annual, it will give you great color immediately—and, at season's end, it will self-sow.

In the manner of many wild species, this Indian blanket's flowers show a fair amount of variation. The jagged-edged petals may be scarlet, red, or russet, may contain stripes of gold or warm orange, and are usually tipped yellow. Sometimes a patch will produce a few solid-color individuals. The effect is exciting, as vibrant and colorful as an Indian saddle blanket.

Galax urceolata
(G. aphylla)

Galax

BLOOM TIME: spring

HEIGHT/WIDTH: 8"–20" × 6"–12" (20–51cm × 15–30cm)

LIGHT: partial shade

ZONES: 5 or 6–8

Galax

If you have a damp spot in shade in your yard, here is the groundcovering plant that will change the site from a problem into a spectacle. And unlike other plants that enjoy these conditions, like certain mints or gooseneck loosestrife, galax will not become an invasive weed.

The plant's best asset is its lovely, leafless wands of tiny white flowers, which appear every spring and last for several weeks. A group planting becomes enchanting. But the leaves are also attractive, and you will appreciate them long after the flowers have passed. They are glossy green, sometimes tinged russet, rounded, and leathery, so they hold up well through the dog days of summer. They also make nice greenery for bouquets or holiday decorations because they are long-lasting. (In the plant's native Appalachian forests, unfortunately, stands have been plundered for these purposes.)

Gaura lindheimeri

Gaura

BLOOM TIME: summer

HEIGHT/WIDTH: 3'–4' × 1'–3' (1–1.2m × 30–90cm)

LIGHT: full sun

ZONES: 5–9

Gaura

All summer long, gaura is a fountain of lovely, delicate-looking white flowers that age to a pretty shade of light, rosy pink. (The harder-to-find species *G. coccinea* features scarlet blooms.) These are carried on the upper part of long, willowy stems. The leaves, which are dark to medium green and spear-shaped, tend to remain low on the plant and not steal the show.

To give of its best, gaura really deserves a place out in the open or a spot in the flower border with room to spread out. It is a wonderful weaver, gently inserting its butterfly-like blooms among the upright stems of taller perennials or flowering shrubs. Try gaura near pink or white roses; you'll appreciate how it softens the stiff uprightness of their canes.

Established gaura plants have a sturdy, fleshy root (like a carrot) and are quite drought-tolerant, but well-drained soil is still an important requirement. Gardeners in the hot, humid South are especially enthusiastic about this terrific plant. It will still do well up north, but may not bloom until later in the summer in cooler areas.

Gentiana andrewsii

Bottle gentian

BLOOM TIME: late summer

HEIGHT/WIDTH: 1'–2' × 6"–12" (30–60cm × 15–30cm)

LIGHT: full sun–partial shade

ZONES: 4–9

Bottle gentian

One of the easiest wildflowers to grow is the curious and beautiful bottle, or closed, gentian. The color is brilliant blue, even more appreciated because the flowers appear in clusters of three to twelve. And the shape is unique—bottle gentian flowers never open fully, but hold their petals closed in a more or less cylindrical shape. There are several plausible explanations for this: it helps keep the pollen dry as the autumn rainy season begins, it permits self-pollination, or it offers late-in-the-year bees shelter if they are visiting the flower and the temperature drops.

In any event, you need not worry about the viability of your bottle gentian plants. They grow easily from seed (though they delay bloom until their second year), transplant readily, can be successfully divided, and are long-lived. They are easy garden subjects, asking only for the moist, rich soil they enjoy in wild meadows and along stream banks. They can grow in some shade, but bloom more profusely in full sun.

As for color combinations with bottle gentian, other primary colors are particularly good choices, such as the cultivated goldenrods or scarlet cardinal flower. If you grow bottle gentian in a shadier spot, ferns make natural and delightful companions.

Geranium maculatum

Wild geranium

BLOOM TIME: spring

HEIGHT/WIDTH: 1'–2' × 10"–12" (30–60cm × 25–30cm)

LIGHT: partial shade–full sun

ZONES: 4–9

Wild geranium

If you already have this plant in your garden, you probably take it for granted. It seems to thrive, and spread, with little or no attention from the gardener. Wild geranium is closely related to many popular cranesbill geraniums, such as 'Johnson's Blue' and 'Claridge Druce'. Its leaves are similar, that is, deeply indented. Unlike those plants, however, its magenta-pink flowers are about an inch (2.5cm) across (the blooms are admittedly small, but not as tiny as those of its weedy cousin, an herb known as Robert [*G. robertianum*]). There is also a lovely white-flowered cultivar called 'Album'.

The plant spreads as its creeping rhizome expands outward. It also self-sows—the beaklike pod matures black and bursts open to hurl seeds in all directions. So once you have this geranium, you will never lack for more. Fortunately, colonies of this perky plant are quite appealing. And if you want to contain it, simply tear out the unwanted plants.

Wild geranium can also be added to a fern glade to good effect. It will weave among the greenery, poking up its bright flowers here and there. It also naturalizes nicely at the bases of trees. Just remember that prolonged dry spells will cause it to go dormant for the rest of the season.

Geum triflorum

Prairie smoke

BLOOM TIME: spring

HEIGHT/WIDTH: 6"–15" × 6"–15" (15–38cm × 15–38cm)

LIGHT: full sun–partial shade

ZONES: 2–7

Prairie smoke

On the prairies of the Midwest, this enchanting wildflower is one of the earliest plants to bloom. The flowers consist of small but stout rosy pink nodding bracts clasped by purplish sepals (the true petals are light brown and hidden within). They look somewhat like fat, unopened rosebuds, and, in fact, the plant is in the rose family. But that's where the resemblance ends.

The seedheads that follow in early summer are what give this unique plant its common name. The flowers ultimately do spring open (once pollinated) and puffs of tiny, slender, soft pink plumes ("smoke") emanate. When the plants are grown in a drift, the effect is enchanting.

The clumping foliage, which is not at all roselike, turns russet or crimson in autumn. It is long and irregularly lobed, a bit like coarser yarrow foliage. Prairie smoke is well able to compete with grasses, so feel free to interplant with your favorite ornamental types, or sedges. The creeping phloxes that also bloom in early spring in pink, lavender, or white (*P. subulata* or *P. bifida*) are nice companions as well.

Grow this stalwart in average or even poor soil, provided it is well drained. If prairie smoke is happy, it will eventually form a large colony. You can dig up and move pieces, but be sure to get a good chunk of the rhizome.

Helianthus annuus

Sunflower

BLOOM TIME: summer

HEIGHT/WIDTH: 3'–12' × 2'–5' (1–3.5m × 60cm–1.5m)

LIGHT: full sun

ZONES: all zones (annual)

Sunflower

Contrary to what you may have assumed from Van Gogh's famous paintings of the French countryside, the sunflower is native to North America. The exchange between the Old World and the New was not even—there are many more European imports to the United States than the reverse. But perhaps the bold golden splendor of this plant tips the scales somewhat.

Of course, a plant this easy to grow and of such dramatic form was quickly seized upon by horticulturists. Some domesticated versions have flower heads more than 12 inches (30cm) wide. The original annual species can be as small as 6 inches (15cm) to 10 inches (25cm) across and has pale yellow petals ("ray flowers"). It has parented a great range of color choices, from the warm red 'Velvet Queen' to the creamy white 'Italian White', and everything in between. In recent years, seed companies have touted towering ones (Burpee sells one called 'Paul Bunyan' that can reach 15 feet [4.5m] tall!) and dwarf ones with jumbo flowers ('Teddy Bear'). It is amazing to realize that all of these annual sunflowers really do go from a small seed to mature size in just a few months. Just be sure to provide all the rich soil and water they need.

Heracleum maximum

(H. sphondylium ssp. montanum)

Cow parsnip

BLOOM TIME: summer

HEIGHT/WIDTH: 4'–10' × 3'–5' (1.2–3m × 1–1.5m)

LIGHT: partial sun

ZONES: 6–8

Cow parsnip

This is one of those plants that causes garden visitors to pause and, after a moment's consideration, exclaim, "Wow! What is that?" It has strong, stout, hollow stems and grows as tall as its relative fennel, with divided, maplelike leaves in threes. Its numerous white, flat-topped umbel flowers, which appear in the second season, are similar to those of many garden herbs and to cultivated parsnip—though they can be enormous, up to 8 inches (20cm) across.

Native to moist, shady spots such as wooded stream banks, cow parsnip prefers similar conditions in the garden, such as a damp back corner, a site on the north or east side of the house or garage, or as a backdrop for a water garden or boggy spot. The large white flower heads are a sensational way to light up dreary areas.

Once considered too large or weedy for gardens, cow parsnip has enjoyed the recent praise of trendy gardeners seeking ever larger and more surprising plant choices. When you give it the conditions it requires, you can count on cow parsnip to provide big drama.

Heuchera americana

Alumroot

BLOOM TIME: late spring

HEIGHT/WIDTH: 2'–3' × 8"–12" (60–90cm × 20–30cm)

LIGHT: full sun–partial shade

ZONES: 5–8

Alumroot

The handsome foliage on this low-growing plant will remind you of maple leaves. Alumroot's leaves begin the year apple green highlighted by darker veins, develop silvery tints or splashes as summer arrives, and change by autumn to russet or bronze (especially in sunnier locations). At 2 to 5 inches (5 to 13cm) across, the leaves are often smaller than some of the fancier garden heucheras, making the plant more useful for rock gardens and tight spaces. Rather tall, slender wands of miniature green or lavender bell-shaped flowers rise above the rosette in late spring and last for a few weeks; they are pretty but, because of their delicacy, not reason enough to grow this plant.

Use alumroot in a spot where its quiet good looks make it a supporting player to spring bulbs or smaller flowering perennials. It also makes a nice groundcover in sun or filtered shade, particularly in combination with ferns. All it needs is rich, fertile soil that drains well. Divide it every few years or when it becomes woody in the center. In mild-climate areas, it should be evergreen over the winter.

Hibiscus moscheutos

Rose mallow

BLOOM TIME: summer

HEIGHT/WIDTH: 3'–6' × 3'–6' (1–1.8m × 1–1.8m)

LIGHT: full sun

ZONES: 5–9

Rose mallow

Bigger and hardier than the familiar houseplant hibiscus (*H. rosa-sinensis*) but smaller and more herbaceous than rose-of-Sharon (*H. syriacus*), this native North American plant may be just the hibiscus for your garden beds. It grows quickly and lustily, with a shrubby profile and enormous, attractive flowers.

The species is white with a crimson eye, but there are many cultivated varieties in the pink and red range, with and without contrasting eyes. The flower form is what you would expect, but the size is impressive. Often the blooms are 6 to 8 inches (15 to 20cm) across, though some are up to 15 inches (38cm) across (prompting the catalog cliché, "flowers as big as dinner plates!"). If this strikes your fancy, look for the Southern Belle strain, the Disco Belle strain, or, the biggest of them all, white-flowered 'Blue River II'.

The maplelike foliage provides a nice green backdrop, and generally cloaks the plant from head to toe. So probably the best uses of rose mallow are as a foundation plant or an informal hedge. It doesn't mind average soil but needs consistent moisture, especially during the heat of summer. Just one caveat: like other mallows, this plant is vulnerable to nibbling Japanese beetles.

Iris cristata

Dwarf crested iris

BLOOM TIME: spring

HEIGHT/WIDTH: 4"–12" × 2"–4" (10–30cm × 5–10cm)

LIGHT: full sun–partial shade

ZONES: 5–8

'Alba' dwarf crested iris

This is a special iris for special spots. Unlike some of its kin, it prefers lean, well-drained, even dry soils. Too much moisture makes it pump out foliage at the expense of flowers, and fertilizer is not necessary. Its petite size makes it suitable for places where larger irises might never be used—try it as an edging bordering a walkway or wall, tuck it into a rock garden, or plant it at the feet of taller plants. Dwarf crested iris does best in ground that drains well, as mentioned above, so a slope or bank might also be a good site. In any event, plant the fleshy roots very near the surface. Over the years, if the plants are happy, they will form a dense patch. Fortunately, this iris is not susceptible to the dreaded iris borer, which can devastate the fancy cultivated varieties.

The lightly scented flowers may be small, but they display plenty of perky color. Petals are marked with royal purple and lavender; the "crest" is yellow and white. (Some wildflower nurseries offer the rare and lovely 'Alba', which is white with a golden crest.) Bladelike, light green leaves carry on the show after the blooms pass; their little tufts, growing en masse, are quite attractive.

Iris pseudacorus

Yellow flag

BLOOM TIME: spring–summer

HEIGHT/WIDTH: 3' × 2'–3' (90cm × 60–90cm)

LIGHT: full sun

ZONES: 4–9

Yellow flag

This is a showy plant for damp to outright wet soils, though it will also grow in ordinary soil. In nature, it skirts wetlands and pond edges, making a striking sight each spring with scores of bright yellow blooms. These are of good size, 3 to 4 inches (7 to 10cm) across.

As with all irises, the stiff, sword-shaped, slightly bluish foliage is handsome when the plant is out of bloom. A variegated one, 'Variegata', has cream-striped leaves that are really gorgeous—splendid in combination with the flowers, a standout in the garden at any time, and a great mixer with many other perennials.

This plant is described in some plant catalogs as "vigorous," which is true. It might be more accurate to say "aggressive," because it self-sows eagerly, especially if you give it a wet area. You can keep it in check over the years by yanking out unwanted clumps. The tall British cultivar 'Roy Davidson' is supposed to be sterile, so it might be a better choice if you want to contain your yellow iris.

Iris versicolor

Blue flag

BLOOM TIME: late spring–early summer

HEIGHT/WIDTH: 1'–3' × 8"–12" (30–90cm × 20–30cm)

LIGHT: full sun

ZONES: 2–9

Blue flag

There are plenty of highly bred, beautiful irises in the world, but there is still something to be said for the good old wild species, blue flag. It is very tough, very hardy, and very low-maintenance, qualities some of its fancier descendants and relatives have lost along the way. It grows in damp areas in nature, and prefers the same in your garden.

The flowers, which measure a modest 4 inches (10cm) or so across, are usually a nice robin's-egg blue, with sunny yellow veins. (Interestingly, these veins have a practical purpose. They guide pollinating bees to the interior of the flower—sort of the same theory as runway lights, if you will.) The flat, pale green to grayish leaves are well in scale with the rest of the plant, at ½ inch to 1 inch (1 to 2.5cm) wide.

In nature, the large rhizomes are evident just below the soil line or maybe emerging slightly from it; you should recreate this condition when planting it in your garden—blue flag that is planted too deeply grows poorly and may be subject to rot. Over the years, a rhizome will elongate, producing lots of leaves and quite a few flowering stalks, so in time it will look like you have a clump of blue flag plants when you really have only one.

Jeffersonia diphylla

Twinleaf

BLOOM TIME: spring

HEIGHT/WIDTH: 8"–10" × 6" (20–25cm × 15cm)

LIGHT: partial shade

ZONES: 5–7

Twinleaf

Thomas Jefferson, as you probably know, was a keen gardener, and not only nurtured plants of all kinds (natives as well as European ones), but also supported the botanists and horticulturists of his day. It is somewhat curious, then, that this quirky North American woodlander is the only genus named in his honor.

The blue-green, red-rimmed foliage, which inspired its species name, *diphylla*, looks like a matched set but turns out to be one large but almost completely divided heart-shaped leaf. One writer describes the leaves as "unfurling as if in prayer," another likens them to "bird's wings poised for flight." Since each plant bears about four leaves, the effect is rather busy. A carpet of twinleaf makes for a real conversation piece, no doubt about it.

The 1-inch (2.5cm) creamy white, eight-petaled flower that appears for a short time in early spring looks like a small bloodroot blossom. Like bloodroot, each plant bears only one, held proudly aloft on a slender, bare stem. Later in the season, you can observe the odd, pear-shaped fruit, which opens with a hinged lid to reveal a full load of tiny, chestnut brown seeds, ready to spread this unique plant. Humus-rich soil inspires the best growth and appearance.

Liatris spicata

Blazing star

BLOOM TIME: summer

HEIGHT/WIDTH: 2'–5' × 18" (60cm–1.5m × 45cm)

LIGHT: full sun

ZONES: 3–9

'Kobold' blazing star

Treasured by butterfly lovers as well as bouquet pickers, blazing star is a champ. It blooms eagerly, bearing wonderful, dense spires of small, usually purple flowers (interestingly, unlike most spike flowers, the top ones open first, then the show proceeds downward). These are carried one-to-a-stem, making harvesting easy. They last a long time in a vase, and dry well, too. But if you can bear to leave them growing, your wildflower garden will soon be hosting flitting butterflies.

A native of the North American prairies, blazing star is a tough plant. It does best in somewhat sandy, fertile soil, and develops a strong tuberous rootstock that stores water for survival during dry spells.

A number of excellent cultivars have been developed from the species. The popular 'Kobold' is shorter, around 2 feet (60cm) tall, and has dark reddish purple blooms. 'Floristan White' has gorgeous pure white spikes.

Lilium canadense

Meadow lily

BLOOM TIME: summer

HEIGHT/WIDTH: 2'–7' × 1'–2' (60cm–2m × 30–60cm)

LIGHT: full sun–partial shade

ZONES: 3–8

Meadow lily

The great thing about the big-flowered Asiatic and Oriental lilies is their uniformity. The great thing about wild species lilies like this one is their variability. The blooms of meadow lily begin as orange buds and flare open to sunny yellow on the outsides of the petals and orange with stippled maroon marks within. Usually. Sometimes, the entire flower is more yellow, sometimes more orange. While some are open, others are still in bud. They are a cheerful sight—brighter and more spontaneous, it seems, than their fancy cultivated cousins.

Meadow lily, as you might guess, likes meadow conditions—that is, full sun and damp soil. It will grow in part-day shade, too, as long as the soil is wet. There is no need to fertilize or otherwise fuss over the plants. Once established, they will bloom lustily every summer for a few weeks.

Keep in mind, however, the size of this lily. It is a tall one, with sturdy stalks, and when well-situated, will end up being taller than the gardener. A single plant, or a small grouping, is a nice choice for the back of a border. Or grow a clump at the edge of a wooded area of your property.

Lilium superbum

Turk's-cap lily

BLOOM TIME: summer

HEIGHT/WIDTH: 3'–7' × 1'–2' (90cm–2m × 30–60cm)

LIGHT: full sun–partial shade

ZONES: 4–9

Turk's-cap lily

This is not a lily for the fainthearted. It towers above most gardeners, displaying dozens of 5-inch (13cm), nodding, orange to red flowers on the upper reaches of its stout stems. These, as the whimsical common name suggests, are "highly reflexed," meaning they curl back almost completely to display the spotted surface of the bright petals, the green throat, and the dangling stamens. The tall habit of Turk's-cap lily is a good thing, then, because you can stand under the plant, look up, and admire the details of these exquisite blooms.

The plant looks best in small groupings. Over the years, it will send out thick runners that generate new little bulbs and, shortly, more plants.

To put on a stellar performance, Turk's-cap lily should be planted in rich, moisture-retentive (but not perpetually soggy) soil, conditions it enjoys in wild meadows. Full sun all day long is not absolutely necessary; some gardeners grow it along a fence or wall that provides a few hours of afternoon shade and some shelter from the wind. Although the stalks are strong, a summer storm can flatten them.

Lobelia cardinalis

Cardinal flower

BLOOM TIME: mid–late summer

HEIGHT/WIDTH: 3'–5' × 1' (1–1.5m × 30cm)

LIGHT: full sun–full shade

ZONES: 2–9

Cardinal flower

This is one of the very best wildflowers for garden use, thanks to its agreeable disposition and beautiful flowers. In nature, cardinal flower appears in damp meadows and along streams, so you can grow it in a damp spot. Lacking that, however, it will be happy with regular watering and a mulch at its feet to preserve soil moisture.

A robust plant, yet not rangy or invasive, cardinal flower has striking flower spires. Perhaps no more than 1½ inches (4cm) long, each blossom has the distinctive fan-like shape you may have observed in the common blue garden lobelias so popular for edgings and window boxes.

The species is scarlet, but variations can be found if you hunt for them (some may be crosses with other, similar, lobelias). 'Ruby Slippers' is an especially gorgeous choice, as is the richly hued, more subtle 'Garnet'. There is also a white ('Alba'), a soft pink ('Heather Pink'), a hot pink ('Pink Parade'), and many others. These are carried on tall stalks that emerge from a low rosette. The leaves are medium to dark green, oblong, and slightly serrated, and they ascend the stalk to just short of the blooms. You can count on cardinal flower to grace either flower borders or wildflower beds for many weeks later in the season.

Lobelia siphilitica

Great blue lobelia

BLOOM TIME: late summer

HEIGHT/WIDTH: 2'–4' × 8"–12" (60cm–1.2cm ×
20–30cm)

LIGHT: full sun–partial shade

ZONES: 6–9

Great blue lobelia

Even gardeners who like the closely related cardinal flower don't always know this wonderful wildflower. But a few nurseries specializing in native plants carry it, and it comes recommended highly. It tolerates less moisture and direct sun better than cardinal flower.

Somewhat shorter than its cousin, great blue lobelia has multibranched stems. The flowers are slightly smaller, and range from periwinkle blue to pale blue—occasionally, a white one appears. They are a pretty sight accompanied by the mint green foliage.

A natural use would be to plant it together with cardinal flower's scarlet blooms—a sweep devoted to them alone would be stunning. But if you want to capitalize on the elegance of its bloom color, try some around a white flower such as 'Snow Queen' bee balm, or combine it with another pastel, like pink obedient plant.

Lupinus perennis

Lupine

BLOOM TIME: late spring–early summer

HEIGHT/WIDTH: 8"–2' × 8"–18" (20–60cm × 20–45cm)

LIGHT: full sun

ZONES: 4–7

Lupine

Lucky residents of Maine have seen and adored the great sweeps that this blue wildflower makes in spring in open fields and road banks. The wild lupine is often easier to grow in the garden than some of its more refined relatives that blaze across the colorful pages of nursery catalogs. Its main requirement is well-drained soil. And you will have better luck if you start with smaller seedlings—seeds may germinate erratically (though presoaking them helps), while larger plants transplant poorly, thanks to their deep root systems.

The racemes are light blue with a touch of purple within, and can be as long as 10 inches (25cm). The plant holds them erect, but the foliage tends to be sprawling, so wild lupine is probably not a good candidate for showcasing in a formal perennial border. Better to take your cue from nature and plant it en masse, perhaps in an area where grass is thin. For companions, try other hardy wildflowers with bright flowers, such as butterfly weed. Unlike the hybrids, this species is long-lived.

Lythrum salicaria

Purple loosestrife

BLOOM TIME: late summer

HEIGHT/WIDTH: 3'–4' × 2'–3' (90cm–1.2m × 60–90cm)

LIGHT: full sun

ZONES: 4–9

Purple loosestrife

Possibly the most controversial wildflower of recent years, purple loosestrife is both lovely to look at and, according to its detractors, a dangerous weed. It is native to Europe and Asia; its fast-sprouting seeds were originally brought to North America by early settlers, inadvertently in either ship ballast or livestock bedding. It wasn't long before the seeds "escaped" and became a pest in wetlands and roadside ditches, and along streambanks.

Nonetheless, present-day gardeners have been susceptible to the plant's bright color and long bloom period, so welcome in late summer and early autumn. Like any self-respecting weed, purple loosestrife is widely adaptable, and will grow well in most soils (provided it gets the moisture it needs). Cultivated varieties have been introduced by the nursery trade, among them the gorgeous pink 'Morden Pink' and 'Rosy Queen'. Allegedly, these produce sterile seeds, though research has challenged this.

And therein lies the problem. Fertile purple loosestrife seed of any kind has come to be regarded as a menace by botanists. A number of states with overrun wetlands agree and have banned the sale of purple loosestrife plants. If it is not illegal to grow it in your state, and you've fallen in love with the beautiful flowers, plant it well away from any wild wet areas and deadhead the blooms before they go to seed.

Mertensia virginica

Bluebells

BLOOM TIME: spring

HEIGHT/WIDTH: 1'–2' × 18" (30–60cm × 45cm)

LIGHT: partial–full shade

ZONES: 3–9

Virginia bluebells

A native of southeastern woodlands but able to grow well much further north, bluebells is a pretty plant. The thin, lance-shaped leaves are mainly basal, though a few ascend the stems on short, succulent stalks. At the top of these stalks are clusters of nodding little bells. They begin as pink buds, but open to lilac-blue flowers. The blue will be darker in deeper shade.

Bluebells are often touted as ideal companions for spring-flowering bulbs, with good reason. This plant likes similar conditions in the garden: organically rich soil in cool shade. Plus, the color seems to go with everything. It is particularly fetching combined with small-flowered yellow or white narcissus.

Like the bulbs, though, bluebells' show ends as summer arrives. The stems die down after bloom, and the plant gradually goes dormant and disappears from view, until the next year. So mark its spot if you wish to move or divide it in the autumn, and to avoid trampling on it or planting something else over it.

Mimulus spp.

Monkey flower

BLOOM TIME: summer

HEIGHT/WIDTH: 1'–4' × 8"–3' (30cm–1.2m × 20–90cm)

LIGHT: full sun

ZONES: 5–7

Monkey flower

The charming, long-blooming flowers look something like a monkey face, hence the common name (amusingly, legend has it that the Latin name refers to a mime actor, Mimus; apparently the word means "buffoon"). There are many species of this wetland wildflower, of varying sizes. Many have yellow flowers, including *M. luteus*, *M. moschatus*, and *M. guttatus*; *M. cardinalis* 'Aurantiacus' has rich orangey flowers. Those of *M. lewisii* are rosy pink. And a monkey flower from the Appalachians, *M. ringens*, is light purple (and, rarely, white).

Whichever ones you choose, be sure to give them damp or constantly wet soil. Because monkey flower plants have a tendency to spread over time, they are a good choice for a boggy area or the perimeter of a water garden. Just remember, if they dry out, you will lose them. Otherwise, they require little attention from the gardener in exchange for many weeks of colorful and intriguing bloom.

Monarda didyma

Bee balm

BLOOM TIME: mid–late summer

HEIGHT/WIDTH: 2'6"–3' × 18' (75–90cm × 45cm)

LIGHT: full sun–partial shade

ZONES: 4–9

Bee balm

This showy wildflower is easy to grow, provided your garden has the rich, moist soil it needs to thrive. It has dark green aromatic leaves, and the big flower heads, up to 4 inches (10cm) across, are a knockout in full bloom. Hummingbirds find them irresistible, and you can expect bees, too, of course.

The original species is reddish, but variation in the wild and in gardens is not unusual. So, not surprisingly, there are a number of named color selections. Most often seen is scarlet ('Cambridge Scarlet', 'Gardenview Scarlet'), but recent years have seen a flurry of new introductions in other colors. 'Marshall's Delight' is peppermint pink, 'Aquarius' is rich mauve-pink, 'Vintage Wine' is a deep zinfandel red, and 'Snow Queen' is pure white.

Bee balm can be an overenthusiastic grower; keep it in bounds by chopping back at the outer perimeter of the roots. Traditionally, this stalwart plant has been susceptible to mildew, which disfigures it later in the season. Fortunately, many of the new varieties mentioned above are, while not immune, touted as "resistant." You can also do your part by offering each plant enough elbow room to allow for air circulation, and spraying if need be.

Oenothera spp.

Evening primrose, sundrops

BLOOM TIME: spring–summer

HEIGHT/WIDTH: 2'–3' × 1'–2' (60–90cm × 30–60cm)

LIGHT: full sun

ZONES: 4–9

Sundrops

A number of similar plants gather under these names; all sport tallish stalks laden, near the tops, with sunny yellow, cup-shaped blossoms. Some open true to their name, in the late afternoon or evening (a desirable quality for those who cannot enjoy their gardens until they get home from school or work each day). These are fragrant, to attract night-pollinating moths. Sundrops are those species, notably *O. fruticosa*, that open in the daytime. None are long-lived, but they all self-sow.

The bright color of evening primrose plants is welcome in casual garden settings, where they bloom reliably, prolifically, and practically all summer long. They aren't fussy about soil, though especially fertile ground causes the stems to become lax and floppy. Let their neighbors offer support (penstemons or campanulas are nice companions), or stake them, as the weight of the blooms can sometimes cause them to lean over.

If you grow this wildflower, you should make it a point to sit out with it some evening (or day, as the case may be) and witness a bloom opening, a process that takes about a half an hour. As the tightly rolled, cigar-shaped buds loosen, the sepals peel back, then the petals spring open to reveal the cross-shaped stigma in the center—a show one writer aptly called "reminiscent of time-lapse photography."

Pachysandra procumbens

Allegheny spurge, American pachysandra

BLOOM TIME: spring

HEIGHT/WIDTH: 10"–12" × 10"–12" (25–30cm × 25–30cm)

LIGHT: partial shade

ZONES: 4–9

Allegheny spurge

Everyone knows this native wild plant's famous Japanese relative, the ubiquitous glossy green groundcover (*P. terminalis*); this one looks different and has different requirements. Allegheny spurge is an easy but offbeat groundcover for your damp shade garden.

One significant difference is the growth rate. This pachysandra is not nearly as rampant, instead spreading slowly and judiciously over the years (so yank out invading weeds in its early years). It languishes in the poor, dry soil its cousin performs so well in. To get the best out of Allegheny spurge, grow it in rich, damp soil like the shady woodlands from which it hails.

And the leaves are significantly different. Individually, they are much larger, up to twice as large. In lighter shade, their coloring tends to be gray-green mottled with silver; under heavier cover, they become darker-hued, and the dappling approaches purple-black. This foliage is also more textured, thanks to puckering along the veins, giving the leaves an appealing quilted look. Unfortunately, they are not evergreen, except perhaps in milder areas. As for the flowers, they appear briefly in spring, little lavender to white bottlebrushes with a sweet scent.

Penstemon spp.

Penstemon

BLOOM TIME: summer

HEIGHT/WIDTH: 1'–4' × 1'–3' (30cm–1.2m × 30–90cm)

LIGHT: full sun

ZONES: 6–8

Penstemon

As a group, penstemons are handsome, shrubby-looking plants of arching stems laden with showy, tubular flowers that attract hummingbirds. Many are native to the mountains of the West, but may be grown in other areas, provided similar conditions are available: full sun and lean, well-drained soil (damp or rich soil causes them to rot). Be advised that they are not long-lived, though they may self-sow.

A few of the most popular garden penstemons are the scarlet-flowered *P. barbatus*, white to pale-purple flowered *P. digitalis*, and *P. gloxinioides (P. hartwegii)*, which comes in a variety of colors. Other species are considered tricky and are better left to collectors and rock-garden specialists.

Arguably the best penstemons, though, are the many hybrids and cultivars, which feature the finest qualities of this species—drought tolerance, heavy flowering, and ease of cultivation. Look for the award-winning 'Husker Red', derived from *P. digitalis*, which owes its name to its reddish foliage and stems; the flowers are white, though sometimes they develop a pink cast. This gorgeous plant would make a stunning addition to a low-maintenance border. Well-stocked nurseries will carry, in addition to white-flowered varieties, ones with lavender, violet, blue, pink, true red, and orange-red blooms.

Penstemon smallii

Beard tongue

BLOOM TIME: late spring

HEIGHT/WIDTH: 1½'–3' × 1' (45–90cm × 30cm)

LIGHT: full sun–partial shade

ZONES: 6–8

Beard tongue

There are many penstemons that have traveled from the wild into our gardens, often with no horticultural improvements or selection—with good reason. These are great plants, in the right spot, tough and drought-tolerant and bringing pretty, long-lasting flowers atop attractive, disease-free, noninvasive plants. *Penstemon smallii* is a favorite because the blooms are especially showy—lavender or pink with creamy white throats. Also, they appear down the stems, not just at the tips, so the plant looks bushier than some of its kin.

And what is the right spot? Well, soil seems to be the most important requirement; grow this and most other penstemons in average ground (overly rich soil shortens the life span) that is well drained. Thin or sandy soil is fine, so beard tongue is a good choice for a rock garden, where its taller profile can be a welcome contrast among more sprawling plants. It may also be tucked in among salvias and lavenders, which thrive in similar conditions.

Phacelia campanularia

Desert bluebells

BLOOM TIME: summer

HEIGHT/WIDTH: 6"–20" × 6"–20" (15–51cm × 15–51cm)

LIGHT: full sun–partial shade

ZONES: all zones (annual)

Desert bluebells

The best way to describe the color of these amazing flowers is electric or navy blue, similar to the color of *Salvia guaranitica* flowers, if you know that ornamental sage. These are little bells, about an inch (2.5cm) long, with protruding yellow stamens. They are carried in loose clusters, giving the plant a jaunty, carefree appearance.

Other features of desert bluebells add to its appeal. The heart-shaped leaves are coarsely toothed and clothe the plant well without overwhelming the flower display. And the stems are reddish, which provides nice contrast.

Although it originally hails from dry hillsides and desert areas from Colorado to California, desert bluebells adapts easily to any well-drained soil. In mild climates, an autumn sowing will give you a head start on early blooms the next spring.

Desert bluebells makes a good filler in casual cottage garden designs. This plant is super in the company of the yellow flowers of coreopsis. And you can't go wrong combining it with that sensational annual, bright orange California poppy.

Phlox paniculata

Summer phlox

BLOOM TIME: summer

HEIGHT/WIDTH: 2'–5' × 2' (60cm–1.5m × 60cm)

LIGHT: full sun–partial shade

ZONES: 3–9

Summer phlox

For a carnival of lively color and sweet scent, summer phlox is hard to beat. The widely available hybrids have completely superseded the wild species and come in a broad range of hues, from snowy white to pink to red to lavender and purple. Many have a contrasting center eye that adds extra sparkle. If you have the space, plant a mixture. Otherwise, you are sure to find at least one or two individual varieties that fit well into your garden's color scheme. One of the best is 'Bright Eyes', pastel pink with a crimson center. If you prefer a solid-color phlox, there are many to choose from. 'Starfire' is red to magenta with dark purple leaves; all-white 'David' is also an excellent choice.

Phlox blooms heavily for weeks on end, provided you have planted it in the same rich, moist soil it thrives on in the wild. Horticulturists have not managed to conquer the plant's one flaw, susceptibility to powdery mildew, which attacks toward the end of the season. A little extra room for air circulation may help—either plant individuals fairly well apart at the outset, or do some thinning after the plants are up and growing in the spring. Spraying with "antitranspirants" (ask at your local garden center) also seems to help. An easier recourse, though, is to plant resistant varieties, of which there are many new ones. Ask, or read catalog descriptions carefully.

Physostegia virginiana

Obedient plant

BLOOM TIME: mid–late summer

HEIGHT/WIDTH: 1'–3' × 8"–2' (30–90cm × 20–60cm)

LIGHT: full sun

ZONES: 3–9

Obedient plant

The curious common name of this wildflower refers to the alleged ability of individual flowers to stay in place when nudged. The plant is related to the snapdragon (the flowers are superficially similar), but, truth be told, it is no more cooperative. Nonetheless, children, especially, like to try tweaking the flowers this way and that.

The real excitement about this plant is its wonderful performance in hot, oppressive, humid summer weather. The stems continue to stand tall through it all, lined with handsome, unflagging dark green foliage and tirelessly producing a dependable supply of pretty flowers for weeks.

Obedient plant is related to mint, and has the same square stems—and the same tendency to grow rampantly in moist soil. If you grow it in average to dry soil, however, you need never see this side of its personality.

The flowers of the species are pink, but some wildflower nurseries offer other choices. Look for darker-hued 'Bouquet Rose' or white 'Summer Snow'. A relatively new selection, 'Variegata', sports cream-striped leaves, a nifty contrast to the pink blooms. Boltonia and wild species of aster have an overlapping bloom time and look lovely with obedient plant.

Polemonium reptans

Jacob's-ladder

BLOOM TIME: spring

HEIGHT/WIDTH: 1'–2' × 1'–2' (30–60cm × 30–60cm)

LIGHT: full sun–partial shade

ZONES: 4–8

Jacob's-ladder

You would never guess that a flower this ferny of foliage and delicate of flower was related to phlox. Yet it is, and it shares with that group sweet scent, soft bloom color, and a clump-forming growth habit. That is where the resemblance ends, however.

The small, dainty flowers are especially sweet: they are airy little China-blue bells accented with tiny white stamens. They appear in clusters at the tips of the plants, so that a patch in full bloom has a fairyland quality. Among the wildflowers that make enchanting companions are foamflower and Virginia bluebells.

It is the leaves that give the plant its common name. They are arranged along the rather brittle stems in pairs, growing smaller as they ascend. They reminded someone of the biblical story of Jacob's dream of ascending to heaven on the rungs of a ladder. Unlike some spring-blooming wildflowers, the leaves of this plant remain all season.

This particular species, native to the East Coast from New York south to Alabama, has a more creeping habit than the more commonly grown *P. caeruleum*, so it is a better choice for planting in sweeps or naturalizing. Grow it in rich, moist soil for best performance.

Polygonatum odoratum

Solomon's seal

BLOOM TIME: spring

HEIGHT/WIDTH: 1'–2' × 1'–2' (30–60cm × 30–60cm)

LIGHT: partial–full shade

ZONES: 4–8

'Variegatum' Solomon's seal

This elegant plant, grown mainly for its foliage, has a wonderful presence in the garden. Strong, graceful stems spread outward, bearing along their length oval-shaped, parallel-veined leaves. Dangling along the underside of the stem in spring is a jaunty row of diminutive, pale green to white, lightly perfumed, bell-shaped flowers. These become blue-black berries by late summer.

The beautiful 'Variegatum' has leaf edges and tips splashed with white markings, which looks fabulous among hostas. If you have the space and want an even bolder show, try Great Solomon's seal (a hybrid of *P. biflorum* or *P. commutatum*), whose arching stems can be 6 feet (1.8m) long.

Solomon's seal has been grown around the world for a long time. The source of the name seems lost to history, though there are several theories. If you examine the tuberous roots, you'll see round scars from the previous year's stalks—these are said to resemble Solomon's seal, or signet. (By the way, you'll be able to determine a plant's age by counting these scars.) Another explanation is that, used medicinally, the plant was useful for healing, or sealing, wounds. Yet another possibility is that the six-pointed flowers were taken to resemble the six points of the Star of David, which was once called "Solomon's seal."

Pontederia cordata

Pickerel rush

BLOOM TIME: late summer

HEIGHT/WIDTH: 2'–3' × 2'–3' (60–90cm × 60–90cm)

LIGHT: full sun

ZONES: 5–9

Pickerel rush

This native of marshes and ponds is an excellent choice for a water garden or boggy area. Unlike some other water-loving plants, it does not look weedy and it is not invasive. Instead, it forms handsome, well-mannered clumps. Pickerel rush is simple to grow, provided its requirement for ample water is met. If you pot it and place it by the edge of a garden pool, immerse it no more than 6 inches (15cm) deep. In other settings, don't let it dry out.

The glossy green leaves are broadly spear-shaped; in the latter part of the summer, they are joined by dense spikes of light blue to royal purple flowers. Aquatics nurseries also offer it in white and, more recently, pink. It will bloom more heavily if fertilized monthly during the growing season, and half-tablets of waterlily fertilizer are fine for this purpose.

Pickerel rush is a valuable addition to a water garden. Its late bloom time brings welcome color at a time when few other accent plants are blooming. The blue combines well with many waterlilies, especially yellow or red ones—the spikes are dense enough to provide significant contrast, and the plant's vertical habit makes the display more interesting. When the plant is not in bloom, the foliage is sufficiently healthy and an effective foil for the flat lily pads and strap-like leaves of many other pondside growers.

Ratibida pinnata

Prairie coneflower

BLOOM TIME: summer

HEIGHT/WIDTH: 2'–5' × 1'–2' (60cm–1.5m × 30–60cm)

LIGHT: full sun

ZONES: 4–8

Prairie coneflower

Tall and showy, the prairie, or gray-headed, coneflower is a fun flower for low-maintenance areas of your yard. It is not fussy about soil, tolerating everything from damp to dry situations—all it requires is plenty of sun. Because of its stature and casual profile, it would be ideal along a fence, toward the back of a wildflower border, or in a meadow planting. Warning: as with many prairie natives, the clumps of this plant form a ranging, fibrous root system, making later transplanting difficult and perhaps requiring stern control measures if it exceeds its allotted space.

The flowers look like little shuttlecocks, with 1- or 2-inch (2.5 or 5cm) bright yellow petals ("ray flowers") swooping back from the prominent center cone. The cone is gray-green to start, but darkens over the course of the summer. The plant pumps these out by the dozens for weeks on end. They are wonderful in flower arrangements, keeping for many days. They also dry well.

Romneya coulteri

Matilija poppy

BLOOM TIME: late spring–early summer

HEIGHT/WIDTH: 6'–8' × 3'–6' (1.8–2.4m × 1–1.8m)

LIGHT: full sun–partial shade

ZONES: 6–9

Matilija poppy

It's taller than you are, it has gray-green, divided leaves, and the huge crepe-paper flowers with the bright boss of golden stamens are unmistakably poppies. What can it be? This exuberant relative of the more familiar Oriental poppies is a California native—though it can be grown in other areas with mild climates. All it requires is sun and soil that drains well (in nature, it is found in dry canyons and washes below four thousand feet [1,200m]). The magnificent flowers are pleasantly fragrant and are followed by those familiar poppy seed capsules.

Matilija poppy is so big and billowing that it is best treated as if it were a shrub. Some gardeners use it as a foundation plant with shorter drought-tolerant plants in front of it. It also makes a good curb-strip plant because it is so tough and so dramatic. Just plant it where you want it to stay, because it is not easily moved. A mature plant has an extensive, fleshy root system that resents being disturbed. It does tend to sucker, and you can dig these up while they are still small and plant them elsewhere or give them away to admiring friends.

Rudbeckia hirta

Black-eyed Susan

BLOOM TIME: summer

HEIGHT/WIDTH: 18"–3' × 2'–3' (45–90cm × 60–90cm)

LIGHT: full sun

ZONES: 4–9

Black-eyed Susan

One of the biggest success stories in wildflowers-gone-to-gardens is the sturdy black-eyed Susan. It pumps out large numbers of especially big, bold flowers, which helps account for its popularity, but also brings with it a natural toughness. Not even the most neglectful gardener can say this plant is difficult to grow. Just give it full sun and ordinary soil. A drought-tolerant plant, it will survive on minimal water. Its only weakness is occasional powdery mildew on the leaves, best avoided by giving it ample elbow room.

There are a number of similar-looking species; *Rudbeckia hirta* is valued because it is reliably perennial, although it will also self-sow. The petals ("ray flowers") are cheerful orange-yellow, and the center cone is chocolaty brown, except when it is dusted with golden pollen. There are many worthy cultivated varieties and relatives.

All rudbeckias bloom over a long period in the garden and retain their color well. They also hold up in bouquets, fresh or dried, and don't readily drop their petals. Picking the hairy, tough stems can be a bit of a struggle, forcing you to resort to a sharp knife or scissors. The stems also remain straight in a vase or outdoors over the winter months. This is because they are lined with fine grooves—as students of architecture will tell you, a fluted column is stronger than a smooth one.

Sanguinaria canadensis

Bloodroot

BLOOM TIME: spring

HEIGHT/WIDTH: 6"–14" × 6"–8" (15–36cm × 15–20cm)

LIGHT: partial–full shade

ZONES: 3–8

'Multiplex' bloodroot

Bloodroot is a familiar sight in wooded areas of the Northeast in early spring, where it thrives in rich, moist, acidic soil. The deeply lobed but heart-shaped leaves are very distinctive, and the creamy white blossoms are lovely. Rock gardeners and connoisseurs of perennials often grow the gorgeous, double-flowered variety 'Multiplex'.

Alas, this pristine beauty has a short moment of glory—in ideal conditions under the shade of high trees, you can expect the blooms to last for only a week or so. They open fully during the day, and fold upward each evening like a closing umbrella; be forewarned that the petals are fragile, and will shatter when disturbed. Make the most of blood-root's show, then, by planting it in an area where no other flowers will compete for attention (until, of course, the blooms are gone), such as among ferns or later-blooming perennial groundcovers such as European or American ginger. Bloodroot's uniquely shaped leaves will linger on for the rest of the season if your soil is not too dry.

By the way, the common name refers to the plant's juicy, orange-red sap, which bleeds from a clipped stem or nicked root and colors skin and fabric easily. It was once used medicinally but is now considered dangerous, due to the presence of a toxic alkaloid.

Sarracenia spp.

Pitcher plant

BLOOM TIME: spring

HEIGHT/WIDTH: 6"–3' × 4"–1' (15–90cm × 10–30cm)

LIGHT: full sun

ZONES: Most are hardy in zones 7–10

Pitcher plant

Yes, they eat bugs, but aren't they gorgeous? Pitcher plants lure bees, flies, and other insects with nectar and scent glands located on the treacherous interior of their lovely, fluted leaf structures; the unsuspecting victims follow deeper and deeper into the plant until they slip into a brew of water and enzymes that consumes them. The theory is that the resulting rich liquid produced nourishes the plants, which grow naturally in an otherwise rather nutrient-poor setting (soggy, acidic wetlands).

In recent years, gardeners have been flocking to pitcher plants because they are beautiful. The leaves come in many colors and patterns, from the green and maroon fili-gree of *S. leucophylla* to the lavender-and-purple veined *S. purpurea* and *S. rubra*. The odd-looking flowers, which appear atop their own slender stalk, may be anything from maroon to acid yellow—they don't last long, however, so the leaves remain the main attraction.

There is no mystery to growing a patch of pitcher plants. If your property lacks an acidic bog, you can mimic one easily enough by filling a shallow container with damp peat moss lightened with some sand for the sake of drainage. Keep the medium wet at all times. If you observe mineral salts building up on the surface, flush out the pot well so the delicate plants aren't adversely affected.

Sedum ternatum

Stonecrop

BLOOM TIME: spring

HEIGHT/WIDTH: 3"–8" × 8"–15" (7–20cm × 20–38cm)

LIGHT: partial shade

ZONES: 4–7

Stonecrop

There are plenty of fancier and showier sedums, to be sure, but the classic species has its virtues. For one, it's simple to grow, requiring only well-drained soil. It establishes itself quickly and forms handsome, spreading mats that require barely any attention except maybe a little tidying early each spring.

It has succulent foliage, like other sedums; its leaves are an attractive shade of blue-green. Stonecrop's sprawling growth habit makes it ideal for banks or slopes in a wild part of the garden, or trailing over rocks or a stone wall in a conventional rock garden setting. Its relatively shallow root system and easygoing nature mean you can tuck other plants in and around it—or let it form a carpet at the base of shrubs.

Each spring, you get the bonus of several weeks of flowers. These are little white stars, less than an inch (2.5cm) across but borne in sprays for greater impact.

Shortia galacifolia

Oconee bells

BLOOM TIME: late spring–early summer

HEIGHT/WIDTH: 6"–8" × 6"–8" (15–20cm × 15–20cm)

LIGHT: partial–full shade

ZONES: 5–8

Oconee bells

When you see this wildflower in bloom, you really do expect to see tiny fairies flitting nearby. The 1-inch (2.5cm) white (sometimes pinkish) bells—actually rather large for a plant this diminutive—have fringed petal edges and sherbet-yellow centers. These bloom for a week or two each spring, and are accompanied by rosettes of durable, glossy green, heart-shaped leaves. There is only one flower per plant, so planting in groups or as a groundcover is wise. It loses impact when you mix it with a lot of other wildflowers or overbearing ferns, though you could slip a few plants into a rock garden here and there. It is also nice in a rhododendron or azalea glade, plants it is seen with in the wild.

This charmer hails from the wildflower-rich Appalachian mountains, but it is winter-hardy as far north as southern New England. As the weather gets colder, the handsome leaves take on a reddish-bronze hue. To succeed with oconee bells, you should simulate the conditions it enjoys in its natural home: acidic, moist, humusy soil and partial shade is ideal. It will adapt to more sun, if you mulch it, and heavier soils, provided you dig in some peat moss or compost prior to planting. It tends to be slow to get established, but long-lived.

Silene virginica

Fire pink

BLOOM TIME: spring

HEIGHT/WIDTH: 1'–2' × 1' (30–60cm × 30cm)

LIGHT: partial shade–full sun

ZONES: 3–8

Fire pink

Here is a wildflower that, when brought into a garden setting, completely outshines its performance in nature. Its native habitat is dry, rocky slopes that receive some shade, conditions difficult to duplicate in cultivation. But plant it in full sun in your garden and you will find that the stems don't flop over nearly as much as they do in the wild. It will do fine in average (not rich) soil. Mulch it, water it regularly, and you will be astounded at its full, bushy profile, and the way the bright flowers literally cover the plant.

You'll welcome the bountiful flowering because the blooms are so terrific. Small tubes flare open to display long scarlet petals. These are slightly notched at their tips, giving away their relationship to carnations and dianthus, otherwise known as "pinks," hence the common name. The plant stays in bloom for several weeks. Try it in the company of white flowers, such as white phlox, dame's rocket, or daisies. In the wild, it consorts with blue phlox and violet wood sorrel, which should also work in the garden. No matter what companions you choose, allow your fire pink some room, as it doesn't enjoy being crowded.

Sisyrinchium angustifolium

Blue-eyed grass

BLOOM TIME: spring

HEIGHT/WIDTH: 6"–18" × 4"–6" (15–45cm × 10–15cm)

LIGHT: full sun

ZONES: 4–9

Blue-eyed grass

Few grasses or grasslike plants have flowers worth mentioning, at least from the point of view of a gardener. This perky little plant is the exception. Its star-shaped flowers are sky blue to periwinkle, centered with a small, cheerful splash of yellow. These appear in clusters rather than one to a stem, adding to their impact. A South American relative, *S. striatum*, has cream-colored flowers.

Nonetheless, you will have to site the plant with care if you want to enjoy the flowers, as they are small, only ½-inch (1.5cm) across. Tuck a few specimens into a rock garden, a mixed container planting, or the front of a flower border.

Despite its name, blue-eyed grass is actually in the iris family, which accounts for its preference for shallow growing conditions and soil that is on the damp side. The soil should also be of average quality (rich soil causes excessive foliage at the expense of flowering). Be sure your plants receive adequate light and elbow room so they don't have to compete for resources. Then, you'll find that your garden-grown plants flower much more lustily than their counterparts in the wild.

Smilacina racemosa

False Solomon's seal

BLOOM TIME: spring

HEIGHT/WIDTH: 1'–3' × 1' (30–90cm × 30cm)

LIGHT: partial shade

ZONES: 3–7

False Solomon's seal

Because this is a relatively tall, erect woodland plant, you may find it better suited to being placed among larger plants than some of the other, lower-growing groundcovering wildflowers. Try false Solomon's seal among rhododendrons and azaleas or big-leaved hostas (it prefers the same moist, acidic soil they do), or skirting the base of a shade tree. It offers long, graceful stems lined with glossy, pleated leaves.

It is known as "false" because it is similar to Solomon's seal (another genus entirely, *Polygonatum*) when out of bloom, though often not as large. Also, the flowers are completely different; they are cream-colored, starry, and borne in clusters at the stem tips; later, they become red, not blue, berries. A drift of false Solomon's seal in bloom is an arresting sight—plus, you will detect the flowers' pleasing fragrance.

Solidago spp.

Goldenrod

BLOOM TIME: midsummer to autumn

HEIGHT/WIDTH: varies

LIGHT: full sun

ZONES: 3–9

'Fireworks' goldenrod

Goldenrod is a real Cinderella story. Long scorned or overlooked as a weed, or avoided because it was falsely thought to cause hay fever (the real culprit is the less showy ragweed, which blooms at the same time), it is now enjoying praise and popularity. And no wonder. In full bloom, it is a glorious sight, and the bright color complements many other late-season bloomers. You'll love goldenrod with the yellow-centered New England asters—both the species and the bigger-bloomed cultivated varieties.

There are now some terrific garden hybrids. The best ones are well behaved enough to stay in bounds in your perennial borders, and feature plush plumes composed of tiny golden flowers. Like their wild cousins, these improved goldenrods are eager to bloom and easy to care for. The aptly named *S. rugosa* 'Fireworks' is a compact, dome-shaped, clump-forming plant (3 to 4 feet [90–120cm] tall) that cascades with bright yellow color. *S. sphacelata* 'Golden Fleece' is a dwarf selection (1½ to 2 feet [45–60cm] tall) that carries its cheery sprays in a tidy, pyramidal fashion. *S. virgaurea* 'Crown of Rays' (2 feet [60cm] tall) has such full, lush plumes that it looks like a golden waterfall.

All of these do fine in poor to average soil—in fact, soil that is too rich will cause them to grow more rampantly than you might wish.

Stokesia laevis

Stokes' aster

BLOOM TIME: summer

HEIGHT/WIDTH: 1'–2' × 1'–2' (30–60cm × 30–60cm)

LIGHT: full sun

ZONES: 5–9

'Cyanea' Stokes' aster

If you like blue flowers and want something that's durable and low-maintenance, consider the lovely Stokes' aster. Its long-lasting blooms are wonderfully intricate and delicate-looking. The flower heads are large, about 4 inches (10cm) across, and feature two rows of numerous petals; the outer ones spray outward in a loose, open fashion, while the shorter, inner ones hug close to the center. The effect is a bit like a Chinese aster, or maybe a bachelor's button. In any event, they're produced one-to-a-stalk, which is a plus for bouquet lovers (also, they tend to have a long vase life). They are usually lavender-blue, but there are also many fine cultivars. 'Alba', of course, has white flowers. 'Klaus Jelitto' has powder-blue blooms. Those of 'Wyoming' are especially dark blue.

The plant is a mound-former, covered in smooth, spear-shaped leaves that make a nice contrast to the interesting flowers. Stokes' aster is wonderfully adaptable and fairly cold-hardy, despite the fact that its natural habitat, the coastal plain of the southeastern United States, is rather restricted. It is happiest in soil that drains well and is neither too fertile nor too poor (it can even be grown at the seashore). Don't overwater it or plant it in a spot that gets waterlogged in the winter months.

Stylophorum diphyllum

Celandine poppy

BLOOM TIME: late spring–summer

HEIGHT/WIDTH: 12"–18" × 10"–15" (30–45cm × 25–38cm)

LIGHT: full sun–partial shade

ZONES: 4–8

Celandine poppy

There's no trick to growing this pretty, long-flowering poppy. It grows well in almost any spot, provided it gets the moisture it needs either from the soil or from the hose. Over the years, it will multiply, but it is not an aggressive plant like lesser celandine (*Ranunculus ficaria*).

The flowers are yellow and glossy, so even though they are small, about 2 inches (5cm) across, they capture your attention. They make a nice stand under the shelter of deciduous trees, mixing well with other spring-blooming wildflowers. But you might also tuck a few individual plants into your sunny flower garden, where their simple, cheery nature and bright color will be welcome. The fuzzy little seedpods (which may be on the plant at the same time as new flowers are opening—a charming sight) are characteristic of poppies. If you leave them be and have no chipmunks in your neighborhood to make off with the seeds, these poppy plants will self-sow.

The much-lobed foliage seems large for the flowers and is an attractive shade of blue-green that intermixes well with other plants. It looks particularly fine among ferns.

Thalictrum aquilegifolium

Meadow rue

BLOOM TIME: spring

HEIGHT/WIDTH: 2'–3' × 1' (60–90cm × 30cm)

LIGHT: full sun–partial shade

ZONES: 5–9

Meadow rue

Each spring, tiny lavender "beads" sway atop slender stalks, opening to enchanting little powder-puff blooms. The cultivar 'Album' has the same buds but—surprise—opens white. There is also a deeper purple one called 'Purple Cloud'.

Shorter than other meadow rues, this species does not require staking, but it is still tall enough to bring a little height to the middle or back of a flower bed. The *aquilegifolium* part of the name refers to the fact that the leaves are similar to those of columbine, that is, dainty and lacy. These are bluish green and clothe the stems at loose intervals, stopping short of the airy flower heads. Thanks to the foliage, the plant maintains a welcome graceful presence in the garden even after the flowers have come and gone.

The key to a sterling performance from meadow rue is moist soil, like that of its native habitat. A light mulch and some afternoon shade are a good idea in especially hot summers.

Thermopsis
caroliniana

Carolina lupine, Carolina bush pea

BLOOM TIME: spring

HEIGHT/WIDTH: 3'–5' × 2'–3' (1–1.5m × 60–90cm)

LIGHT: full sun

ZONES: 5–8

Carolina lupine

A tallish, erect plant with striking flowers, Carolina lupine deserves to be more widely grown. It is well behaved enough to join a formal perennial border (imagine it with China blue campanulas) and easygoing enough to chime in with other bold-flowered plants in a more casual scheme (try it with baptisia or penstemon). Its needs are easily met: full sun, rich soil, supplementary water and/or mulch during dry spells.

It begins its season with bushy, dark green, cloverlike foliage and is soon joined by the dense flowering stalks, which rise above the leaves. The large sunny yellow flowers, which last for weeks and weeks, look a great deal like lupine blooms. Later, they fade to flattened brown seedpods.

A couple of minor caveats: young plants are slow to bloom, spending their first season or two on root development instead—so you have to be patient. Also, Carolina lupine forms a deep taproot, so site it where you want it to stay, as later transplanting may not be possible.

Tiarella cordifolia

Foamflower

BLOOM TIME: spring

HEIGHT/WIDTH: 6"–12" × 6"–12" (15–30cm ×
15–30cm)

LIGHT: shade

ZONES: 3–8

Foamflower

No doubt this irresistible woodland wildflower gets its common name from the way it literally foams with airy white blossoms for many weeks each spring—a sight best enjoyed when it is growing in large groups. You can reproduce this show easily in your own shady garden, provided you have humus-rich soil (naturally found under deciduous trees).

Foamflower's blooms aren't actually pure white. Tiny golden stamens shoot outward amid the white petals, giving individual blooms a starry look and the entire spike a full yet exuberant appearance. The leaves are equally handsome, and carry on well after the flowers are gone, as long as you remember to water the plants during the heat of summer. They are heart-shaped, somewhat furry, and in the variety *T. cordifolia* var. *collina* (also known as *T. wherryi*) feature accenting red veins. Foamflower leaves gain an attractive bronze hue as cold weather arrives.

So agreeable and good-looking is foamflower that native-plant nurseries have been answering the call for variations. Among the alternatives you may find are clump-forming 'Dunvegan', with pink-tinted flowers and sage-green leaves, and delicate-looking but eager-growing 'Slickrock', with smaller, deeply lobed forest green leaves and light pink blooms.

Tradescantia virginiana

Spiderwort

BLOOM TIME: summer

HEIGHT/WIDTH: 1'–2' × 3' (30–60cm × 90cm)

LIGHT: full sun–partial shade

ZONES: 5–8

'Concord Grape' spiderwort

Clumps of grassy leaves that may remind you of daylily foliage will enthusiastically cover a bank, line a pathway, or serve as a foundation planting, with the added bonus of a constant supply of flowers. Spiderwort leaves can be a foot or more long and interweave and overlap, generally to the exclusion of weeds. The distinctive, three-petaled flowers look a bit like little tricorner Colonial hats, are centered with a small boss of yellow-tipped stamens, and are carried in umbels. Between 1 and 2 inches (2.5–5cm) across, they are usually blue. Deadheading is not necessary—the petals fade and drop unobtrusively each evening to be replaced by others coming into bloom the next morning. If the show begins to dissipate or the foliage starts to sprawl, simply cut back the entire plant hard; by autumn, you should get a repeat performance.

The native spiderwort is a tough plant, prospering in sun or part shade; some shade makes the color of the leaves and flowers darker. It tolerates all sorts of soil and moisture conditions. In damp spots, it will grow rampantly. It also self-sows, so plan for its eager growth by putting it in a spot where you want a lot of ground covered.

Trillium grandiflorum

Large-flowered trillium

BLOOM TIME: spring

HEIGHT/WIDTH: 12"–18" × 8"–12" (30–45cm × 20–30cm)

LIGHT: partial–full shade

ZONES: 3–9

Large-flowered trillium

Alas, this is one wildflower we may have to live without—in our gardens. It is undeniably beautiful, and familiar to anyone who has taken a walk in shady, moist woods in early spring. There, it looks both sturdy and plentiful, displaying its broad white flowers with grace as it carpets large areas.

But trilliums are endangered plants in many areas. It's not the depredations of an occasional admiring hiker that threaten the wild populations (though the plant makes a poor cut flower and is very unlikely to survive transplanting back home), it's the pillaging done by wildflower poachers.

Professional horticulturists are desperately seeking a fast, easy way to propagate them. Unfortunately, offsets naturally produced by the rhizomes are few and slow to get established. Tissue culture (raising clones in laboratory test tubes) does generate more little trilliums but there is about a five-year wait for blooming-size plants. Trillium can also be grown from freshly harvested seed, but blooms may be up to nine years away! So, needless to say, an inexpensive trillium plant from a local or mail-order nursery should be viewed with great suspicion. Your best bet, if you simply must have trillium, is to check the plant sales of botanical gardens—and pay the high price willingly. Otherwise, if demand for trillium continues unabated, we won't have them in the woods *or* our gardens.

Uvularia sessilifolia

Wild oats, sessile bellwort

BLOOM TIME: spring

HEIGHT/WIDTH: 1' × 1' (30cm × 30cm)

LIGHT: partial shade

ZONES: 3–8

Wild oats

Dry shade? No problem. Here's a sweet little groundcover that you can plant, give a little mulch, let spread, and leave alone. It may remind you somewhat of Solomon's seal, thanks to its arching stems lined with oval, tapering leaves, but this is a smaller plant, generally with fewer leaves to a stem. Wild oats has the curious habit of leaning in one direction, something that becomes more noticeable and actually quite charming when you grow it en masse.

The dainty, 1-inch (2.5cm), bell-shaped flowers, which appear at the ends of the stems, are soft yellow.

Unfortunately, they hang downward, so they're not very noticeable, though they do last for several weeks. In and out of bloom, wild oats looks good in the company of smaller, airy ferns and wildflowers of similar stature, such as Virginia bluebells.

Related species are larger of stem and flower. Straw-bells, *U. perfoliata*, reaches 2 feet (60cm). Merrybells, *U. grandiflora*, is taller, grows up to 30 inches (76cm), and also has a more erect growth habit.

Verbascum spp.

Mullein

BLOOM TIME: summer

HEIGHT/WIDTH: 4'–8' × 3' (1.2–2.4m × 90cm)

LIGHT: full sun

ZONES: 5–9

Mullein

If you've been dismissing this stately plant as a roadside weed, you're missing out. Granted, it grows as easily as weed (all it wants is well-drained or dry soil), but don't let that blind you to its virtues. Mullein's profile is husky enough to make an important contribution to a cottage garden scheme. And it looks wonderful in the company of roses, particularly the old-fashioned ones. Gardeners in the Southwest and West sometimes group three or so plants center stage or as a foil to boulders or a wall; mulleins certainly have the presence to succeed in such settings.

Most are biennials, so all you see their first summer is a large, felted, gray-leaved rosette hugging the ground. Their second summer, though, is worth waiting for. Then, substantial spires rise up and display their blooms for many, many weeks. Some species have branched spires for a candelabra effect, desirable if you want maximum impact.

A tour of the flower colors may further persuade you. A number of mulleins (among them *V. bombyciferum*, *V. olympicum*, and *V. thapsus*) are a pleasant primrose yellow. Some are white-flowered, a soft duet with the silvery foliage (*V. chaixii 'Album'*, *V. × hybridum 'Mont Blanc'*). The variable *V. phoeniceum* ranges from red to pink to white, but is usually seen lavender. The 'Southern Charm' hybrids are pastels from apricot to soft pink to light purple.

Vernonia novaboracensis

Ironweed

BLOOM TIME: late summer

HEIGHT/WIDTH: 5'–8' × 2'–4' (1.5–2.4m × 60cm–120cm)

LIGHT: full sun

ZONES: 5–7

Ironweed

Have you read the Pulitzer prize–winning novel by William Kennedy named after this plant? He did his homework: the introduction, adapted from the Audubon Society's wildflower guide, notes that ironweed owes its name to the toughness of its stem. Kennedy's hero, Frank Phelan, has great tenacity in the face of all sorts of misfortunes.

In addition to the strong, erect stem that sees this towering wildflower through wind and weather, ironweed has another laudable asset. The electric purple flowers, borne in clusters, are probably the most vivid shade of purple you can expect to see at that time of year (did Kennedy also want to point out Phelan's intensity?).

Ironweed is not at all particular about soil. It will do fine in lean soil, and be a bit bigger and lusher in more fertile spots. Set some of the newer, abundant-flowering goldenrods at its base for a great shout of late-season color. Or line it up along a garage wall or back fence with tall sunflowers. It is not an especially good self-sower.

Veronicastrum virginicum

Culver's root

BLOOM TIME: summer

HEIGHT/WIDTH: 4'–7' × 1'–3' (1.2–2m × 30–90cm)

LIGHT: full sun

ZONES: 3–9

Culver's root

Where your sunny garden can use the height, this slender, graceful plant will be a wonderful addition. As you might guess from the name, it is closely related to the familiar garden perennial veronica (in fact, it was formerly classified as one). The difference, of course, is the size, and the habit as well; veronica is often a mound, wider than tall, while this plant is taller and much more narrow.

Otherwise, the blooms are quite similar to those of Veronica—pretty, tapering spires composed of tiny flowers. The species is either white or a soft blue; the blue hue is especially apparent when you view a large planting from a distance.

Horticulturists have made an effort to select for consistent color, and, if you wish, you can choose pristine 'Album' (also known as var. album) or pale pink 'Roseum' (also known as var. rosea). Whatever the color, the spires hold up well in a vase and also dry well for arrangements.

Like so many other native wildflowers, Culver's root thrives in fertile soil that drains well; a mulch is advisable where summers are long and hot. You would do well to plant it in groupings so the flowers stand out well. Then give it some attractive, taller companions that like similar conditions, such as bee balm or Joe-Pye weed.

Viola pedata

Bird-foot violet

BLOOM TIME: spring and autumn

HEIGHT/WIDTH: 4"–10" × 4"–6" (10–25cm × 10–15cm)

LIGHT: full sun–partial shade

ZONES: 4–9

Bird-foot violet

All the wild violets are sweet, delicate things, but the bird-foot may be the loveliest. Its name comes from its unique leaves, which, rather than the usual heart shape, are finely divided (between nine and fifteen points) to look a bit like a many-toed small bird's foot.

The flowers of this violet are also bigger than some of its near relatives, up to an inch and a half (4cm) across. And unlike the ubiquitous Johnny-jump-ups, they're violet, though sometimes the three lower petals are a contrasting lighter hue. Tiny stamens are golden to orange. Bird-foot violet flowers have a soft, romantic fragrance. They bloom in the spring, and often again in the autumn, especially if you remember to cut back the plants to within a few inches of the ground several weeks after flowering.

To thrive in a garden setting, bird-foot violet must have sharply drained soil. It languishes in rich soil, and develops crown rot if its spot is too damp. So perhaps the best place for it is a pathside, slope, or bank that is sandy or gravelly — a site where few other plants will grow anyway. If you'd like to include it in the garden proper, you can line its planting hole with a handful of sand or grit. Its graceful, rather lacy character is pretty among spring-flowering bulbs.

1 0 0

*F*AVORITE

*P*LANTS

FOR SHADE

Introducing Shade Plants

Judging from many gardening books and magazines, a beautiful garden is full of sunshine and colorful flowers. Does this mean that shade on your property means no garden? Not at all! Here are one hundred plants that will prosper in shade, from a woodland's deepest gloom, to the space under a small grove of trees, to areas that get morning sun and afternoon shade. Many plants appropriate for shade have extraordinarily beautiful leaves—there's amazing variety in shape, texture, and even color. And you may be pleas-

antly surprised to discover, as you thumb through the following pages, that many also have attractive flowers.

Shade actually is a benefit to many plants. Lack of direct sun means their leaves look healthy and lush, without burned edges or tips, without drying out and wilting. Sunlight also tends to bleach out the beauty of variegated leaves, leaves that are marked or rimmed in white, cream, or gold, whereas in shade such foliage thrives and lights up the scene.

Shelter from the sun's hot rays also preserves flower color, so shade bloomers often hold their color very well. And if you have the impression that plants that flower in shade come only in white, feast your eyes on the upcoming pages: you'll see every hue of yellow, blue, pink, purple, and red. Such variety, both in foliage and flower, suggests all sorts of exciting possibilities. Rather than wondering what on earth to grow in shade, you are invited to view a range of tantalizing choices.

TYPES OF SHADE

Before you start landscaping your shade garden, take a moment to analyze it. Each entry in this chapter addresses what sort of shade is best for the plant in question. Of course, there is always latitude, and something described as ideal for "dappled shade" may well please you growing in half-day shade, or more.

That said, here are the three main types of shade gardeners contend with.

Full shade: This is defined as an area where foliage from overhead trees or an adjacent structure (house, outbuilding, deck) effectively blocks out practically all light, all day. If the shade comes from trees, the deprivation to plants below is more severe because their dense or overlapping leaves may also keep rainwater from reaching the ground, and their roots may suck out moisture and nutrients from the soil at their feet (common culprits are Norway and silver maples, oaks, and many evergreens). Full shade is not easy to garden in, no doubt about it. But with some soil improvement (described in the following pages), regular watering, and carefully chosen plants, you have every chance of beautifying such a spot.

Dappled, filtered, or partial shade: You find this pleasant condition under deciduous trees with lighter-textured foliage (such as birches, locusts, olives, and shorter growers like dogwoods and hawthorns). A pergola or overhead lathwork also will cause this effect. The constant shifting of light and shadows goes on for most of the day, giving shade plants below the best of both worlds—sufficient light to photosynthesize and bloom, but protection from the sun's damaging rays.

Half shade: As alluded to above, many shady gardens actually get several hours of full sun. At other times of the day, the sun moves around the house, garage, wall, fence, or bordering wooded area, and shadows fall over the area. Shade plants seem to do best when the sunny period is in the morning, rather than the reverse, because afternoon sun tends to be hotter and more intense. Lots of plants like half

shade, even ones usually billed as sun lovers. But every yard is different, so experiment and find out what works and what you like.

CHANGING SHADE

No matter what type of shade you have, expect it to change. The situation often just gets darker and darker as your trees grow taller and broader (or vines envelop your pergola). Sometimes an unexpected storm takes out limbs or an entire tree and suddenly there's light where there never was any before. If your shade plants become established where you've planted them, they likely will adapt. If light becomes too dim, they may flower less or cease flowering, grow lanky as they stretch toward a bit of sun, or roam into areas that suit them better. Take all this in stride. In the words of the late great garden writer Henry Mitchell, "If you stop and think of it ... [plants] would be much better off if we stopped pestering them all the time."

There may be times when you tamper with the shade you've been given. Sometimes you simply have to. Lower limbs on your evergreens lose all their needles and eventually die; you might as well remove them. Damaged or diseased branches on evergreens and deciduous trees alike should be removed promptly. First-aid pruning can generally be done at any time, though evergreens tend to bleed if cut in late spring or early summer when their sap is running. Better to wait until late summer or early autumn when the evergreen is heading into dormancy.

TOO MUCH SHADE

If you want to admit more sunlight into a wooded area and don't want to take out entire trees, judicious pruning will help. Don't get in there and hack away indiscriminately. Most trees recover well from pruning as long as no more than a quarter or at most a third of their growth is removed in any one growing season. So, if you have major thinning in mind, spread the work over several seasons.

It is admittedly painful to cut down a tree to make way for a garden. But you ought to consider it if the area you have in mind hosts a black walnut or ailanthus; both of these secrete chemicals that harm or kill neighboring plants. If you decide to leave them, the situation is not hopeless, but you will have to do research and endure plenty of trial and error until you succeed in calling the area in their vicinity a shade garden.

Less obvious roadblocks to success are shallow-rooted trees, among them maples, cottonwoods, and spruce. These are resource hogs, sapping moisture and nutrients from the top layers of soil. And your shade plants need only the first six to twelve inches (15 to 30cm) of soil to grow in. Your options? Remove some (but not all?) such trees. Make raised beds or place plants in containers around the area. Or garden well away from the root zones of the trees.

TOO LITTLE SHADE

Suppose you want to make shade. You've just built a new house or moved into a new housing development, and the lot is distressingly bare. You need some relief from the blasting rays of the sun.

Quick coverage, of course, can be provided by building something. A pergola, with slats that admit some sun, is attractive. If you can, site it on the south side of the house, where the light is strongest.

Alternatively, plant some shade trees. While none can truly be termed "fast growing," some are quicker than others, so you can hope to enjoy shade—and a shade garden—sometime in the next decade. Good choices are dogwoods, Japanese maples, Russian olive, sourwood, and chaste tree. For more ideas, and for information on proper planting techniques (soil amendments will be key), consult your local nursery.

DON'T TOUCH!

One thing you should never do with your shade area is to remove autumn leaves. In nature, they aren't raked up, are they? Instead, they break down and contribute valuable humus to the soil. If you observe that they have fallen in overwhelming numbers or their broad leaves are forming a slimy, smothering mat, intervene by gently raking out some piles and composting them or dicing them up with the lawnmower or in a shredder—then, return this precious resource to the place it came from. Your shade plants will be ever so grateful.

GROWING SHADE PLANTS

The secret to successful shade gardening is the same as with any other type of gardening: good soil equals happy plants. You cannot just plunk in a groundcover or shade-loving wildflower, walk away, and expect it to thrive. The unfortunate fact is that the soil under trees or on the north side of the garage may not be very good, and when you have plans for the area, you should invest some effort in initial improvement and be prepared to keep at it in ensuing seasons.

Many shade plants adore humusy soil, which helps retain soil moisture and improves soil texture. So dig in organic matter in the form of compost, damp peat moss, decomposed leaves, or dehydrated manure. The result will be hospitable ground that gets seedlings off to a good start and nurtures them in years to come. Note that young plants often don't bloom or appear to grow much at all in their first season; this is because they are busy forming roots that will fuel future growth.

You'll notice that the descriptions of some of the plants in this chapter point out special requirements—damp or moist soil is recommended, or acidic soil is preferred. You may have such conditions naturally on your property, but a little soil preparation prior to planting is still wise.

Soil moisture can become a real issue. It seems spring is often damp, and, when summer ushers in, the soil dries out. Some shade plants respond by going dormant, disappearing until the next year; others simply die out. To a certain extent, the soil improvement recommended above will improve moisture retention. Mulching also can help. But you may have to visit your shade garden with the hose or a sprinkler—so, hopefully, water is within reach. Some gardeners choose to lay down soaker hoses, which by virtue of the dimmer light don't seem as obtrusive in the shade as they do in sunny spots.

One last note about the care of your shade plants: Feeding, generally speaking, is not mandatory. If the light is right, the soil is good, and the moisture levels are adequate, you can be sure your shade plants will thrive and contribute interest and glory to your garden.

Aegopodium podagraria

Bishop's goutweed

HEIGHT/WIDTH: 1'–2' (30–60cm)/spreading habit

FLOWERS: white umbels

BLOOM TIME: early summer

ZONES: 4–9

'Variegatum' bishop's goutweed

This is a common plant that sophisticated horticulturists love to hate. "Weedy," they say, "ugly," they sneer. Well, beauty is in the eye of the beholder—and there are times and places when bishop's goutweed is just the plant you need. It is one of the few plants that will grow in terrible soil in complete or partial shade, with no attention from you. It's suitable for a neglected or problem area on your property that needs quick and thorough coverage.

Bishop's goutweed is most often seen in its variegated form, 'Variegatum', and the leaves are actually rather pretty. They're usually lime green and edged liberally with creamy white, making them "pop" in gloomy spots. The flower heads are plentiful and attractive enough, though too small to be dramatic. To control the plant, yank out or whack back unwanted growth and, if you're willing to take the time, cut out the flowers before they go to seed. If you like the plant's look and want to enjoy it in controlled circumstances, containers are the way to go.

The plant is originally from Europe and must owe its name to the fact that it grows around medieval monasteries and churches. It was probably deliberately planted long ago as a medicinal plant, and used to treat gout as well as sore joints and other aches.

Ageratum houstonianum

Ageratum

HEIGHT/WIDTH: 6"–14" × 6"–14" (15–35.5cm ×
15–35.5cm)

FLOWERS: blue, pink, or white

BLOOM TIME: summer

ZONES: all zones (annual)

'Blue Horizon' ageratum

For fast color in dappled shade, few plants beat this bullet-proof annual. It forms small, compact mounds of mint green leaves and, for the entire summer and well into autumn, displays loads of neat color. All it requires is decent, well-drained soil; it survives in drier soils, too, but is not as attractive.

Ageratum's flower heads are clusters of up to forty little fluffy blooms. Most of us have seen the plant in blue or lilac-blue, and sometimes this hue is exactly what you need—as an edging for a hosta border, perhaps, or skirting some spring-flowering shrubs after their blooms have gone by. But it also comes in perky white ('Album', 'Hawaii White') and even pink (the dwarf 'Swing Pink'), suggesting other planting possibilities. A combination of these, rib-boned through a shady perennial bed or along a path, would be lovely.

If you need further persuasion: ageratum attracts butterflies, creatures not often seen in shady spots.

Ajuga reptans

Ajuga, bugleweed

HEIGHT/WIDTH: 4"–8" × 8" (10–20cm × 20cm)

FLOWERS: purple or blue spikes

BLOOM TIME: late spring–early summer

ZONES: 3–8

'Burgundy Glow' ajuga

As a groundcover, this plant has become a bit of a cliché and can spread quite aggressively. But it really has many good and useful qualities, and it should not be written off altogether. Ajuga often grows very well where few other plants thrive, even sites with thin or poor soil, or areas of deep shade. It spreads out well, by means of creeping runners. Its only shortcoming is susceptibility to fungus and rot, but these can be avoided by planting it in well-drained soil.

Nowadays, ajuga comes in a variety of intriguing forms, so if you search the nurseries or catalogs diligently, you can make yourself the proud owner of a truly handsome,

unique, low-maintenance planting. Among the many choices are 'Burgundy Glow', whose leaves are splashed with pink and cream; 'Pink Surprise', with lance-shaped leaves of bronze-green (and pinkish flowers); and 'Purple Brocade', sporting especially ruffled duotone leaves of purple-bronze and forest green. The most interesting one is 'Catlin's Giant', which has extra-big, dark bronze–purple leaves and taller flowers (it originated in the garden of a fellow who accidentally sprayed weed killer on his ajuga patch—most of the plants died, but one clump survived and came back in this jumbo size).

Alchemilla mollis

Lady's-mantle

HEIGHT/WIDTH: 1'–2' × 1'–2' (30–60cm × 30–60cm)

FLOWERS: tiny sprays; chartreuse

BLOOM TIME: late spring–early summer

ZONES: 4–8

Lady's-mantle

As a foliage plant, lady's-mantle is especially desirable. The large, scallop-edged leaves (up to 4 inches [10cm] across) are lime green and have a soft, felted texture. When it rains or when early morning dew gathers on the leaves, the water beads up like quicksilver—a truly enchanting sight. The leaves are borne in clumps and lend an immediate grace and softness to semishady areas.

The frothy flowers also make a welcome contribution. They are a sharp, clear shade of yellow-green, best described as chartreuse. They appear in profusion each spring, and continue to a lesser extent for the rest of the season. Short stalks hold them slightly above and away from the leaves. Their form and color mix nicely with other shade bloomers, particularly violet or rosy flowers, such as those of creeping phlox and some violas.

Lady's-mantle is simple to grow. All it needs is moist but well-drained soil. If your summers become hot and dry, provide a mulch and supplemental water.

Amsonia tabernaemontana

Bluestar

HEIGHT/WIDTH: 2'–3' × 2'–3' (60–90cm × 60–90cm)

FLOWERS: clusters of blue stars

BLOOM TIME: early summer

ZONES: 3–9

Bluestar

At maturity, bluestar gains an appealingly soft, shrubby appearance that is welcome in semishady spots. And its blooms are that hard-to-find shade of true blue. They are about half an inch (1.5cm) across and star-shaped, and appear in domed clusters at the tops of the stems. The tidy foliage, between 3 and 6 inches (7.5 and 15cm) long, is narrow and willowy and encircles the erect stems.

Despite its seemingly delicate appearance, bluestar thrives in moderately fertile soil and proves itself to be drought tolerant over long summers. If it gets leggy, trim it back occasionally to keep growth dense. Bluestar is also usually free of disease and pest problems. Autumn foliage is a real plus: instead of fading away, the leaves turn a vibrant shade of gold that brings a welcome glow.

This handsome plant is probably best grown in groups or sweeps, so its fine texture won't be lost and the wonderful shade of blue has a chance to really stand out. It's a striking companion for orange- or red-flowered deciduous azaleas, which generally bloom at the same time.

Anemone nemorosa

Wood anemone

HEIGHT/WIDTH: 3"–6" × 6"–12" (7.5–15cm × 15–30cm)

FLOWERS: blue or white

BLOOM TIME: spring

ZONES: 4–8

Wood anemone

While other members of the vast anemone tribe may tolerate light or part-day shade, the wood anemone, a wildflower of European origins, is particularly prized. It is not a tall plant, though it presents its lovely, starry blooms to advantage above its palmate foliage. Moderately moist, rich soil, as is often found in woodland gardens, inspires it to grow lustily. As such, it is ideal for naturalizing.

There are quite a few cultivars to choose from—your best bet is to comb specialty catalogs—but most are in the white or blue range. 'Robinsoniana' (named for the renowned English plantsman William Robinson) is widely regarded as a classic and features large, ½-inch (4cm) blooms in pale lilac, with silvery undersides and a puffball of soft yellow stamens in the middle. Also lovely is the shining white 'Alba' (an heirloom variety that has been around since 1771!) and its double form, 'Alba Plena'.

Although it doesn't grow from a bulb, but rather from a stoloniferous rootstock, this anemone is best planted in autumn, about 3 inches (7.5cm) deep in humusy soil. This gives it a head start, and it may just bloom for you its first spring. It generally dies down (goes dormant) during the summer months.

Aquilegia × hybrida

Columbine

HEIGHT/WIDTH: 2'–3' × 1'–2' (60–90cm × 30–60cm)

FLOWERS: various colors

BLOOM TIME: spring–early summer

ZONES: 3–9

McKana Giants columbine

Columbine flowers are so lovely that no shade gardener should do without them. The plants do best in decent, well-drained soil, and like a little morning sun or dappled sunlight. They make charming companions for hostas and ferns. Just bear in mind that, even in the best settings, they are short-lived. But the species will self-sow; and, if you grow one of the hybrids, you won't hesitate to run right out and replace it.

The original red-and-yellow wild columbine (*A. canadensis*) has small, nodding, upside-down blossoms. Generally, the spurred outer petals are red and the fluted inner ones bright yellow.

There are a host of fabulous, tall, multicolored hybrids to choose from. Many are bicolors, which makes for a lively display. Perhaps the best of the hybrids are the McKana

Giants, which grow to between 2 and 3 feet (60 and 90cm) tall and carry lots of extra-big flowers, in many color combinations. The durable 'Biedermeier' strain is about half as tall, but has an equally diverse color range. If you prefer solid-color columbines, there are plenty to choose from, from sherbet yellow 'Maxistar' to pristine white 'Snow Queen'.

Columbine's only flaw is that its lacy foliage is prone to leaf miners, which weave their trails inside the leaves until little green is left. The flowers keep on blooming, though, seemingly unaffected. Remove all affected foliage, or wait until flowering is over and cut the entire plant down. A fresh flush of new foliage will appear shortly after.

Arisaema triphyllum

Jack-in-the-pulpit

HEIGHT/WIDTH: 2'–3' × 1' (60–90cm × 30cm)

FLOWERS: spadix, color varies

BLOOM TIME: spring

ZONES: 4–8

Jack-in-the-pulpit

This North American woodland native has an eccentrically elegant look that has captured the imaginations of adventurous shade gardeners. Good news: it is also relatively easy to grow. A sheltered spot in moist soil is essential. It is slow and tedious from seed, taking up to four years to reach blooming size. Better to start with a seedling that has already developed its small bulblike root, called a corm. These are available from nurseries in the spring.

Each Jack-in-the-pulpit plant grows two stalks; one bears a pair of leaf-topped stems, the other bears the odd-looking flowering structure. A green and maroon striped hood that curves over at the top, the "pulpit," shields "Jack," a slender, dark red-brown, greenish yellow, or white spadix.

The true flowers lurk at the bottom of the spadix and are very tiny. Through it all, the broad leaves, borne in leaflets of three, form a canopy over and nearly hide this show.

In autumn, if the plant is growing in rich, moist soil and prospering, a cluster of oval red berries appears, sheathed in a papery cylinder. The berries are not edible.

If this plant captures your fancy, you will be intrigued to learn that it has many Asian relatives that are only now making it into the offerings of specialty catalogs. Some have textured or marbled foliage and stems (marketed as "snake-like"!). There are dramatic variations in the "Jack" and "pulpit" colors, and a few have orange autumn berries.

Aruncus dioicus

Goatsbeard

HEIGHT/WIDTH: 4'–7' × 3'–4' (120–210cm × 90–120cm)

FLOWERS: white panicles

BLOOM TIME: late spring–early summer

ZONES: 2–6

Goatsbeard

No, it's not a big astilbe, though you would be pardoned for thinking so the first time you see goatsbeard. It even likes the same conditions of full to partial shade and moist soil. But goatsbeard is a much larger plant, attaining a size and stature that is downright shrublike. Staking is not usually necessary.

Goatsbeard's flowers are not as long-blooming as those of astilbe, but the show is so magnificent you may not mind. For a couple of weeks in late spring or early summer, the stately, feathery wands of creamy white flowers rise in a flurry above the light green foliage. The male and female flowers are borne on separate plants; the male flowers are fuller and the female ones are more greenish. Unfortunately, nurseries don't differentiate, and you won't know until it blooms. Better to plant several, then.

After the dramatic flowers pass, you'll still appreciate the plant for its foliage. The delicate, textured leaves are compound, dissected, and toothed, and they clothe the plant from head to toe. They are untroubled by pests and look fresh all season. If the species is too big for your purposes, seek out the shorter cultivars 'Child of Two Worlds' (3 to 4 feet [90–120cm]) or 'Kneiffi' (3 feet [90cm]).

Asarum canadense

Wild ginger

HEIGHT/WIDTH: 4"–12" × 4"–6" (10–30cm × 10–15cm)

FLOWERS: tiny; purplish brown

BLOOM TIME: spring

ZONES: 4–8

Wild ginger

This is the native North American version of the similar European ginger. Like its relative, it has handsome, dark green, heart-shaped leaves and likes to grow in moist, rich soil. But its leaves are usually larger, up to 6 inches (15cm) across, and have a slightly furry (thus, less glossy) texture. The broader leaves give the plant, as a groundcover, a bolder presence. For instance, it is better able to hold its own in the company of hostas, or to make a dramatic pathside swath. American ginger, unfortunately, seems to be a bit more susceptible to slug damage, so be on the lookout.

Another significant difference is that the leaves of the American ginger are not evergreen over the winter. Even so, they return with gusto each spring. And, generally speaking, the plant is tougher than its European counterpart. Although it is deciduous, it is hardier—gardeners in the North will have better luck with it. It also has proven to take the heat and humidity of a southern summer better.

The small flowers, nondescript, purplish brown, bell-shaped curiosities, are borne in the spring and are well hidden by the foliage. The plant may self-sow, but it spreads mainly by creeping roots. Speaking of the roots, they have a distinctly gingerlike scent and flavor, and were used by native tribes in cooking and medicinally. But the plant is not related to commercial ginger root.

Asarum europaeum

European ginger

HEIGHT/WIDTH: 3" × 8"–12" (7.5cm × 20–30cm)

FLOWERS: tiny brownish bells

BLOOM TIME: spring

ZONES: 4–8

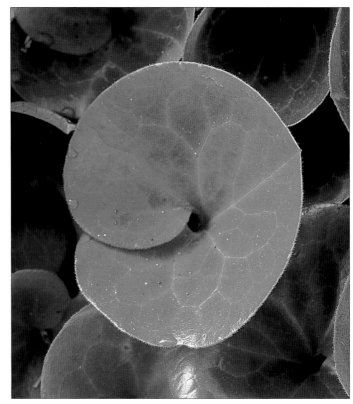

European ginger

If you're looking to densely carpet a shady area with an evergreen groundcover that looks great all season, resists pests and diseases, and requires little or no attention, European ginger is an elegant choice. The kidney-shaped leaves are rich green and wonderfully glossy. Plus, the plant grows and multiplies quickly.

The only catch is that the soil must be right in order to get a good performance. It should be on the moist side, humusy, and yet well drained, so the plants don't suffer from "wet feet." Furthermore, European ginger tends to prefer slightly acidic conditions. Woodland gardens in the Northeast probably fit this bill the best; gardeners else-where can try their luck by meeting as many of these conditions as possible.

Ginger's flowers are not a reason to grow the plant, for they are hidden under the leaves; but they are fascinating. They are tiny things, reddish inside, gray-green outside; one botanist aptly likened them to "little brown stone crocks." They last many weeks, and, when they pass, the seeds are carried off by small rodents.

The plant gets its name from its root, which has an appealing, gingerlike scent and flavor. It is not related to commercial ginger root.

Astilbe × arendsii

Astilbe

HEIGHT/WIDTH: 1½'–4' × 1½'–2½' (45–120cm × 45–75cm)

FLOWERS: plumes (many colors)

BLOOM TIME: spring–summer

ZONES: 4–9

'Gloria Purpurea' astilbe

Where they can be grown—in fertile, moist, well-drained soil, in parts of the country not given to extremes of heat or humidity—there are no finer shade-loving plants than astilbes. A great many of the best varieties were bred in Germany at the turn of the century by accomplished plants-man George Arends. The magnificent feathery plumes, actually masses of tiny flowers, come in a range of colors, from white to lavender to pink to red. Bloom times vary, so if you plan carefully, you can enjoy a long period of color.

Planted in a sweep in a woodland setting or even as a formal circle around the base of a tree, astilbes are delight-ful. They are also a popular choice for along the banks of a pool, pond, or stream.

After the flowers go by, the plant remains attractive. A clump-former, astilbe is clothed in toothed leaflets that look somewhat ferny. Problems with diseases and pests are rare.

Athyrium goeringianum 'Pictum'

(A. niponicum 'Pictum')

Japanese painted fern

HEIGHT/WIDTH: 1'–2' × 6"–10" (30–60cm × 15–25.5cm)

FLOWERS: none

BLOOM TIME: not applicable

ZONES: 5–8

Japanese painted fern

Unlike the vast majority of ferns, Japanese painted fern has handsomely variegated foliage. The fronds are pewtery-silver with a green border; the veins are plum or wine red. Although Japanese painted fern still needs shade to truly thrive, the more light the fronds receive, the more intense the coloring appears. You can experiment with this quality by moving a plant around from one year to the next (or in a container, certainly), or by observing the changes it makes from early spring to late summer, assuming the type of shade it receives varies. The show is enhanced by reddish stems.

This is not an especially hardy fern, and it will not only brown but also die back in a cold autumn and winter. If you are growing it in a marginal climate, either dig it up and bring it in for the winter, or try a heavy protective mulch. Either way, it won't remain evergreen over the winter, though you can look forward to a fresh flush of growth the next spring, heralded by the appearance of new, tiny, rosy-red fiddleheads.

This attractive fern is a favorite with gardeners who grow spring-blooming bulbs and wildflowers. You can see why: the fronds expand just in time to hide and distract from the dying-back foliage. Japanese painted fern also adds fascination to hosta beds, and makes a neat and lovely edging for a somewhat formal shady border.

Begonia grandis

Hardy begonia

HEIGHT/WIDTH: 1'–2' × 1'–2' (30–60cm × 30–60cm)

FLOWERS: sprays, pink or white

BLOOM TIME: summer

ZONES: 6–10

Hardy begonia

It looks like a houseplant begonia, perhaps one of the angelwing types, but this is truly a hardy plant, suitable for growing outdoors and leaving out over the winter in many places. The leaves are big and jagged in form; their top sides are dappled with rich purple, with a velvety red reverse. The dainty little flowers, usually pink, sometimes pink-tinged white, appear later in the season in clusters, when color is often in short supply. (There is a white-flowered variant, 'Alba'.)

To keep hardy begonia looking good, grow it in moist but well-drained soil. Yes, this versatile plant will do well even in full shade. If happy, hardy begonia will spread eagerly by means of little bulbils that are shed by the stems later in the season. You can intercept these if you have other plans for them (you may wish to plant them in another spot or give some to a friend) or want to control the plant's expansion.

If you are at all concerned about your plants making it through the cold weather, give them a mulch in late autumn. As long as the tuberous roots don't freeze, they'll return in full glory the next year.

$\mathcal{B}egonia \times tuberhybrida$

Tuberous begonia

HEIGHT/WIDTH: 1'–2' × 1'–2' (30–60cm × 30–60cm)

FLOWERS: color varies

BLOOM TIME: summer

ZONES: 9–10 (grown as an annual)

Tuberous begonia

These are the jumbo-flowered sensations you see so vigorously advertised every spring in nursery catalogs and garden centers. They are touted as a dependable source of bold color for partial to full shade, which is true. The plump, 4- to 5-inch (10 to 13cm) blooms come in a range of bright colors (red, orange, yellow, hot pink) as well as white and picotee (white or cream petals, with colorful edging) and lace (colorful petals, white or cream edging). A happy plant will bloom like gangbusters.

Many gardeners like to grow these in containers, window boxes, hanging baskets, and so forth. As long as the plants get what they need, namely a good, rich soil mix, adequate moisture, and decent air circulation, they do well. You can also plant the tubers in the ground, realizing that they are tender and will die over the winter unless you overwinter them in a cool (not freezing) place in baggies of sawdust or moss.

If you get hooked on using these in your shade garden, it might behoove you to do some shopping around. Not all tuberous begonias are created equal. Some are propagated vegetatively to assure uniformity, others are seed-grown, with the expected variations. Some have smaller flowers, some bloom longer. The best are the Blackmore & Langdon strain, from England but available abroad from select nurseries. Also worthwhile are the widely available U.S.-bred tuberous begonias out of the Santa Cruz, California, area.

Bergenia cordifolia

Bergenia

HEIGHT/WIDTH: 1'–1½' × 1' (30–45cm × 30cm)

FLOWERS: pink, red, white

BLOOM TIME: spring

ZONES: 3–8

'Redstart' bergenia

Looking almost tropical in its lushness, bergenia forms big, bold, cabbagelike clumps with sturdy, glossy leaves. Each leaf is oval or heart-shaped, and can be as wide as a foot (30cm) across. The texture is leathery and shiny, and the foliage develops brown edges only if the plants get too much sun in the summer or if you neglect to mulch them for a harsh winter. Otherwise, bergenia is handsome in all seasons, remaining evergreen in most parts of the country. The onset of cool autumn weather inspires the leaves to turn an attractive shade of bronze, russet, or purple. This plant is a dramatic choice for mass plantings, such as under a tree, at the base of a shrub border, or along a walkway.

The flowers appear just above the leaves in spring, on strong stalks, and consist of lush trusses of bright pink blossoms. There are a number of worthy hybrids. The handsome Bressingham selections, 'Bressingham Ruby', 'Bressingham Salmon', 'Bressingham White', hail from England and can be found in some U.S. nurseries. Widely available hybrids include 'Abendglut' ('Evening Glow'), with flowers that are nearly crimson and foliage that turns maroon in winter; 'Perfecta', with rosy-red flowers and purplish leaves; and 'Silberlicht' ('Silver Light'), with pink-blushed white flowers with red centers.

Browallia speciosa

Browallia

HEIGHT/WIDTH: 1'–2' × 8"–10" (30–60cm × 20–30cm)

FLOWERS: usually blue

BLOOM TIME: summer

ZONES: 9–10 (annual in all other zones)

Browallia

Since browallia, also called bush violet, is of tropical origins, it's best grown in the Deep South, Gulf Coast, or mild areas of the West. The rest of us can envy those gardeners, or enjoy it as an annual. Because of its arching, drooping stems, it's also suitable for containers or hanging baskets, perhaps on a protected porch. In any event, don't allow it to be exposed to hot afternoon sun, which causes leaf-tip burn. Filtered shade is best, and the soil should be evenly moist.

The somewhat sticky leaves are long (up to 4 inches [10cm]), with pointed tips, and browallia is more upright than spreading—though this characteristic is not obvious when it is grown in a grouping or as a groundcover.

Browallia is blanketed in bell-shaped, 1- or 2-inch (2.5 or 5cm) blooms for much of the summer, and they are beauties. Usually lilac blue, they are also available in deep violet-blue ('Marine Bells', 'Blue Bells') and white, which really lights up semishady areas ('White Troll', 'White Bells'). Newly introduced 'Vanja' has vivid blue flowers with white eyes.

Brunnera macrophylla

Brunnera, Siberian bugloss, perennial forget-me-not

HEIGHT/WIDTH: 1'–2' × 1'–2' (30–60cm × 30–60cm)

FLOWERS: sprays of tiny blue flowers

BLOOM TIME: late spring–early summer

ZONES: 3–7

Brunnera

If you love forget-me-nots, try this vigorous-growing perennial charmer. Loose sprays of tiny (¼-inch [6mm]), star-shaped, brilliant blue flowers appear early, along with the spring bulbs and forsythia, and bloom with abandon for up to a month. The plant makes a wonderful "weaver" in areas where you've planted a variety of flowers, because the color goes with almost everything. It also brings fresh excitement to hosta or fern beds in semishade. White-flowered brunneras are available, as are ones with variegated leaves (ivory-banded 'Hadspen Cream' is a stunner). Note that the plant will self-sow, though it's simple to pull out unwanted volunteers.

Even if it didn't flower, brunnera would be a valuable addition to a lightly shaded garden as a groundcover, because its heart-shaped leaves are attractive in their own right. They start out small, form a pretty carpet that disguises fading bulb foliage, and expand in size (sometimes to nearly 8 inches [20cm] across) as the summer goes by. Watch out for nibbling slugs, though, and set out bait if they start to disfigure the planting.

Caladium bicolor

(C. hortulanum)

Caladium, elephant's ears

HEIGHT/WIDTH: 1'–2' × 1'–2' (30–60cm × 30–60cm)

FLOWERS: greenish-white spathes

BLOOM TIME: spring

ZONES: 9–10 (annual elsewhere)

'Fannie Munson' caladium

Northerners may think of caladium as a houseplant, but gardeners in the South know better. It is one of the most valuable, lush-growing foliage plants for shade, because it brings a range of bright, attractive color and because it is so easy to grow.

Each plant grows from a small, chubby tuber. The broadly heart-shaped leaves are carried on short stalks. They usually feature dappled patterns accented with solid-color margins and veins, in handsome variations of pink, white, red, and green.

Plantings devoted to one cultivar are breathtaking—try a band of, say, white-and-green ones ribboning under the shade of live oaks. Mixed plantings are equally attractive, perhaps in planters on a porch or in a semishaded eastern or northern exposure. Feeding monthly with an all-purpose fertilizer guarantees a super display.

Caladiums are generally trouble-free, rarely bothered by pests or disease. They thrive in moist, humusy soil and do well in hot, humid summers, but may suffer from rot if the soil doesn't drain well. If you grow them in containers, be sure to attend to the drainage requirement (a hole in the bottom of the pot, and good, rich potting mix). Either way, you'll see that your caladiums slow down in the autumn and go dormant for the winter. If you are at all concerned about their cold-hardiness, simply dig up the dormant tubers and store them for the winter in a cool, dry place indoors.

Caltha palustris

Marsh marigold

HEIGHT/WIDTH: 12"–18" × 9"–12" (30–45cm × 23–30cm)

FLOWERS: yellow buttercups

BLOOM TIME: spring

ZONES: 4–10

Marsh marigold

Damp or wet shade is often difficult to landscape, but your troubles are over—marsh marigold is a splendid candidate for a starring role in such conditions. The succulent, cabbagelike leaves will thrive, and spread by means of runners, until the whole area is covered.

Each spring you will be treated to a short but exuberant flowering show. Marsh marigold flowers really are sensational. They are sunny yellow, about 2 inches (5cm) across, and carried in clusters; they look a great deal like buttercups, to which they are related. A cultivar, 'Plena', has double flowers. Their brightness makes them a pleasant companion for spring bulbs that don't mind similar conditions (such as camas or winter aconite); and, after all the flowers fade, marsh marigold foliage stays around to cover up and carry on.

If your soil begins to dry out as summer advances, the leaves will gradually die down and fade from view and the plant will go dormant. If this leaves you with a bare area, be sure to plant marsh marigold in the company of other things that continue the show, like cardinal flower or irises.

Campanula spp.

Bellflower

HEIGHT/WIDTH: 1'–4' × 6"–2' (30–120cm × 15–60cm)

FLOWERS: blue, purple, pink, or white bells

BLOOM TIME: summer

ZONES: 4–8

Bellflower

Many members of the campanula tribe will do well in some shade, which preserves the flower color. The taller, upright-growing ones are probably best for attracting notice — in dappled, not deep, shade, such as at the edge of a woodland or in a spot that receives some morning sun and is shielded from hot afternoon rays. For the most part, they require moist, well-drained soil that is not acidic.

Among the top choices are great bellflower (*C. latifolia*), clustered bellflower (*C. glomerata*), and milky bellflower (*C. lactiflora*). The first has small racemes of tubular flowers atop thick, unbranched stems that don't require staking. There are some nice cultivars of this one, including handsome white 'Alba', atmospheric 'Gloaming', with pale, smoky blue flowers, and 'Macrantha' (also known as *C. lactiflora* var. *macrantha*), with larger, royal purple blooms.

Clustered bellflower, as the name suggests, carries its funnel-shaped flowers in large, loose clusters. The plant blooms lushly, so it is a good choice where you really want a show. It, too, hosts a number of worthy selections, among them dark periwinkle blue 'Joan Elliot' and the taller 'Superba', as well as white 'Crown of Snow'.

As for milky bellflower, it is a tall plant, sometimes reaching as much as 5 feet (1.5m), and laden with large, heavy panicles that look from a distance like scoops of ice cream. You will have to stake this flower, or set it adjacent to plants it can lean on. The lovely 'Loddon Anna' has soft pink blooms.

Caulophyllum thalictroides

Blue cohosh

HEIGHT/WIDTH: 1'–2' × 6" (30–60cm × 15cm)

FLOWERS: tiny, brownish

BLOOM TIME: spring

ZONES: 3–8

Blue cohosh

Grow this plant for its autumn berries, which are sensational. There is a buildup to get them, but it is always interesting. First, in early spring, the tiny, ½-inch (1.5cm) flowers emerge; they're brownish green to brownish purple with yellow stamens and pistils—not very attractive. Shortly, the small flowers are joined by tufts of dark purple foliage that will remind you of columbines. As the season progresses, the odd flowers fade and the foliage expands and turns deep blue-green, a color match for the leaves of some hostas.

At last, in autumn, the round, peasize berries pop out of the seed capsules. They are green at first, but one day you stop dead in your tracks and gasp at their beauty—they've become magnificent, rich, bright violet-blue. You can't miss them, nor will anyone else who visits your garden at this time of year.

For best results, grow blue cohosh in moist, fertile, acidic soil. Part shade is fine; full shade is too. The plant doesn't tend to spread much, because the seeds embedded in those fabulous berries germinate slowly and erratically.

Centranthus ruber

Red valerian, Jupiter's beard

HEIGHT/WIDTH: 2'–3' × 2'–3' (60–90cm × 60–90cm)

FLOWERS: red or white

BLOOM TIME: summer

ZONES: 5–8

Red valerian

A wanderer at heart, red valerian may begin life in your garden in a sunny border but eventually seed its way into semishady nooks and crannies. No matter where this plant grows, you'll enjoy the remarkably long-lasting, sweetly fragrant blooms, which in the species are rosy crimson. (A white version, 'Albus', is easy to find, and a little hunting in specialty nurseries will turn up the lovely pink-hued 'Roseus'.)

Individual blooms are only about half an inch (1.5cm) across, but the flower heads are dense with them. Butterflies adore these flowers. They also make terrific bouquets.

This adaptable plant is also easygoing about its soil preferences. It doesn't care for extremes of wet or dryness but otherwise will grow just about anywhere. Established plants are quite drought-tolerant, and drier soil also seems to inspire more compact growth. Only very hot, humid summers cause this exuberant plant to flag.

Since valerian is in bloom for practically the whole summer, it is probably best planted solo, so it doesn't steal the show. To vary things a bit, just grow more than one color. You'll notice that the sage green foliage shows up well against the dark background of shrubs and hedges.

Chrysogonum virginianum

Goldenstar, green-and-gold

HEIGHT/WIDTH: 4"–1' × 1'–2' (10–30cm × 30–60cm)

FLOWERS: small yellow daisies

BLOOM TIME: late spring–summer

ZONES: 5–9

Goldenstar

Few other groundcovers for partial shade bloom as brightly and continually as little goldenstar. A low, spreading (but not aggressive) plant, it has dark green, heart-shaped leaves and bears marvelous, glowing yellow, 1½-inch (4cm) daisy-like blooms on short stalks. If you grow it in soil that is neither boggy nor dry, it will bloom generously for many weeks and thereafter produce occasional blooms until cold weather arrives. A cultivar, 'Pierre', is smaller than the species and prized for its especially long bloom period.

A wildflower native to the area from the Appalachians south to Florida, goldenstar will surely thrive in gardens in that part of the United States. But it does just fine further north, provided you give it a good winter mulch.

Mass plantings, as along a woodland walkway or bordering a line of shrubs, always look great and call attention to the vivacious though small flowers. You can successfully combine goldenstar with other flowers—make a lively carpet of color by growing it with columbine or Virginia bluebells.

Cimicifuga racemosa

Bugbane

HEIGHT/WIDTH: 3'–6' × 3' (90–180cm × 90cm)

FLOWERS: white spires

BLOOM TIME: midsummer

ZONES: 3–8

Bugbane

A tall, full plant, bugbane is magnificent in the right setting. It is best employed in back of shorter plants, where its imposing presence enhances rather than overwhelms; some gardeners like to place it in the middle of an "island bed," where it can be admired from all sides. A solo performance under deciduous trees, perhaps with ferns at its feet, is guaranteed to be dramatic.

The dark green, much-divided foliage creates a bushlike form up to about 3 feet (90cm) tall and wide. The creamy white flower plumes, 6 inches (15cm) or longer, rise up an additional 2 or 3 feet (60 or 90cm) above the foliage and are a sight to behold: they are branched, rather than individual, spires, so the effect is like candelabras. Bugbane puts on a regal show for several weeks in midsummer, and never needs propping up. Some nurseries don't mention the scent, while others tell you it's "rank," but the truth is that it's not very obtrusive.

Cimicifuga is long-lived and trouble-free, unfussy about soil and asking only for sufficient moisture. The more shade it receives (although it is not suitable for deep gloom), the longer-lasting those remarkable blooms will be.

Coleus × hybridus

Coleus

HEIGHT/WIDTH: 1'–3' × 1'–3' (30–90cm × 30–90cm)

FLOWERS: purple spires

BLOOM TIME: summer

ZONES: all zones (annual)

'Color Pride' coleus

Although often thought of as a houseplant, coleus can be grown outdoors anywhere the summers are warm—just consider it an annual, and tear it out before cold weather comes. It adapts well to any shady location, even deep, dark shade, provided its soil is moist and well drained (dry soil causes it to become leggy, look increasingly awful, and finally expire).

There are now literally hundreds of crisply colorful varieties on the market, and a bed devoted to coleus alone or in tandem with other foliage plants can be quite an appealing sight. You've probably seen the ones sporting plain red leaves with green borders everywhere, but there are also some unusual beauties, such as ones with eggshell white, claret red, or gold-bronze interiors and lighter or richer green borders or veination. Some of the new dwarf varieties don't need any pinching to grow naturally bushy.

A word to the wise about finding these interesting coleus selections: shop for seeds. Most large seed companies offer several intriguing choices, and coleus is a cinch to grow from seed.

Comptonia peregrina

Sweetfern

HEIGHT/WIDTH: 2'–4' (60–120cm)/spreading habit

FLOWERS: tiny yellow-green catkins

BLOOM TIME: summer

ZONES: 4–7

Not a fern at all, but rather a deciduous shrub with lush, aromatic foliage and inconspicuous flowers, sweetfern is prized for its ability to tolerate difficult conditions. It grows in sandy, acidic, infertile soil in the wild, and tolerates the abuses of wind, weather, and even pollution. It is rarely bothered by any pests or diseases, and unlike some shrubby plants, it requires little pruning to remain the same height.

Once established, however, sweetfern will not stay within its bounds to the sides. Its species name, *peregrina*, refers to the fact that it "peregrinates," or wanders and spreads at will. So it would be an appropriate choice for landscaping a partially shaded, naturalistic area with poor soil. It is one of the few plants able to tolerate seaside areas with aplomb.

Sweetfern

The long, lance-shaped leaves more or less resemble skinny fern leaves, though they are mostly carried in loose clusters that give the plant a carefree profile. They are dark green above and lighter below. On hot days, or when you rub your hands on them, they radiate an enchanting spicy-fern fragrance

The only thing that has kept this fine plant from being grown more widely is the difficulties of propagating and transplanting it. Fortunately, some nurseries have succeeded in raising some from root cuttings, and you should look for these and plant them while they're young.

Convallaria majalis

Lily-of-the-valley

HEIGHT/WIDTH: 4"–8" × 8"–12" (10–20cm × 20–30cm)

FLOWERS: tiny white bells

BLOOM TIME: late spring

ZONES: 2–9

Lily-of-the-valley

Ah, what would springtime be like without the gentle, romantic scent of lily-of-the-valley wafting across the yard? When it has the right conditions—humusy soil and part to full shade—this old favorite makes a superb groundcover, blanketing broad areas with its glossy lilylike foliage and excluding weeds.

The deliciously fragrant small bells line separate stems that rise above the carpet of green leaves. They have a waxy texture, which helps them tolerate the vagaries of springtime weather, allows them to last many weeks in the ground, and makes it possible for them to transfer with grace to a petite vase indoors.

Much as you may adore the original species, some of the newer cultivars are worth considering. 'Albostriata' has white-striped leaves that are very attractive. Larger-flowered cultivars also are available, including 'Fortin's Giant' and the double-flowered 'Flore Pleno'. The one with pale pink bells may also win your heart (it's called var. *rosea*). Any of these are worth growing on their own or mixing together. Note that lily-of-the-valley is sold as "pips," which are simply pieces of fleshy rhizome. Don't let them dry out—plant them immediately upon arrival at your home, or soak them in a bowl of water until you're ready. Hopefully, they will flower their first year.

Cornus canadensis

Bunchberry

HEIGHT/WIDTH: 3"–9" (7.5–23cm)/spreading habit

FLOWERS: white

BLOOM TIME: spring

ZONES: 2–6

Bunchberry

In its native woods, bunchberry grows in broad colonies, lighting up the gloom with its large (for the plant's size) white flowers—a sight you can imitate in your garden. It must have humus-rich, moist, well-drained soil to do well, however, so it is happiest under deciduous trees or a combination of deciduous and evergreen ones (the ground under a grove of shallow-rooted evergreens is often too dry and infertile). It is also nice at the feet of acid-soil-loving shrubs such as rhododendrons and azaleas.

The flowers look just like dogwood-tree flowers, or rather "bracts," which is no surprise, as this plant is the same species. The orange-red berries that follow by autumn are also characteristic and, while pulpy to our taste, are beloved by birds. As for the leaves, they grow in a loose whorl around the stem and are a nice, shiny green. In sheltered locations, they may last all winter.

Some gardeners have had trouble establishing bunchberry, so here are a few tips to ensure success. Obviously, the site should be suitable, as described above. Your best bet is to start with young seedlings; although bunchberry can be grown from seed, this is a tedious process best left to the nursery. Also, older plants tend to be woodier and resent transplanting. Keep your crop well watered its first season, and add a moisture-retaining mulch. If your plants are happy, over the years they will spread far and wide throughout your shade garden; extras are easily removed.

Corydalis lutea

Golden corydalis

HEIGHT/WIDTH: 12"–16" × 12" (30–40.5cm × 30cm)

FLOWERS: yellow

BLOOM TIME: spring–autumn

ZONES: 4–8

Golden corydalis

A champion for cool, moist soil in partial shade, golden corydalis blooms heartily all summer long. Its small, tubular, rich yellow flowers are held aloft in lush racemes. At season's end, they shed plenty of seeds. Let them—new plants will turn up in unexpected places (even hugging a stone wall!). A border, pathside, or woodland turned over to them is always a cheerful sight, especially on gray days.

The plant forms a low mound of lacy, ferny foliage that looks very much like bleeding heart foliage (the two plants are not related, however). It is evergreen, though in the northern reaches of its range winter protection is advisable.

In recent years, fabulous blue-flowered versions of this plant have appeared in North America and Europe; they hail from China's Sichuan province. The most popular of the blue-flowered cultivars is electric blue 'Blue Panda', which blooms over just as long a period as golden corydalis, if not longer. While 'Blue Panda' tolerates light shade, less sun tends to make it grow a bit leggy.

Cyclamen hederifolium

Ivy-leaved cyclamen, baby cyclamen

HEIGHT/WIDTH: 3"–5" × 5"–8" (7.5–13cm × 13–20cm)

FLOWERS: pink or white

BLOOM TIME: autumn

ZONES: 5–9

Ivy-leaved cyclamen

Gardeners who fancy late-flowering bulbous plants agree, this hardy cyclamen is the prettiest of them all. The flowers look just like those of the florist cyclamen, its cousin, they are just much smaller, about an inch (2.5cm) across. Perched atop graceful, bare stems, they are usually pink and sometimes white, and a patch of them in bloom, with all their swept-back petals, is a truly enchanting sight.

But perhaps the greatest attraction of ivy-leaved cyclamen is its magnificent foliage. Each individual leaf is a study in light and dark green, with silver highlights and purplish-green undersides. Occasionally you'll notice an all-green

one, or an almost entirely silver one, but this variability just enhances the value of the plant as a beautiful groundcover.

Like all cyclamen, it grows from a stout little tuber. Plant it in the spring, shallowly, in ground that is loamy and well drained. The high shade under deciduous trees is ideal. Ivy-leaved cyclamen is a tough little customer; it will manage to thrive in dry shade and survive hot, dry summers by going dormant. When conditions are right, the plant self-sows freely, enlarging the size of the patch you've now become so enamored of.

Darmera peltata
(Peltiphyllum peltatum)

Umbrella plant

HEIGHT/WIDTH: 3'–6' × 2'–3' (90–180cm × 60–90cm)

FLOWERS: pink flower heads

BLOOM TIME: spring

ZONES: 5–9

Umbrella plant

Want a bold plant in your semishady garden, bolder than the broadest-leaved hosta? Try umbrella plant, which earns its name from its tall stems bearing large, prominently veined, spreading leaves, a foot or two (30 or 60cm) across. You almost expect a mischievous troll or hobbit to appear under their shelter. For today's smaller gardens, this plant is certainly a realistic alternative to the massive *Gunnera manicata*, which has a similar form but is easily twice as large—and not as hardy.

The first, and probably only, requirement for success with this handsome plant is moist soil. In nature, it is found along streams and pond edges. It tolerates periods of standing water, so you could put it in a boggy area that tends to dry up a bit as summer progresses. It also prospers in heavy clay soil, where few other things will grow.

The flowers precede the leaves in early spring. They are borne on tall leafless stems and are bright to lilac pink, occasionally pinkish white. They are fleeting, but pretty while they last.

At season's end, the gardener gets another treat, particularly if the summer has been mild. The leaves turn a flaming coppery orange-red, highlighted with yellow veins.

Dicentra spectabilis

Bleeding heart

HEIGHT/WIDTH: 2'–3' × 2' (60–90cm × 60cm)

FLOWERS: pink-and-white

BLOOM TIME: spring

ZONES: 3–9

'Alba' bleeding heart

This beloved plant is a shade garden classic, with good reason. It has truly stood the test of time, with no need for improvement by plant breeders. It looks terrific solo, in a spot where it has adequate elbowroom. It's also nice massed under shade trees or on the north or east side of a house or garage, though it's too tall and full to be considered a groundcover per se. Another favorite use for it is among spring-flowering bulbs or wildflowers, because it comes on a bit later, taking over the show just as the other plants begin to flag, and covering up or distracting from dying foliage. Moist soil is required for bleeding heart to prosper.

The plant's ferny, much-divided foliage forms a beautiful, loose mound about as wide as it is tall, and the endearing, 1-inch (2.5cm) locket-shaped flowers line arching stems. The plain species is pink-and-white flowered. A cultivar, 'Alba', has all-white blooms, and is not quite as vigorous a grower. Both will stay in bloom for as long as six weeks, provided your spring weather is not too capricious. Afterward, the attractive foliage remains and holds its own pretty well for the rest of the season; in warmer areas or drier soils, however, it may simply throw in the towel and go dormant by midsummer.

Digitalis grandiflora
(D. ambigua)

Yellow foxglove

HEIGHT/WIDTH: 2'–3' × 1'–2' (60–90cm × 30–60cm)

FLOWERS: yellow bells

BLOOM TIME: summer

ZONES: 3–8

Yellow foxglove

This pretty foxglove not only is perennial (unlike many of its relatives), but also blooms over many weeks each summer. Shade becomes it, preserving the longevity of the flowers and highlighting their soft, appealing glow.

This one is not as formal-looking as some of its kin. Its growth is shaggier and it always produces lots of lopsided flower spikes. While the color is subtle enough to mix with other shade-tolerant bloomers—imagine it among yellow-rimmed hostas or at a woodland's edge with red cardinal flower or poppies—perhaps its best use is its natural inclination. Yellow foxglove doesn't just return year after year, it also spills its seeds to generate more plants. Let it naturalize.

Close inspection reveals that the flowers are dotted and striped inside with chocolate brown. Bring them indoors for bouquets so everyone can admire them—just remember to pick early, when they're half open, for best results.

Disporum spp.

Fairybells

HEIGHT/WIDTH: 2'–3' × 1' (60–90cm × 30cm)

FLOWERS: white or yellow bells

BLOOM TIME: early spring

ZONES: 4–9

Fairybells

Sometimes wonderful woodland plants come from unexpected places. In recent years, plant explorers have found a bonanza of garden-worthy ones in Korea and Japan, and these introductions have made their way into specialty plant catalogs and nurseries. One such prize is a number of new fairybells.

If you've encountered fairybells at all, you've most likely seen the broad-leaved *D. sessile* 'Variegatum', which has liberally striped foliage that makes a splash in shady places. With oblong or lance-shaped foliage lining the stems, this plant is superficially similar to Solomon's seal. The 1-inch (2.5cm) pendant, tubular flowers, however, are

carried on their own stalks, in pairs or clusters. In the case of 'Variegatum', they're off-white. Those of the less common but equally enchanting *D. flavens* are soft yellow (the foliage is shiny green). In autumn, the flowers yield to blue-black berries. The green-leaved *D. hookeri* has greenish bells and orange-red berries.

A spreading clump-former, this amiable plant has a lot going for it. The shiny, heavy-textured leaves are quite attractive and keep up appearances even in dry shade. The only potential problems, slugs and leaf-disfiguring fungi, may be kept at bay if fairybells is grown in well-drained soil.

Dryopteris marginalis

Wood fern, marginal shield fern

HEIGHT/WIDTH: 2'–3' × 1'–2' (60–90cm × 30–60cm)

FLOWERS: (not a flowering plant)

BLOOM TIME: (not applicable)

ZONES: 3–8

Wood fern

For many people, this is the ideal fern. The fronds are dark blue-green, are neat and uniform, and have a crisp texture. Wood fern is popular with florists, who prize it as handsome, long-lasting greenery to embellish bouquets, and you can certainly harvest your homegrown fronds for the same use. Because it is shorter than some other garden-worthy ferns, and because it doesn't tend to spread much, wood fern is a nice choice for mixing with flowering plants without over-whelming or overarching them. Celandine poppy and foam-flower are two suitable companions.

In the wild, wood fern grows on rocky woodland slopes, which hints at its most critical need besides shade: well-drained soil. It does not appear to be particular about soil pH, tolerating both acidic and alkaline spots equally well. Moisture, though, is key. If your wooded area dries out in the summer months, help your ferns along with a lit-tle extra moisture and/or mulch. In milder climates, wood fern is evergreen over the winter. Elsewhere, you'll look forward to fiddleheads announcing this fern's revival each spring.

Epimedium spp.

Epimedium, bishop's-hat, barrenwort

HEIGHT/WIDTH: 6"–1' × 1'–2' (15–30cm × 30–60cm)

FLOWERS: small clusters; color varies

BLOOM TIME: spring

ZONES: 4–8

Red epimedium

Here is a plant that looks delicate but is tough and versatile. It will grow equally well in damp or dry shade. It does well carpeting the ground under trees and shrubs, seemingly untroubled by the competition. It also makes a good-looking edging along a shady garden path. Epimedium's only drawback is that it is not a fast increaser, so you should plant individuals fairly close together, say, a foot (30cm) apart.

Generally speaking, these plants have pretty, oblong-heart-shaped leaflets on wiry stems. The leaves are red or bronze when they emerge in early spring, change to red- or chocolate-tinged green over the course of the summer, and may also be rimmed in red. Some are evergreen over the winter, some are not, so if this characteristic matters to you, ask the nursery before you buy.

The spurred flowers, which appear for a brief but generous display in spring, are small, borne in clusters, and vary from white to yellow to bright pink to scarlet, sometimes with contrasting spurs of white or yellow. They are not the prime reason to grow the plant, and in some species they are even hidden by the foliage.

Some choice epimediums to look for include red epimedium (*E.* × *rubrum*), which has contrasting bicolor red or pink and white blooms; yellow-flowered, lime green–leaved Persian epimedium (*E.* × *versicolor* 'Sulphureum'); and the smaller, green-leaved *E. youngianum* cultivars ('Niveum' has white flowers, 'Roseum' has pink ones).

Erythronium spp.

Trout lily, fawn lily

HEIGHT/WIDTH: 5"–12" × 5"–12" (13–30cm × 13–30cm)

FLOWERS: yellow, white, or pink

BLOOM TIME: spring

ZONES: 4–8

'Pagoda' trout lily

The best place for this appealing native wildflower is high, open shade under deciduous trees. The soil should be organically rich and well drained. There, your trout lilies will thrive and multiply, filling your woodland with beauty each spring.

Trout lilies probably get their whimsical name from their distinctive foliage; each plant sports just two simple, lance-shaped leaves, mottled or speckled with brown, purple, or even cream markings. One botanist suggests that the other common name, "fawn lily," is inspired by their resemblance to the perked-up ears of a young deer.

The bloom rises above the pair of leaves on a slender, wiry stem. It's a pretty thing, between 1 and 3 inches (2.5 and 7.5cm) across and looking very much like a nodding, slightly flared lily flower (the plant is in the same family as cultivated lilies). The flowers of *E. americanum* are chiffon yellow brushed with chocolate brown marks. Because those of the enchanting *E. revolutum* vary from rosy pink to soft pink to white, selections were inevitable. 'Rose Beauty' and 'White Beauty' are available from bulb suppliers and specialty nurseries.

But perhaps the most popular cultivar, apparently derived from *E. tuolumnense*, is the sunny yellow 'Pagoda'. Its flowers and leaves are much larger than those of the others, and it is an eager, robust grower. A patch of these makes a marvelously cheery golden carpet over the dull brown ground of early spring.

Euonymus fortunei

Wintercreeper

HEIGHT/WIDTH: 4"–6" (10–15cm)/spreading habit

FLOWERS: inconspicuous; greenish white

BLOOM TIME: early summer

ZONES: 5–9

'Emerald Gaiety' wintercreeper

You know this plant—it is that tough-leaved, fast-growing, spreading vine, low shrub, or groundcover. It has been extensively hybridized, perhaps too much so, as some cultivars are rather similar to others. Many are variegated, which accounts for the plant's enduring appeal in part to full shade. 'Variegata' or 'Variegated' may have white or yellow markings or margins. 'Silver Queen' has pronounced white edges. Compact-growing 'Emerald Gaiety' is generally viewed as one of the best, with rounded green leaves that are liberally rimmed in white; these turn reddish in colder weather. Still another popular one is 'Colorata' (or var. *coloratus*), which has a plum-purple color in autumn and winter. Others have brighter, splashier yellow-and-green

variegation, larger leaves, smaller leaves, and so on. All are tolerant of most soils (except downright boggy conditions).

Opinions on this overused plant vary. The accomplished gardener and author Sydney Eddison, who grows 'Emerald Gaiety' in her Connecticut garden, gratefully calls it "a godsend" because it not only survives but also thrives in a difficult site among rocks and tangled tree roots. Meanwhile, the ornamental plant expert Michael Dirr can barely contain his scorn, saying: "From seventeen feet [5m] away, [the cultivars] all look the same." Given its fast growth and rather coarse appearance, this euonymus is probably best used where nothing else does well.

Eupatorium coelestinum

Mist flower

HEIGHT/WIDTH: 1'–3' × 1'–2' (30–90cm × 30–60cm)

FLOWERS: small purple heads

BLOOM TIME: late summer—autumn

ZONES: 5–10

Mist flower

If you are careful with the siting of this pretty, late-blooming plant, you will be more than delighted with its performance. A naturally rampant grower in damp soils, it becomes perfectly manageable in dry shade. If you must grow it in moist ground, you can control its spread by occasionally digging out and discarding or giving away unwanted offspring. Another trick is to cut the plant low in early summer. It will rebound but be of more compact habit, and still bloom at the usual time.

Mist flower's late summer to early autumn bloom period is a real asset, especially since the flowers are so long-lasting—up to eight weeks! They look quite a bit like the familiar annual ageratum, with profuse, flattened flower heads in blue or lilac. But individual blossoms are fluffier and more spidery. Also, the fact that they are borne on a taller plant, not a groundcovering bedding plant, means that you can enjoy them in semiwild borders or woodland edges. They also make pretty cut flowers.

The cultivar 'Wayside' is available from Wayside Gardens. It is virtually the same as the species, but shorter-growing, to only 2 feet (60cm), which might tempt you to include it in a more controlled border situation.

Galium odoratum

Sweet woodruff

HEIGHT/WIDTH: 6"–1' × 1' (15–30cm × 30cm)

FLOWERS: white stars

BLOOM TIME: spring

ZONES: 3–9

Sweet woodruff

Shade gardeners have long cherished this plant, and it is easy to see why. It is a charmer, from its long, thin, apple green leaves (which occur in whorls along the slender stems) to its small, dainty white flowers. The name refers to the fact that the entire plant exudes a sweet, spicy scent when dried—some people have likened it to vanilla. Craftspeople like to add clumps to the stuffing in pillows and mattresses, and sweet woodruff also has been used to flavor homemade wine.

Easygoing to a fault, this plant will take to almost any soil and spread slowly but surely. Moist soil inspires faster growth. Sweet woodruff is ideal for banks, along pathways, under trees, or as an edging. It is durable enough to withstand some foot traffic or the occasional wayward soccer ball, so some gardeners use it in shady curb-strip plantings and even in the gaps between walkway stones. No matter where you grow sweet woodruff, "volunteers" that appear beyond their bounds are easily pulled out.

Gaultheria procumbens

Wintergreen, checkerberry

HEIGHT/WIDTH: 4"–6" (10–15cm)/spreading habit

FLOWERS: tiny white bells

BLOOM TIME: spring

ZONES: 4–8

Wintergreen

For the longest time, this native North American woodlander was appreciated mainly as a medicinal and culinary herb. The leaves, particularly when bruised or chewed, emit an invigorating menthol scent. The oil, which may be extracted with a lot of time and effort, was used in cough and cold remedies, chewing gum, salves for sore muscles, and even real root beer. It has been upstaged by synthetic imitations or the more easily extracted oil from black birch trees (*Betula lenta*).

Useful or not, wintergreen certainly makes a nice groundcover, preferably under the high shade of deciduous trees—it likes humusy, acidic soil. The small, 1 to 2-inch (2.5 to 5cm) roundish leaves form an attractive, glossy green, somewhat shrubby mat. The tiny, nodding white bell flowers are attractive while they last. And when the round, bright red berries appear, wintergreen looks downright festive. Often both leaves and berries persist over the winter months.

Wintergreen has a creeping rootstock, and self-sows as well. So a few plants ought to become a nice colony after a few seasons.

Gaylussacia brachycera

Box huckleberry

HEIGHT/WIDTH: 6"–18" (15–45cm)/spreading habit

FLOWERS: tiny white or pinkish bells

BLOOM TIME: late spring

ZONES: 5–7

Box huckleberry

You want a groundcover in your rhododendron or azalea patch or at the base of some pine trees, but nothing seems to grow well there. Your search is over: box huckleberry adores such shady, acidic-soil conditions.

Once established, this attractive evergreen will spread its glossy foliage slowly but surely to form a glorious mat of dark green. The flowers, though small, are pretty while they last. These are followed in late summer by tiny bluish berries (technically drupes) that look like blueberries and, while edible, are full of crunchy seeds. In the cold months, the leaves take on a rich bronze or wine-red hue.

This plant has an interesting legend attached to it. Apparently, there is a massive, mile-long patch in central Pennsylvania that is said to have originated from a single plant thousands of years ago. If you grow it, you will observe firsthand its spreading habit. True or not, the story does give testimony to box huckleberry's incredible durability!

Geranium spp.

Cranesbill geranium

HEIGHT/WIDTH: 1'–2' × 1'–2' (30–60cm × 30–60cm)

FLOWERS: many colors

BLOOM TIME: varies

ZONES: 5–9

'Johnson's Blue' cranesbill geranium

Pretty flowers and a long bloom period recommend this group highly to anyone who desires color in their shade garden. Cranesbills look wonderful massed (which makes a virtue out of their mounding or sprawling habits); lower-growing ones can even be used as groundcovers. They thrive in good, not overly rich, soil.

The saucer-shaped flowers come in a range of colors from white to pink to blue, and the dainty petals often have darker-colored veining. The leaves are usually palm-shaped and deeply lobed or cut, and may turn red in autumn, adding a welcome late splash of color when you least expect it.

Perhaps the most popular cranesbill geranium is a hybrid called 'Johnson's Blue'. It produces loads of vivid blue, 2-inch (5cm)-wide flowers. Another choice selection is the lovely and vigorous *G. endressi* 'Wargrave Pink'; the 1-inch (2.5cm) blooms are bright pink. *G. sanguineum* 'Album', a lower-growing type, has pure white 1½-inch (4cm) flowers against a backdrop of dark green leaves.

There are many, many other choices—feast your eyes on the selections at any good perennials nursery, local or mail-order, and treat yourself to a few lovely cranesbill geraniums.

Hakonechloa macra 'Aureola'

Hakonechloa, wind-combed grass

HEIGHT/WIDTH: 6"–18" × 6"–18" (15–45cm × 15–45cm)

FLOWERS: tiny, pale green spikelets (not grown for flowers)

BLOOM TIME: late summer

ZONES: 5–9

'Aureola' hakonechloa

Ornamental grasses have been in vogue for a while now, and some of them tolerate less than full sun. But, one might argue, does the shade garden need more foliage plants? If you feel this way, you still ought to consider making an exception for this plant. Hakonechloa, of Japanese origins, is an unusual and unusually beautiful grass.

The long, tapering leaves display a golden glow from a distance. Up close, they are more complex: they are a fine shade of yellow or off-white, generously striped with rich green that contains hints of bronze. (The flowers are incon-spicuous.) Hakonechloa is deciduous, but before it closes down for the winter, its foliage turns reddish, then soft tan.

The plant has a graceful, low-growing habit that arches and spills over itself like a waterfall. It spreads slowly by means of creeping rhizomes, but if expansion is not your wish, simply rein it in by planting it in a container that is sunk into the ground. A whiskey barrel of it in a shady corner or courtyard would be fabulous. It must have fertile, evenly moist soil that is slightly acidic.

Hedera helix

English ivy

HEIGHT/WIDTH: climbing vine or sprawling ground-cover

FLOWERS: tiny, yellowish green (rarely appear)

BLOOM TIME: autumn

ZONES: 5–9

English ivy

If you still think of English ivy as a plain, congested groundcover or "tree eater," it's time for a fresh look. It's true that the broadly heart-shaped leaves of the species are not terribly distinctive (though if you simply want a wall or fence covered, you may still resort to planting it). But nowadays there are dozens of intriguing alternatives.

Perhaps the most exciting new cultivars are the ones with variegated leaves; note that they do prefer a bit more light. 'Adam' has beautiful sage green leaves rimmed and marked with creamy white. 'Calico' leaves are mainly white, bordered in rich green. The bizarre 'Harrison' has smoldering dark leaves defined with white veination; in cold weather, they turn royal purple—a breathtaking sight.

Ivy leaves that are bred to be yellow are also in vogue. 'Sulphur Heart' and 'Gold Heart' have golden interiors. 'Buttercup' has an almost entirely yellow leaf.

You will also find ivies with unusual leaves. 'Curlytop' has fairly full leaves, but they are whimsically curly. 'Fan' has spreading foliage with scalloped edges. These and others bring unexpected texture to your garden.

Consult mail-order catalogs, which offer the best selections, and you may get the best of both worlds—a vigorous, climber with surprising beauty. Remember that most ivies are self-clinging and will attach themselves to fences, walls, trellises, and tree trunks with little help from you.

Helleborus spp.

Hellebore, Lenten rose, Christmas rose

HEIGHT/WIDTH: 2' × 2' (60cm × 60cm)

FLOWERS: color varies

BLOOM TIME: early spring

ZONES: 4–8

Lenten rose

These exquisite flowers are among the earliest signs of life each spring, an unorthodox alternative to all the spring bulbs. Their nodding blooms are sometimes carried singly, sometimes in clusters. Slightly cup-shaped, up to 4 inches (10cm) across, they come in shades of pristine white, cream, lime green, pink, rose, lavender, purple, even blue-black. The lighter-colored ones are often blushed, speckled, or edged with a darker hue. All are centered with a boss of dainty yellow stamens. At first glance, hellebores are reminiscent of single-form roses—hence the common names. The attractive leaves are carried in compound leaflets, and may be evergreen if your winters are not too harsh.

The hellebores you are most likely to find in nurseries are Christmas rose (*H. niger*), which can be tricky to grow well, and the smaller-flowered Lenten rose (*H. orientalis*). The so-called stinking hellebore (*H. foetidus*) actually only releases its scent if bruised, and it's really not that offensive; the flowers are enchanting green bells edged with purple-red.

Named cultivars are hard to come by, but there's nothing wrong with planting some seed-grown ones in a shady spot and waiting to see what blooms. Pamper them by making sure their soil is cool, moist, and slightly alkaline. It should also be very fertile, with plenty of organic material; provide top-dressings at least once a season as well.

Heuchera spp.

Coralbells, alumroot

HEIGHT/WIDTH: 1'–3' × 1'–2' (30–90cm × 30–60cm)

FLOWERS: delicate bells; pink, red, or white

BLOOM TIME: spring–summer

ZONES: 3–9

Coralbells

You can have it all with these shade lovers: stunning foliage and attractive flowers. The durable leaves are produced in mannerly clumps, and look a bit like those of ivy, though more rounded. They remain good-looking all season long, making the plant an ideal choice for a semishady perennial border or even a naturalized groundcover.

Recent years have seen a flurry of new introductions featuring gorgeous foliage variations (frequently a result of breeding with various closely related species). The popular 'Palace Purple' features rich, maroon to royal purple leaves. Other selections are bronze, russet, or silvery, or have these colors on their veins only for a rich, tapestrylike appearance.

The names are mouthwatering: 'Cappuccino', 'Cathedral Windows', 'Chocolate Ruffles', 'Plum Pudding', 'Velvet Night'.

Certain hybrids are treasured for their petite but splendid flowers, arrayed along tall, graceful stalks above the leaves in spring or early summer. These remain in bloom for several weeks, and can even be used as cut flowers. 'Mt. St. Helens' has glowing red flowers, 'Coral Cloud' has pinkish coral flowers, and there are a few white-flowered selections ('June Bride', 'White Cloud'). Planted in groups, coralbells in bloom brings an enchanting, fairyland quality to the shady garden.

Hosta spp.

Hosta, plantain lily

HEIGHT/WIDTH: varies

FLOWERS: white or lavender

BLOOM TIME: varies

ZONES: 3–9

Hosta

Admittedly, hostas are a shade garden cliche, but before you decide to do without them, take a look at the offerings in a specialty nursery catalog or at a well-stocked perennials nursery. You will be amazed at the variation, and may be tempted to create a planting that uses several different ones for a richly hued, many-textured carpet. Certain ones also make excellent accent plants. In any case, for a sterling performance, plant your hostas in dappled shade, in cool soil that is fertile and moist.

When shopping for hostas, consider size first: there are small, mounding types that stay less than a foot (30cm) across as well as great broad-shouldered ones that spread

out at maturity to almost 3 feet (90cm) across. There is also great diversity in leaf color, perhaps more so than with any other foliage plant, from a soft blue-green to a bright minty green. Many have leaves that are white- or gold-rimmed or marked with light green variegation. And last but not least, there is texture—some hosta leaves are sleek, some are ribbed or quilted, and some are quite puckered.

Although hosta's greatest value is as a foliage plant, don't overlook its flowers, which come in either white or lavender. These line arching stalks and appear from late spring to late summer, depending on the variety. They can be quite a show in their own right, especially planted in a grouping.

Houttuynia cordata 'Chameleon'

Houttuynia, chameleon plant

HEIGHT/WIDTH: 6"–12" (15–30cm)/spreading habit

FLOWERS: white

BLOOM TIME: early summer

ZONES: 4–9

'Chameleon' houttuynia

If you seek a multicolored, low-growing carpeter for your shade garden, there is no finer plant than this. The heart-shaped green leaves are liberally splashed with cream and pink or red, no two alike. So a patch is a picture in varying hues. This plant is particularly welcome in deep gloom, where few other plants thrive.

The flowers, when they appear, are nothing to write home about. They're only half an inch to an inch (1.5 to 2.5cm) across, and consist of a prominent little white spike and four small white bracts ("petals").

Houttuynia loves moist soil and greedily spreads far and wide in such a setting, given half a chance. It can even grow in shallow, standing water, as at a streamside or bordering—or even wading into—a pool. Ground that is drier seems to rein it in a bit. But if you find it wandering where it shouldn't, simply mow off or tug out unwanted sections.

Allegedly, there are other cultivars of this plant, but the situation appears to be confused, though whether the fault lies with the nurseries or the botanists is unclear. 'Tricolor' is virtually indistinguishable from 'Chameleon'.

Impatiens walleriana

Impatiens, busy Lizzie

HEIGHT/WIDTH: 1'–2' × 1'–2' (30–60cm × 30–60cm)

FLOWERS: color varies

BLOOM TIME: summer

ZONES: grown as an annual

'Super Elfin Twilight' impatiens

Few plants are as utterly dependable in shade as impatiens. They are simply remarkable performers, never failing to pump out a constant supply of neat flowers week after week, month after month, in all but the heaviest shade. The lance-shaped foliage, which varies from light to dark green, is reliably attractive. (The original, red-flowered species from which the many modern hybrids are derived is a tender perennial native to tropical Africa, where it prospers on the forest floor.)

Recent years have seen an explosion of terrific new impatiens, generally in "series," meaning you can buy mixed seed packets or seek out specific colors or color combinations in the bedding plant section of your local nursery. The superb Super Elfin series, as the name suggests, is a group of compact-growing plants, and the color range is wide: every pastel imaginable, as well as more vivid hues of orange, pink, red, and violet-purple. There are also bicolor impatiens, and ones with a central white star or eye. And there is still a lot to be said for planting plain white ones; a ribbon of these through a dim area under oaks or other shade trees never fails to brighten the scene.

Note that the New Guinea impatiens group, with its variegated leaves and larger flowers, can take more sun. However, in especially long, hot summers, impatiens of all kinds must have shelter from the sun.

Imperata cylindrica 'Rubra'

Japanese blood grass

HEIGHT/WIDTH: 1'–2' × 1'–2' (30–60cm × 30–60cm)

FLOWERS: short, silvery spikelets

BLOOM TIME: summer

ZONES: 5–9

Japanese blood grass

Grasses are an unorthodox choice for a shade garden, but there are a few that do just fine in limited light. Japanese blood grass is one. The long, casually upright, flat blades are not uniformly red; instead, the bases are greenish and the color gradually segues to increasingly intense crimson at the tips. The effect is like a small bonfire.

In a smaller garden, a mature plant makes a fabulous accent plant. When Japanese blood grass is grown en masse, of course, its sensational beauty is magnified—but you had better have the space to devote to it, because it will be a scene-stealer.

You often see Japanese blood grass photographed backlit, which dramatizes the glow. You won't get this effect in your garden if you site one or more plants behind others, of course. Better, then, to place it in a more open setting, where shade is light or filtered, perhaps in a west- or east-facing bed or along a pathway. Wherever you grow it, be sure the soil is moist but well drained.

This grass is not as tall or vigorous as some others, and spreads slowly over the years by means of creeping rhizomes. Also, it is rarely troubled by any insect pests or diseases, so, overall, you may find it quite easygoing.

Iris cristata

Dwarf crested iris

HEIGHT/WIDTH: 4"–12" × 2"–4" (10–30cm × 5–10cm)

FLOWERS: small iris, usually lavender

BLOOM TIME: spring

ZONES: 4–8

'Summer Storm' dwarf crested iris

It is true, almost any iris can be grown in partial shade, but do you want to expend the large, magnificent beardeds and Louisianas and the classically beautiful Siberians and Japanese this way? Better to let them take their glory out in the sun—and turn the shade over to this diminutive but utterly enchanting species.

Crested iris is shade tolerant, and it prefers lean, well-drained, even dry soils. Be sure to plant the fleshy roots very near the surface. Then, sit back. Don't fertilize, and don't water except during periods of drought. Over the years, if it is happy, it will form a dense patch. You will also

be pleased to learn that this iris is not attacked by the dreaded iris borer, which can devastate its fancy cultivated relatives.

Its lightly scented flowers may be small, but they display plenty of perky color. Petals are marked with royal purple and lavender; the "crest" is yellow and white. (There is also a rare and lovely 'Alba', which is white with a golden crest.) Bladelike, light green leaves carry on the show after the blooms pass; their little tufts, growing en masse, make an attractive groundcover. Alternatively, crested iris is a terrific addition to a semishady rock garden.

Kirengshoma palmata

Kirengshoma

HEIGHT/WIDTH: 2'–4' × 2'–3' (60–120cm × 60–90cm)

FLOWERS: yellow bells

BLOOM TIME: late summer

ZONES: 5–9

Kirengshoma

Here's a pretty plant that blooms later in the season, a time when your shade garden could use some color. A native of Japanese woodlands, it requires damp, acidic soil and protection from drying winds. So a spot under deciduous trees, which can also offer the benefit of their decomposing leaves to the soil, would be ideal.

Kirengshoma is a rather tall, multistemmed plant, so it should be grown in small groups or toward the back of a shade border. Its arching stems, which are dark red or pur-

ple, display pairs of maplelike leaves that get smaller as they ascend. So it is a striking plant, even when not in bloom.

When they finally debut, the flowers are lovely things, little drooping, butter yellow, tubular bells, somewhat reminiscent of campanula blooms. They are carried in threes, generally, which helps them to stand out, for individually they are only between 1 and 2 inches (2.5 and 5cm) long. The blooms last for many weeks, so the wait is well worth it.

Lamiastrum galeobdolon

Lamiastrum, golden dead nettle, yellow archangel

HEIGHT/WIDTH: 1'–2'/spreading (30–60cm/spreading)

FLOWERS: yellow

BLOOM TIME: spring

ZONES: 3–9

'Herman's Pride' lamiastrum

An attractive, spreading choice for dry shade, lamiastrum is closely related to the more common lamium. Like lamium, its leaves are opposite and rather heart-shaped; they may be mint green or variegated with silver or pewter. Individual plants are mounding and spread quickly in the right conditions: semishade and decent soil. The upside is that lamiastrum naturally forms nice, uniform patches that have a tidy demeanor, so a glade devoted to this plant need not look out of control or unkempt. To further exercise control, you can cut the plant back after flowering.

The springtime flowers are a tempting reason to grow this plant. The cultivar you usually see, 'Herman's Pride', is spangled with dense clusters of golden yellow flowers (a color you won't see in lamium, and a main reason this plant was separated off from that genus). The flowers in conjunction with the silver-flecked foliage make a vivacious show.

Lamium maculatum

Lamium, spotted dead nettle

HEIGHT/WIDTH: 1'–2' × 1' (30–60cm × 30cm)

FLOWERS: small clusters; white or pink

BLOOM TIME: summer

ZONES: 4–8

'White Nancy' lamium

Especially good-looking variegated foliage is the reason to invite this justly popular groundcover into your shade garden. The oval leaves are a fresh green, spotted, ribbed, or marked with white, light green, or silver. 'White Nancy' and 'Beacon Silver', the most commonly seen cultivars, have green-rimmed foliage that is otherwise entirely silver. The newer, luscious 'Chequers' has heavily marbled leaves; the background is rich red, and the veins are silvery.

A nice plus about these plants is their flowers, which nearly steal the show when they appear for several weeks each summer. Each is less than an inch (2.5cm) long, with a hooded shape. The flowers are borne in tight little clusters that stand slightly above the foliage. Those of the aforementioned 'White Nancy' are white, which in combination with the leaves really make the plants "pop" out of the shade as you walk by. 'Beacon Silver' and 'Chequers' have pretty pink to rose flowers.

Essentially a trouble-free plant, lamium will obligingly carpet great areas, even in deep shade. Moist, well-drained soil is best, but the plant will manage even without perfect conditions.

Ligularia × przewalskii

Ligularia

HEIGHT/WIDTH: 4'–6' × 2'–3' (120–180cm × 60–90cm)

FLOWERS: yellow stars

BLOOM TIME: mid- to late summer

ZONES: 4–8

'The Rocket' ligularia

This is an imposing plant for the edge of a wooded area or a shady border that gets some morning sun. No doubt about it, ligularia is a big plant; at maturity, it is likely to be taller than you. The leaves, which can measure up to a foot (30cm) across, are palmlike but highly dissected. The plant is a clump-former, and the erect stems are dark purple. So it has a somewhat tropical look to it. Ligularia needs moist, rich soil to give of its best.

Near the middle of the summer, the impressive flower-stalks appear. They, too, have purple stems, and carry cheery little yellow flowers, each less than an inch (2.5cm) across, in tall, loose spikes. These last for many weeks, igniting a dim area with welcome color. (Close inspection reveals that the flowers are like tiny daisies—in fact, the plant is closely related to asters.)

'The Rocket' is the most commonly seen edition of this dramatic plant (though it is sometimes listed as a cultivar of *L. stenocephala*). The flower stems are quite dark, nearly black, making a magnificent contrast for the sunny yellow blooms. It generally doesn't grow quite as tall as *L. × przewalskii*, usually topping out at 4 feet (120cm).

Lilium martagon var. alba

White Martagon lily

HEIGHT/WIDTH: 3'–6' × 1'–2' (90–180cm × 30–60cm)

FLOWERS: white bells

BLOOM TIME: summer

ZONES: 3–7

White Martagon lily

It's true, most lilies do best out in the open, perhaps only with some protection from the withering heat of the noonday sun. But here is a modest, graceful species lily that makes a genuinely appropriate and lovely choice for partial shade. Derived from the Turks-cap lily, this white-flowered version has even smaller flowers (about 1½ inches [4cm] across), but with the same highly swept back ("recurved") petals. Yellowish green stamens dangle down, and each petal is flushed with a little soft green at its base. It's an unforgettably beautiful flower.

When this lily is grown well, you can count on it to produce flowers in large quantities, in tiered racemes of as many as forty. One nursery rhapsodizes that "it is simply peerless at dusk, especially when planted in groups of five to ten, creating a grove of candelabras with their glowing flames." Catalog hyperbole? Perhaps not!

The key to success with white Martagon lily is well-drained soil; "wet feet" spells sure death for it (and many other lilies, for that matter). Unlike some, it will tolerate slightly alkaline soil, good news for Western gardeners.

Like its red-flowered parent, this white lily is not, however, sweetly fragrant; in fact, some noses find it unpleasant. But that need never become an issue if you are growing it for show in a semiwild shady area.

Liriope muscari

Lilyturf

HEIGHT/WIDTH: 1'–2' × 1'–2' (30–60cm × 30–60cm)

FLOWERS: purple spikes

BLOOM TIME: late summer–autumn

ZONES: 6–10

'Variegata' lilyturf

If you want to edge a shady walkway or devote a bed to one plant that can be relied upon to always look neat and demand little effort from you, perhaps lilyturf is your best bet. Assuming, of course, that it is hardy where you live — this tufted groundcover prospers best in areas with long, hot, humid summers; it cannot tolerate lengthy, snowy winters.

The spiky, narrow leaves are grasslike but a bit more substantial. White- and yellow-striped versions are available. A naturally compact grower, lilyturf usually remains less than 2 feet (60cm) tall, and some of the cultivars are even shorter (one, 'Christmas Tree', is a mere 8 inches [20cm] tall). Its only drawback is its vulnerability to snails and slugs. So if these pests frequent your garden, be prepared to protect this plant.

As the name suggests, the blooms look like taller versions of those of the spring-flowering bulb *Muscari*, also known as grape hyacinth. They appear on narrow, 10- to 20-inch (25.5 to 51cm) spikes late in the season, and are usually purple, though white varieties exist ('Monroe White').

Lobelia cardinalis

Cardinal flower

HEIGHT/WIDTH: 3'–5' × 1' (90–150cm × 30cm)

FLOWERS: red

BLOOM TIME: mid–late summer

ZONES: 2–9

Cardinal flower

If you have a shady spot with moist or even perpetually wet soil, here's a tall, beautiful native wildflower that will dress it up in style. Cardinal flower is all the more welcome because it blooms later in the season, when most of the color is gone from the shady garden.

A robust plant, yet not rangy or invasive, it has striking flower spires. Perhaps no more than 1½ inches (4cm) long, the individual blossoms have the distinctive fanlike shape you may have observed on the common blue garden lobelias so popular for edgings and window boxes. The species is a fabulous shade of scarlet, but variations can be found if you hunt for them (some are crosses with other, similar lobelias). 'Ruby Slippers' is an especially gorgeous choice, as is the richly hued, more subtle 'Garnet'. There's also a white ('Alba'), a soft pink ('Heather Pink'), a hot pink ('Pink Parade'), and many others.

Flowers are carried on tall stalks that emerge from a low rosette. The leaves are medium to dark green and oblong, are slightly serrated, and ascend the stalk to just short of the blooms. Planting cardinal flower in groups or even broad patches will call still more attention to it.

Lobularia maritima

Sweet alyssum

HEIGHT/WIDTH: 2"–12" × 8"–12" (5–30cm × 20–30cm)

FLOWERS: white, pink, or purple balls

BLOOM TIME: summer

ZONES: all zones (annual)

Sweet alyssum

There is probably no more agreeable annual "filler" plant than this one. Sweet alyssum is justly valued for its tireless flower production, manageable mounding habit, and undemanding care requirements. Tuck it in anywhere you need quick color—a new semishady rock garden, a shade border, or as an underplanting for bigger plants that are out of bloom. Then relax. It will get right to work.

If you haven't looked lately, you will be pleasantly surprised to discover that white flowers are just the beginning of your choices. (And if you still want sweet alyssum in white, look for 'Snow Crystals', which has perhaps the neatest blooms.) Nowadays sweet alyssum also comes in purple,

red, and pink, and variations of these shades. Grow them individually or try a blend, which, owing to the flowers' small size and lacy texture, weave a charming, almost tapestrylike display.

No matter which ones you grow, count on your sweet alyssum to reseed prolifically. That is, this year's tidy rows or ribbons will eventually lose their definition and the odd plant will pop up in a walkway, crack, or wall many feet away. In other words, unless you intervene and assiduously yank out volunteers, this plant will play a major role in paving your maturing garden's way to a more casual, informal look.

Lysimachia nummularia

Moneywort, creeping Jenny

HEIGHT/WIDTH: 2"–4" × 1'–2' (5–10cm × 30–60cm)

FLOWERS: small, yellow

BLOOM TIME: late spring

ZONES: 3–8

Moneywort

There are those who decry this plant as an odious pest, never to be invited into a garden. They are alarmists. True, it grows fast and thickly. Of course it will be invasive in certain settings—common sense counsels against planting such a vigorous plant adjacent to a perennial bed or manicured lawn. But if you have a shady area with damp soil that really needs coverage, moneywort will do the trick.

This is a tough plant for tough locations. It even can withstand some foot traffic. So a shady slope or bank with moist soil that has been lying fallow or weed-infested for years might as well be turned over to moneywort.

The plant is actually perfectly attractive. The common name perhaps refers to the rounded, coin-shaped, glossy leaves. The bright yellow flowers, which appear in profusion in late spring and often repeat on and off through the summer months, are between half an inch and an inch (1.5 and 2.5cm) across. Moneywort spreads by means of long trailing stems; it roots at the nodes where they touch earth.

There is a yellow-leaved form, 'Aurea', but it loses its luster in shade (the foliage turns a sickly pale green) and really is better grown in full sun.

Lysimachia punctata

Yellow loosestrife, circle flower

HEIGHT/WIDTH: 2'–3' × 2' (60–90cm × 60cm)

FLOWERS: yellow cups

BLOOM TIME: summer

ZONES: 5–8

Yellow loosestrife

Sure, it can become invasive. But if you simply want to turn over a shady, wild area to just one plant, and you want color practically all summer, yellow loosestrife is a good choice. It grows rampantly in moist soil, but unlike some of its near relatives, it can also tolerate somewhat drier soil, particularly in deeper shade.

The plant's form is a bit unusual. Ever-smaller leaves ascend the erect stems, and the 1-inch (2.5cm), cup-shaped flowers somehow manage to wedge their way in between, also encircling the stem. As they do, they steal the show. Individually, the plants burst with bright color, and a colony of them is a festival of cheer.

Recently, an intriguing yellow loosestrife cultivar has been making its way into the catalogs. Called 'Alexander's', it has creamy white–variegated leaves that help it stand out in the shade and provide striking contrast for the golden flowers when they appear.

Mahonia aquifolium

Oregon grape

HEIGHT/WIDTH: 3'–6' × 3'–6' (90–180cm × 90–180cm)

FLOWERS: yellow

BLOOM TIME: spring

ZONES: 5–8

Oregon grape

In its native Pacific Northwest, this glossy-leaved plant often can be seen growing along highways and in roadside ditches, a testament to its natural toughness. Those settings, of course, expose plants to all sorts of abuse, including poor, dry soil, wind, weather, and pollution. But bring this shrub into your shade garden, and you will be gratified at how beautifully it domesticates and how eager it is to please.

Truly a shrub with four seasons of value, Oregon grape maintains its lush, green, hollylike foliage for months on end. In the spring and summer, it drenches itself in clusters of bright yellow flowers. These are powerfully fragrant and attract lusty bees. By autumn, the plant is draped in small,

blue-black berries, not exactly big or sweet enough to pass as grape substitutes, but certainly safe to eat and attractive to some birds and animals. The autumn foliage is often gorgeous, anywhere from a dusky red to a fiery orange-red, a sensational contrast with the berries. In all but the harshest cold, the foliage will remain over the winter.

Oregon grape would be an easygoing addition to a landscape that is partially shaded by evergreen trees. Its handsome color and texture might also be welcome among broad-leaved evergreen shrubs such as rhododendrons. Be moderate about placement: deep shade may cause it to be too leggy; too much exposure to sun may dry out the leaves.

Matteuccia struthiopteris

Ostrich fern

HEIGHT/WIDTH: 2'–6' × 2'–3' (60–180cm × 60–90cm)

FLOWERS: (not applicable)

BLOOM TIME: (not applicable)

ZONES: 3–8

Ostrich fern

There are good reasons why this vase-shaped fern is popular with shade gardeners. It's easy to grow, it spreads quickly to give your woodland area a naturally lush look, and it is free of pest and disease problems. Its clump-forming fronds are tall, neat, and always bright green. In short, it's foolproof.

Take a closer look at this fern over the course of a growing season. In early spring, you'll welcome the stout fiddleheads. After they unfurl, the outer fronds will reveal themselves as sterile (no spores on the backs of the individual leaves) and rather lacy. They looked like the tail feathers of the ostrich to someone, hence the common name. In mid- to late summer, dark brown, inrolled interior fronds appear. They are a bit smaller and, lower down, are laden with little black to brown spots that, under the right conditions, shed spores on the ground and form new little plants in years to come. Like other ferns, ostrich fern spreads by its creeping roots—new plants may pop up several inches to a foot (30cm) away.

Ostrich fern needs moist soil to prosper. If the soil dries out too much, the leaf edges brown and curl unattractively and the plant struggles. Fertile, humus-rich ground also is desirable. Anything from partial to dark shade will suit it fine. Some gardeners like to plant it with their spring-flowering bulbs and wildflowers because the fronds start to unfurl just as those flowers are passing, hiding and distracting from the end of that show while making one of its own.

Mazus reptans

Mazus

HEIGHT/WIDTH: 2"–5" × 12"–18" (5–13cm × 30–45cm)

FLOWERS: purple or white tubular bells

BLOOM TIME: late spring

ZONES: 4–8

Mazus

This is a very tough, spreading groundcover for partially shaded areas. It can even withstand some foot traffic, so some people tuck it in the gaps between stones on shady garden paths, including flagstone paths where sun lovers like creeping thyme won't thrive. The small, toothed leaves are lime green and grow densely to form a large, impenetrable (to weeds) mat.

Given the reliable, iron-strong constitution of mazus, the exuberant flowering each spring is simply a nice bonus to rejoice in. Hundreds of tiny (half an inch to an inch

[1.5 to 2.5cm]), tubular blooms in soft purple carpet the foliage. They are vaguely reminiscent of tiny foxglove flowers, which is not surprising given that they are in the same family. A white-flowered version, called 'Albus' or var. *albiflorum*, also is available.

The only "catch" here is that mazus must have moist but well-drained soil. In ground that is too damp, there is a risk that the plants will become overenthusiastic. But that may be just what you have in mind.

Meconopsis cambrica

Welsh poppy

HEIGHT/WIDTH: 12"–18" × 8"–10" (30–45cm × 20–30cm)

FLOWERS: yellow

BLOOM TIME: summer

ZONES: 6–8

Welsh poppy

Most poppies prefer to be waving their pretty, crepe-paper blooms out in the bright sun, but this European import is happier in partial shade or in a spot that gets morning sun and afternoon shade. And it is surely a welcome sight there—imagine a glade of deciduous trees, perhaps with some ferns, and small patches of these merry golden flowers spangling the area. If you want even more impact, look for the golden-orange, double-flowered variety, prosaically called var. *aurantiaca* 'Flore Pleno'.

Welsh poppy will grow in soil of average fertility and doesn't mind if it's even a bit alkaline. Shelter from hot sun and drying winds, plus supplemental water in dry spells, of course, is beneficial. If Welsh poppy settles in, you can expect this charmer to self-sow liberally in the coming years, which may be exactly what you wish.

To get started, you can sow fresh seed. However, the contents of packets that have been sitting around for many months or years aren't likely to germinate well, if at all. Alternatively, you can pay a little more and buy seedlings. Once they are up and blooming, you are in for a treat—the flowering continues for many weeks, sometimes all summer long. And, yes, Welsh poppy is perennial, so the flowers will be back the next year.

Mertensia virginica

Virginia bluebells

HEIGHT/WIDTH: 1'–2' × 1½' (30–60cm × 45cm)

FLOWERS: small clusters of blue bells

BLOOM TIME: spring

ZONES: 3–9

Virginia bluebells

Virginia bluebells is a plant whose show is confined primarily to spring, but it is so pretty that many shade gardeners cannot resist it. A native of southeastern woodlands but able to survive much further north, it is easy to grow. The thin, lance-shaped leaves are mainly basal, though a few ascend the stems on short, succulent stalks. At the top of these stalks are clusters of nodding little bells. They begin as pink buds but open to lilac-blue flowers. The blue will be darker in deeper shade.

This wildflower is often touted as an ideal companion for spring-flowering bulbs, with good reason. It likes similar conditions in the garden: organically rich soil in cool shade. Plus, the color seems to go with everything. It is particularly fetching combined with small-flowered yellow or white narcissus.

Like the bulbs, though, its show ends as summer arrives. The stems die down after bloom, and the plant gradually goes dormant and disappears from view until the next year. So mark its spot if you wish to move or divide it in the autumn, and to avoid trampling on it or planting something else over it.

Microbiota decussata

Russian (Siberian) carpet cypress

HEIGHT/WIDTH: 2'–3' (60–90cm)/spreading habit

FLOWERS: minute cones

BLOOM TIME: summer

ZONES: 3–7

Russian carpet cypress

A shrubby evergreen from Siberia must be a tough plant. And so it is. It is extremely cold tolerant, rarely troubled by any diseases or pests, and requires little of the gardener, not even pruning. The color is usually bright green, often turning bronzy purple over the winter. It is not a shade lover per se, but it appreciates some shelter from the glare of midday sun and will do well in settings of light or dappled shade.

To say this plant sprawls may be an understatement. Its goal in life is not to grow up, but outward, and, over the years, you will be amazed at how well it stays with this plan. As such, it has received great praise as an unorthodox groundcover or pathside plant. You might also try it in a shrub border or as a row along the east side of your house.

Although it bears a superficial resemblance to the overused juniper, it is not a substitute. Its cultural requirements are different—not just the preference for less than full sun, but also a need for fertile, well-drained soil. Siberian carpet cypress also has a much softer profile.

Mitchella repens

Partridgeberry

HEIGHT/WIDTH: 2"–3" × 9"–12" (5–7.5cm × 23–30cm)

FLOWERS: tiny, white

BLOOM TIME: spring

ZONES: 4–9

Partridgeberry

This groundcover has an irresistibly elfin look. Its tiny, chubby leaves, sometimes marbled with white, appear in pairs along the trailing stems. The miniature scented flowers are tubular; they are light pink in bud and open to white. But partridgeberry really comes into its own by autumn. Then, the bright crimson berries sprinkle the glossy green mat with festive color. Birds and other wildlife absolutely adore them.

To grow this sturdy little plant well, site it in moist, acidic soil under the dappled shade of trees or deciduous shrubs. It can be slow to establish, but over the years it will spread out luxuriously via runners to form great carpets.

Partridgeberry's rather dainty features suggest that it is best used in a pathside or rock garden setting, rather than relegated to a back corner, so its charms can be appreciated at closer range.

Myosotis sylvatica

Forget-me-not

HEIGHT/WIDTH: 6"–12" × 6" (15–30cm × 15cm)

FLOWERS: tiny, blue

BLOOM TIME: spring–early summer

ZONES: 5–9 (usually grown as a biennial)

'Ultramarine' forget-me-not

As an adorable plant best suited to informal semishady areas, forget-me-not is hard to beat for agreeable character and low maintenance. In spring, it foams with dozens of tiny, blue-petaled, yellow-centered blooms. They have a very appealing, nosegay appearance that is welcome among smaller hostas or any low-growing, green-foliaged groundcovers.

Forget-me-not is not long-lived and, indeed, may not bloom its first season. But once established, it sows its seeds throughout your garden, ensuring that you'll never be without it. To be honest, it can begin to take over, crowding out other plants or moving into open areas. Fortunately, unwanted seedlings are easily dug up and either discarded or moved.

While it is a fairly adaptable plant, it looks its best when growing in somewhat moist soil. It even can take "wet feet," perhaps along the edges of a garden pool or bog. The sentimental legend behind its common name is that a gallant knight drowned while fetching a bouquet for his lady love (crying out "forget me not!" as he slipped under), but you have to wonder just how deep the water was!

Myrrhis odorata

Sweet cicely

HEIGHT/WIDTH: 3'–6' × 2'–5' (90–180cm × 60–150cm)

FLOWERS: white umbels

BLOOM TIME: spring–early summer

ZONES: 3–7

Sweet cicely

Although it becomes rather large and rambling, sweet cicely never overwhelms a shade garden, thanks to the lacy delicacy of its finely divided foliage. Instead, it weaves itself in among other, shorter, plants or makes a pleasant grove along a path, the back of a wall or fence, or in a glade of deciduous trees. Through the the heat of summer and all the way up to the first frost, it remains a fresh, crisp green. Both the leaves and the hollow stems are edible and have a sweet, celery-anise flavor that enhances salads and soups.

The frothy white flower heads, which look like those of many other herbs, appear early, in spring to early summer, attracting the attention of early foraging bees. They're an appealing sight in light or filtered shade, but, alas, don't last long. The small, thin seeds that follow are edible and can be used in baking, whole or powdered.

Sweet cicely prefers moist soil; if the spot you've chosen dries out when summer comes, supplemental watering will be necessary. Note that it forms a thick, gnarled taproot, so plant it where you want it to stay. The plant is best raised from store-bought seedlings or from divisions donated by another gardener, as the seeds germinate slowly and erratically.

Nemophila spp.

Nemophila, baby blue eyes

HEIGHT/WIDTH: 6"–12" × 6"–12" (15–30cm × 15–30cm)

FLOWERS: saucer-shaped, color varies

BLOOM TIME: summer

ZONES: annual (all zones)

Nemophila

Originally known primarily to botanists and native plant enthusiasts of the western United States, this unsung wildflower somehow captured the attention of plant breeders. Perhaps the fact that it is an annual that does well in partial shade recommended it (the genus name *Nemophila* means "grove loving"). Perhaps its eagerness to bloom, especially when brought into the more comfortable surroundings of garden life, had something to do with it as well.

At any rate, you can now grow this low, ground-hugging beauty with flowers in a variety of intriguing colors. Those of *N. maculata* 'Five Spot' most closely resemble the wild version, with white petals tipped with a violet spot and violet veining. Those of *N. menziesii* 'Baby Blue Eyes' are sky blue. But, for sheer novelty, you can't beat two recent introductions, *N. menziesii* 'Pennie Black', which has deep purple blooms edged with creamy white, and its counterpart 'Snowstorm', with black-speckled white petals.

The saucer-shaped flowers are never large, generally only between 1 and 2 inches (2.5 and 5cm), but they are borne individually on swaying stalks, and they cover the plants, nearly hiding the small, scrubby, lyre-shaped green to gray-green leaves. Nemophila prospers in fertile, well-drained soil.

Nicotiana alata

Flowering tobacco

HEIGHT/WIDTH: 3'–5' × 8"–1' (90–150cm × 20–30cm)

FLOWERS: various colors

BLOOM TIME: summer

ZONES: 10–11 (grown as an annual)

'Starship Lemonlime' flowering tobacco

Delicious fragrance is the main reason to grow this easy-going plant. Because they are pollinated by night-flying insects, the long-tubed, five-petaled flowers release their scent at full force when they open late in the day—a plus for gardeners who are away all day at work or school. Yes, flowering tobacco can also be grown in the open, but shade gardeners know this plant's other secret: shelter from the sun's rays coaxes the plants to bloom in the daytime as well.

This justly popular plant comes in a tantalizing array of colors, from red to pink to white to yellow to lime green, colors you will be eager to include in your semishady beds, either individually or in mixed groups. The plain species, freshly appreciated by those who like to cultivate an old-fashioned look in their garden, is soft white with a blush of light green.

Flowering tobacco tolerates heat and cold, and blooms literally from early summer to the first autumn frost. Start the seeds indoors a month or two before you want to plant them outside (note that you should sow them on top of a flat of soilless mix; light hastens germination).

Omphalodes cappadocica

Navelwort

HEIGHT/WIDTH: 10"–12" × 14"–16" (25.5–30cm × 35.5–40.5cm)

FLOWERS: blue

BLOOM TIME: early spring

ZONES: 6–9

'Cherry Ingram' navelwort

Admittedly an undistinguished, mounding plant when not in bloom, navelwort is utterly charming when covered with sprays of tiny, ¼-inch (6mm) flowers each spring. The species flowers are blue with a white center, slightly reminiscent of forget-me-not and pretty enough in their own right. There's a larger-flowered cultivar called 'Cherry Ingram' with flowers that are even deeper blue. But the most desirable version is a true bicolor, also with larger flowers, dubbed 'Starry Eyes'. Each petal is rimmed in palest pink (which fades to white) and has a bold swathe of lilac-blue down the middle.

No matter which version you grow, expect waves of flowers for many weeks each spring. The flowers coupled with the lance-shaped leaves make the plant quite a splendid groundcover for partial shade. Later, when the flowers have passed, the plant devotes its energy to spreading slowly by creeping rhizomes.

As you might guess, navelwort thrives in woodland settings. It prefers moderately fertile soil that is moist. Unfortunately, these are also heavenly conditions for slugs and snails. If these pests lurk in your damp, shady garden, they will damage the leaves.

Pachysandra spp.

Pachysandra

HEIGHT/WIDTH: 10"–12" × 10"–18" (25.5–30cm × 25.5–45.5cm)

FLOWERS: small bottlebrushes, white to lavender

BLOOM TIME: spring

ZONES: 4–9

Pachysandra

Good old Japanese pachysandra (*P. terminalis*): if you have a spot that has average or even dryish soil, in deep, dark shade, few other plants will cover it as dependably, year in and year out. The coarsely toothed leaves, borne in whorls on strong stems, are always a rich shade of green. (The small flowers, usually white bottlebrushes, are insignificant.)

Pachysandra is evergreen in most climates, and may even be seen stubbornly poking a glossy green head out of the first few snows of the season. Try it in your holiday decorations—it holds up well, especially when the cut ends are immersed in water.

If you appreciate this plant but are feeling more adventurous, consider a few alternatives. 'Silver Edge' and 'Variegata' have white-rimmed leaves and are not quite as fast-spreading. 'Green Carpet' has even shinier leaves and grows more compactly than the species. And a related native North American species, known as Allegheny spurge (*P. procumbens*), is gaining in popularity. It is not evergreen, is more particular about soil (it must have moist, fertile ground), and spreads more slowly, but its attractive gray-green leaves are more than twice as large.

Paxistima canbyi

Cliff-green

HEIGHT/WIDTH: 12"–18" × 2'–3' (30–45cm × 60–90cm)

FLOWERS: tiny, white

BLOOM TIME: summer

ZONES: 3–7

Cliff-green

If you're landscaping a woodland floor, you might consider cliff-green an intriguing alternative to the ubiquitous pachysandra. It, too, has glossy green foliage, spreads by means of branching, rooting stems, is impervious to pests and diseases, and requires little or no attention once established. Its tiny leaves are less than an inch (2.5cm) long and have toothed margins—they look a bit like miniature holly leaves. When colder weather arrives, they become an attractive shade of red-tinged bronze.

To look its best, cliff-green ought to be grown in well-drained soil. It tolerates acidic conditions, such as under pine or oak trees. The site should also remain moist over the summer; drought does in this little groundcover.

Because of the small leaves and neat appearance of cliff-green, a flourishing patch looks somehow less overbearing than pachysandra. You might even invite cliff-green into a semishady rock garden. Plant it in a pot sunk into the ground, or remove the unwelcome sprouts from time to time.

Phalaris arundinicea 'Picta'

Ribbongrass

HEIGHT/WIDTH: 2'–3' × 1'–2' (60–90cm × 30–60cm)

FLOWERS: white or pale pink seedheads

BLOOM TIME: summer

ZONES: 4–9

Ribbongrass

No, it's not a bamboo, though if you have never seen ribbongrass before, you would be pardoned for thinking so at first. It's a bushy, mounding, perennial "ornamental grass," valued for its neatly striped blades of cool white and mint green. The seedheads, when they appear, are carried in loose clusters on their own stems.

Able to tolerate even the most wretched soil, wet or dry, ribbongrass is sometimes used as an erosion-control plant on banks or slopes. Partial shade suits it fine and in fact best preserves the quality of the foliage. If it should begin to look raggedy by midsummer, simply cut the plant back by half—or entirely—and await a fresh flush of growth.

It must be admitted that ribbongrass does have a deserved reputation (like bamboo) for vigorous growth; it spreads eagerly by creeping rhizomes. So gardeners who want to curb it must grow it in containers. It's large enough to warrant a half-whiskey barrel or something of comparable size and, when thriving, will be your pride and joy. Otherwise, if massing is your plan, great masses of ribbongrass you shall have.

Phlox divaricata

Wild sweet William

HEIGHT/WIDTH: 1' × 1' (30cm × 30cm)

FLOWERS: blue or white

BLOOM TIME: spring

ZONES: 4–8

Wild sweet William

This little charmer is a world away from its big, bold-flowered cultivated cousin, garden or summer phlox (*P. paniculata*). It enjoys partial or half-day shade and has an informal, easygoing way about it. It is short, topping out at only 1 foot (30cm), and covers itself in loose, airy clusters of sweet little 1-inch (2.5cm) powder-blue blossoms for several weeks each spring.

It also has a wild heart. Its creeping stems take off in all directions, spreading the plant quickly. Some gardeners, therefore, like to use it as a groundcover, on a bank or path-side. It also makes a good companion for later-blooming spring bulbs (particularly other pastels or white ones), weaving the display together while giving it an air of spontaneity.

You may prefer to grow one of the cultivars. Best known is the pure white 'Fuller's White', which has deeply notched petals, lending it a lacier appearance than the species. 'Mrs. Crockett' is lavender, 'Barb's Choice' is baby blue, and 'Louisiana' is rich violet-purple.

Phlox stolonifera

Creeping phlox

HEIGHT/WIDTH: 4"–6" × 12" (10–15cm × 30cm)

FLOWERS: many colors

BLOOM TIME: spring

ZONES: 3–8

'Violet Vere' creeping phlox

Few shade groundcovers are as lovely as this sweet-scented, low-growing creeper. For up to a month every spring, it smothers itself in 1-inch (2.5cm)-wide blooms. The species is soft lavender, but there are many worthy selections available, among them the classic 'Bruce's White', the delicately colored 'Pink Ridge', and the rich gentian blue 'Sherwood Purple'. The fragrance is as arousing as that of lilies, and, naturally, gains power in larger patches.

Because this is such a dependable plant and comes in a range of colors, it makes a wonderful stage for spring-flowering bulbs; the possible combinations are many.

Creeping phlox also makes a pretty skirt at the base of spring-flowering shrubs and trees; it may lap at their bases or trunks.

Creeping phlox's habit is short and spreading. It expands by runners (stolons), but maintains a tidy, dense appearance that discourages weeds from interjecting. You will be glad to learn that, unlike other phloxes, this one is impervious to mildew and is untroubled by nibbling slugs. Fertile, moist soil will encourage it to prosper—sometimes too well. But unwanted seedlings are easily yanked out.

Polemonium reptans

Jacob's-ladder

HEIGHT/WIDTH: 1'–2' × 1'–2' (30–60cm × 30–60cm)

FLOWERS: little bells, usually blue

BLOOM TIME: late spring

ZONES: 4–8

Jacob's-ladder

The small, delicate flowers of this low grower are especially sweet: they are airy little China-blue bells accented with tiny white stamens. They appear in clusters at the tips of the stems in late spring. A patch in full bloom has a fairyland quality. And, since Jacob's-ladder self-sows, you can look forward to an ever-growing carpet.

It is the fernlike leaves that give the plant its common name. They are arranged along the rather brittle stems in pairs, growing smaller as they ascend; they reminded some-one of the Biblical story of Jacob's dream of ascending to heaven on the rungs of a ladder. Unlike with some spring-blooming plants, the leaves of Jacob's-ladder remain all season long.

This particular species has a more creeping habit than the more commonly grown *P. caeruleum*, so it is a better choice for planting in sweeps or naturalizing. Gardeners in areas with cooler summers have better luck with it. In any event, for best results, grow it in rich, moist soil.

Polygonum odoratum

Solomon's seal

HEIGHT/WIDTH: 1'–2' × 1'–2' (30–60cm × 30–60cm)

FLOWERS: tiny pale green to white bells

BLOOM TIME: spring

ZONES: 4–8

'Variegatum' Solomon's seal

No shade garden is complete without this elegant plant— and it will tolerate drier soil. Its strong, graceful stems arch outward, bearing along their length oval-shaped, parallel-veined leaves. Dangling along the underside of the stem in spring is a jaunty row of diminutive, pale green to white, lightly perfumed, bell-shaped flowers. These become blue-black berries by late summer.

The beautiful, sought-after cultivar 'Variegatum' has leaf edges and tips splashed with white markings. If you have the space and want an even bolder show, try Great Solomon's seal (a hybrid of either *P. biflorum* or *P. commutatum*), whose arching stems grow up to 6 feet (1.8m) long.

This plant has been grown around the world for a long time. The source of the name seems lost to history, though there are several theories. If you examine the tuberous roots, you'll see round scars from the previous year's stalks—these are said to resemble Solomon's seal, or signet. (By the way, you'll be able to determine a plant's age by counting these scars.) Another explanation is that, used medicinally, the plant was useful for healing, or sealing, wounds. Yet another possibility is that the six-pointed flowers were taken to resemble the six points of the Star of David, which was once called "Solomon's seal."

Primula japonica

Japanese primrose, candelabra primrose

HEIGHT/WIDTH: 1'–2' × 1' (30–60cm × 30cm)

FLOWERS: color varies

BLOOM TIME: spring

ZONES: 5–8

Japanese primrose

If you've ever seen a semishady glade given over to Japanese primroses, you'll never forget it or cease longing to re-create it at home. Assuming you garden in a cooler climate (they simply cannot take long, hot, humid summers) and have an appropriate setting, you may get your wish. The best spot is one that is naturally damp, though not sodden, with humusy soil. Partial or dappled shade is best, such as under the shade of high trees.

The good news is that Japanese primroses, unlike some of their relatives, are fairly easy to grow. In fact, once their basic needs are met, they will flourish and even self-sow. So you might as well plan to devote a broad area to this enthusiastic plant.

The fabulous flowers line the stalks on all sides, in whorls, and appear in tiers, not just at the top. Individual blossoms are merely half an inch (1.5cm) across, but they are clustered so that there is no missing them. The color range is from white to pink to lavender, accented with contrasting eyes (darker pink or red, sometimes yellow). As with other primroses, the leaves remain basal and are broadly paddle-shaped.

Combine Japanese primroses with other shade lovers if you like, but try to stay with foliage plants like ferns or hostas. You won't want anything to distract from these remarkable, colorful flowers.

Primula ×
polyantha

Polyanthus primrose, English primrose

HEIGHT/WIDTH: 6"–15" × 9"–12" (15–38cm ×
23–30cm)

FLOWERS: color varies

BLOOM TIME: spring

ZONES: 6–8

Polyanthus primrose

These bright-eyed beauties are sure to warm the heart of any winter-weary gardener. Usually yellow-centered, the flowers range from purple to pink to red to white; they are carried in pert umbels of several 1- to 2-inch (2.5 to 5cm) blooms. Enjoy them in pots in early spring, or, if your weather is not too harsh, plant them outside. Tuck some in among the flowering bulbs for extra bursts of color.

Unlike other primroses, these are far from temperamental. They like organically rich soil, and are at their best in partial or light shade. They've certainly stood the test of time—versions of them have been grown since the seventeenth century. Their parentage is complex (apparently a mixture of *P. eliator, P. veris,* and *P. vulgaris*) and worth mentioning only because they seem to have gathered together the best of their forebears in terms of ease of culture and vibrant color.

Once the flowers pass, you're left with the foliage, which is not especially appealing. The rosettes consist of long, floppy green leaves, almost corrugated in texture. If you're not wild about this phase of the plant's life, or have other plans for the area in which you tucked them, it wouldn't be a crime to pull them out and start over with new ones the next year.

Primula vialii

Orchid primrose

HEIGHT/WIDTH: 1'–2' × 1' (30–60cm × 30cm)

FLOWERS: purple-red spikes

BLOOM TIME: late spring

ZONES: 5–8

Orchid primrose

The poetic garden writer Ann Lovejoy once described orchid primrose in bloom as "a sizzling display of Szechuan fireworks." It's an image you don't soon forget. And this exciting little plant, when planted in drifts in part shade, delivers on Lovejoy's promise.

A native of China, orchid primrose will remind you of neither an orchid nor a primrose. However, botanically it is indeed a primrose, and shares with that group large, paddle-shaped leaves and soft, sweet fragrance. Its form is a bit more like that of another carpeting spring bloomer, grape hyacinth, which also bears spikes composed of tiny, densely packed individual blooms. But these flowers are so remarkable, they'll stop you in your tracks. They begin bright red and flare open from the bottom up, revealing violet-blue interiors.

Moist, humus-rich soil is a must for this plant. To highlight the drama of the blooms, site some of the plants near contrasting-color astilbes—white ones would be nice; red ones will help call out the unfurling show. If orchid primrose is content in your shade garden, it will self-sow.

Pulmonaria saccharata

Pulmonaria, lungwort, Bethlehem sage

HEIGHT/WIDTH: 9"–18" × 1'–2' (23–45.5cm × 30–60cm)

FLOWERS: blue, pink

BLOOM TIME: spring

ZONES: 3–8

Pulmonaria

Foliage dappled and splashed with silvery spots and blotches really makes this groundcovering classic stand out in the shade. The leaves are mostly at ground level (that is, basal) and lance-shaped, and they grow up to a foot (30cm) long and half as wide. In mild climates, pulmonaria may weather the winter. When planted en masse, it forms an elegant, luminous carpet.

The blossoms, while fleeting, are lovely. They are carried in loose clusters and start out as rosy-pink buds before opening to sweet, violet-blue bells. The most widely available variety, 'Mrs. Moon', has pink flowers that age to blue and more prominently spotted leaves. 'Sissinghurst White' has white flowers. The beautiful 'Dora Bielefeld' has green-and-silver variegated leaves and pink flowers.

Should you wish to combine pulmonaria with other plants, it is an agreeable mixer. It is a good addition to a spring bulb display; the leaves will remain to help disguise the fading bulb foliage. It is also nice with other spring-bloomers, particularly white-flowered bleeding heart.

Sarcococca hookerana var. humilis

(S. humilis)

Dwarf sweet box

HEIGHT/WIDTH: 1'–2' × 2'–3' (30–60cm × 60–90cm)

FLOWERS: small clusters; pinkish-white

BLOOM TIME: spring

ZONES: 6–9

Dwarf sweet box

Yes, it's in the same family as boxwood—and it's no hardier, so is best grown in milder climates. It also has boxwood's signature glossy green foliage, but the leaves of dwarf box are not tiny; they are oblong and up to 3 inches (7.5cm) in length, more closely resembling the foliage of laurels or rhododendrons. And it does very nicely in shade and semishade.

Unlike its cousin, it is a natural as a dense-growing groundcover. It never gets very tall, and while it spreads by creeping runners, it is not aggressive in this capacity. It is never troubled by insect pests or leaf diseases. Probably its best use would be under deciduous trees, where the soil is moist, organically rich, and drains well.

As a pleasant bonus, early each spring dwarf box spangles itself in tiny pinkish white flowers that are richly fragrant—the sweet scent wafts outward and is irresistible as you stroll through the garden. They're not especially pretty, and, indeed, you may have to get close and sift through the foliage just to get a better look. Sometimes, but not always, they become small black fruits—again, you have to seek them out to truly appreciate them.

Senecio × hybridus
(Pericallis × hybrida)

Cineraria

HEIGHT/WIDTH: 1'–3' × 1'–2' (30–90cm × 30–60cm)

FLOWERS: daisies; various colors

BLOOM TIME: spring–summer

ZONES: 8–10 (annuals elsewhere)

Cineraria

A daisy for shade? Sounds unlikely, but it's true. Cineraria can't tolerate full shade, but in partial shade or a place that's sheltered from the rays of midday and afternoon sun, it will grow and flower bountifully. Technically a perennial, it originally hails from the Canary Islands off the west coast of Africa and the Azores. Thus it is not cold-hardy. However, it grows quickly and blooms reliably—so it's most sensible to enjoy it during the spring and summer, pull it out each autumn, and plant new ones the next spring.

Cineraria blankets itself in perky 2-inch (5cm) flowers and is long-blooming. It comes in a wide range of vivacious colors, from royal purple to copper to crimson to baby pink, and some cultivars have contrasting white eyes. You can either buy individuals as plants or sow a packet of mixed colors.

For best results, grow these daisies in well-drained soil, or in pots or window boxes of a light soilless mix. They make nice bedding plants, or can be used to provide spots of color where needed. If kept too damp or too dry, or in a spot that has poor air circulation, they can fall prey to insects such as aphids and whiteflies; tear out affected plants right away so the problem doesn't spread.

Smilacina racemosa

False Solomon's seal

HEIGHT/WIDTH: 1'–3' × 1' (30–90cm × 30cm)

FLOWERS: tiny white stars

BLOOM TIME: spring

ZONES: 3–7

False Solomon's seal

If you're composing a mixed-foliage shade display, don't forget to include false Solomon's seal. It is a relatively tall, erect woodland plant, perhaps better suited to planting among larger plants than some of the other, lower-growing groundcovers. Try it with rhododendrons and azaleas, or big-leaved hostas (it prefers the same moist, acidic soil they do), or skirting the base of a shade tree. Its long, graceful stems are lined with glossy, pleated leaves.

It is known as "false" because it is similar to Solomon's seal (another genus entirely, *Polygonatum*) when out of bloom, though it is often not as large. Also, the flowers are completely different; they're cream-colored, starry, and borne in bowing clusters at the stem tips; later, they become red, not blue, berries. A drift of false Solomon's seal in bloom is an arresting sight—plus, you will detect the flowers' pleasing scent.

Stylophorum diphyllum

Celandine poppy, wood poppy

HEIGHT/WIDTH: 12"–18" × 10"–15" (30–45cm × 25.5–38cm)

FLOWERS: yellow buttercups

BLOOM TIME: late spring–summer

ZONES: 4–8

Celandine poppy

This pretty, long-flowering poppy grows well in almost any spot, provided it gets the moisture it needs either from the soil or from the hose. Over the years, it will multiply, but it is not as aggressive as lesser celandine (*Ranunculus ficaria*).

The flowers are yellow and glossy, so even though they are small, about 2 inches (5cm) across, they command attention. They make a nice stand under the shelter of deciduous trees, mixing well with other spring-bloomers.

The fuzzy little seedpods (which may be on the plant at the same time as new flowers are opening—a charming sight) are characteristic of poppies. If you leave them be and have no chipmunks in your neighborhood to make off with the seeds, this poppy will self-sow extensively.

The much-lobed foliage seems large for the flowers and is an attractive shade of blue-green that intermixes well with other plants. It looks particularly fine among ferns.

Tiarella cordifolia

Foamflower

HEIGHT/WIDTH: 6"–12" × 6"–12" (15–30cm × 15–30cm)

FLOWERS: spikes of small white stars

BLOOM TIME: spring

ZONES: 3–8

Foamflower

No doubt this irresistible woodland native gets its common name from the way it literally foams with airy white blossoms for many weeks each spring—a sight best enjoyed when it is growing in large groups. You can reproduce this show easily in your own shady garden, provided you have humus-rich soil (naturally found under deciduous trees).

Foamflower's blooms aren't actually pure white. Tiny golden stamens shoot outward amid the white petals, giving individual blooms a starry look and the entire spike a full yet exuberant appearance. The leaves are equally handsome, and carry on well after the flowers are gone, as long as you remember to water the plants during the heat of summer. The leaves are heart-shaped, somewhat furry, and, in the variety *T. cordifolia* var. *collina* (also known as *T. wherryi*), feature accenting red veination. Foamflower leaves gain an attractive bronze hue as cold weather arrives.

This agreeable, good-looking plant is also available in other forms. Among the alternatives you can find are clump-forming 'Dunvegan', with pink-tinted flowers and sage green leaves, and delicate-looking but eager-growing 'Slickrock', with smaller, deeply lobed, forest green leaves and light pink blooms. The vivacious 'Tiger Stripe' features glossy leaves liberally splashed and striped with purple; its flowers are pink.

Tradescantia × andersoniana

Spiderwort

HEIGHT/WIDTH: 1'–2' × 1'–2' (30–60cm × 30–60cm)

FLOWERS: purple, blue, red, or white

BLOOM TIME: summer

ZONES: 5–9

'Snowcap' spiderwort

Because this grassy-leaved, low-growing plant tends to grow in large, full drifts, it is not an especially good mixer. But if a monoculture is what you need in a certain area, it may suit you quite well. It is often used as a low-maintenance underplanting for trees and shrubs.

Spiderwort forms a dense bed of foliage and covers itself in blooms over a long period, often for the better part of the summer. Individual leaves can be as long as a foot (30cm), and they interweave and overlap, effectively excluding weeds. The distinctive, three-petaled flowers, about 1½ inches (4cm) across, look a bit like tricorner colonial hats. In the species, they are purple or blue, but there are many cultivars. 'Valour' is bright red, 'Innocence' and 'Snowcap' are white, 'Rosie' is lilac pink, and so on. All are centered with prominent yellow stamens, which give the blooms an appealing perkiness.

Although spiderwort grows well in sun, it really fares best in partial or light shade. Here, it is less inclined to become raggedy looking, and it seems to stay in bloom even longer. It's not fussy about soil quality, but appreciates some moisture. If need be, cut back flowering stems after their show is over, both to prevent self-sowing and, hopefully, to inspire a second round of color before the season is through.

Tricyrtis hirta

Toad lily

HEIGHT/WIDTH: 2'–3' × 1'–2' (60–90cm × 30–60cm)

FLOWERS: white with purple spots

BLOOM TIME: late summer

ZONES: 4–9

'Miyazaki' toad lily

The unfortunately unappealing common name of this plant doesn't begin to hint as its elegance. The funnel-shaped flowers have flaring or outwardly curving petals that are usually creamy white, speckled and dabbled in violet, curiously evocative of an orchid. These appear in great numbers, all over the plant, singly and in clusters, at the end of the summer and on into early autumn, when the shade garden could use a little color. Because they are not very big, though, perhaps an inch (2.5cm) or so across, they are best admired at close range. So although they can grow further back in a woodland, do yourself a favor and locate some plants close to the path or at the perimeters of a border, so you can admire them more easily.

The foliage, as is typical of members of the lily family, is lance-shaped and has parallel veins. The plant is a clump former, but its creeping rootstock will lead to more plants in the seasons to come.

To get a satisfactory performance out of toad lily, grow it in slightly acidic soil that is evenly moist and well drained. If you're thinking of combining it with other plants, try it with one of the smaller-flowered, autumn-blooming asters — or anything with smaller flowers, so it is not overwhelmed.

Trillium grandiflorum

Large-flowered trillium

HEIGHT/WIDTH: 12"–18" × 8"–12" (30–45cm × 20–30cm)

FLOWERS: white

BLOOM TIME: spring

ZONES: 3–9

Large-flowered trillium

Although this gorgeous white wildflower is a knockout in woodland settings and familiar to many people, it is not an easy garden candidate. For starters, trillium is difficult to propagate. Offsets naturally produced by the rhizomes are few and slow to get established. Tissue culture (raising clones in laboratory test tubes) does generate more little trilliums, it too is slow—about a five-year wait for blooming-size plants. Trillium can also be grown from freshly harvested seed, but blooms may be up to nine years away!

Impatient nurseries and impatient gardeners have turned to wild collection, but this tack is unethical, for the plants are becoming endangered in many areas. It's not the depredations of an occasional admiring hiker that threaten the wild populations (though the plant makes a poor cut flower and is very unlikely to survive transplanting back home). It's the pillaging done by wildflower poachers, who dig up great patches of the rhizomes and sell them to unscrupulous nurseries.

So, needless to say, an inexpensive trillium plant from a local or mail-order nursery should be viewed with great suspicion. Your best bet, if you simply must have trillium in your "back forty," is to check the plant sales of botanical gardens—and pay the high price willingly. Otherwise, if demand for trillium continues unabated, we won't have them in the woods or our gardens.

Vancouveria hexandra

Vancouveria, northern inside-out flower

HEIGHT/WIDTH: 12"–16" × 12"–16" (30–40.5cm × 30–40.5cm)

FLOWERS: long sprays, tiny, white

BLOOM TIME: late spring–early summer

ZONES: 5–9

Vancouveria

As you might guess from the name, this plant hails from the forests of the Pacific Northwest (technically, it honors the explorer Captain George Vancouver). There it can be seen carpeting the ground under redwoods and mixed hardwoods. The good news is that it adapts well to gardens in that region as well as other parts of North America. Though deciduous, it is fairly winter-hardy and grows best in partial shade and humusy, moist soil.

Up close, the plant has dainty features. The tiny, bright green, bluntly lobed leaves are actually carried in leaflets of nine or more. The white flowers, which appear in late spring or early summer, wave above the foliage in airy sprays. Individual flowers are merely half an inch (1.5cm) across. If you crouch down to examine one, you'll see that the petals (technically, sepals) flare back, like the flower of shooting star *(Dodecatheon)*, perhaps—hence the other common name, inside-out flower.

Vancouveria tends to get off to a slow start, but after a few years it grows and spreads vigorously (by creeping rhizomes). An established patch excludes weeds well and becomes self-sufficient, even weathering summer dry spells.

Veronica spp.

Veronica, speedwell

HEIGHT/WIDTH: 1'–2' × 1'–2' (30–60cm × 30–60cm)

FLOWERS: blue or white

BLOOM TIME: summer

ZONES: 5–8

'Crater Lake Blue' veronica

Sometimes the shade gardener longs to grow traditional perennials, not just woodland natives. Some garden favorites, among them certain lilies, campanulas, and bee balms, will oblige, as long as they are situated in light shade or get morning sun. Perhaps one of the best choices is good old veronica.

Veronicas, as you may know, flower in spikes. The leaves, generally lance shaped, are a deep mint green that can get lost in shadows, so planting a cluster of plants works best, as it masses the color for maximum impact.

Among the veronicas that tolerate some shade are the beautiful, gentian blue 'Crater Lake Blue' (a cultivar of *V. latifolia* or *V. austriaca* ssp. *teucrium*, depending on which botanical reference you subscribe to) and the white *V. spicata* 'Icicle'. Both grow quickly in fertile, well-drained soil, but remain less than 2 feet (60cm) tall. The blue one blooms in early summer, the white one a bit later. Both hold their color well when sheltered from hot sun, and flowering may continue for a month or more, especially if you deadhead (remove spent flowers).

Vinca minor

Periwinkle, myrtle

HEIGHT/WIDTH: 4"–8" (10–20cm)/spreading habit

FLOWERS: blue, violet, or white

BLOOM TIME: spring

ZONES: 4–9

Periwinkle

Perhaps you associate this rambling groundcover with long-neglected gardens, cemeteries, woods, and schoolyards, and have never given a thought to its many virtues. It certainly is no trouble to grow, in any sort of shade, even upon the knobby roots of big old trees. It doesn't seem to care whether the soil is acidic or alkaline, dry or wet (though it will expire in downright sodden ground). The foliage tolerates foot traffic and is impervious to diseases. Once several plants merge to form a patch, weeds are virtually banished. All this, and the flowers are pretty, too.

Time to take a fresh, appreciative look at this old standby. The original species, dubbed "periwinkle" because of its soft purple-blue blooms, was widely planted by early settlers to North America. A cultivar, 'Bowles' Variety' (sometimes, and more correctly, called 'La Grave'), is a more vigorous plant with larger flowers of a darker, true-violet, hue. Not surprisingly, there are also white editions, which bring sparkle to dark corners. Double-flowered ones, which are somewhat fluffy, also are available.

You may be equally interested in growing this extremely reliable plant for its foliage. That of the species is dark green, and perfectly handsome in its own right. The cumbersomely named 'Aureovariegata' has olive green leaves with golden centers (and white flowers), and 'Argenteovariegata' ('Sterling Silver') has rich green leaves rimmed in white (charmingly paired with lilac-blue flowers).

Viola odorata

Sweet violet, English violet

HEIGHT/WIDTH: 3"–8" × 6"–12" (7.5–20cm × 15–30cm)

FLOWERS: color varies

BLOOM TIME: spring

ZONES: 6–9

'Thalia' sweet violet

Some violets are best featured in containers or window boxes, or placed in a perennial flower bed or rock garden. This one is small and grows eagerly, making it more useful as a novel or old-fashioned groundcover. It grows beautifully in partial or dappled shade.

The dainty, fragrant flowers are less than an inch (2.5cm) across, but appear in great numbers, wafting such an evocative scent into the air that you almost forget how small they are. Unlike with some other violets, the flowers rise directly from the center of the plant on short stems. Traditionally light purple, *Viola odorata* also can be found in a range of other colors—'White Czar' is pure white, 'Rosina' is rose pink, 'Royal Robe' is deep, dark blue, and 'Thalia' is yellow and purple. 'Alba Plena' has larger, double white flowers. The accompanying leaves are also adorable. They are heart-shaped and between 2 and 3 inches (5 and 7.5cm) across, well in scale with the flowers.

For best results, grow sweet violet in rich, moist soil and be sure to water if the summer is dry. In a few years, thanks to rooting runners and self-sown seeds, you'll have a sweet little carpet.

Viola × wittrockiana

Pansy

HEIGHT/WIDTH: 6"–9" × 9"–12" (15–23cm × 23–30cm)

FLOWERS: color varies

BLOOM TIME: summer

ZONES: all zones (grown as an annual)

'Melody Purple and White' pansy

For quick and exuberant color in partially shaded locations, tough, long-blooming pansies are unbeatable. They are simple to grow, asking only for average soil and supplemental water when rain is scarce. Purchase bedding plants from your local nursery, or try growing some from seed—the seed catalogs offer a tantalizing variety of harder-to-find colors and bicolors.

Among the many, many worthy types, certain ones stand out from their fellows. The Fama series sports especially large flowers that come in every color of the rainbow. An All-America Selections winner from years back, the charming 'Jolly Joker', has stood the test of time; it has royal purple petals contrasted with a bright orange face marked with purple whiskers. If you prefer solid-color pansies (no bicolors, no "faces"), look for the Clear Crystal series. Or try the lovely, award-winning golden-orange 'Padparadja'.

All of these pansies are technically perennials, but they seem to run out of steam after one season, growing leggy and flowering less. They are inexpensive enough to replace each year, certainly.

Creative use of pansies can bring fresh excitement to a shady garden or border. They look terrific among ferns, are great in rock garden settings or along walls, and provide color when the flowers of neighboring shade bloomers have passed.

Waldsteinia ternata

Barren strawberry

HEIGHT/WIDTH: 4"–6" x 18"–24" (10–15cm x 45–60cm)

FLOWERS: small, yellow

BLOOM TIME: spring–summer

ZONES: 3–8

Barren strawberry

Dry shade? Perhaps this plant is the answer. It's quick to form a lush, low-growing carpet of green, with shiny three-part leaves that look somewhat like tiny, rounded, toothed maple leaves. Good soil is not a requirement; in fact, if the soil is too moist or fertile, the plant can become invasive. It spreads by means of creeping rhizomes and stolons that root as they extend their reach. It is never troubled by pests or disease. Weeds rarely get a foothold where barren strawberry is established.

The small but bright yellow flowers appear for several weeks each spring. They do look like strawberry flowers (the plant is in the same family) but don't produce any berries, hence the name. While the plant is in bloom, it certainly lights up your shade garden.

Although barren strawberry survives cold winters, it does not remain evergreen. So clean up the planting if need be each spring, and expect a fresh round of green foliage.

PLANT HARDINESS ZONES

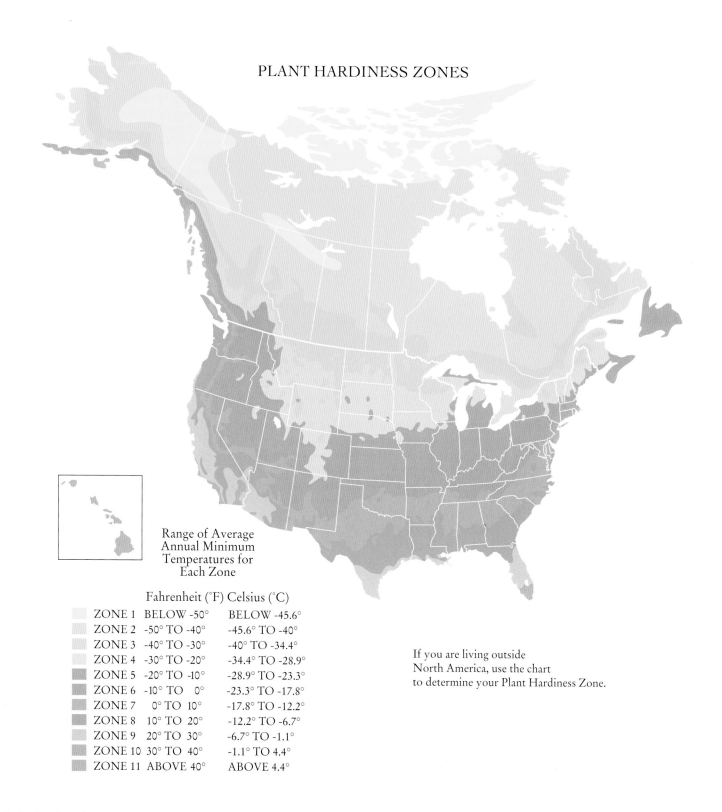

Range of Average
Annual Minimum
Temperatures for
Each Zone

Fahrenheit (°F) Celsius (°C)

		Fahrenheit (°F)	Celsius (°C)
	ZONE 1	BELOW -50°	BELOW -45.6°
	ZONE 2	-50° TO -40°	-45.6° TO -40°
	ZONE 3	-40° TO -30°	-40° TO -34.4°
	ZONE 4	-30° TO -20°	-34.4° TO -28.9°
	ZONE 5	-20° TO -10°	-28.9° TO -23.3°
	ZONE 6	-10° TO 0°	-23.3° TO -17.8°
	ZONE 7	0° TO 10°	-17.8° TO -12.2°
	ZONE 8	10° TO 20°	-12.2° TO -6.7°
	ZONE 9	20° TO 30°	-6.7° TO -1.1°
	ZONE 10	30° TO 40°	-1.1° TO 4.4°
	ZONE 11	ABOVE 40°	ABOVE 4.4°

If you are living outside
North America, use the chart
to determine your Plant Hardiness Zone.

Sources

Here is a list of mail-order nurseries. Note that many of these companies are small operations, and cannot afford to send out free catalogs, so please remember to include a check for the fee when requesting a copy.

Perennials

Bluestone Perennials
7237 Middle Ridge Road
Madison, OH 44057
Free catalog

Busse Gardens
5873 Oliver Avenue SW
Cokato, MN 55321
Catalog $2

Carroll Gardens
444 E. Main Street
Westminster, MD 21158
Catalog $3

Klehm Nursery
4210 N. Duncan Road
Champaign, IL 61821
Catalog $4

Milaeger's Garden
4838 Douglas Avenue
Racine, WI 53402-2498
Catalog $1

Andre Viette Farm & Nursery
Route 1, Box 16
Fisherville, VA 22939
Catalog $3

Wayside Gardens
P.O. Box 1
Hodges, SC 29695-0001
Catlog $1

White Flower Farm
P.O. Box 50
Litchfield, CT 06759-0050
Free Catalog

Roses

Antique Rose Emporium
Rte. 5, Box 143
Brenham, TX 77833
Catalog $5

Blossoms & Bloomers
E. 11415 Krueger La.
Spokane, WA 99207
Catalog $1

Carroll Gardens
444 E. Main St.
Westminster, MD 21157
Catalog $3

Edmunds' Roses
6235 S.W. Kahle Rd.
Wilsonville, OR 97070
Free Catalog

Hardy Roses for the North
Box 273
Danville, WA 99121-0273
Catalog $3

Heirloom Old Garden Roses
24062 N.E. Riverside Dr.
St. Paul, OR 97137
Catalog $5

Jackson & Perkins Co.
One Rose La.
Medford, OR 97501
Free Catalog

Justice Miniature Roses
5947 S.W. Kahle Rd.
Wilsonville, OR 97070
Free Catalog

Lowe's Own-Root Roses
6 Sheffield Rd.
Nashua, NH 03062
Catalog $2

Nor' East Miniature Roses
P.O. Box 307
Rowley, MA 01969
Free Catalog

The Roseraie at Bayfields
P.O. Box R
Waldoboro, ME 04572
Catalof free for first-class stamp

Royall River Roses
70 New Gloucester Rd.
North Yarmouth, ME 04097
Catalog $3

Wayside Gardens 1 Garden La.
Hodges, SC 29695
Free Catalog

White Flower Farm
Rte. 63
Litchfield, CT 06759
Free Catalog

Herbs

Bluestone Perennials
7237 Middle Ridge Road
Madison, OH 44057
Free catalog

Companion Plants
7247 N. Coolville Ridge Rd.
Athens, OH 45701
Catalog $3

Filaree Garlic Farm
Rte. 2, Box 162
Okanogan, WA 98840-9774
Catalog $2

Goodwin Creek Gardens
P.O. Box 83
Williams, OR 97544
Catalog $1

Greenfield Herb Garden
P.O. Box 9
Shipshewana, IN 46565
Catalog $2

Herban Garden
5002 2nd St.
Rainbow, CA 92028
Catalog $1

Herbs-Licious
1702 S. Sixth St.
Marshaltown, IA 50158
Catalog $2

High Altitude Gardens
P.O. Box 1048
Hailey, ID 83333
Catalog $3

Le Jardin du Gourmet
Box 275
St. Johnsbury Center, VT 05863
Catalog $1

Logee's Greenhouses
141 North St.
Danielson, CT 06239
Catalog $3

Moonrise Herbs
826 G St.
Arcata, CA 95521
Catalog $1

Nichols Garden Nursery
1190 Old Salem Rd. NE
Albany, OR 97321
Free catalog

Plants of the Southwest
P.O. Box 11A
Santa Fe, NM 87501
Catalog $3.50

Rasland Farm
Rte. 1, Box 65C
Godwin, NC 28344-9712
Catalog $3

Richters Herbs
357 Hwy. 47
Goodwood, Ontario
L0C 1A0 Canada
Catalog $2

Sandy Mush Herb Nursery
Surrett Cove Rd.
Leicester, NC 28748-9602
Catalog $4

Tinmouth Channel Farm
Box 428B
Tinmouth, VT 05773
Catalog $2

Well-Sweep Herb Farm
205 Mt. Bethel Rd.
Port Murray, NJ 07865
Catalog $2

Westview Herb Farm
P.O. Box 3462
Poughkeepsie, NY 12603
Catalog $1

Wrenwood Nursery
Rte. 4, Box 361
Berkeley Springs, WV 25411
Catalog $2.50

Woodside Gardens
1191 Egg & I Rd.
Chimacum, WA 98325
Catalog $2

Flowering Shrubs

Canyon Creek Nursery
3527 Dry Creek Road
Oroville, CA 95965
530-533-2166

Eastern Plant Specialties
Box 226
Georgetown, ME 04548
207-371-2888
Catalog $3

Forest Farm
990 Tetherow Road
Williams, OR 97544-9599
541-846-7269
Catalog $4

High Country Gardens
2902 Rufina Street
Santa Fe, NM 87505-2929
505-438-3031

Klehm Nursery
4210 North Duncan Road
Champaign, IL 61821
217-373-8400
Catalog $4

Musser Forests, Inc.
P.O. Box 340
Indiana, PA 15710
800-643-8319

Northwoods Nursery
27635 S. Oglesby Road
Canby, OR 97013
503-266-5432

Oikos Tree Crops
P.O. Box 19425
Kalamazoo, MI 49019
616-624-6233

Raintree Nursery
391 Butts Road
Morton, WA 98356
800-845-1124

Weiss Brothers Nursery
11690 Colfax Highway
Grass Valley, CA 95945
916-272-7657

Garden Wildflowers

Donaroma's Nursery
P.O. Box 2189
Edgartown, MA 02539
Free catalog

Heronswood Nursery
7530 N.E. 288th St.
Kingston, WA 98346
Catalog $5

J.L. Hudson, Seedsman
Star Route 2, Box 337
La Honda, CA 94020
Catalog $2

Moon Mountain Wildflowers
P.O. Box 725
Carpinteria, CA 93014
Catalog $3

Native Gardens
5737 Fisher Lane
Greenback, TN 37742
Catalog $2

Niche Gardens
1111 Dawson Rd.
Chapel Hill, NC 27516
Catalog $3

Plants of the Southwest
Route 6, Box 11A
Santa Fe, NM 87501
Catalog $3.50

Prairie Nursery
P.O. Box 306
Westfield, WI 53964
Free catalog

Seeds Trust/High Altitude
Gardens
P.O. Box 1048
Hailey, ID 83333
Free catalog

Shooting Star Nursery
444 Bates Road
Frankfort, KY 40601
Catalog $2

Sunlight Gardens
174 Golden Lane
Andersonville, TN 37705
Catalog $3

Vermont Wildflower Farm
P.O. Box 5
Charlotte, VT 05445
Free catalog

We-Du Nurseries
Route 5, Box 724
Marion, NC 28752
Catalog $2

Wildseed Farms
425 Wildflower Hills
Fredericksburg, TX 78624
Catalog $2

Shade Plants

Heronswood Nursery
7530 N.E. 288th St.
Kingston, WA 98346
Catalog $5

Plant Delights Nursery
9241 Sauls Rd.
Raleigh, NC 27603
Catalog $3.50

Shady Oaks Nursery
112-10th Ave. S.E.
Waseca, MN 56093-3122
Catalog $4

Underwood Shade Nursery
P.O. Box 1386
North Attleboro, MA 02763
Catalog $2

Andre Viette Farm & Nursery
P.O. Box 1109
Fishersville, VA 22939
Catalog $5

Australian Sources

Country Farm Perennials
RSD Laings Road
Nayook VIC 3821

Cox's Nursery
RMB 216 Oaks Road
Thrilmere NSW 2572

Honeysuckle Cottage Nursery
Lot 35 Bowen Mountain Road
Bowen Mountain via Grosevale NSW 2753

Swan Bros Pty Ltd
490 Galston Road
Dural NSW 2158

Canadian Sources

Corn Hill Nursery Ltd.
RR 5
Petitcodiac NB EOA 2HO

Ferncliff Gardens
SS 1
Mission, British Columbia
V2V 5V6

McFayden Seed Co. Ltd.
Box 1800
Brandon, Manitoba
R7A 6N4

Stirling Perennials
RR 1
Morpeth, Ontario
N0P 1X0

Organizations

American Rose Society
P.O. Box 30,000
Shreveport, LA 71140-0030
318-938-5402

Canadian Rose Society
10 Fairfax Cresent
Scarborough, Ontario M1L 1Z8
Canada
416-757-8809

Herb Society of America, Inc.
9019 Kirtland Chardon Rd.
Kirtland, OH 44094
Send a long SASE for information on dues and benefits

International Herb Association
P.O. Box 317
Mundelein, IL 60060-0317
Send a long SASE for information on dues and benefits

National Wildflower Research Center
4801 LaCrosse Ave.
Austin, TX 78739
512-292-4200
www.wildflower.org

New England Wild Flower Society
Hemenway Road
Framingham, MA 01701
(508) 877-7630
www.newfs.org/[tilde]newfs/

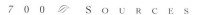